OXFORD REVISION GUIDES

A Level

S ... Y
s

OXFORD

UNIVERSITY PRESS

OXFORD
UNIVERSITY PRESS

Great Clarendon Street, Oxford OX2 6DP

Oxford University Press is a department of the University of Oxford.
It furthers the University's objective of excellence in research,
scholarship, and education by publishing worldwide in

Oxford New York
Athens Auckland Bangkok Bogotá Buenos Aires Calcutta
Cape Town Chennai Dar es Salaam Delhi Florence Hong Kong Istanbul
Karachi Kuala Lumpur Madrid Melbourne Mexico City Mumbai
Nairobi Paris São Paulo Singapore Taipei Tokyo Toronto Warsaw
with associated companies in Berlin Ibadan

Oxford is a registered trade mark of Oxford University Press
in the UK and in certain other countries

British Library Cataloguing in Publication Data

Data available

ISBN 0 19 913409 X

Typeset by Hardlines, Charlbury

Printed in Great Britain

CONTENTS

SPECIFICATIONS FOR AQA AND OCR

AQA

Level Unit	STRUCTURE	Total marks	%	Exam time
AS 1	**Unit 1** *One structured data response from choice of 3 sections* • Families and Households (Section A) • Health (Section B) • Mass Media (Section C)	60	17.5	75 mins
AS 2	**Unit 2** *One structured data response from choice of 3 sections* • Education (Section A) • Wealth, Poverty and Welfare (Section B) • Work and Leisure (Section C)	60	17.5	75 mins
AS 3	*Either:* **Unit 3W** *One compulsory structured data response* • Sociological Methods *or:* **Unit 3C** • Coursework task	60	15	60 mins / course work
A2 4	**Unit 4** *One short compulsory structured data response and one essay from a choice of 2, from one of 3 sections* • Power and Politics (Section A) • Religion (Section B) • World Sociology (Section C)	20 + 40	15	90 mins
A2 5	*Either:* **Unit 5W** *One compulsory structured data response and one essay from a choice of 2* • Theory and Methods *or:* **Unit 5C** • Research study	20 + 40 or 60	15	90 mins / course work
A2 6	**Unit 6** *Three-part synoptic question from one of 2 sections:* • Crime and Deviance (Section A) • Stratification and Differentiation (Section B) **This is a synoptic unit**	60	20	90 mins

OCR

STRUCTURE	Total marks	%	Exam time
Unit 1 *One from two four-part structured data response* • Individual and Society	90	15	60 mins
Unit 2 *Two two-part structured essays chosen from the same or different options* • The family (Option 1) • Mass Media (Option 2) • Religion (Option 3) • Youth and Culture (Option 4)	60 × 2	20	90 mins
Either: **Unit 3** *Compulsory structured data response question* • Sociological Research skills *or:* **Unit 4** • Research report	90	15	60 mins / course work
Unit 5 *One unstructured essays from a choice of 2 from one of 6 options* • Crime and Deviance (Option 1) • Education (Option 2) • Health (Option 3) • Popular Culture (Option 4) • Social Policy (Option 5) • Protest and Social Movements (Option 6)	90	15	60 mins
Either: **Unit 6** *Two compulsory structured data response questions* • Applied Sociological Research skills *or:* **Unit 7** • Personal study	90	15	90 mins / course work
Unit 8 *One from two structured data response questions* • Social Inequality and Difference **This is a synoptic unit**	120	20	90 mins

SPECIFICATIONS WITH LINKS TO SECTIONS OF THE BOOK

Level	Unit	AQA TOPIC	AQA SECTION OF BOOK	OCR TOPIC	OCR SECTION OF BOOK
AS	1	Families and Households (Section A) Health (Section B) Mass Media (Section C)	• Families and Households • Health • Mass Media	Individual and Society	• Culture and Identity
AS	2	Education (Section A) Wealth, Poverty and Welfare (Section B) Work and Leisure (Section C)	• Education • Wealth, Poverty and Welfare • Work and Leisure	The family (Option 1) Mass Media (Option 2) Religion (Option 3) Youth and Culture (Option 4)	• Families and Households • Mass Media • Religion • Culture and Identity • Crime and Deviance (6, 10)
AS	3	Sociological Methods	• Methods • Topic chapter from units 1 or 2	Sociological Research skills *or:* Research report	• Methods • Topics specific chapter
A2	4	Power and Politics (Section A) Religion (Section B) World Sociology (Section C)	• Power and Politics • Religion • World Sociology	Crime and Deviance (Option 1) Education (Option 2) Health (Option 3) Popular culture (Option 4) Social Policy and Welfare (Option 5) Protest and Social Movements (Option 6)	• Crime and Deviance • Education • Health • Culture and Identity • Wealth, Poverty and Welfare (3, 4, 10, 11, 12, 13, 14, 15) • Health (13, 14) • Religion (part) • Power and Politics (part)
A2	5	Theory and Methods *or:* Research study	• Theory • Methods • Topic specific chapter	Applied Sociological Research skills *or:* Personal study	• Theory • Methods • Topic specific chapter
A2	6	Crime and Deviance (Section A) Stratification and Differentiation (Section B)	• Crime and Deviance • Stratification an Differentiation	Social Inequality and Difference	• Stratification and Differentiation • Wealth, Poverty and Welfare (1, 2, 5, 6, 7, 8, 9) • Work and Leisure (part)

SKILLS AND ASSESSMENT

ASSESSMENT OBJECTIVES (AO)

Knowledge and Understanding AO1	Identification, Analysis, Interpretation and Evaluation AO2
• Theoretical knowledge of the main points of view and arguments of an issue • Knowledge of the major sociologists who have contributed to the debate • Empirical knowledge of the main points of important studies • Understanding of the historical context of the debate • Understanding of concepts and ideas • Understanding shown through clarity and coherence in the presentation of an answer • Extraction of information from tables / graphs	• Identification of social trends • Recognise the perspective of a writer • Selection and application of relevant material • The use of social theories and concepts to analyse social issues and personal experience • Display an awareness of two or more sides to a debate • Strengths and weaknesses of evidence and arguments of sociological and non-sociological material • Assessment of how convincing or true to life a particular viewpoint is • Making connections between different areas of sociology • Demonstrating the nature of relationships between two institutions • Recognition of the impact of change • Offering explanations for patterns or changes • Interpretation from qualitative and quantitative data • Use evidence to support and sustain arguments
ACTIVITY WORDS THAT INDICATE WHICH SKILLS YOU ARE REQUIRED TO SHOW	
• list • suggest • outline • what is meant by • define • how many / much • state • what percentage • name • describe • which • examine • explain	• identify • to what extent • assess • summarise • evaluate • give examples / reasons • how far • compare / contrast • discuss • critically discuss /assess • show how

WEIGHTING OF ASSESSMENT OBJECTIVES

module / level	AQA			module / level	OCR		
	AO1	AO2	Total		AO1	AO2	Total
1	8.75%	8.75%	17.5%	1	8%	7%	15%
2	8.75%	8.75%	17.5%	2	11%	9%	20%
3	7.5%	7.5%	15%	3 or 4	8%	7%	15%
Total AS	**25%**	**25%**	**50%**	**Total AS**	**27%**	**23%**	**50%**
4	6.0%	9.0%	15.0%	5	7%	8%	15%
5	6.0%	9.0%	15.0%	6 or 7	7%	8%	15%
6	8.0%	12.0%	20.0%	8	9%	11%	20%
Total A2	**20%**	**30%**	**50%**	**Total A2**	**23%**	**27%**	**50%**
Overall	**45%**	**55%**	**100%**	**Overall**	**50%**	**50%**	**100%**

SYNOPTIC ASSESSMENT – the explicit assessment of the understanding of the connections between different elements of the subject.

AQA	OCR
Crime and Deviance or Stratification and Differentiation are examined using the 'higher level' skills to show the connections between: • the nature of sociological thought • methods of sociological enquiry • substantive areas of sociology	Draws together the skills which have been learnt by examining: • the pattern of inequality in contemporary Britain with an emphasis on class, gender and ethnicity • the underlying processes which shape the life chances of individuals and groups • the relationship between social inequality, the nature of sociological thought and methods of social enquiry

REVISION TIMETABLE

Number of weeks to exam…

	Morning	Afternoon	Evening
Monday			
Tuesday			
Wednesday			
Thursday			
Friday			
Saturday			
Sunday			

- Photocopy or reproduce 6 copies of the timetable above for the last 6 weeks of revision
- Enter all your fixed time commitments, e.g. lectures, paid work, family obligations.
- Keep at least one session per day clear for revision (preferably two in the last two weeks leading to the exam).
- Take at least one session every other day for leisure.
- Work backwards from the last week before the exam entering in the topics in rotation into the available sessions.
- The last revision sessions should be re-reading the relevant sections of this book.
- Earlier revision should be active and have a specific goal, e.g. learning the theories of poverty in Wealth, Poverty and Welfare 6, 7 and 8.
- You are better going through all your pages once and then returning to them a second or third time than trying to remember a particular topic with 100% recall.
- When you have completed a whole topic once build in a review session.

TYPES OF EXAMINATION QUESTION

	STRUCTURED DATA RESPONSE	STRUCTURED ESSAYS	UNSTRUCTURED ESSAYS
AQA	✓ AS & A2	✗	✓ A2
OCR	✓ AS & A2	✓ AS	✓ A2
Description	You will be provided with one or more pieces of data that may take the form of: • prose • statistical tables • diagrams • pictures There will be from 3–7 related questions of varying mark allocations.	These are two-part questions on a single or connected theme. The second part usually carries more marks than the first part. Both parts must be answered.	These are single questions which carry a single mark allocation. Although called 'unstructured' there will be indications of structure embedded within the question. This should be decoded to ensure that you answer all aspects of the question.
Advice on mark and time allocation, planning	• There will be some time allowance to enable you to read the data provided. • Marks will vary between parts of the question. Use this information to assess how much time to spend on each. • Try to answer the lower mark questions in a shorter time as higher mark questions are like mini-essays and require more time to construct an answer. • Careful and accurate responses to the short answer questions that require you to interpret and apply material from the items can produce full marks. Then you are well on the way to a pass grade answer before you begin the more substantial questions. • Plan all parts of the question before you start writing and avoid using the same material for two answers. • Make sure you answer **all** the question parts.	• Choose between alternative structured questions by comparing your ability to answer the higher mark part rather than your preference in the lower mark part. • Marks cannot be reallocated for between parts so be sure to use your knowledge the most appropriate section. This means you should plan both parts of the answer before starting to write. • Allocate your time between the two parts in proportion to the marks available and make sure you stick to this time plan.	• A large number of marks will rest on this one question, so it is very important not to misinterpret the question or to respond to a trigger word without reading the whole question carefully. • There is flexibility within the mark schemes for answers which address one part of the question more than another, but no marks will be given for irrelevant material. • Ten minutes spent planning before you start writing can help to avoid both problems and prevent you running out of material halfway through your time allocation. • Overrunning your time is also dangerous as it is easier to accumulate marks in the bottom bands of a mark scheme than to improve your marks once in the top bands, so move on to your next question whether you have finished or not. You can return to this question later if you have time.
For each exam	Familiarise yourself with the format of the exam paper: • the number of questions to be answered • the style of the questions • the choice you have in revision.	• the choice you will have in the exam room (Specification for AQA and OCR on page vi) and check with your teacher • use the length of the exam and the marks available to work out how long you should spend per mark per question.	

1 Culture and Identity

1. DEFINITIONS

[Kroeber and Kluckholm (1952) uncovered 200 definitions for 'culture']

Culture and structure

- Culture is all that can be learned and transmitted to next generation.
- Culture is differentiated from structure, that is seen as a relatively stable set of social relationships.
- Culture includes the beliefs of a society and all the creative activities engaged in by social groups.
- Distinctions are often made between 'high culture' (which includes art, classical music and literature) and 'popular culture' which is enjoyed by mass audiences (such as TV, football, bingo, pop music, tabloid newspapers and romantic fiction).
- Culture links the individual to the structural relationships within society. All societies have kinship networks but they are structured differently.

Identity

- Identity is the way we see ourselves in relation to others.
- Roles we take on also define our identities as they relate to our gender, ethnicity, region, nationality, family, occupational status, able-bodied/disabled status etc.
- Identities are inseparable from our place within society and how we are defined by our culture.
- Difference between social identity and personal identity: *social* marks out people in relation to their social groups, being like others; *personal* = individual as unique with their own set of characteristics, e.g. our names denote our uniqueness.

DEFINITIONS

Raymond Williams' three approaches to culture:

1. *Ideal* = high culture, the best in intellectual and artistic endeavour. The study of culture involves the application of universally applied criteria or rules – separating 'good' from 'bad'.

✗ Separates elite from masses and assumes elite culture is better.

2. *Documentary* = this is broader as it includes high culture but extends the definition to other examples of the best in creative activity. Seen in schools curriculum approach to English heritage.

✗ Still elitist as it distinguishes between 'good' and 'bad', e.g. Shakespeare vs. soap opera.

3. *Social definition* = a more sociological definition which includes all aspects of life which are created and consumed by individuals within local communities as well as opera houses.

✗ Difficulty of discriminating between aspects of culture as all seen as being of equal value. This has danger of becoming completely relativistic.

✗ It becomes impossible to judge one culture superior as there are no absolutes. May lead to ideologies of extremism.

However, sociobiology sees social behaviour as directed by natural instincts and biological drives which enable individuals to survive and reproduce.

✗ This assumes that individuals all respond in the same way, thus it cannot account for **cultural diversity**.

✗ There may well be biological needs in order for individuals in society to survive, but the way these needs are met is cultural.

Primary and secondary identities

- **Primary identity** is ascribed at birth, especially gender and ethnicity and infant's names.
- Children take an active part in the acquisition of primary identities of personhood and growing sense of self.
- Kinship identity is established as the nature of a child's own family and their place within it is learned. Ethnic identity is constructed as child learns customs, beliefs and values of social group.
- **Secondary identities** are acquired during secondary socialisation processes.
- Major secondary identity is occupational status – through entering the labour market, people adopt the relevant characteristics of their occupational role.
- Leisure and consumption-based identities are gradually becoming as important or even more important than occupational ones. People identify themselves as football fans, ballroom dancers, antique collectors, gardeners etc.
- National identity: this has been enhanced in specific historical contexts, e.g. Israel vs. Palestinian, Serbian vs. Kosovan etc.
- Nationality remains an important secondary identity in the UK and USA for white majorities. For ethnic minorities, often, ethnic identity remains primary and they are reinforced by those who oppress or exclude them.
- Sexual identity: this has become more significant with the increasing openness and acceptance of gay, lesbian and bisexual choices.

An individual's identity changes over time, as the balance of primary and secondary identity construction varies with experience.

✗ It is difficult to establish the precise balance of influences which affect an individual at any one time.

2. THEORIES OF SOCIALISATION

ROLE-LEARNING THEORY	SOCIAL-CONSTRUCTION THEORY	PSYCHOANALYTIC THEORY

Functionalist approach to socialisation
- Rejects idea of inbuilt social responses in favour of idea that infants are born with potential for social action which will be developed through socialisation.
- Through socialisation children learn contents of their culture and normative expectations that define their social roles. Individuals become social by learning social roles.
- Social roles are institutionalised social relationships which act as forms of external constraint.
- Socialisation is the process through which the individual learns how to perform social roles. Role-taking involves taking on culturally given roles and acting them out.
- Individuals learn conformity to role expectations via rewards and punishment, first by immediate family members, later by other members of society. The individual learns to internalise the norms and values of their society during this period.
- Period of primary socialisation lays down guidelines for later secondary socialisation process in schools, through friends, religion, work and media.

Symbolic interactionist approach to socialisation
- Stems from work of G.H. Mead on the meanings of social interaction. Development of self occurs during socialisation through social interaction.
- Play is very important to development of self, it is the way children develop into social beings. Taking the role of the other enables the child to take into account the social reactions of others.
- Significant Others play an important part in enabling the child to see how its actions generate specific social reactions.
- 'Self is split into 'I' and 'me' where the 'I' is the active aspect and the 'me' is the reflective part – Cooley's 'looking-glass self'. The 'me' is the reservoir of social experiences which are drawn upon in social action.
- Social self develops by 4–5 years of age. Later, child is able to detach from significant others to 'generalised other' by which time they have internalised the rules and norms of social behaviour.
- Goffman argues that play continues throughout life. Roles are not fixed entities but 'actors' create their role-style. Individuals present many different selves to the world depending on the social context.

Psychological (Freudian) approach to socialisation
- Focus not on cognitive meanings but emotions. Human behaviour can be understood as relationship between conscious and unconscious aspects.
- Early socialisation crucial for adult emotional development – in some cases psychoanalysts argue that basis for adulthood is laid down in first 24 months of life.
- Carer (usually mother) of infant is critical in personality development of the child. Bonds of attachment made early secure emotional satisfactions of child.
- Anxieties laid down in early infancy generate specific personality disorders in adulthood. Examples include phobias, reaction formation, projection etc.
- Freud (1856–1939) argued that there were two unconscious drives – Eros and Thanatos – which ensured the survival of the individual. One was a drive towards pleasure and the other to aggression and eventual death.
- Id = unconscious anti-social desire, controlled by conscious Ego which is in contact with real world. Superego develops as a conscience controlling individual's moral behaviour.

Evaluation

✓ Challenges biological assumptions of social behaviour.

✓ Differentiates between primary and secondary socialisation.

✗ No theory of the mechanisms of socialisation.

✗ Over-socialised view of individuals – no place for construction of identity by individual.

Evaluation

✓ Allows for action by individual in the process.

✓ Development of self is outcome of individual interpreting role of others and their reactions.

✗ Assumption that developmental stages are universal.

✗ Fails to explain how meanings are generated in the first place and who they may benefit most.

Evaluation

✓ Discovery of role of unconscious in social behaviour.

✓ Links made between personality and social behaviour.

✗ Insufficient emphasis placed on cultural factors in socialisation.

✗ Doesn't allow for significance of secondary socialisation.

3. THEORIES OF CULTURE

CONSENSUS THEORY (STRUCTURAL FUNCTIONALISM)

- Consensus sociologists identify 4 sub-systems: economic, political, kinship and cultural.
- These play a role in determining the culture of a society, but cultural institutions such as media, religion and education are more significant.
- Importance of socialisation process – learning of norms and values.
- Functionalists emphasise cultural rules which structure people's actions and interactions.
- Individuals are constrained by cultural rules – behaviour is channelled by external forces which promote conformity.
- Culture includes roles, statuses, values and norms all of which help to produce social order.
- Through socialisation individuals learn to adopt the value consensus as we are all socialised into the same set of societal values etc.

Evaluation

✗ Does not account for difference – individuals do not all behave like robots and they disagree over values.

✓ Consensus theorists argue that this can be countered by sub-cultural theory which takes into account different groups within society which have specific rules, values etc. transmitted in the socialisation process. Merton's work (1968) shows that there are different adaptations to society's goals and means and while most people are conformist, others may be ritualists, retreatists, innovators or rebels.

✗ It is not clear how conformity is achieved or why some individuals refuse to conform.

CONFLICT THEORY (MARXISM)

- Culture affects people's behaviour, by structuring the way individuals are able to think and act.
- Contrary to consensus theory, it assumes that conflict not consensus is at the heart of social interaction. Individuals are in competition rather than in co-operation with each other.
- Society is characterised by inequalities of wealth, power, status mediated through factors like gender, ethnicity and most significantly, social class.
- Conflicting interest groups arise from ownership/non-ownership of private property in the means of production. Those with greatest economic power socialise the rest into acceptance of this inequality.
- This occurs through cultural socialisation and the promotion of cultural ideologies. Ideological State Apparatuses such as family, religion, media and education serve to promote the dominant ideology of the owners of the most powerful groups. If this fails Repressive State Apparatuses such as the police and armed services can be called upon to maintain control.
- Those who control access to those resources considered by the society to be culturally valuable will have power over those who wish to gain access to those resources.
- Hegemonic Marxists argue that the subject groups would not accept a dominant ideology without questioning or rebellion, so the powerful groups win over their consent by offering concessions which makes them feel that they have some purchase on the system. This is done culturally by the marginalisation of 'unacceptable' groups such as foreigners, feminists, ethnic minority youth, unemployed and welfare scroungers. In this way the majority feel themselves to be respectable members of society.

Evaluation

✓ Stresses the relationship between control of economic resources and the ability to dominate cultural forms.

✓ Highlights the importance of intermediate organisations and structures in transmitting culture and ensuring ideological control.

✓ Hegemony is a useful concept because it provides understanding of cultural diversity and dynamic cultural struggle. Allows us to see that cultural forms evolve and change over time as societies encounter new issues to dealt with.

✗ It is not made clear how economic power leads to cultural power, except as a simplistic correspondence.

✗ Relationship between Ideological and Repressive State Apparatuses not explained fully, especially the circumstances in which the RSA are brought into play.

✗ Still does not overcome the idea that individuals have choices and free will as pluralists would argue. Does not account for cultural variance between different genders and ethnic groups.

INTERACTIONISM (SYMBOLIC INTERACTIONISM)

- Culture is maintained through interaction based on communication of signs and signals. Meaning is transmitted symbolically and is generated through the process of interaction.
- Society is socially constructed, it is an elaborate fiction maintained by individuals in social interactions.
- Culture is part of the universe of meaning created by individuals which is transmitted through socialisation.
- By categorising the social world we attribute meaning to it and give a semblance of order, but this order is always negotiable and open to different interpretations.

Evaluation

✓ Sees social reality as a construction rather than as an objective reality imposed on individuals so allows agency to the individual.

✗ Does not explain how some groups manage to have their culture valued above others (e.g. elite culture).

✗ Underplays the material base of society and over-emphasises symbolic aspects.

4. SOCIAL CLASS

> • Twenty years ago it was possible to relate culture and taste to class background.
> • There were clear distinctions between elite and popular cultures.
> • Today those distinctions are more problematic:
>   1. Media have made high culture accessible to wide audience
>   2. Relationship between class and culture varies widely across the world
>   3. Concept of 'class culture' is subject to considerable sociological debate.

WORKING-CLASS CULTURE

• **Marxism** – sees the cultural aspects shaped by the economic infrastructure. Close correspondence between class and education: hierarchies, fragmentation, alienation and obedience shapes working-class consciousness (Bowles & Gintis, 1976).

• **Gramsci** (1971) questioned relationship between economic and cultural systems. Counter-culture of working class can stand in opposition to ideology of ruling class.

• **Bourdieu** (1990) saw cultural tastes as influenced by social class. Cultural capital = set of cultural competences and dispositions including tastes and lifestyle. Process of transmission involves Habitus – everyday practices and assumption of a particular social environment. Conflict of cultures for working-class child at school as they are unprepared for middle-class culture.

• **Embourgeoisement thesis** maintained affluent working class starting to adopt cultural commodities and lifestyle of middle-class.

✗ No clear evidence apart from normative convergence.

• 'Resistance' of working-class culture to dominant culture (Centre for Contemporary Cultural Studies (CCCS)) but evidence that capitalist institutions incorporate such resistance – commercialisation of working-class fashion and professional football.

✗ Failed to address gender dimension. Women may have different cultural agenda, seen more recently with increased sexual freedoms for young working-class women.

✗ Neo-Weberians completely challenge notion of dominant ideology. Ethnographic studies show that working-class attitudes are contradictory, they are critical of capitalism but reluctantly accept it. Workers face unemployment or poverty if they do not accept situation.

MIDDLE-CLASS CULTURE

• The concept of cultural capital characterises middle-class culture. In education middle-class children have necessary attitudes, motivation and resources to succeed.

• Habitus of middle class enables them to adopt positions on matters of cultural taste as if 'second nature'. This excludes the working class.

• So patterns of consumption become more important than simply income and class.

• Neo-Weberians accept that no single dominant ideology exists. They see middle-class as socially and culturally fragmented so that there are multiple, overlapping middle-class lifestyles (Savage et al, 1992).
  1. *Postmodern:* Section of middle-class who experiment and innovate with lifestyle. Likely to be young professionals in private sector (advertising executives, stockbrokers). Expensive cars, holidays and food but 'healthy' lifestyle.
  2. *Ascetic:* High in cultural capital, low in economic capital (teachers, social and health workers). Likely to pursue ascetic lifestyle – less expensive tastes but intellectual and individualistic activities.
  3. *Undistinctive:* Managers and administrators. Leisure pursuits of golf, fishing and visiting country houses.

DEATH OF CLASS?

✓ Post-modernists argue that class is no longer a signifier of identity or culture.

✓ Consumption is dictated by lifestyle rather than class. This has been generated by media images of possible lifestyle options (and copying of designer goods by high street outlets).

✗ Marxists still see working-class as duped by ruling class hegemony but with potential for revolutionary action.

✗ Studies still show people identify themselves with a specific social class even though they may hold contradictory attitudes and ideologies (Marshall et al, 1990).

> Foucault as a post-structuralist denies a link between structure and identity. Social factors like class do not produce identities. **Discourses** affect how we come to view ourselves and the world.

5. ETHNICITY

Census 1991 asked respondents to assign themselves to an ethnic group.

✗ Options were not exhaustive (Irish category not included).

✗ Figures based on self-assigned groups = subjective.

✗ Question mixed skin colour with nationality.

✗ Did not distinguish between groups from same national origin.

✓ Still most reliable source for sociologists.

Terminology
- Categorisation is problematic for race and ethnicity.
- Racial categories were used to identify groups by skin colour and have been used as justifications for discriminatory practices and racism.
- Ethnicity focuses more on groups who share a common culture and is a more flexible, dynamic category.

- Over 3m described themselves as ethnic minority (5.5%).
- Of these, 30% described themselves as black, black African or other.
- 28% described themselves as Indian.
- More than 50% live in South East England.
- 60% of black population and 30% Indian population live in London.
- High density of ethnic population also in Midlands, W. Yorks., Lancashire and Manchester.

Ethnic differences are social differences reflecting different origins of social groups. This creates a sense of identity as an 'imagined community'. Ethnic groups may construct a common identity and sense of community even if widely dispersed.
Nationalism is a form of ethnic identity.

SOCIAL CONSTRUCTION OF ETHNICITY
- Ethnic groups are not fixed entities but dynamic with no fixed boundaries.
- Individuals can synthesise different cultural forms to create individual identities using commodities from culture industries.
- **Diaspora** describes the process of cultural dispersal of norms and values which produces new forms of meaning and identity. African diaspora has indirectly influenced Caribbean and UK cultures e.g. music styles have drawn upon both black and white influences.

- Produces **hybridisation** of culture – incorporation of aspects of different cultural traditions. Spread of cultural influences through global media undermines nationalist values systems and a specific 'way of life'.
- Hall (1992) sees that with cinema, ethnicities have intersected with age, gender, sexual orientation and class (films like *My Beautiful Laundrette, Buddha of Suburbia, Bhaji on the Beach* all achieved mainstream success while reflecting complexity of ethnic identity).
- Influences in the social construction of identity include: mainstream culture; minority cultural traditions; synthesis of different ethnicities.

ETHNICITY AND MATERIAL CULTURE
- Consumption is important in reproduction of identity where commodities can express individuality (and group solidarity).
- Ethnic identity can be seen as arising from specific socio-cultural situations and experiences.

- Case study = Leicester Asian community (Hides, 1995). Ethnic minorities use material culture like clothing, jewellery, home decor and other goods to define a sense of ethnic identity. Wearing traditional dress is symbolic affirmation of membership and links with tradition. Gender differences also apparent. Artefacts possessed symbolised role or status of individual within the community. Conflicts with individualistic values of 'English' society.

GENDER AND ETHNIC IDENTITY
- For some young women their ethnic identity is paramount, especially young Muslims.
- Islam was an important guide to their lives, but they were able to choose aspects of both British and Asian cultures in order to construct identities which gave them freedom and choice (Butler, 1995).

- Sub-cultural studies have focused on young Afro-Caribbean men, Rastafarianism, rude boys and hip-hoppers with distinctive music and dress styles.
- Asian youth have been subject to fewer studies, but there is evidence of hybridisation of Asian/Western music styles.

6. GENDER

- Different and unequal gender roles have been traditional part of Western culture.
- Social positions involving leadership, power, decision-making have been taken by men.
- Roles focusing on dependency, family concerns, caring for others have gone to women.
- Men and women still expected to behave differently because of their genders.
- Women have traditionally been concerned with their physical appearance.
- Although these ideas have been challenged, especially by feminist sociologists, the ideological assumptions still exist and influence cultural expectations.

Parental behaviour differentiated by gender of infant (gender identity acquired by 5 years).

Process of gender socialisation = manipulation, canalisation (encouraged into gender appropriate behaviour), appellation (e.g. 'she's a good girl'; 'he's a good boy'), activities.

Schooling: earlier research showed reasons for underachievement of girls – subjects were gender specific, teachers favoured boys, girls had lower self-esteem, 11+ weighted against them, limited occupational opportunities etc.

Concern is now with *underachievement of boys* = anti-school culture, lack of adequate role models, male unemployment, rise of women's consciousness, girl power etc. (see **Education 9**)

Girls behaving 'ladly' – deviancy, girl gangs, sexually more liberated, girls as role models in popular culture.

SOCIALISATION PROCESS

Changes in gender roles are impacting on consumption and production of popular culture:

Consumption
Women become more economically independent and gain more recognition as consumers of goods and of popular cultural products.

Production
Women securing positions in cultural industries as journalists, editors and as senior managers.

But not all good news:

✗ In families women do not share equally in consumption of goods and services.

✗ Media and cultural services still largely focused on men (from sport to pornography).

✗ Men still occupy top position in media/cultural industries, only 2 national newspapers edited by women, and by 1995 only 20% of BBC senior executives were women.

✗ In cinema films, top earners are still predominantly male.

Explanations
- Feminism: important differences between various branches of feminist thought (see **Sociological Theories 7**). Some are more optimistic than others about women having greater say in production and consumption of culture.
- Radical feminists are least optimistic – women in senior positions in media/cultural industries will bring little change.

✓ Liberal feminists most optimistic, seeing gradual improvements leading to real change in women's position in cultural consumption.

- Commercial pressures will still demand that magazines, films and other cultural products use women's bodies to sell products and services (whether women made editorial decisions or not).
- Patriarchal ideology so embedded that we all consume through the 'male gaze'.

BUT

✗ Emergence of **male** bodies as sexualised objects used to sell commodities.

✗ Rise of fashion industry, glossy magazines and stores selling to men as they used to sell to women.

✗ Rise of gender identity as fluid and flexible. Challenge to compulsory heterosexuality allows for homoerotic imagery and gender liminality.

7. AGE AND GENERATION

SOCIAL STRUCTURING OF AGE IN CONTEMPORARY BRITAIN

Stage	Relevant aspects of structure	Contemporary issues
Childhood	Parents, State & legal processes	Child abuse, poverty, education – pre-school and school-age, consumption
Youth	Parents, peer groups, education, work & training, sexual relationships	Deviance, criminality, control, conformity, commitment
Young adulthood	Work & career, partnerships, children	Separation/divorce, lone-parenthood, responsibility, equality (gender, ethnic, sexual)
Middle age	Parental role, high point of career, financial security	Commitment to partners/children, redundancy, early retirement
Early old age	Retirement, leisure, financial (in)security	Loss of role, grandchildren?, loss of status, increased numbers of old people, greater political and economic power
Late old age	Retirement, single living, finance	Loneliness, frailty, gender differences, care/cost, community

FOUR AGES OF LIFE
1. *First age* = period of childhood, characterised by socialisation and dependency
2. *Second age* = period of full-time employment, family-building, and adult responsibility
3. *Third age* = period from 50–74, the age of active independent life, post-work and post-parenting
4. *Fourth age* = old age, characterised by increasing dependence on others

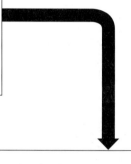

CHILDHOOD
- Idea that childhood is a social construction. In medieval society, no recognition of childhood as a separate stage of development. In traditional society (pre-1800) children not clearly differentiated from adults (Aries, 1972). Childhood developed in tangent with capitalism as part of the rise of maternal love and domesticity (Shorter, 1976).
- 19th century legislation distanced world of children more and more from adult responsibilities.
- Child labour less necessary and increasingly disapproved of. Educational reforms, initially for moral guidance of working-class children, ensured further segregation of children. School-leaving age raised to 16 in 1972.
- Rise of ideology of 'child development' as critical stage in adult personality and stability led to child-centredness at home and school.
- Rise of children's rights – especially after increased knowledge of child abuse by family members and institutionalised carers (Children Act 1989).

BUT
✗ Child as consumer. Adverts targeted towards children; merchandising of TV programmes and films.

✗ Children and violence: fears over children as vulnerable and open to influence by violent content of media. Cases (such as James Bulger's murder and Nathan Martinez's killing of step-mother and half-sister) placed focus on children being potentially as criminal as adult.

✗ Nowadays a paradoxical position between seeing children in need of protection against drugs, television, sexual exploitation and children as a threat to social order (especially working-class boys).

8. YOUTH AND YOUTH SUB-CULTURES

THREE KINDS OF CULTURE (MEAD, 1930)

post-figurative which takes authority from the past, little change takes place.	**configurative** in which change occurs and model of behaviour taken from peers.	**pre-figurative** in which change is rapid and youth hold key to new knowledge.

YOUTH

- Adolescence or youth can also be seen as a social construction as it is culturally variable.
- In the UK, universal education helps to shape experience of youth as it does with childhood.
- Identified by social psychologists as time of 'storm and stress' – puberty generates problematic behaviour.
- Informal peer groups become important in socialisation process and in development of youth sub-cultures.
- Influence of media on youth in fashion, music and consumerism generally.

- Increased earning power
- Increased consumption
- Market geared to youth fashion, music, cosmetics, magazines etc.
- Emergence of different youth styles – class, gender, ethnicity, region

| Teddy boys |
| Mods |
| Rockers |
| Hippies |
| Skinheads |
| Punks |

Youth sub-cultural types

Response	Working-class	Middle-class
Deviant	Strong	Weak
Pleasure-seeking	Strong	Less strong
Political	Weak except Higher Education	Stronger among Higher Education students

EMERGENCE OF YOUTH CULTURE (1950s)

Creation of moral panics over youth (see **Crime and Deviance 9**)
- Press reports of battles between Mods and Rockers
- Exaggeration of trouble
- Label of 'folk-devils' as threat to social order
- Public concern expressed by media
- Call for more legislative controls

SOCIOLOGICAL EXPLANATIONS OF YOUTH SUB-CULTURES

Functionalist	**Marxist**
In absence of any clear rites of passage, sub-cultures help young people to manage transition from childhood to adulthood.	Uses concept of hegemony to explain youth behaviours. Youth as relatively autonomous and can set out their own behavioural strategies.
Sub-cultural membership helps youth to cope with pressures and stresses generated by need to compete and achieve, but assumes most youth are conformist.	Importance of concept of resistance to understand youth. Dress styles reflect social circumstances of the different groups – often rejection of or resistance to the capitalist system.
Sub-culture offers validation for who you are, not what you can achieve.	Example of appearance of skinhead youth demonstrates adherence to traditional working-class values and patriotism.
✓ Highlights category of youth as socially constructed, as there are clear differences between and across cultures.	✓ Helps to explain class differences: structural location of youth groups with middle-class youth as potentially part of bourgeoisie whereas working-class youth seen as a threat by those in power.
✓ Sees youth culture as a phase that is achieved and then discarded. Most panics are misconceived as sub-cultures are actually functional in a healthy society.	✓ Makes connections between social structure and sub-cultural styles. Uses semiological analysis to interpret dress codes etc.
✗ Not always a means of tension management but source of disorder.	✗ Emphasis on 'spectacular' youth styles not on 'ordinary' youth.
✗ Theory is gender-blind, there is an emphasis on problems of adolescent boys and only passing reference made to young girls.	✗ Not all working-class youth became Teds, skinheads, Rockers etc. Class structure is not so deterministic as some middle-class youth also joined these groups.
✗ Theory is blind to social class differences. Most of the work focuses on working-class males and assumes all working-class sub-cultures are similar.	✗ Hebdige (1979) challenges earlier work of CCCS and ✓ produces concept 'bricolage' to show that sub-cultures are actually quite complicated.

9. OLD AGE

Changes in population during this century have led to an age imbalance

The UK has an increasingly ageing population. By 2021 nearly one in five will be over 65 and one in two over 50.
Between 1991–2031 the overall size of UK population will increase by 8%.
- Those aged 85+ will have increased by 138%.
- Those aged 75–84 will have increased by 48%.
- Those aged 60–74 will have increased by 43%.
Old are not homogeneous but divided by class, gender, ethnicity and age.

- Lower birth rates
- Longer life expectancy
- Immigration – population tends to be younger

CONSEQUENCES OF AN AGEING POPULATION

→ *Income* = differentials have created two nations; those on state provision vs. private pensioners.

→ *Housing and care* = shift to private provision. Rising costs to state (in 1992 £2000m).

→ *Health* = perceived as frail and unhealthy but differences by class.

→ *Dependency* = retirement makes old dependent on rest of working population and while working population is declining for other reasons, numbers of elderly at work is also falling. Dependency ratio is expected to change from 63:100 to 79:100 by 2031.

→ *Family life* = some elderly may be burden on family carers, others may provide mutual support.

AGE IN TRADITIONAL AND CONTEMPORARY WESTERN SOCIETY

Traditional society	Contemporary western
Gerontocracy gives status to elders	Low status – seen as vulnerable and burdensome
Elders are heads of families and kinship networks	Tend not to be heads of family and kin
Knowledge and skills are valued by young	Privatised nuclear families independent of elderly
Knowledge is based on experience and tradition	Knowledge and experience is outdated
Pre-figurative culture (knowledge held by elders)	Post-figurative culture (knowledge with younger generation)

- Most studies of ethnicity have concentrated on youth at expense of old.
- UK's ethnic population is ageing and ethnicity is a factor in discrimination.
- Ethnic elderly experience of ageing is affected by their expectations from country of origin.
- Ethnic elderly are more likely to be female and working-class.
- Triple jeopardy of racism, ageism and material disadvantage.

- Work processes impact on women's later lives.
- Women have greater longevity than men and make up a large proportion of the 'very old'.
- Women are more likely to suffer financial hardship in later years because of their lower (occupational) pension entitlement.
- Life expectancy: women 77.9; men 72.3.

ETHNICITY

GENDER

ASPECTS OF AGEING

EUROPE

POPULAR CULTURE

Ageing population in Europe (1990–2040)
(People aged 65+ as % of total population)

Germany	29.6
Netherlands	24.8
Denmark	24.7
Italy	24.2
France	22.7
Spain	22.7
Belgium	21.9
Greece	21.0
Portugal	20.4
UK	20.4
Ireland	16.9

Ageing and popular culture

✗ Stigmatised social identity of age shown by TV and press.

✗ Elderly as vulnerable, in need of care and special equipment (e.g. stair lifts).

✗ Elderly as sexless and physically unattractive.

✓ Increasing number of heroes on film played by elderly (men).

✓ Some elderly have become very wealthy and powerful.

10. SEXUAL IDENTITY

| Socialisation process | ➡ | gender roles | ➡ | sexual orientation | ➡ | heterosexual
homosexual
bisexual
transsexual |

ISSUES
- Nature vs. nurture debate. Human sexuality is culturally specific.
- Ideas of 'normal' sex vary over time and from society to society. Socialisation teaches norms of sexual identity. Earlier in this century Western society emphasised 'compulsory heterosexuality'.
- Diversity in sexual practice – people engage in wide range of sexual practices.
- Homosexuality may be learned and reinforced by social experiences. Many individuals engage in homosexual behaviour in adolescence but do not pursue it.
- Important factor in shaping homosexuality is labelling and stigmatisation.
- Nowadays gayness is more acceptable and subcultural support is available.
- Sexual identity is not fixed but fluid and open to choice.

REGULATION OF SEXUALITY

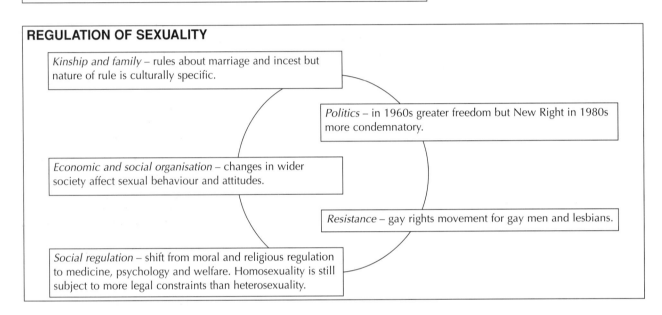

Kinship and family – rules about marriage and incest but nature of rule is culturally specific.

Politics – in 1960s greater freedom but New Right in 1980s more condemnatory.

Economic and social organisation – changes in wider society affect sexual behaviour and attitudes.

Resistance – gay rights movement for gay men and lesbians.

Social regulation – shift from moral and religious regulation to medicine, psychology and welfare. Homosexuality is still subject to more legal constraints than heterosexuality.

HOMOSEXUALITY AND HETEROSEXUALITY
- Foucault argued that sexual behaviour was classified and regulated by governments from 18th century.
- New discourses around sexuality were influenced by new scientific ideas. Homosexuality defined as deviant in 1860s and from then onwards scientists sought explanations for it from biological abnormality to problems in psycho-social development.
- Freudian psychology emphasised lack of identification with father figure or over-identification with mother. Nowadays most experts dismiss theories of homosexuality as illness or abnormality. American Psychiatric Association rejected it as a psychiatric disorder in 1972.

  ✗ However, still regarded as deviant (Clause 28 still on statutes in 2000).

  ✗ Compulsory heterosexuality implies that society tries to compel individuals into heterosexuality.

  ✗ Homophobia is still evident in institutions like schools and places of work.

  ✓ Cultural diversity – some evidence to show that homosexuality is revered in other societies from Roman times to present day.

  ✓ Gay sub-culture – more acceptance of gayness:

1. Pink Pound – middle-class gay men targeted as consumers by magazines, advertisers and stores. Emergence of gay villages in major cities in UK.
2. Increased representation of gay and lesbian images in popular culture. Mainstream cinema and television programmes representing homosexuality as acceptable. Idea of gay audiences targeted by TV companies (*Gaytime TV; Queer as Folk; Out* etc.).

Post-modernism
- Gender is simply a 'performance', so sexual identity is constructed, learned, performed.
- Identity is free-floating = the dramatic effect not cause of our performance.
- Sexuality is fluid and implies choice.

11. MASS CULTURE DEBATE

	Pessimists: Radicals and Romantics	Optimists: Pluralists and Post-modernists
What was working-class culture like in early industrial society?	*Romantic Right:* paternalistic view of working-class culture as authentic, folk culture. They passed on traditions by word-of-mouth. Held fairs and folk-gatherings – culture based on locality and community. *Radical Left: Frankfurt School of Marxism:* working-class culture was vital, radical and dynamic. Trade unions and other working-class associations gave possibility of challenge to Establishment.	*Pluralists:* working-class life was harsh and often brutalised. Pleasures were limited, health and sanitation often poor. Employment was uncertain and conditions in work unsafe. Time available for cultural activity was restricted. *Post-modernists:* no clear view of traditional culture, but no acceptance that things were better in the past.
What is it like now?	*Romantic Right:* depressing picture of a mass culture which is plastic, uncreative and mass-produced. Americanisation of cultural products. *Radical Left:* alienation, commodity fetishism, and a lifeless working-class who have lost their sense of revolution. Media produce a 'diet of trivia' and 'bread and circuses'. Working-class culture has lost its authenticity.	*Pluralists:* Better for working-class as they have choice. Media has produced a more informed populace who are media literate and politically literate. Audiences have wide-ranging options – different newspapers, magazines, TV programmes, including OU broadcasting. Satellite, digital and cable TV all offer audiences choice. *Post-modernists:* As above and the collision of high and mass culture. Elite culture has become a commodity too and is as easily available, hence football and opera. A 'pick and mix' culture full of choices.
What caused the changes?	Industrialisation, mass production and large corporate interests. Marxists also blame capitalism rather than industrialisation.	Industrialisation, media industries especially. Mass consumption allowing people to make choices.
What will the future offer?	More homogenisation, more commodity consumption. A semblance of choice, but actually limited choice between similar poorly produced, commercialised cultural products – owned by mega-corporations interested only in profitability and large audiences.	Hybridity within and across cultures. An increased diversification of cultural products and identification. Role of new technologies – as yet unknowable.

Pessimistic View

Radical Left Frankfurt School
- Mass commodities and mass consumption
- Inauthentic plastic culture
- Commodity fetishism
- Diet of trivia – 'bread & circuses'

Right-wing conservatives
- Folk culture lost, big business provides diet of Americanisation
- Working-class apathetic – cannot discriminate
- Junk tastes

MASS/POPULAR CULTURE

Optimistic

Pluralists
- More freedom of choice
- High culture available to all
- Enlightenment for working-class
- Enhances political and social awareness

Post-modernists
- No distinction between high and mass culture
- Popular culture available to all
- Audience media literate interpreters of texts
- 'Pick-and-Mix' culture via consumption.

12. GLOBALISATION AND NATIONAL IDENTITY

- Globalisation, nationalism and the individual are all closely related.
- Living in 'late-modern' era our cultural choices have global consequences.
- Structural changes within process of globalisation have consequences for identities.

Compression of time and space
- Traditional societies experienced time and space as fixed and stable.
- Time measured by natural events (sunrise, harvest-time etc.).
- Nowadays, time is separated from space and locality.
- Speed of modern communication and transportation compresses both time and distances – 'time–space distanciation' (Giddens, 1991).
- '24-hour society'.

Disembedding' mechanisms
- In traditional society relationships were located in face-to-face situations.
- Nowadays relationships have become impersonal, often via computers (e.g. Internet communication).
- Symbolic tokens such as credit cards etc. (disembedding mechanisms) lift social relations out of local contexts.
- We depend on globalised systems far from local control.
- Reflexivity of self-identity – late-modernity allows individuals to be more proactive in construction of new identities.

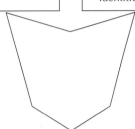

NATIONALISM AND IDENTITY
- Counter-movement to globalisation has been rise of nationalism, national identity and pride.
- Devolution in the UK – a move to fragment Britain into ethnic nationalisms.
- Former Yugoslavia, Bosnian and Kosovan conflicts have demonstrated assertion of ethnic identity after unification period lasting many decades.
- 'Nationalism' is fairly recent invention – a result of the development of a common culture in modern society. Traditional societies were not united in a common national identity.
- Nations and nationalism can be seen as social constructions. Nations = 'imagined communities' which emerged in Europe mainly after Reformation with invention of printing as common language was a powerful unifying force (Anderson, 1983).
- Dissemination of national identity through the following (Schudson, 1994):
1. *Language, print and education* – with spread of state education a common language was taught and common texts used.
2. *Consumer culture and national markets* – mass production generated national markets and fashion, food and sport became organised on national lines.
3. *National rituals* – civic religion promotes social solidarity: coronations, royal weddings, but also political rallies such as Nuremberg.
4. *Mass media* – especially broadcast media reinforce national identity. TV has become part of global village. National rituals and televised sporting competitions also serve to unite nations.

THEORIES OF NATIONALISM
- *Functionalism* – nationalism acts to integrate large-scale heterogenous societies. Importance of national symbols and rituals for a sense of collective belonging.
- *Marxism* – nationalism as an example of hegemony, a means of winning over the working-class. Can be seen in zeal of English working-class soccer fans abroad, i.e. status acquired through soccer team. Idea of traditional symbols is essentially an invented tradition (like construction of monarchy as House of Windsor).
- Typology of nationalism.
→ *Classical:* emergence of nation state in Europe from 18th century (usually elitist)
→ *Post-colonial:* independence of former colonial states (used nationalism as unifying movement)
→ *Sub-cultural:* movements within nation-states often as breakaway movements.

13. MODERNISM AND POST-MODERNISM

	CHARACTERISTICS OF MODERNISM	CHARACTERISTICS OF POST-MODERNISM
In Social Science	• Post-Enlightenment. The idea of progression towards a 'better' society. Early sociologists (e.g. Comte, Durkheim, Marx and Weber) emphasised that with increased scientific approaches, rationality and positivism society would progress towards a state which could be better understood and controlled.	• The decline of the metanarrative. Science has not provided answers. We have not conquered poverty, ill-health or abuse. Theories become discourses with no absolutes. Marxism especially has been shown to be inadequate with the breakdown of the old Soviet Bloc and the westernisation of China.
In culture	• Culture and society analytically separate. Media would reflect culture (like a mirror) but be separate from it. • Assumption that there was a reality separate from the images of it.	• Breakdown of distinction between culture and society. Media-saturated society where advertising has become ubiquitous. Consumption is increasingly influenced by popular culture. Image is all-important.
High vs. popular culture	• High culture assumed to belong to elite groups and not accessible to or appreciated by the 'masses'. Included opera, ballet, classical literature and music.	• Breakdown of the distinction between them. Introduction of classical music into areas such as sport and pop charts. Popularity of soaps and football – enjoyed by wider audiences.
Knowledge	• Assumption that knowledge could reveal truths and establish a rational standpoint from which reality could be described and analysed.	• Assumption that no absolutes existed, relativism rules. Post-modern writers like Jameson, Lyotard and Baudrillard embraced fragmentation and diversity.
Time and space	• Assumption of clear, linear narratives in literature and film. • Travel takes time, news may take some days to arrive. Personal experience of other countries may be limited.	• Possibility of fracturing narratives and reversing conventions previously accepted. • Contraction of world into global village. Air travel, satellites and cable have shrunk the world. We have international news events shown on our TV sets almost as they take place.
In the arts	• Modernism refers to set of cultural and aesthetic styles at beginning of the 20th century. Search for 'inner truth' behind surface experience. Names associated are: Joyce, Yeats, Proust, Kafka in literature; Cezanne, Picasso, Matisse and the Expressionist, Futurist, Dadaist and Surrealist movements in art. • Architecture emphasised 'the modern' with high-rise apartments which were like cities in the sky.	• Post-modernism refers to movement in advanced capitalist societies especially in the arts. Erasure of boundary between art and everyday life, collapse of distinction between high and popular art. Emphasis on surface not depth. • Destruction of many of these tower blocks as people refused to live in them – they were associated with isolation, vandalism and lack of playing spaces for children.

14. DEBATES ABOUT MODERNITY

LYOTARD

- Lyotard's argument: In primitive society knowledge based on narratives or meaningful accounts. Narratives play a key role in socialisation by conveying rules and norms of society. Narrators use their position to assert truth of their account = language games.
- With Enlightenment, narrative language games replaced by scientific 'denotative' games where statements are subjected to proof via evidence and rational argument. Problems of objectivity – science rests on metanarratives which give meaning to other accounts.
- Since WW2 there has been increasing doubt about metanarratives, science now justified by practical, commercial application.
- However, new information technology will allow more access to information. Knowledge will be more widely distributed not simply held by those in power.

  ✓ Sees knowledge as relative – no absolute truth. Knowledge is a social construct.

  ✗ Lyotard's own knowledge has no greater validity than any other.

  ✗ Scientists still have to demonstrate proof. Continuities between early modern and contemporary society still significant.

BAUDRILLARD

- Baudrillard sees society as having entered new phase related to language and knowledge.
- Society moved from economic production to being shaped by consumption. We live in a society of **signs** where cultural commodities like TV programmes, music and computer games have as much importance as food.
- The media fabricate 'non-communication' – a form of relativism where each viewpoint is given same weight as every other. Audiences receive one-way communication.
- Images of commodities become as significant as the commodities themselves. The advertising image of a car, for example, bears no relation to the reality of driving a real car. The sign bears no relation to reality, it becomes its own simulacrum.
- A simulacrum is an image of something that does not exist. Modern society is filled with images which have no connection to reality.
- Pessimistic towards possibility of political change and of social theory acting to change society.

  ✗ Vague as to development of post-modern societies – apart from intrusion of TV into our lives.

  ✗ Highly abstract view which is difficult to operationalise.

JAMESON

POST-MODERN SOCIETY
→ Jameson sees post-modern society as superficial – lacking real emotion.
→ It is ahistoric and immediate – no links to historical experience.
→ It is timeless – lack of linear plot or narrative.
→ New technology like TV, computers, produce 'flat' images – no explanation, only immediacy.
Criticisms

  ✓ Combines a Marxist analysis with post-modern social theory.

  ✓ Demonstrates continuities and changes in contemporary societies.

  ✗ Fails to give enough credence to relations of production.

  ✗ In danger of producing another metanarrative in place of the others.

THE END OF METANARRATIVES?

  ✓ Fall of Communism seemed to challenge viability of Marxism.

  ✓ Political parties have merged (imploded) into centre.

  ✓ Consumerism seems to define individual identity – shallow, narcissistic and transient.

  However

  ✗ Still evidence of strongly-held beliefs – political and religious examples:

  → *Fundamentalism* – New Christian Right in USA fight against reforms like divorce, gay, black and women's rights.
  → *Islamic fundamentalism* strong in Iran, Afghanistan.
  → *Ethnic cleansing* in former Yugoslavia and independence of states from former USSR.

  ✗ Any new theory is in danger of becoming itself a metanarrative.

  ✗ In danger of producing another metanarrative in place of the others.

15. LOCATION AND IDENTITY

EMILE DURKHEIM (1893)

- Mechanistic and organic solicarity distinction

	Mechanistic	Organic
Associated with	Rural life	Urban life
Relationships	Face-to-face	Anonymous
Division of labour	Simple, varied roles	Complex, specialised
Place in society	Clear, accepted	Mobile
Identity	With group	With self
Solidarity	Of sameness	Of difference

- Change in solidarity occurs not because cities are industrial but because they are more dense.
- Urbanisation multiplies possibilities of contact, making each contact more fleeting.
- But ironically makes individuals more dependent on each other, because of specialisation.
- Danger was anomie where no strong moral code bound individuals together.

Criticisms

✗ Attitude to cities ambiguous.

✗ Over-simplifies rural living.

FERDINAND TONNIES (1890)

- Gemeinschaft and Gesellschaft relationships

Gemeinschaft	Gesellschaft
Intimate and enduring	Large-scale, impersonal
Based on mutual understanding of each other's position in society	Based on inter-dependent need for the other to meet own individual needs
Holistic	Segmental
Involves whole being, relating more fully	More superficial, involving only part of being
Greater mutual involvement and caring	More calculation of interest and contractual obligation

- Gemeinschaft and Gesellschaft have no moral dimension, one is not better than the other.
- Gemeinschaft not just associated with rural living, but could be ethnic groups, ghettos, totalitarian nation.

Criticisms

✗ Often taken up with moral overtones.

✗ Distinctions too tightly drawn.

MAX WEBER (1921)

- Medieval cities were innovative centres of commerce, with strong merchant class.
- Were forerunners of modern society, containing many features of modernity, such as bureaucracy.
- Under industrialisation, cities degenerated as they lost their independence and innovative capacity.

Criticisms

✗ Narrow view of role of cities.

✗ Pessimistic about future of urban life, seeing it as controlled.

✗ Denies that industrial cities are also innovative centres in modern societies.

KARL MARX (1867)

- Rise of the industrial city a sign of progress.
- Rural life represented backwardness.
- Cities were the locality for the rise of socialism, and thus preferred to 'idiocy' of rural life.
- Cities were the furnaces where class unity was forged, the preconditions for the working class to become a 'class in itself'.
- But cities also were squalid because unfettered capitalism held sway.

Criticisms

✗ Stereotyped view of rural life.

✗ Focused on economic conditions as basis of urban life.

GEORG SIMMEL (1922)

- Adopted a social psychological approach.
- Urban living produces a distinctive type of personality, forged by social forces.
- Distinctive feature of city is 'over-stimulation', which leads to the 'blasé attitude'.

Rural way of life	Urban way of life
Emotional	Rational
Barter economy, where exchange is personalised – based on identity	Money economy, where even people are treated as potential commodities
Habitual thought, as things have always been thought	Calculative thought, based on self-interest and main chance
Wonder and naivety	Urban sophistication
Involvement with others	Reserved with others

- Saw the city as poor substitute for the vibrant caring communities of rural life.

Criticisms

✗ Stereotypes of rural and urban life.

✗ Often crudely drawn dualisms illustrate contrasts.

✗ Had moral attitude towards urban sophistication.

✗ Developed series of virtual caricatures of urban types – city slickers, urban cowboys and drop-outs.

Criticisms of classical tradition

✗ Most, though not all traditions, had a romantic and conservative view of rural living, the 'Golden Age of the Village Community'.

✗ Saw countryside as idyllic community, untouched by conflict, ignoring peasant unrest.

✗ Saw cities as repositories of inequality, ignoring fact that great inequality preceded growth of cities.

16. COMMUNITY AND IDENTITY

COMMUNITY

This is one of the central concepts in sociology, but the hardest to pin down exactly. Used by classical sociologists and has long tradition right up to present day.

Why is it so difficult to define?	
? Not value-free concept, but associated with images of idyllic peaceful, happy living.	
? Has an ideological dimension, in that appeals to 'community' often made by politicians.	
? Has implication of conflict – those not of 'our' community are somehow the 'other'.	

Ways in which it has been defined	
1. As geographical locality	A definable area which forms basis of identifiable social organisation, members of which identify with each other.
2. As local social system	A set of relationships, usually but not always within a defined geographical area, in which members relate to each other.
3. As a type of relationship	A distinctive way of interacting which produces a strong set of shared identity, unconfined by geographical location.

Different types of community		
Local e.g. village or city area	National e.g. British	Ethnic e.g. Irish
Religious e.g. Muslim	Sexual e.g. gay	Virtual e.g. cybercommunity

Gemeinschaft – relationships which are close, enduring, warm and deeply felt

Gesellschaft – relationships which are fleeting, calculative, cold and quickly forgotten

A dualism which is typical of the area, which contrasts rural living with urban living and sees them as opposites.

Other Dualisms

PATTERN VARIABLES BETWEEN RURAL AND URBAN LIVING (TALCOTT PARSONS)

Ascription	Status given at birth, e.g. caste position as parents	⟷	Achievement	Status given according to talent and effort
Role diffuseness	Roles undertaken are broad and varied	⟷	Role specificity	Roles are undertaken for particular purposes
Particularism	Personal and family contacts are of prime importance	⟷	Universalism	Rules are applied equally to all, whether family or not
Affectivity	Life is lived on an emotional and public level	⟷	Affective neutrality	Emotions are controlled, especially in public
Collective orientation	Shared interests are important and actions geared to them	⟷	Self-orientation	Personal success and individualism are paramount

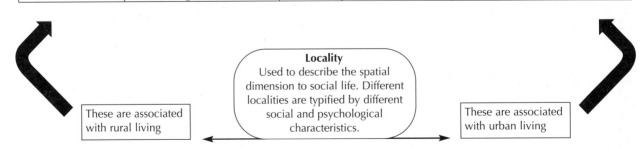

Locality
Used to describe the spatial dimension to social life. Different localities are typified by different social and psychological characteristics.

These are associated with rural living

These are associated with urban living

17. SOCIOLOGICAL PERSPECTIVES ON COMMUNITY, NEIGHBOURING, AND IDENTITY

STRUCTURALIST / **INTERACTIONIST**

STRUCTURAL FUNCTIONALIST

- Communities function to maintain solidarity ties between individuals.
- Communities are moral orders which exercise social control over members.
- Individualistic behaviour is restricted in communities to establish social order.
- This creates tensions in community between privacy and the collective.
- Leads to 'surveillance' of neighbours as well as mutual support networks BUT

✗ Has romantic view of community, even where surveillance is end-result.

UTILITARIAN THEORY

- Emphasis on conflict over scarce resources between neighbours and communities.
- Individuals and communities pursue interests in rational way, seeking the greatest benefit.
- Choices made for mutually beneficial exchanges (reciprocity) between individuals and communities BUT

✗ Rationality of individuals overemphasised

✗ 'Modern neighbourhoodism' displays much less social exchange for mutual benefit

✗ Does not explain areas where little interaction takes place.

INTERACTIONIST

- Focus on the way groups produce identity.
- Emphasis on in-groups and out-groups, insiders and outsiders.
- Gossip is one of the mechanisms by which status as outsider or insider is established.
- Stereotypes operate to maintain boundaries between included and excluded BUT

✗ Ignores wider social and economic processes which affect outcomes e.g. racism

✗ Tends to polarise social locations rather than see them as diverse mixtures of people

✗ Focus on the now rather than historical processes.

COMMUNITARIANISM

- Individualism of free market New Right breaking up communities, threatening stability.
- Need to re-establish a moral order in which citizens actively engage with others to create the 'good society'.
- Both parents to teach morals to children, reinforced by schools.
- Government to support community webs and empower locales to actively construct society, while defusing conflicts BUT

✗ New Right argues this removes individual choices

✗ Ignores corporate responsibilities (Marxists)

✗ Feminists dislike criticism of non-traditional family forms.

POST-STRUCTURALIST

Individuals reveal themselves to others in gradients, with other community members likely to see full 'disclosure'. With strangers, enclosure is more likely. Communities may also be experienced as oppressive, with members not disclosing true identity so as not to offend official community values BUT

✗ Not clear how 'official' community values known

✗ Degree of disclosure in any situation not explained.

MARXIST/CONFLICT

- Traditional Marxist sees community as 'residual', that is, unimportant in class societies.
- Neo-Marxists argue that class conflicts have micro and macro economic aspects.
- Neighbourhood is thus important variable in understanding nature of class society BUT

✗ Emphasis still firmly on economic processes rather than social or political aspects of community

✗ Social polarisation implied by housing segregation is over-played

✗ Process whereby neighbourhood feeling intersects with class consciousness not made clear.

FEMINIST

- Emphasis on patriarchy and the way communities are structured according to gender.
- Looks at imbalance of power between men and women in communities, especially economic power.
- Focuses on role of women as keepers of the history of the locality.
- Examines role of women in 'policing' communities in terms of notions of respectability.
- Stresses pivotal role of women in maintaining neighbourhood relations BUT

✗ Tends to see all problems stemming from patriarchy

✗ Underplays men's role in maintaining and servicing communities.

POST-MODERNIST

- Community can be expressed as a 'symbolic boundary', that is, boundaries which appear only in the mind.
- They vary from person to person and time to time.
- Important because traditional boundaries have dissolved, e.g. as countryside becomes more like town.
- New communications technology and geographical mobility have expanded potential limits of symbolic boundaries.
- Communities can and do engage in their own transformation, by getting involved in policy BUT

✗ Degree of engagement overdone

✗ Existence of symbolic boundaries not shown.

18. SYNOPTIC OVERVIEW

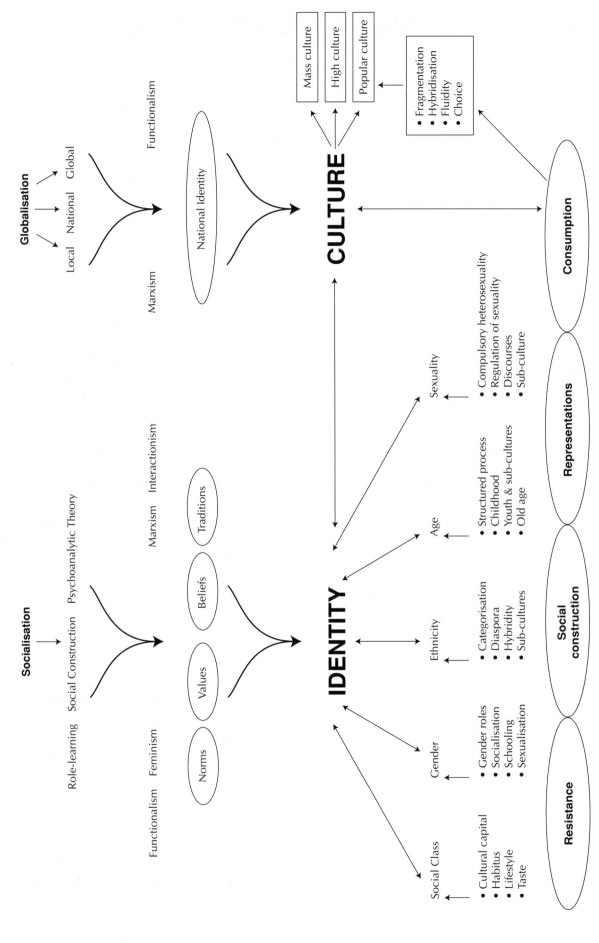

2 Families and Households

1. FAMILY AND HOUSEHOLD STRUCTURES

Nuclear [conjugal] **'cereal packet'** type, parents and unmarried children, small family size is a feature of the 20th century.

Nuclear family, larger family size was more common in the later 19th century.

Vertically extended (consanguine) family, i.e. three generations in one household. Becoming more common with increased life expectancy and the policy of community care.

Matrifocal family: two or more generations of women in the same household with their dependent children. Identified among the black poor of the Caribbean and southern states of the USA, also found among black British.

Horizontally extended by the inclusion of the families of siblings in one household. Found amongst rural / agricultural communities.

Reconstituted, (blended) horizontally extended by step relationships, becoming more common with high rates of divorce and remarriage.

$O = \Delta$ or O O

or Δ Δ

Couples with **no dependent children** either before or after family building stage.
Growing number of same-sex partnerships.

O

Single-person households, commonly found among the old (these are more often women); after the desertion of a partner; or with increasing numbers of young adults leaving parental home before marriage.

Single-parent family: mother or less commonly father, with dependent children. Often a temporary arrangement before entering a reconstituted family.

O Δ

O O

House share: same or mixed sex groups sharing accommodation for practical reasons rather than emotional bonds.

KEY   O = female   Δ = male

2. IS THE NUCLEAR FAMILY UNIVERSAL?

CROSS-CULTURAL EXCEPTIONS	MURDOCK'S CLAIM (1949) THAT THE NUCLEAR FAMILY IS UNIVERSAL	CONTEMPORARY HOUSEHOLDS THAT DO NOT FIT THE DEFINITION
• In the Nayar (Mexico) the husband did not live with the wife and her children and had no social contact. • In a kibbutz the children live in dormitories.	**DEFINITION** The family is a social group characterised by: • common residence	• Families can be separated by prison or immigration restrictions.
• Nayar husbands gave token gifts but had no obligation to provide maintenance. • In the kibbutz the community share property, and children are the responsibility of the whole group.	• economic co-operation (implies a division of labour between male and female partners based on male hunters and female gatherers and homemakers)	• Domination of economic resources can occur when one partner uses family money for personal gain, e.g. gambling social security benefits. • Role reversal households.
• The Trobriand islanders (Papua New Guinea) had no understanding of how children were procreated. • In the Nayar any one of the visiting warriors may father the child.	• and reproduction.	• Excludes foster families and those created by surrogacy and IVF.
• Matrifocal New World black families were accepted and expected as a positive adaptation to a situation of poverty.	It includes adults of both sexes,	• Large number of lone parent families some of whom will not remarry.
• Rules of exogamy and incest are variable, e.g. in the Tikopia (Pacific Ocean) marriage closer than a second cousin was frowned upon.	at least two of whom maintain a socially approved relationship,	• Lesbian and gay relationships are not recognised in law in Britain but are in some American states.
• The Ashanti of Ghana had no permanent conjugal arrangement.	and one or more children, own or adopted, of the sexually cohabiting adults.	• Does not include reconstituted families.
• The family is socially constructed and varies from one culture to another.	The nuclear family is universal in the sense that it exists as the building block and so recognises the possibilities of family beyond the nuclear structure, e.g. extended and polygamous families.	• Does not recognise reductions to a smaller unit, e.g. married couple with no children.
• These functions have been performed by traditional kibbutz communities.	Murdock found the nuclear family in each one of 250 societies studied. It is universal because it performs 4 essential functions necessary for survival and continuity.	• Does not consider alternatives to the family that could fulfil these functions, e.g. communes.

Whether the family is universal depends on how the family is defined. If a broad definition is used then all social arrangements are included but it does not tell you very much about families. If a narrow definition is used there are too many exceptions to claim universality.

3. CONTRASTING VIEWS ON THE FUNCTIONS OF THE FAMILY

	FUNCTIONALIST	MARXIST	MARXIST – FEMINIST	RADICAL FEMINIST	LIBERAL FEMINIST
Sex, marriage and reproduction	• Provides for the satisfaction of sexual needs of both partners. • Produces the children for the next generation, these children are helpless and dependent so need adults to survive.	• Monogamy is a way of ensuring men transmit ownership of private property to their own offspring.	• Marriage gives men property rights over women. • Reproduces the labour power for work in a capitalist society at no cost to the capitalist employer.	• Patriarchal power controls women's sexual activity, many wives are dominated by violence. • Women are handicapped by their biology and forced into dependence on men.	• Men benefit more from marriage as shown by health statistics, income and status. • Fathers should also have rights to a close relationship with their children.
Socialisation and social control	• Passes on the shared culture without which society would cease to exist. • Prepares children for adult roles.	• Suppresses individuality to produce a compliant workforce that is passive, subservient and uncritical of the inequalities which prop up capitalism.	• Children learn to submit to parental authority and are thus prepared to take their place in the hierarchy of a capitalist society.	• Sex role socialisation maintains patriarchy, children are powerless and subject to age patriarchy.	• Gendered socialisation of children produces rigid and inflexible expectations.
Stabilisation	• A loving relationship in marriage provides warmth, security, emotional support and fulfilment for adults, the family is a haven from the outside world.	• Private life of the family provides the opportunities for satisfactions unavailable in work, thus cushioning the effects of capitalism.	• Wives make husbands more productive workers by acting as a safety valve and shock absorber to handle the tensions and frustrations generated at work.	• Marriage is the theft of women's labour, women are the 'takers of shit'.	• Women express more dissatisfaction with marriage and initiate more divorce proceedings.
Economic and welfare	• Males and females have different capabilities so a division of labour is an efficient way of organising family life.	• Unit of consumption essential to capitalist production. • Family responsibilities constrain men not to withdraw their labour.	• Women provide free domestic labour without cost to capitalism, they are 'slaves of the wage slaves'. • Capitalists use the housewife role to depress wages by acting as a reserve army of labour.	• Division of labour allows men to dominate women. • Being a housewife is a low status, unpaid position.	• Women's potential is limited by accommodating men's needs. • Being a housewife literally makes women sick.
Evaluation	✗ Only looks at the positive aspects ✗ Assumes that the family benefits everyone ✗ Does not recognise diversity and alternatives to the family ✗ Ignores the interaction process between parent and child ✓ Shows how important the family is to social life ✓ Emphasises continuity across generations ✓ Has strong ideological hold over many individuals	✗ Concentrates on the effects of capitalism to the exclusion of other factors ✗ Does not explain the similarities in capitalist and non-capitalist societies ✗ Engel's ideas based on unreliable anthropological evidence ✓ Identified a source of gender inequality on which later theories have expanded ✓ Shows the relationship between capitalism and the family	✗ Does not explain the subordination of women in pre-capitalist society ✗ Many women like the domestic role in family life and this is not false consciousness ✓ Identifies exploitation of women as the key feature of family life ✓ Shows the family is ideologically and socially constructed	✗ Ignores the real satisfactions the family can give to many women ✗ Anti-men stance does not reflect real life ✗ Ignores the dimensions of class and ethnicity ✗ Assumes that gender unites women ✓ Shows that housework is real work ✓ Reveals the extent of marital violence ✓ Challenges notions of symmetry ✓ Introduces issues of power to family relationships, class and race and assumes gender unites women from all backgrounds	✗ Tries to bring about more equality without changing social structures ✗ Too soft in thinking everything will be put right in time ✗ Does not recognise the all-pervasive nature of patriarchy ✓ Helps to understand the process of sex role socialisation in the family ✓ Recognises that men also need to be more free ✓ Aims for gradual change is more realistic

4. FOUR VIEWS OF THE TRADITIONAL FAMILY MODEL

NEW RIGHT

The traditional family model is the 'natural' unit and the cornerstone of society. The model has been undermined by permissiveness, feminism and the welfare state. Social policy (see **Family 5**) is needed to support the traditional family model and return to traditional family values.

Tolerance of deviation has produced pathological families and moral decline in society. The social problems that originate in one-parent families in particular are criminality, under-achievement of children, fecklessness, and illegitimacy in the next generation.

The traditional family model is desirable

 **Model is weak in society**

FUNCTIONALISTS

The reality fits the image and that is good because this fits industrial society. Chester suggests a neo-conventional family (in which wives are periodically employed outside the home), as the more usual arrangement in modern society. He argues that the nuclear family is numerically dominant if people are counted rather than households. It is most people's experience of family and it is also ideologically dominant. It suits people because it provides intimacy without oppression.

 **Model is powerful in society**

THE IMAGE OF THE TRADITIONAL FAMILY MODEL

Male breadwinner
with patriarchal control

Heterosexual couple

Married,
dependent wife

Two children

Everyone happy

LIBERALS AND SOME HISTORIANS

The model is irrelevant as it only represents 25% of all households. The family has always been characterised by diversity. This is to be celebrated for the freedom of choice it brings. Diversity is found in the organisation of families, e.g. lone parents, reconstituted etc.,(see **Family 1**).

There are cultural variations, e.g. extended families of Asian background, matrifocal of Afro-Caribbean; class differences e.g. middle class dispersed or attenuated extended, working class local extended; stage of life cycle; cohort, e.g. patriarchal families in grandparents' generation more symmetrical amongst new families.

FEMINIST

The pervasiveness of the image in the media, consumer packaging, and government policy is damaging because people are misguided into believing this structure is the only appropriate one in which to live. The image obscures and neglects the reality of family life with its violence, oppression and exploitation. It encourages an ethnocentric view of family life and assumes the domestic role of women and the power of men is correct and necessary. The family is the mechanism for passing inequalities to the next generation. Women in particular are disadvantaged in the traditional model, as their needs are subsumed by their 'duty' to the family.

The traditional family model is undesirable

5. SOCIAL POLICY AND THE FAMILY

> **SOCIAL POLICY** refers to the actions (or inaction) of government and its agencies in relation to the lives of the population. Although there is no government department responsible for family policy, legislation and decisions in the areas of housing, taxation, employment, social security, and judicial decisions all have an impact on family life.

Characteristics of the traditional family model	POLICY SUPPORTING THE MODEL	POLICY AGAINST THE MODEL
Heterosexual	<ul><li>Only legal form of union</li><li>No teaching or promotion of homosexuality in schools</li><li>Same-sex couples not afforded same rights as heterosexuals</li></ul>	<ul><li>Lowering age of consent for homosexual relationships</li><li>Abolition of "Clause 28"</li></ul>
Married	<ul><li>Green Paper 1998 'Supporting Families' suggests that marriage is best</li><li>Divorce law requiring counselling and cooling-off period</li><li>Promotion of marriage in sex education lessons in school</li></ul>	<ul><li>Green Paper does not criticise alternative arrangements</li><li>Perverse tax incentives to remain single, e.g. tax relief for children of single-parent families</li><li>Removal of the barriers to divorce</li></ul>
Two children	<ul><li>Free contraception</li><li>Legalisation of abortion</li><li>IVF programmes supported by NHS</li><li>Housing priority when children are present</li></ul>	<ul><li>Child benefit payable for all children under 16 or in full-time education has been said by some to encourage large families</li></ul>
Male breadwinner	<ul><li>Child Support Agency (CSA) requires absent parent (usually father) to maintain children</li><li>Cohabitation rules in social security assume that a cohabiting man is financially supporting the woman and her children</li><li>No paternity leave</li></ul>	<ul><li>CSA undermines the ability of the father to support a new family</li><li>Welfare state benefits for single parents</li><li>Equal Pay Act</li><li>Separate tax assessments for husbands and wives</li><li>Removal of married man's tax allowance in 1989</li></ul>
Dependent wife	<ul><li>Factory Acts of the 19th century excluded women from certain forms of work</li><li>Maternity leave</li><li>Lack of nursery places and after-school care</li><li>Care in the community relies on the informal caring of relatives (mainly women)</li><li>Reduced national insurance contributions for married women under the Beveridge plan 1945</li></ul>	<ul><li>Tax relief on childcare makes it easier for women to work</li><li>Welfare-to-work programmes encourage single mothers to be independent</li><li>Abolition of reduced national insurance contributions by married women</li><li>Abolition in 1986 of the ruling that a married woman could not claim Invalid Care Allowance when looking after a sick or disabled relative</li></ul>

6. IS THE FAMILY IN DECLINE?

Functions	FAMILY IN DECLINE/LOSING ITS FUNCTIONS (position taken by right-wing politicians)	FAMILY NOT IN DECLINE (misconceptions of the past and re-interpretation of current statistics)
Sex	• Permissive attitudes towards sex • Pre-marital and extra-marital relationships • Illegitimacy rate going up	• Double standards existed in the past • Concealed in the past by marriage after conception • Births increasingly registered to both parents suggesting a common-law marriage arrangement
Marriage	• Total number of marriages down and marriages do not last as long • Period of cohabitation is lengthening suggesting an alternative to marriage • Rising divorce rate • Growth in single-person households	• 90% of people marry at some time • Re-marriage rate up • Cohabitation is a trial *before* marriage rather than a substitute • People usually marry before the birth of the first child • More opportunities to escape unhappy marriages • Marriages broken by death of one partner in the past
Reproduction	• Couples choosing not to have children • Smaller family size • Access to IVF treatment suggests state has become involved even in this area of family life • Increasing number of single women choosing parenthood without male support	• More couples in the past were infertile • Families in the past not large because of later marriage and high infant mortality
Child rearing	• Large number of child abuse cases • Increase in cases of child neglect	• Uncovering what was previously hidden • Standards of care higher today
Socialisation	• State has taken over the education role and more children go to pre-school education • Lack of male role models weakens family discipline	• Families more child-centred than in the past and family life continues to be the most formative influence on a child's life • Parents spend quality time with their children
Stabilisation	• Increasing numbers of dysfunctional families as shown by domestic violence	• Uncovering problems that have always been there
Economic	• Reduced to a unit of consumption • State provides family benefits in cash (child benefit) and kind (education and health)	• Family still an important economic group because of the economic value of domestic activities such as cleaning, food preparation and care • Family is major part of 'grey economy'
Welfare	• State has taken over the health and income support role • Law establishes rights of state agencies to intervene in family life	• Family still provides first line care in sickness and childbirth • Extended family provides for mutual aid and help in crises • Family still offers 'home' to members from time to time

24 Family and household structures

7. NEGATIVE ASPECTS OF FAMILY LIFE

Above the water the alligator, like the family, presents a calm and unthreatening face.

Below the surface the animal, like the family, has the power to destroy.

	Psychiatric disorders		Overloaded	Violent	Emotional scapegoating
	RADICAL PSYCHIATRISTS		**ANTHROPOLOGIST**	**FEMINIST**	**FUNCTIONALIST**
	Laing	Cooper	Leach	Dobash & Dobash	Bell & Vogel
Ideas	• Claimed to reveal the reality behind normal family life. • Concluded the family is damaging and can cause schizophrenia. • Behaviour disorders as a response to intolerable family situations such as the conflicts of parents. • 'Mad' people come from 'mad' families. • Behaviour that may appear bizarre has meaning for the individual.	• Adds a Marxist perspective to Laing's ideas. • Family seen as an ideological conditioning device reinforcing the power of the ruling class and crushing individual identity. • Tensions and guilt in the family are caused by capitalism and it is these chains that have to be broken to produce a creative and independent individual.	• Studied pre-industrial societies where extended kin provide emotional and practical help. • This led him to believe isolated nuclear family is emotionally overloaded, it internalises problems and expects too much of members. • Claimed the 'family with its narrow and tawdry secrets is the source of all our discontents'.	• Argue that the family is not a secure, happy or peaceful place. • Family is the most violent group to which a person will belong. • Demonstrate the under-reporting and widespread nature of domestic violence and show that it is not restricted to one social class. • Show marital conflict is also associated with child abuse.	• Focus on the emotionally disturbed child. • Unresolved tensions and conflicts of the parents are projected onto the child. • This relieves parents' frustrations, enabling them to carry out other roles, e.g. work. • What is dysfunctional for the child is functional for the parents.
Criticisms	✗ Untypical families studied ✗ No normal control families for comparison ✗ Laing retracted many of his controversial ideas before he died	✗ Impossible to validate ✗ Assumes the child is powerless ✗ Focuses exclusively on the negative aspects of family life	✗ Lack of empirical evidence. The family is the haven from the tension in the outside world ✗ If people choose to live in families they must be good	✗ Data collected by informal interviews is subjective, value-laden and may contain interviewer bias ✗ Tends to assume violence is only male on female	✗ Assumes gains to parents and society outweigh costs to child ✗ Ignores the fact that an emotionally disturbed child may become an inadequate parent

8. FAMILY AND SOCIAL CHANGE

MARX'S CONFLICT THEORY

Revolutions		Agricultural		Industrial		Political	
Stages in family development	**Primitive communism** No private ownership, society is classless and matriarchal.	⇨	**Feudalism** Land ownership creates primogeniture, and monogamous marriage.	⇨	**Capitalism** Nuclear patriarchal family meets the needs of the bourgeoisie for profit-making.	⇨	**Socialist** Society will become classless and family roles equal.

PARSONS' FUNCTIONALIST THEORY OF 'FIT'

Isolated nuclear family fits industrial society because it is:

- **Structurally differentiated** from the pre-industrial multi-functional extended family as the result of pressures from factory production
- **Geographically mobile**, it is not tied down by kinship obligations and can move to towns for work
- **Socially mobile** as the two-generation structure avoids conflict between father and son which might occur when social status is no longer ascribed and differentials occur in levels of achievement
- Small and economically **self-sufficient**
- Performs two irreducible functions of **socialisation** and **stabilisation**
- Non-essential functions are taken over by outside agencies.

Critique of 'fit' theory

1. Cause and effect are the reverse, the nuclear family's practice of primogeniture provided the impetus for industrialisation. Non-inheriting sons had to make their own way in life and so were a mobile labour force with the values of hard work and achievement necessary for industrialisation to develop.

2. Parish records in pre-industrial England showed only 10% of households were extended beyond the nuclear family due to late marriage and early death.

   x Ignores variations as averages oversimplify

   x Kin may have been in co-operative social groups although not co-resident

   x Accuracy of the records themselves can be questioned

3. Early industrial period showed an increase in the number of extended family households as people's dependence on kin increased. The family could help to get jobs; provide childcare for working wives; protect against poverty. The 1851 census data from Preston showed 23% of households with extended kin. Only in mid-20th century did the reduction of the power of kin to speak for relatives, fewer singles in search of work, and the cushioning effect of the welfare state bring about the nuclear family.

   x Preston had high unemployment and no welfare so generalisation may be inappropriate

4. Extended family remains important in industrial society in a modified form because of affectional ties and choice, i.e. the family is not isolated.

MARCH OF PROGRESS (EVOLUTIONARY) THEORY

The family develops through a process of **stratified diffusion**, i.e. change filters down through the class structure. The structure and function of the family changes as a result of new technology and work patterns, housing and leisure.

Stage 1 ⇧
pre-industrial:
nuclear (pre-1750): late marriage and parents dying early so few families had surviving grandparents

Stage 2 ⇧
industrial extended (1750–1900): children and grandparents survived to create three-generation families which acted as mutual support

Stage 3 ⇧
symmetrical nuclear family: a home-centred unit with partners taking an equal share in domestic duties

Stage 4
asymmetrical family: found among the top classes and assumed to be the pattern of the future, work is the central life interest of men, and women revert to an exclusive domestic role

9. MARRIAGE ISSUES

FORMS OF MARRIAGE
- **Monogamy** (one spouse for life)
- **Serial monogamy** (one spouse at any one point in time but two or more over the course of a lifetime)
- **Polygyny** (more than one wife): this can confer status and bring economic rewards of children as labour
- **Polyandry** (more than one husband): often fraternal where brothers share a wife
- **Common law partnerships**

REASONS FOR MARRIAGE

In the wider social group:
- Economic alliances
- Co-operative alliances
- Ensuring offspring

For the couple and their children:
- Legitimation of offspring
- Companionship
- Emotional/love matches

STATE CONTROLS ON FAMILY BUILDING
- Laws on who you can marry, e.g. sex and familial relationship
- At what age you can marry
- Under what conditions or whether the marriage can be broken by divorce
- Compulsory registration of births
- Number of children (e.g. China)

REASONS FOR THE CONTROL OF FERTILITY
- Availability of reliable contraception
- Preference for small families because of costs of children
- Delayed childbirth until the establishment of a career
- Fall in infant mortality, each pregnancy is likely to result in child reaching adulthood
- Sex in marriage is no longer seen as for the procreation of children
- Women have taken control since the availability of the contraceptive pill in the 1960s

CHANGES IN FAMILY BUILDING PATTERNS
- Increase in the median age of all marriages
- Decline in the median age of first marriage
- Marriage rates have fallen
- One-third of marriages are re-marriages, but fewer women remarry after divorce
- Delay in first pregnancy, mean age of mother 28 years
- Increase in joint registrations
- Average family size below 2 children, but class and ethnic variations
- Shorter gap between pregnancies
- Increase in abortions
- Growing number of women never married
- More couples childless by choice

INTERPRETIVIST APPROACH

Social construction of reality in marriage:
- Couples arrive at a common view through socialisation
- Children are socialised into the same view.
- Views of marriage emerge from day-to-day interaction of couple and their children.

Becoming a parent:
- A learning process involving trial and error in bringing up children
- Making sense of children's behaviour in terms of phases and stages of development.
- Parents draw on their own experience and 'folk wisdom' of their own parents to negotiate child-rearing.

Types of marriage
- Drifting – couples with no long-term plans
- Surfacing – at least one partner with a previous marriage that continues to be a problem
- Establishing – conscious planning often saving money to buy a house
- Struggling – experiencing financial problems usually because of unemployment, made worse by unplanned pregnancies.

10. MARRIAGE BREAKDOWN

Causes ← → **Consequences**

Center: **MARRIAGE BREAKDOWN** / **DIVORCE (legal termination of a marriage)** / (legal separation, desertion, empty shell marriages)

Rings: **INDIVIDUAL** · **PARTNERS** · **FAMILY** · **SOCIETY**

Causes

- Decline in religion
- Permissive legislation
- Change in social values, less stigma
- Benefits for the single parent
- Growth of urban communities
- Employment opportunities
- Wars
- Longer life expectancy
- Less influence of extended family
- A child of divorced parents
- Shortage of money/ unemployment
- Sharing accommodation with relatives
- Increased independence of wives
- High expectations of marriage
- Conflicts with spouse
- Love unions are more unstable than economic alliances
- Differences in social class, age or ethnicity
- Occupations involving time spent apart
- Teenage marriage
- Pregnancy at marriage

Individual (causes): Depression and stress; Loneliness

Consequences

- Avoidance of marriage
- Counselling services
- Remarriage
- More chance of second broken marriage
- More single parents
- Impact on children, e.g. emotional and educational
- Interventions by social workers
- Reconstituted families and step relations
- Demands for tighter legislation
- Tax burden for the state
- Housing needs
- Serial monogamy

11. DOMESTIC LABOUR

THE SOCIAL CONSTRUCTION OF THE HOUSEWIFE ROLE DURING 19TH & EARLY 20TH CENTURIES.

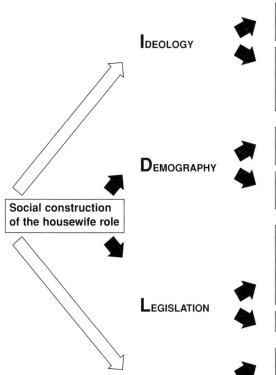

IDEOLOGY

The concept of 'maternal instinct' was used to justify the child-rearing arrangements that subordinated women to the mother–child bond.

Middle-class women were expected to stay at home as a mark of status and a sign that the man could provide for the family. Working-class women were expected to take in homework so they could combine paid work with childcare.

DEMOGRAPHY

The stage of child-bearing and rearing was lengthy due to a lack of reliable contraception.

Life expectancy was shorter so there was little time after family building before death to start paid work outside the home.

Social construction of the housewife role

LEGISLATION

Factory acts restricted child labour so children became dependent on parents for care.
Employment acts excluded women from work in some industries. This was partly philanthropic and partly in the interests of male workers to protect their jobs.

1925 Guardianship of Infants Act gave women control of children.

ECONOMY

Male unions used their power to demand a 'family wage' sufficient to support a wife and children.

Women's wages came to be seen as a secondary source and spent on family extras, whereas a man's money was his own property once he had provided the housekeeping.

SIMILARITIES AND DIFFERENCES IN UNSKILLED MANUAL WORK AND HOUSEWORK

COMPARISON Both:	CONTRAST	
	UNSKILLED MANUAL WORK	HOUSEWORK
are social obligations	is contractual and linked to pay through hours worked or output achieved	is non-contractual, based on personal obligation
have time implications	has specified clocking in and out with rest periods and paid holidays	has unlimited time commitment: 77 hours per week or more when there are young children, with no time off
are productive or offering a service	is a central part of the economic system	has no recognised economic role
are alienating	is dull, monotonous and fragmented	is repetitive, unfulfilling and no end product, but the absence of supervision gives women some autonomy
make use of technology	uses technology to increase productivity or remove the physically demanding aspects of the job	uses technology that leads to higher expectations of cleanliness
have quality standards	set by employers or industry watchdog	'standards' arrived at informally through comparisons with neighbours
operate in a set of social relationships	gives social support from work mates and supervision down the hierarchy	is socially isolating by being limited to family and has no union for protection
are subject to exploitation	Low pay	Unpaid

12. CONJUGAL ROLE RELATIONSHIPS

ARGUMENTS AND EVIDENCE OF INEQUALITIES IN RELATIONSHIPS	SUBJECT OF DEBATES SHOWING DEGREE OF INEQUALITY	CRITICISMS
F U N C T I O N A L I S T S		
Biological differences reflected in the division of labour in 250 societies studied suggests evidence of the universality of feminine tasks.	BIOLOGY V CULTURE	✗ Re-analysis showed no universality, rather cultural relativity
Instrumental (male provider) and expressive (female carer and giver of affection) roles are based on group responses to social organisation which are both natural and efficient.	TRADITIONAL ROLES	✗ No basis for the sex-specific roles and fixed distinction between the instrumental and expressive roles ✗ Idea based on work with temporary groups not families
Segregated conjugal roles occur when the couple have separate social lives. Differentiation of roles and joint roles occur where there is more sharing and joint decision-making. Pattern varies with the connectedness of the couple's social networks.	ROLES AND SOCIAL NETWORKS	✗ Based on data from only 20 couples not randomly selected ✗ Invalidity of the social indicators used to measure connectedness and role segregation
As women work, less time is spent with kin and men spend more time with their families. 72% of men did housework other than washing up in the last week before the survey.	SYMMETRY	✗ Based on one question which exaggerated the contribution men make by including those who iron their own trousers
F E M I N I S T S		
Women retain primary responsibility for child-care. Role reversal is only found in a small number of households. In dual career families the wife dealt with the problems created by her working, e.g. childcare.	CHILDCARE	✗ More fathers attend the birth of their children and have a continuing involvement in their care
Women still do most of the housework and the least desirable jobs with the lowest status, e.g. cleaning the toilet. In households where there is an unemployed man women are unlikely to further undermine the traditional masculine role by expecting help with housework. In households of two full-time doctors the women did the majority of the shopping and took time off when children were ill.	HOUSEWORK	✗ Men do more when their wives are working. If a wider range of tasks is included then men's involvement is greater, although specialisation does occur ✗ Total number of hours in paid and unpaid work between men and women is not that different
Pooling resources conceals inequality and husband-controlled pooling strengthens the power of the earner. Women more often control the money when the family is on benefits, and she uses this position for the benefit of the family rather than her own needs.	MONEY	✗ Small sample size means that representativeness cannot be guaranteed
In middle-class couples men alone make the important decisions and set the agenda over what can be discussed.	DECISION-MAKING	✗ Women may not be passive victims of male power in intimate relationships
Women often support men in their jobs, by acting as secretaries, messengers or entertaining clients. They are socially dependent when they have no work contacts. In dual income families women's jobs are seen as secondary to their partners.	DEPENDENCE	✗ Many women actively choose this type of relationship
Wife battering is an extension of men's domination and control over women and a reflection of wider social inequalities.	VIOLENCE	✗ Actions of a few disturbed individuals not a normal pattern.

13. CHANGES IN FAMILY RELATIONSHIPS FROM THE MID-TWENTIETH CENTURY

RELATIONSHIP	Nature of the change	Positive Consequences	Negative Consequences	Criticism
MOTHER – CHILD	• Increase in employed mothers both full-time and part-time • Returning to work when children are younger	• Positive role model especially for daughters • Essential income for families • Encourages father – child bond • Improved mental health for women	• Maternal deprivation results in pathological personalities and juvenile delinquency • Creates role conflict and guilt • Lack of childcare and after-school provision	• Not a new pattern, working-class women have always had to work • Cultural variations in child-rearing do not have harmful effects
LONE PARENT – CHILD	• Doubling of numbers of families in 20 years, 1.6m children • Created by choice, divorce, separation and desertion rather than death of spouse as in the past	• A new emerging family that signifies changing structures, and a sign of women's independence • Better than a child living in a family of conflict and violence	• New Right claim that the welfare state offers perverse incentives to become single parents, e.g. queue-jumping the housing list • No male role model for children who become delinquent and underachieve educationally	• Figures are only a snapshot and do not recognise this family type as a transitional phase • Effects on children are from the break-up of families not single-parenting • Problems relate to the poverty of single parents not their inability to parent
WIDER KIN	• Reduction in links with extended family, through geographical and social separation • Communication at a distance	• Strengthens conjugal bonds • Creates the small mobile unit that fits industrial society (see **Family 8**)	• Overloads the nuclear family (see **Family 7**) • Difficulties in caring for elderly relatives, see below	• Operates in upper class for economic reasons • Mother – daughter ties for mutual aid and emergency help • Cultural diversity
ELDERLY IN THE FAMILY	• People living longer • Children now old themselves when their parents need care • Fewer siblings to share care • Children may not live close to parent	• Free of work obligations and fit and healthy to enjoy retirement • Creates new family relationships across three generations	• Burden of care falls to women • Institutionalisation of the dependent elderly	• Misrepresentation of the past as a golden age, only 5–6% of elderly cared for in institutions, the same as 100 years ago

14. SOCIAL CONSTRUCTION OF CHILDHOOD

HISTORICAL CHANGES IN THE CONCEPTION OF CHILDHOOD

Before 1600	1700–1800	1800–1900	1900–1950	1950–onwards
The child of 5 years old belonged to the adult world of work, leisure and sex, but the interpretation from paintings used as evidence has been challenged. Information about role of children is very limited and evidence is often not direct. Interpretation is open to dispute.	Children were an economic asset, new industry depended on the skills of the young, and they provided insurance for their parents in later life. There was little love or affection shown to children. Children's wages, though small, were an important financial asset to the family.	Children's economic role became marginalised with restrictions on child labour and the imposition of compulsory schooling. Middle-class children were assumed to lack the competencies of adults and were in need of protection and guidance. Under the influence of religion the working-class child was assumed to be born corrupt and wicked and had to be taught and controlled.	Children became economically worthless but emotionally priceless. Children needed love and attention and the realities of life were hidden from them. Children have their own culture that is impenetrable to adults. Childhood became idealised, as a magical time of innocence and fun.	Growing awareness of children's rights and empowerment. Children are seen as active family members and make a more democratic contribution to the family through contributions to housework. Young people form a growing economic force in society and in the family. Children targeted by commerce in own right.

CULTURAL VARIATIONS

Ik people of E. Africa treated their children harshly in the hope they would die and therefore be one less mouth to feed. At 3 years old they were thrown out of home.

Child labour is widespread in the developing world where it is estimated there are 145m children involved in commercial production. Street children are also a feature of poorer societies.

Legal age of marriage, e.g. in Turkey a young person can marry at 14.

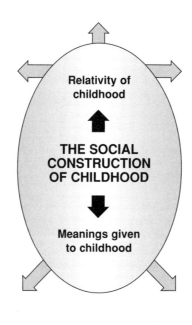

Relativity of childhood

THE SOCIAL CONSTRUCTION OF CHILDHOOD

Meanings given to childhood

LAWS WHICH DEFINE CHILDHOOD ACCORDING TO THE ACTIVITY

At the following ages you can:
- 5 – drink alcohol in private
- 7 – draw money from a bank account
- 10 – be convicted of a criminal offence
- 12 – buy a pet without a parent
- 13 – work a restricted number of hours
- 14 – go into a pub but not drink alcohol
- 15 – see a '15' film
- 16 – buy a lottery ticket, leave school, have sex
- 17 – drive a car, be sent to prison
- 18 – vote

CHILDHOOD IS DISAPPEARING

Good – Libertarians
- Children's interests are and should be put first in custody and adoption cases
- They must be listened to in allegations of abuse and should have rights to divorce parents
- Children make a contribution to the family
- They share the same television programmes, food and clothes as adults

Bad – New Right
- Children know all adult secrets through the media and Internet
- They need to be protected from abuse and exposure to inappropriate materials
- They are becoming parents, sports and media stars whilst still children themselves
- They are undisciplined and lack respect for adult authority, e.g. police and teachers

CHILDHOOD IS NOT DISAPPEARING

Good – Functionalists
- Children are innocent and need protection so they are banned from adult places and activities
- The complexity of society requires a long period of socialisation, hence schools and university
- Resources spent on children, e.g. on toys, are specialised for their needs
- They have their own self-contained culture

Bad – Marxists and Feminists
- Childhood is an artificial period of dependence and a form of oppression
- Age patriarchy is evident in the differential distributions of power, work, violence and rewards within the family
- Toys amplify gender roles and commercialise childhood
- Children should not be protected from the realities of life e.g. death and wars

15. SYNOPTIC OVERVIEW

	MODERNITY	SOCIAL CHANGES	POST-MODERNITY
Key concepts	**Family** – characterised by closeness and a sense of obligation. **Kinship** – network of relatives connected by common descent or marriage.		**Families** – may or may not live as households. **Households** – a group of people who share facilities at the same residential address.
Emphasis on	• **uniformity** of structure and functions • unitary prescription of how family life should be lived • the objective virtue of the nuclear family • non-traditional family forms as the cause of social problems.		• **diversity** of structures • the need to understand roles and relationships and how obligations are negotiated, honoured and abandoned • relativism – accepts the rightness of different ways of living • impossibility of judging the superiority of one over another.
Assumptions	• **life cycle** – family formation a predictable pattern: starts with marriage; develops by the birth of children; contracts as children depart; death of a partner ends the family • Monogamous heterosexual marriage normal and everything else a perversion or deviance • Mothering a natural instinct • Need to prop up ailing families, e.g. family therapy.		• **life course** – the individual rather than the family is the basic unit, and a person can experience a variety of social situations which are socially constructed and cumulative in character, thus the way a person starts the course and moves through it can affect the way they finish it. • love and affection may be a requirement for human happiness but there are many ways to experience this. • parents should be urged and enabled to be good parents.
Important theories	**Functionalists** – idealised model of family life. **Marxists** – features of nuclear family that have pay-offs for capitalism and people persuaded that this is the right way to live.		**Action theory** – recognises the ability of the individual to determine and choose different lifestyles. **Post modernism** – social worlds are made up of competing and contradictory discourses.
Links to other areas	**Health** – definitions of illness, e.g. female hysteria was claimed to be brought on by a lack of family membership; medicalisation of family life through reproductive technologies. **Crime** – maternal deprivation and family socialisation as a cause of juvenile delinquency. **Wealth poverty and welfare** – community care assumes the services of unwaged female carers. **Stratification** – class differences in patterns of child-rearing. **Politics** – use of government policy to influence family life in ways they approve.		**Crime** – households as victims of crime. **Wealth, poverty and welfare** – distribution of resources within and between households. **Stratification** – ethnic diversity in family and household roles and relationships. **Locality** – gentrification linked to household formation and composition; gay villages. **Work** – growth of homeworking. **Media** – use of role reversal images in advertising.

SOCIAL CHANGES

- ☐ **Demographic changes**
  - longer life expectancy
  - smaller families
- ☐ **Employment opportunities**
  - greater for women
  - reduced for male manual workers
- ☐ **Sexual revolution**
  - redefinition of female sexuality
  - spread of contraception
- ☐ **New technologies**
  - effects on housework
  - leisure/work in the home
- ☐ **Immigration**
  - introduces ethnic diversity
- ☐ **Feminism**
- ☐ **Decline in the influence of religion**
- ☐ **Changing laws**
  - divorce
  - decriminalisation of homosexuality
- ☐ **Growth of education**

3 Health

1. DEFINITIONS AND MEASUREMENT

Definitions

HEALTH – the ability to function effectively within a given environment

			MORBIDITY – socially recognised sickness			MORTALITY
HEALTH – the ability to function effectively within a given environment			Unwell, but not socially recognised			
Complete physical, mental and social well being – WHO (World Health Organisation)	Absence of symptoms	Symptoms seen as normal or to be expected	Subjective experience of being ill	A temporary disease or malfunction	A permanent infirmity that is not life-threatening	A time limited condition	Brain stem death / Loss of pulse

Health – death continuum

HEALTH	PRE-SYMPTOMATIC	SYMPTOMS, NO ACTION	SYMPTOMS, NON-MEDICAL ACTION	ACUTE	CHRONIC	TERMINAL	DEATH

(continuum arrow)

Example

PRE-SYMPTOMATIC	SYMPTOMS, NO ACTION	SYMPTOMS, NON-MEDICAL ACTION	ACUTE	CHRONIC	TERMINAL
pathological cell division	smoker's cough, hangover	head cold	infectious diseases	diabetes, arthritis	some cancers

Measurements

- BMI (Body Mass Index) desirable height-to-weight ratio
- Prevalence revealed by screening tests
- Self-report data
- Self-certification of absence from work
- GP visits or sick notes
- Hospital in- and out-patient records
- Notifiable diseases
- Prescriptions dispensed
- Death rates, e.g. Infant Mortality Rates (IMR)
- Life expectancy
- SMRs (Standardised Mortality Ratios)

Evaluation

BMI
- ✓ Ideal type for comparison
- ✗ Culturally relative

Prevalence revealed by screening tests
- ✓ Reflects future morbidity
- ✗ Under-recording: not available for all conditions
- ✗ Not used by all who are entitled

Self-report data
- ✓ Reveals some of the under-recording by other methods
- ✗ Subjective

Self-certification of absence from work
- ✗ Often reflects work dissatisfaction rather than ill-health
- ✗ False claims of illness
- ✗ Only covers working population

GP visits / records etc.
- ✓ Reliable
- ✗ Medical decision rule, preference by doctors for diagnosing ill-health
- ✗ Double counting, one patient may have many episodes
- ✗ Large unknown figure of unreported ill-health

Death rates etc.
- ✓ Objective
- ✓ Allows international comparisons
- ✗ Nothing about the quality of life

2. HEALTH INEQUALITIES – EXPLANATIONS, SOLUTIONS, AND CRITICISMS

Explanation	Causality	Solution	Criticism
ARTEFACT			
The relationship between social variables (such as class, gender, ethnicity, age and region) and health is spurious and evidence is invalid.	Social group → Health	There is no problem, therefore no action needs to be taken. Care needs to be exercised in interpreting health statistics.	The existence of inequalities is denied despite repeated demonstrations of their existence and increase. Excludes any analysis of health statistics by social groups.
NATURAL/SOCIAL SELECTION			
The association is real. Natural selection is the result of genetic or biological factors. In social selection, ill-health is a cause of inequality.	Genes → Social group/Health **or** Health → Social group	Both processes are seen as beneficial to society. Thus no action is required. Interference in natural, biological and social processes is seen as dangerous.	Nothing is done to remove the inequalities in health. Too deterministic. Leads to fatalistic acceptance of ill-health.
BEHAVIOURAL			
Differences in health status are attributable to differences in norms, values, attitudes and style of living.	Social group → Way of life → Health	Resocialisation through education and the media is needed to change the behaviour of certain groups. If these messages are ignored people have only themselves to blame.	Many factors contribute to health which are outside the control of the individual. The behaviour patterns may be rational if the context is understood.
STRUCTURAL			
People have unequal material/environmental circumstances and access to education.	Inequality → Social group → Health	Redistribution is required to remove the underlying inequality. Only by addressing fundamental causes of ill-health will solutions be found.	People are absolved from responsibility for their own health status. Calls to redistribute creates resistance among those who lose out.
HEALTH CARE INEQUALITIES			
Inverse care law – those most in need of medical care have less access because of institutional practices which discriminate against them.	Social group → Unequal health care → Health	A reallocation of resources to remove unfairness. Positive discrimination to compensate for past inequalities.	People generally will not accept a worsening of their position in order to benefit another group. Positive discrimination contradicts equal opportunities.

3. CLASS INEQUALITIES

SOCIAL CLASS GRADIENTS FOR SELECTED HEALTH MEASURES

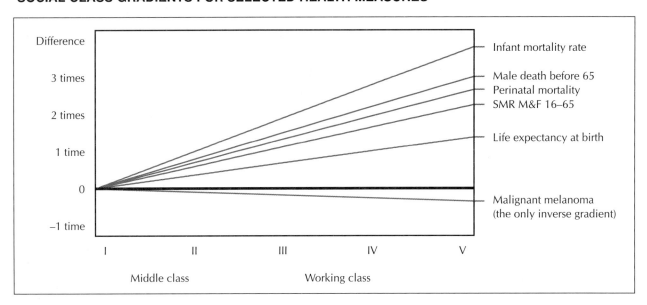

EXPLANATIONS FOR SOCIAL CLASS PATTERNS

	Evidence and arguments	Criticisms
Artefact	• Changes to the occupational structure – with fewer people in social class V who are older and therefore more unhealthy – produce a spurious association. • Definition and classifications used for social class inflate the class differences.	• Social gradient is present across all social classes. • Social class V is a large group of people despite declining proportion of the population. • Differences still clear among Whitehall civil servants whose status can be recorded accurately.
Social selection	• Life course studies show that selection by health does occur, particularly downward mobility among older workers. • Taller and healthier women are more likely to be upwardly mobile at marriage.	• Social mobility cannot explain most of the differences as most ill-health occurs in middle life when a person's social class position is already established. • Education is more important than health in explaining mobility.
Behavioural	Working class: • smoke more, drink more, have a poorer diet • take less exercise in leisure • have fatalistic attitudes that make participation in prevention less likely.	• Class differences remain even when behavioural patterns accounted for. • Behaviour may be rational, smoking relieves the effects of stress; a healthy diet is more expensive. • A victim-blaming view.
Structural	Working class: • experience poorer housing in more polluted areas of cities • are exposed to industrial disease and injury • have lower pay and less job security.	• Does not identify the underlying cause of the inequality. • Ignores the individual's responsibility for their own health.
Health care inequalities	• Working class get shorter time and less information in doctor consultations. • Private medicine produces a two-tier system. • Variations in time and costs to visit doctor.	• Health care is freely available to all. If the working class fail to make full use of the service that is their fault (see behavioural explanation).

4. ETHNIC AND REGIONAL INEQUALITIES

	Ethnic differences	Regional differences
PATTERNS	Infant Mortality and Ethnicity, UK, 1990 *Source*: Hunt 	North SMRs < 100 South SMRs > 100

Infant Mortality and Ethnicity, UK, 1990
Source: Hunt

Mother's place of birth	Still births	Neonatal deaths (in first 28 days)
	(per 1000 live births)	
UK	4.4	4.3
Bangladesh	8.6	3.9
India	5.3	5.1
Pakistan	9.1	7.8
E. Africa	6.9	5.6
Caribbean	5.7	8.4

	Ethnic differences	Regional differences
ARTEFACT	• Differences reflect factors in the person's country of origin, but do not explain differences in second-generation immigrants. • Misdiagnosis especially of mental illness. • Differences in reporting behaviour (see **Health 6**).	• Differences are not related to the geography of the area but to the people who live there, e.g. ageing population in the north as migration of the young to the productive centres of the south.
NATURAL/SOCIAL SELECTION	• Thalassaemia (Asian and Middle East) and sickle cell anaemia (Caribbean) are genetic conditions that confer advantage in some locations, but condition not exclusive to these ethnic groups.	• Healthy and fit more likely to move to more prosperous south in search of work.
BEHAVIOURAL	• Cultural practices, e.g. preference for traditional remedies. • Low take-up of antenatal services. • Larger family size spreads infection. • Use of toxic lead in eye make-up. • High fat intake, e.g. from use of ghee.	• 'Northerners drink more beer and eat fish and chips and they do not take exercise in their leisure' (Edwina Currie when Minister for Health) • Northerners also smoke more
STRUCTURAL	• Racism and discrimination lead to higher unemployment, low pay, poorer housing, overcrowding, poor working conditions.	• Related to the distribution of industry, employment and urbanisation which has an impact on the environment and brings changes to the socio-economic, ethnic or demographic structures of the area.
HEALTH CARE INEQUALITIES	• Fewer doctors in inner city areas where high proportion of ethnic minorities live. • Lack of understanding by professional staff of cultural differences and requirements, although there has been progress made on provision of interpreting services and appropriate diets for in-patients.	• London teaching hospitals received more funding when NHS first set up, now they are centres of excellence which attract the top professionals and new technology. • Poorer areas are less well served by GPs and hospitals as they are not attractive places to work.

5. GENDER AND AGE INEQUALITIES

	Gender	Age
PATTERN	Premature mortality Morbidity	Death rate per 1000
ARTEFACT	• Women report more ill-health. • Women live longer so have more periods of sickness, but this cannot account for the mortality differences.	• No case made for this view.
NATURAL SELECTION	• Biological theory suggests the female XX chromosome is stronger than the male XY, but this does not explain the morbidity pattern or cross-cultural variations in gender mortality.	• Ageing process inevitable. • High rates of perinatal and infant mortality are nature's way of ensuring only the fittest survive.
BEHAVIOURAL	• In the past males smoked and drank more than women, but differences are diminishing and may equalise in the future. • Men take more risks in leisure and life. • Women look after themselves by watching their weight and taking advantage of screening programmes. • Contraception has reduced maternal mortality.	• Elderly fail to take care of themselves by not keeping warm and eating well. • Their independence may prevent them seeking the help they need. • Some child-rearing practices may put the child at risk, e.g. a baby in parents' bed can get smothered.
STRUCTURAL	• Laws have prevented women from working in mines and in other life-threatening occupations. • Working mothers have a double role which may explain higher morbidity, but is not yet showing in mortality data.	• Inequalities of working life are carried into old age. • The old are more likely to have low incomes and live in the worst housing. • Retirement creates an artificial end to working life and leads to a loss of social role. • The young are dependent on adults for survival.
HEALTH CARE INEQUALITIES	• Well-women clinics and female screening programmes prevent early death and find more morbidity, despite feminists' view of a largely patriarchal medical profession.	• Priority for the young and those with dependants. • Care of the elderly is a 'Cinderella service'. • Emphasis on acute rather than chronic or palliative care.

6. SOCIAL CONSTRUCTION OF HEALTH AND ILLNESS

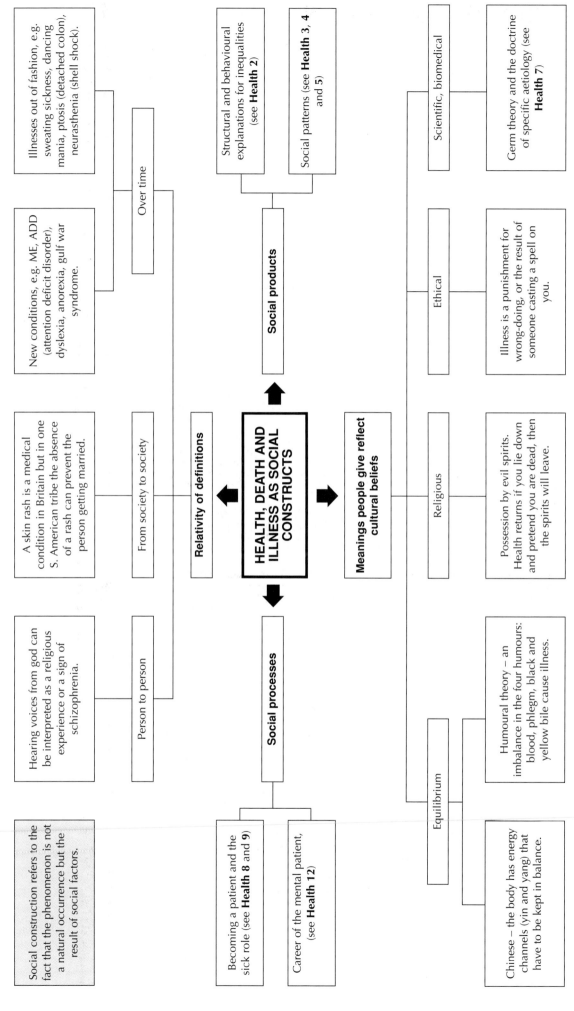

Social construction refers to the fact that the phenomenon is not a natural occurrence but the result of social factors.

HEALTH, DEATH AND ILLNESS AS SOCIAL CONSTRUCTS

Relativity of definitions

From society to society

A skin rash is a medical condition in Britain but in one S. American tribe the absence of a rash can prevent the person getting married.

Over time

Illnesses out of fashion, e.g. sweating sickness, dancing mania, ptosis (detached colon), neurasthenia (shell shock).

New conditions, e.g. ME, ADD (attention deficit disorder), dyslexia, anorexia, gulf war syndrome.

Person to person

Hearing voices from god can be interpreted as a religious experience or a sign of schizophrenia.

Social products

Structural and behavioural explanations for inequalities (see **Health 2**)

Social patterns (see **Health 3, 4** and **5**)

Social processes

Becoming a patient and the sick role (see **Health 8 and 9**)

Career of the mental patient, (see **Health 12**)

Meanings people give reflect cultural beliefs

Scientific, biomedical

Germ theory and the doctrine of specific aetiology (see **Health 7**)

Ethical

Illness is a punishment for wrong-doing, or the result of someone casting a spell on you.

Religious

Possession by evil spirits. Health returns if you lie down and pretend you are dead, then the spirits will leave.

Equilibrium

Humoural theory – an imbalance in the four humours: blood, phlegm, black and yellow bile cause illness.

Chinese – the body has energy channels (yin and yang) that have to be kept in balance.

Health 39

7. MODELS OF HEALTH

		BIOMEDICAL MODEL (characteristics and mnemonic)	CHALLENGE TO THE BIOMEDICAL MODEL	THE SOCIAL MODEL
P		The *professional* is the only person with the expertise to diagnose. The doctor can diagnose sickness without the patient feeling unwell.	Doctors lack the knowledge to treat the major causes of death in the 21st century. The role of the doctor is merely to legitimate illness for the benefit of others. These include the patient, employers, and the state.	*Lay definitions and judgements* of what is needed and when are just as valid as professional assessment. Much illness is diagnosed in the family (see **Family 6**).
A		Health is *absolute*, i.e. a person is either healthy or sick. If someone claims sickness without evidence the doctor may define them as 'malingerer' or 'hypochondriac'.	There is a *continuum of ill-health* from conditions that are unknown to the person through illness that is only recognised by the sufferer, to socially recognised illness (see **Health 1**). Even death is relative depending on the definition used.	*Illness is relative* and represents a deviation from some norm. It is also judgmental and varies from time to time, place to place and person to person (see **Health 6**). Different people will interpret the same symptoms differently.
I		The object of treatment is the patient as an *individual*.	The decline in death rates has been achieved through *environmental* improvements rather than by the medical profession treating individual patients. Sewers have been more important than diagnosis.	*Social relationships* have to be understood to explain why the death rate is higher on bank holidays, or why men are at risk of premature death in the first year of retirement.
D		Each *disease* has a specific cause and it occurs randomly in the human population.	Multiple causation is more realistic. Ill-health occurs in *patterns* in the population (see **Health 3**, **4**, and **5**). Ill-health is therefore socially, not randomly, distributed.	Emphasises the personal experience of *illness* and the need to understand an individual's perception and social circumstances.
T **O**		Illness is a *temporary condition* producing a physical symptom ...with an *organic cause*.	Bacteria are more likely to produce the symptoms of a sore throat when there are high levels of stress.	Much illness is long-standing or *permanent* and can only be understood if the *social dimension* of health is considered.
C		The illness can be *cured* by treating the body like a machine and fixing the broken parts in a medical setting, e.g. a hospital.	Doctors can be responsible for causing ill-health, i.e. *iatrogenesis*. Hospitals are sources of infection as well as curing people.	*Care* of the patient and their family within the community may improve the quality of life more than a partial cure.
O		Ill-health is an *objective* condition established by scientific procedures. The diagnosis and tests are observable and verifiable.	Many treatments have not been tested scientifically. A randomised control trial of heart patients revealed that those receiving home care recovered just as well as those in coronary care units.	Ill-health is a *subjective* condition that is influenced by the social definitions and meanings attached to particular events (see **Health 6**).
N		Health is defined in a *negative* way as an absence of symptoms.	95% of people asked reported symptoms in the previous two-week period, i.e. ill-health is normal.	Ill-health is *normal* if a positive definition is adopted, e.g. World Health Organisation (see **Health 1**).

8. SOCIAL PROCESS OF BECOMING A PATIENT

Factors influencing the process

Stages in the process of becoming a patient

Removal from the process

All people

All people
• Cultural differences in tolerance to conditions, e.g.
1. Italians and Jews are more demanding and dependent on doctors
2. In some societies the practice of couvade operates in which women show no distress in childbirth but their husbands get into bed and groan!

Those who have unpleasant bodily sensations, are uncomfortable or unhappy

No problems

• Cultural explanations for ill-health, e.g. religious or scientific (see **Health 6**)
• Speed of onset of symptoms
• Perceived risk

Interpret their condition as possible illness

Interpret their condition as normal, e.g. period pains, hangovers

• Costs and benefits of being labelled as ill, e.g. absence from work or other obligations
• Interference with social, personal or physical activity

Self-diagnosis as ill

Assume it is trivial and will go away

• Availability and costs of doctor
• Faith in western medicine
• Sanctioning by others
• Giving symptoms a specified time to improve

Decision to consult a doctor

Self-medication

• Knowledge of the medical profession, e.g. ptosis (detachment of the colon) now discredited due to misinterpretation of X-rays
• Availability of diagnostic facilities
• Stereotypes of patient, e.g. malingerer, or based on gender and age
• Medical decision rule, if in doubt impute illness

Doctor diagnoses illness

Doctor diagnoses no illness

• Judgement of seriousness
• Fashion in medicine e.g. anaemia and low blood pressure are not now routinely treated

Decision to treat or refer

No action taken

• Level of specialisation
• Competence of the doctor

Illness given a label

Effects of label
• Legitimation of illness
• Help to get appropriate treatment
• Stigmatisation, e.g. AIDS
• Change in people's behaviour towards person, e.g. physical impairment can make people treat the patient like a child

PATIENT

Social reaction creates a self-fulfilling prophecy, e. g. passivity and compliance of blind person is the result of treatment by those who see blindness as a psychological adjustment rather than a technical handicap.

PATIENT BECOMES PATIENT!

PARSONS' FUNCTIONALIST THEORY

Sick role / Doctor role

Description

Sick role:
- *Vulnerable* because of symptoms and open to exploitation by others. *Deviant* because it interrupts normal role performance and is a threat to society.
- Temporary *exemption* from normal role functioning.
- Patient incapable of curing themselves so given *no responsibility* for cure. They are assumed to need care.

Doctor role:
- *Gatekeeper* controlling entry to the sick role.
- *Examination* of patient's physical and personal life.
- *Authority* over the patient and *autonomy* in practice.

Rights

Obligations

Sick role:
- *Motivation* to get well because it is recognised that the condition is undesirable.
- *Willingness* to seek medical help and *co-operate* in the recovery by adopting a degree of *passivity*.

Doctor role:
- *Patient's needs first* before self-interest.
- *Restoring health,* through specialist help and expertise.

Doctor – patient relationship

Harmonious and functional for the individual and society

Criticisms (left side)

- Some patients can become more knowledgeable about new or rare conditions than their doctor.
- Some conditions can give power by the threat of transmission of infectious diseases.

- Adoption of the sick role to avoid work is dysfunctional.

- Chronically ill may need to maintain normal role for rehabilitation process.
- Patient may need to effect a lifestyle change, e.g. diabetic, anorexic.
- Patients can be held responsible for their condition and denied care, e.g. heart patients who smoke.

- Chronic conditions cannot be cured.
- Seeking medical help may not be preferred option (see **Health 6**).

- Patients are expected to know when to seek medical help, hence are active at the stage of consultation.
- Many prescribed medicines not taken.
- Patients are not always passive.

Criticisms (right side)

- Medical decision rule imputes illness, therefore letting people in rather than keeping people out.

- Difficult for the patient to make a complaint.

- Possibility of abuse of position.
- Patient may become dependent on authority of doctor.
- Autonomy can hide incompetence.

- Doctors are not objective – they have their own career interests.

- Doctors do more harm than good by creating ill-health and dependency.
- Doctors are not all-knowing; there are limits to what they can cure.

EVALUATION

Relationship full of conflict and tension, e.g. privileged access to body; doctor's concern for organic cause, patient's for pain and incapacitation.

10. THEORIES OF THE POWER OF MEDICINE

	FUNCTIONALIST Parsons (1951) (see Health 9)	WEBERIAN Friedson (1970), Wilding (1981)	MARXIST Navarro (1976), Doyal (1979)	FEMINIST Oakley (1984), Graham (1984)	FOUCAULDIAN Foucault (1963, 1976)
Whose interests are served?	Society as a whole	Medical profession	Capitalist	Men	Medical profession
How is this achieved?	• Protecting the public from unscrupulous practice. • Acting as a gate-keeper to the sick role, which if over-used could become dysfunctional.	• Collective organisation that controls entry to the profession. • Competition securing monopoly of right to practice. • Organisation of health around professional skills rather than client needs.	• Maintaining a healthy workforce. • Disguising the true cause of ill-health, i.e. capitalism. • Supporting the profit-making of the drugs industry.	• Branding female healers as witches. • Demotion of midwifery to an ancillary occupation. • Medicalisation of pregnancy, childbirth, conception and even beauty.	• Provide definitions of normality and sickness and the vocabulary through which needs and remedies are defined. • Powers of examination create discourse.
Source of power	• Legitimate authority, which is attained on merit because doctors have scarce knowledge and skills which are crucial for a healthy population.	• Rational – legal authority which can control information to the patient. • Ideological control through the mystique of professional expertise and belief that doctors are trustworthy and know best.	• As the servants of the ruling class they have delegated power which has been passed on through family connections. • Doctors are becoming proletarianised as they come under the control of managers.	• Patriarchal medical practice. • Medical knowledge is gendered, e.g. anatomy texts do not represent the clitoris correctly.	• Surveillance and regulation of both the individual and the collective 'body' of society.
Role in social control	• Limiting abuse of the sick role by acting as a gate-keeper. • Legitimates absence from work for individuals.	• Defining needs and problems. • Attaching (stigmatising) labels.	• Defining illness as an inability to work. • In USSR, political opposition was defined as mental illness. • Making health an individual rather than a social problem.	• Women dominated in subordinate roles as low paid or unpaid carers. • Drugs 'treatment' of depression in women is based on gender stereotypes.	• Anatomical control of human bodies particularly through control of sexuality by the medicalisation of the sexually peculiar and the treatment by psychiatrist of perverse pleasure.

11. THEORIES OF MENTAL ILLNESS

STRUCTURAL THEORY
Lower class lifestyle stimulates the development of psychotic disorders.

SOCIAL FACTORS
Life events are important as provoking agents, but it is the meanings these events have for the individual that are the causal force. Protective factors (having a partner or a job) create vulnerability if absent.

ECOLOGICAL THEORY
Areas of social disorganisation, e.g. inner cities are conducive to schizophrenia.

Criticisms
- Focuses on class to the exclusion of other factors
- Does not link the findings to the position of women
- Socially constructed medical diagnosis which interactionists would say is invalid in society

INTERACTIONIST
- In a pseudo patient experiment 8 healthy people were diagnosed as insane on the fake presentation of hearing voices. This mistake was recognised by other patients but not the staff.
- An individual's self concept is shaped by others' reaction (see **Health 12**); behaviour is changed under the influence of a total institution. Decarceration is recommended to avoid these harmful effects (see **Health 13**).
- Diagnoses of mental illness are not objective but influenced by financial, ideological and political motives.

Criticisms
- Neglects the needs of the mentally ill
- Putting people back into the community where their problems originated does not help to cure them
- There are symptoms and behaviour which are widely recognised as illness

PSYCHO DYNAMIC (FREUD)
People have drives which if not given full expression, can lead to regression or fixation at an earlier stage of development. The solution is psychoanalysis to bring these problems to consciousness.

PSYCHIATRY
Assumes a neurological disease causes mental illness. Classifies according to symptoms, i.e. psychotic (out of touch with reality) and neurotic (in touch). Patients are treated with drugs and surgery like physical illnesses.

BEHAVIOURAL
Mental illness is learned inappropriate behaviour or the absence of appropriate learning. The solution is to condition new patterns by behaviour modification therapy (using rewards) or aversion therapy (using punishments).

Criticisms
- An unfalsifiable theory
- Studying abnormal cases does not help an understanding of the normal condition
- Little evidence of effectiveness of treatments
- A young science that is still classifying
- Causation not established
- Some of the treatments are of doubtful value
- Assumes the patient also learns the symptomatic behaviour patterns

RADICAL PSYCHIATRY
Oppressive family relationships are the cause of schizophrenia. Also mental illness is potentially liberating, like a spiritual journey.

Mental patients lack the capacity for self-delusion, they can see right through to the awful truth about the human condition. Most people exist in a state of false consciousness.

Mental illness is a myth, it is a label that acts as a mechanism of social control that can be applied to any behaviour that does not make sense, e.g. political dissidents in the old USSR.

Criticisms
- Both these stages of R.D. Laing's work have been retracted
- Does not explain the causes of family dysfunctions
- Case study data has dubious generalisability
- Ignores the pain mental illness can cause and offers no help

POSITIVIST (illness is real and has a cause which can be identified)

ANTI-POSITIVIST (challenges the existence of the illness)

SOCIOLOGICAL

NON-SOCIOLOGICAL

12. THE CAREER OF THE MENTAL PATIENT (AFTER GOFFMAN)

Actions and reactions of the 'patient' | **Actions and reactions of significant others**

Actions and reactions of the 'patient'	Actions and reactions of significant others
A particular pattern of behaviour emerges.	Defined by others as odd or unacceptable.
Behaviour continues.	Family can no longer cope i.e. their tolerance has changed not the behaviour of the 'patient'.
Behaviour occurs in public places.	Other agencies become involved, e.g. police.
May feel let down or betrayed.	Medical consultation arranged.
	Passage from home to hospital made easy by next of kin: • 'They are the experts' • 'It is for the best' • 'They know what they are doing'.
This account may not be accepted and patient perceives an alienative coalition against him.	Consultation in which a case history is constructed on patients past life to show how he became sick.
Makes a different case/explanation.	Discounted as the patient is ill and may be used as evidence of being out of touch with reality.
	Doctor accepts that patient needs professional help and will be admitted to hospital.
Feels further separated from the people he trusted.	Next of kin made guardian so that transition to the institution is made simple.
Is stripped both physically and metaphorically of personal identity.	Admission to the institution takes the form of a *degradation ritual*, i.e. removal of personal possessions and valuables, change of clothes and bathing, use of alternative form of address, e.g. first name not surname.
Tries to reassert identity through *adaptive responses*: • *Situational withdrawal*: refusal to communicate with other patients because he denies that he is one of them • *Intransigence*: wilful refusal to co-operate with staff • *Conversion*: adopts the staff view of how he should behave • *Playing it cool*: varying behaviour between other three adaptations so unpredictable.	These anti-social behaviours are further evidence of mental illness and dealt with by punishment or force in a *mortifying process*: • the patient is denied comforts, e.g. cigarettes • removal of privacy in bathing and toileting • lack of freedom in movement • regularised timetables • staff talk about the patient not to the patient • visits from next of kin denied as unsettling.
Mortification and degradation lead to complete loss of self-concept and the removal of the old personality and power of self-determination. Patient becomes *institutionalised* as he has lost the habits considered normal in a wider society.	Process of *rehabilitation* can begin now that patient has accepted his condition.

13. INSTITUTIONAL CARE VERSUS COMMUNITY CARE

	INSTITUTIONAL CARE	COMMUNITY CARE
Description	• A place where all daily activities are planned and controlled by staff and are carried out in the company of other inmates. • Sign of the social surveillance and regulation of the individual and collective body of society.	• Looking after those in need of care in society rather than in hospitals and other institutions. • Can mean care by professionals in the community setting or care by the community i.e. informal caring.
Background	• Asylums and workhouses were a common feature of C19th welfare. • 1990s proposed return to institutional care for those with psychopathic personalities who may pose a threat to society.	• Adopted in the 1960s. • Rapid expansion during the 1980s of private hostels and care homes, with government encouragement.
Reasons for C20th policy	• Solution to the growing problem of groups of homeless ex-patients. • Crisis of order. • Moral panics concerning the well-publicised, but occasional, incidents of violence.	• Dehumanising effects of old-style institutions. • New drugs made it easier to treat patients in the community. • Shift from a medical to social model of psychiatric care (see **Health 7**). • Financial crisis in welfare spending.
Arguments for	• Specialist staff available. • Protects the patient from own actions of self-destruction. • Gives protection to the public. • All a person's needs are met. • Ensures that patients take their medication. • Gives family security knowing their relation is secure.	• Allows people to stay in their own home. • Avoids the person becoming 'institutionalised'. • People's needs are assessed and they are given some choice. • Society learns to be tolerant. • Cheaper to provide. • Better way of looking after people.
Arguments against	• Creates institutionalised dependency which does not aid rehabilitation. • Removes people's freedom without a democratic process. • Wide use of untrained and inadequately supervised staff. • Physical and psychological abuse can occur at the hands of the staff. • Loss of dignity. • Stigmatises patients.	• In practice it can mean placement in private residential homes or hostels that are similarly institutional. • Locating people in the most run-down areas of the city can perpetuate their problems. • Needs are *not* always met or are means tested. • Much of the burden can fall on unpaid (often women) carers. • Rarely is 24-hour cover provided and there is a limited amount of after-care services. • Incidents of violence by unsupervised patients can create more intolerance.

14. METHODS OF DELIVERING HEALTH CARE

	Description	Arguments for	Arguments against
PUBLIC	**NHS 1945–1990:** Universal coverage funded through general taxation free at point of use.	✓ No financial barriers, care provided on the basis of medical need ✓ Everyone benefits from the health of the whole community ✓ Can successfully run preventive and health education projects ✓ Provides a co-ordinated and fast emergency service	✗ High taxation required to fund the demand ✗ People pay for a service they may never use ✗ Rationing by long waits for elective procedures ✗ People use the service wastefully when they do not have to pay ✗ Bureaucratic and impersonal system
INTERNAL MARKET	**NHS Reforms 1990:** Market principles in a state-funded service achieved by: • Separating purchasers (GPs, health authorities) from providers (hospitals, ambulances, community services) • Use of private contractors to provide services, e.g. laundry and cleaning.	✓ Introduces choice for purchasers ✓ Competition between providers keeps costs down ✓ Attaching a cost to each service limits demand for healthcare ✓ More responsive to local needs ✓ Contracts give the purchasers some control over health expenditure	✗ Inequalities between adjacent Health Authorities ✗ Some procedures e.g. IVF, tattoo removal, may not be bought by the purchasers ✗ Produces a two-tier state system ✗ Expensive drugs or treatment denied when purchasers run out of money ✗ Growth of managers and accountants at expense of doctors and nurses ✗ Competition leads to duplication of expensive equipment and treatment ✗ No co-operation between institutions in medical developments
PRIVATE	**USA health care** and growing in the UK: Commercial organisations provide a service paid for by individuals or by insurance cover privately arranged or through employers.	✓ Patient choice ✓ Claims to better and quicker treatment ✓ Reduces the waiting lists on the NHS ✓ Generates money for health care ✓ Provides services not available on the NHS e.g. cosmetic surgery ✓ Doctors content, thus preventing a brain drain ✓ People take responsibility for their own health care	✗ Preferential treatment for those who can afford to pay, queue jumping over people in greater medical need ✗ Patient lacks knowledge to make rational choices ✗ Doctors have a financial motive to recommend treatments which are profitable but not the most effective ✗ Only provides in profitable areas of medicine, not for chronic sick and elderly ✗ Creates its own accounting and legal industry ✗ Uses doctors and nurses trained at public expense

15. MEDICALISATION AND DE-MEDICALISATION

Criticisms

M — More areas of social life are subject to the 'medical gaze'.
- ✗ A sign of the increasing surveillance in society

E — Evidence of sickness claimed in Soviet Union for unacceptable political views.
- ✗ Suggests a spurious scientificity

D — Doctors have become the arbiters of who will receive a treatment or procedure, e.g. abortion and ....
- ✗ Undermines the power of ordinary people to make their own decisions

I — IVF (in vitro fertilisation) programmes which may not be available to the unmarried or those of a certain age.
- ✗ Clinical iatrogenesis from medical interventions which are damaging or unnecessary; e.g. thalidomide babies

C — Childbirth and pregnancy are subject to routine medical interventions in what is usually a natural process.

A — Ageing is becoming medicalised as family and community structures are no longer in place to take the responsibility.
- ✗ Social iatrogenesis from the creation of an artificial dependency on the medical profession

L — Law and religion have been replaced by psychiatry e.g. . . .
- ✗ Structural iatrogenesis – people's autonomy is undermined when they lack the ability to care for themselves and others or to withstand pain

I — In dealing with alcoholism
- ✗ Medical treatments may be coercive without the democratic process

S — Sexuality is controlled by labelling sexual practices as disorders.

A — Attention deficit disorder in children is ...

T — Treated by drugs.

I — Idle or nervous women were said to be suffering hysteria, which means literally a 'disorder of the uterus'.

O — Orthodox medicine has the power to label other systems as 'alternative'.

N — New technologies have expanded the influence of medicine over life and death issues.

BENEFITS OF MEDICALISATION
- ✓ Offers a treatment rather than a punitive solution
- ✓ People are living longer
- ✓ Childbirth has become much safer for mother and baby
- ✓ Doctors are in the most favourable position to make rational allocation decisions

DEMEDICALISATION

The process whereby sections of society turn away from traditional orthodox medicines to alternatives.

ALTERNATIVE MEDICINES
- Acupuncture
- herbaLism
- osTeopathy
- homEopathy
- chiRopracture
- hypNotherapy
- yogA
- aromaTherapy
- faIth healing
- ayurVeda
- rEflexology
- Shiatsu

EVIDENCE FOR THE GROWTH OF ALTERNATIVE MEDICINE
- There are 11000 therapists in alternative medical associations, plus 17,000 non-registered practitioners.
- Once used by lower social groups/uneducated, now respectable and used by wealthy and royalty.
- Government-appointed junior minister responsible for alternative medicine.
- More patients seeking help because of limitations of orthodox medicine.

POSITIVE CONTRIBUTIONS OF ALTERNATIVE MEDICINES
- ✓ Represents a new philosophy of naturalism
- ✓ Popular when conventional methods fail
- ✓ Deconstructs traditional forms of authority
- ✓ Sign of the onset of post-modernism by challenging rational scientific medicine
- ✓ Recognition of psychological, emotional or spiritual dimension to health
- ✓ No power imbalance of doctor–patient relationships

Criticisms of alternative medicines
- ✗ Medical orthodoxy remains firmly entrenched in institutional practice
- ✗ Unregulated practice that preys on the vulnerable and lacks scientific credibility
- ✗ Losing their alternative identity as they have adapted to requirements of orthodox medicine by:

1. Accepting the terms of orthodox medicine by offering complementary rather than alternative treatments.

2. Practising under the direction of orthodox medicine but remaining under the control of the consultant.

3. Accepting the authority of orthodox medicine when patients are advised to seek surgical treatment.

4 Mass Media

1. DEVELOPMENT OF MEDIA INDUSTRIES

C14th	
C15th	
C16th	
C18th	
C19th	
C20th	
Late C20th	

PRINT REVOLUTION

- Invention of printing press in 1450 by Gutenberg – creation of movable type.
- Print revolution took place in Europe although printing had existed in China for many centuries.
- Publishing in Europe was organised on capitalist lines.
- Only a small minority of the European population was literate, but book production increased rapidly (by 1500 twenty million volumes had been printed).
- Publishers became interested in popular volumes and others went out of circulation.
- Cultural impact was increase of national languages. Early books were written in Latin, but increasingly translations into national languages were made.
- So printing stabilised status of national languages, national literatures were established in 16th century.

NEWSPAPERS

- First established in 18th century in Britain.
- Mainly for middle-class readers with interest in business, soon became possible for radical press to educate working-class.
- 1820s – introduction of popular (Sunday) press.
- *Daily Telegraph*, *Daily Mail*, *Daily Express* and *Daily Mirror* followed in late 19th century.
- Advertising became major source of revenue for press.
- Technological changes led to mass-production, mass-circulation industry and concentration of ownership.

Integration

- → *Horizontal* – merging of similar industries.
- → *Vertical* – buying up of other industries at different levels of the production process.
- Era of press barons – Lord Northcliffe and Lord Beaverbrook.
- By 1910 67% of national daily circulation was owned by three individuals and 69% owned by another three = concentration of ownership.
- Press barons used newspapers to influence public and politicians. Since then the process has continued:

⬇

- Concentration within media – by 1988, 3 newspaper groups accounted for 81% of national Sunday and 73% national daily circulation.
- Cross-media ownership – growth of conglomerates like News International.
- Ownership across delivery systems – cut across existing interests, e.g. terrestrial TV companies having shares in satellites and digital media.
- Transnational ownership – transnational companies with global reach may undermine national and local production.

BROADCASTING MEDIA

Radio

- Crawford Committee recommended new broadcasting service funded by licence fees. John Reith appointed Director General of British Broadcasting Corporation in 1927.
- Public service radio broadcasting attempted to educate working-class listeners, but soon lost out to commercial radio stations.
- Independent radio attracted younger and working-class audiences; forced BBC to change its own content.
- Broadcasting Act 1990: independents are regulated by Radio Authority. Radio ownership also concentrated.

Television

- Introduced 1936 but did not become popular medium until after WW2.
- Introduction of commercial TV in 1954 under control of Independent Television Authority.

Problems

✗ Increased commercialisation put pressure on ITV and BBC to be commercially successful – led to debates about 'dumbing down' of television programmes, playing to lowest common denominators of public taste.

✗ Content and advertisements – breakdown of barrier between adverts and content of programmes with sponsorship of TV and product placement so advertising becomes more integrated.

✗ Concern expressed that only advertising of cigarette brands now appears with sponsorship of sport on TV.

✗ Growth of 'infotainment', a mixing of news and light entertainment (like Breakfast TV). Encourages human interest stories of lives of rich and famous – personalities rather than politics in political sphere.

Benefits (?)

✗ Widening of choice from increase of satellite and digital TV as well as terrestrial.

✓ Pluralists and New Right theorists hold this free market position. Increased technology is said to enhance democracy of the media.

✓ Possibilities for increased democratic participation.

✗ Marxists argue that it is only the *perception* of choices, really just more of the same.

✗ Media-rich and media-poor. People can only consume what they can afford to buy.

✗ Pessimistic view of future of broadcasting = possible end of Public Service Broadcasting and quality TV but simply repeats of cheap imports = no effective choice for audiences.

2. OWNERSHIP AND CONTROL DEBATE

Instrumentalist Marxist	Hegemonic Neo-Marxist	Pluralist

ROLE OF MEDIA PROPRIETORS

Instrumentalist Marxist	Hegemonic Neo-Marxist	Pluralist
• Concentration of ownership of media products into very few hands through processes of integration, diversification, internationalisation and globalisation.	• Proprietors may be powerful, but they do not have direct control over all their products.	• Proprietors may be powerful, but they cannot have direct control over all their products.

ROLE OF MEDIA PROFESSIONALS

Instrumentalist Marxist	Hegemonic Neo-Marxist	Pluralist
• Owners are also controllers; proprietors of newspapers have direct influence on content. • Managers do not run organisations independently of proprietors. They only have discretion within framework set by owners.	• Media professionals have day-to-day control of running of media industries. • Media professionals share a world view. They are white, middle-class, middle of the road politically, and male.	• Power is not zero-sum but dispersed throughout many different interest groups. • Media professionals come from different backgrounds and present a wide spectrum of opinion.

MEDIA AND IDEOLOGICAL BIAS

Instrumentalist Marxist	Hegemonic Neo-Marxist	Pluralist
• Media serve to legitimate the power of ruling groups through dissemination of a dominant ideology. • As owners concentrate on large markets for their cultural products, audiences receive a media diet which is unchallenging and trivial.	• Many groups which threaten the hegemony are marginalised by the media by stereotyping, ridiculing and presenting them as threats. • Ideological bias is not conscious but part of the inferential structures of the media, i.e. the taken-for-granted ways in which media content is produced.	• Market forces and forms of regulation ensure diversity of content and Public Service Broadcasting. • There is no obvious bias. • Consumer sovereignty remains supreme. Consumers are active audiences who engage in selective exposure, selective perception and selective retention.

EVALUATION OF DEBATE

Instrumentalist Marxist	Hegemonic Neo-Marxist	Pluralist
✗ Owners not an identifiable class. ✗ Assumes audiences are easily manipulated. ✓ Evidence that proprietors do appoint personnel who share their viewpoint (e.g. Rosie Boycott appointed by Lord Hollick as editor of *Daily Express*). ✓ Places media industries within framework of capitalist enterprise.	✗ Sometimes difficult to separate hegemony from Althusser's Ideological State Apparatuses. ✗ Looks at ways in which media professionals 'learn' the media. ✓ Does allow us to see that media messages are differentiated. ✓ Emphasises cultural struggle rather than manipulation.	✗ Overly optimistic. ✗ Media diversity does not mean wide choice but more of the same. ✗ Left-of-centre newspapers do not get same support from advertisers. ✓ Emphasis is on active audiences. ✓ Allows us to see that media do not speak with one voice.

PROPONENTS OF THE APPROACHES

Instrumentalist Marxist	Hegemonic Neo-Marxist	Pluralist
• Miliband, Althusser.	• Gramsci, Hall, Glasgow Media Group.	• Whale, journalists and broadcasters.

3. MARXIST THEORIES OF THE ROLE OF THE MEDIA IN SOCIETY

INSTRUMENTALIST MARXISM
(also known as Manipulationist and Classical Marxism)

- Mass media seen as agent of social control similar to that operating in education system and religion, a part of the Ideological State Apparatus.
- Media create false class consciousness to distract people from realities of capitalist oppression and exploitation. Media content is little more than propaganda.
- Dominant ideology is transmitted through the messages of the media – media have become more important than religion as source of ideological control.
- Proprietors of media industries have control over the output of the media.

Evaluation

✗ Idea of a dominant ideology fails to account for diversity of ideologies and ideas in society and the many contradictions within and between them.

✗ Assumes passivity in audiences – as if they simply soak up the ideological content without question.

✗ Overly deterministic. Ownership of media industries does not necessarily assume specific effects on audiences.

✓ As a structural approach it enables us to analyse media industries as part of capitalism.

✓ It links the production of the dominant ideas of the time to those who wield economic power. The question 'who benefits?' becomes very significant.

STRUCTURALIST MARXISM
(also known as Hegemonic Marxism and Neo-Marxism)

- Concept of hegemony used to demonstrate that the powerful have to engage in a cultural struggle to maintain their control (Gramsci).
- Ruling class has to win consent over working class to stay in power. The media operate in several ways to enable this to happen.
- News production: world view of media professionals – editors, journalists, broadcasters etc. – is represented by structuring of newsworthy items.
- Representation – some groups perceived as threatening to white, middle-class males are marginalised, i.e. portrayed in negative, stereotypical ways and even ridiculed.
- A Marxist position which allows us to see subtlety of the process of capitalist control.

Evaluation

✗ Pluralists would argue that things are improving and groups who were previously marginalised are getting fairer representation (e.g. women, gays and ethnic minorities).

✗ Media professionals are not completely free to run the media. Proprietors still have hiring and firing control and will bring in editors who support their viewpoints (e.g. Lord Hollick employed Rosie Boycott as editor of *Daily Express*).

✗ Empirical evidence is inconclusive on whether audiences accept definitions and representations of marginalised groups.

✓ Does engage in empirical research on the content of the media. GMG have been researching within hegemonic framework for decades.

✓ It can also be linked with feminist and anti-racist theory in gender/ethnic representations.

FRANKFURT SCHOOL OF MARXISM

- Includes Adorno, Horkheimer and Marcuse. Left Europe in 1930s and went to USA.
- Witnessed increasing mass production and mass consumption of USA society after WW2.
- They maintained society was becoming a mass society.
- Media as part of socialisation process creates 'one-dimensional' people who are consumption driven.
- Loss of working-class communities with rise of plastic culture. They are fed diet of trivia which they think gives them freedom of choice.
- Lack of intellectual challenge to capitalism and loss of revolutionary fervour among working class.

Evaluation

✗ Again assume that audiences are manipulable – happy robots complying with authority of the powerful.

✗ Value-laden assumptions placed on high + low culture.

✗ Paradoxical that they see hope for revolution within the hands of a non-working-class cultural and intellectual elite.

✗ Does not explain how they are able to see through the system whereas others cannot.

✓ Applied social theory to the analysis of popular culture – as a subject to be taken seriously.

✓ Linked false consciousness to the growth of the culture industries, hence linking individuals to structure; escapism offered to working class as relief from boredom and alienation.

4. THEORIES OF THE ROLE OF THE MEDIA IN SOCIETY (CONTINUED)

FEMINIST THEORIES

Liberal feminists	Socialist feminists	Radical feminists
• Reformist approach which emphasises equal opportunities. • Content analysis (quantitative) research to examine numbers, roles and frequency of appearance of women in the media – especially TV. • Findings typically show a cultural lag: women appear less often in dramatic roles apart from soaps. • Sex-role stereotyping still evident in 1990s broadcasting.	• Does not focus exclusively upon gender but incorporates class, ethnicity etc. into the discourse. • The work of Gramsci has been particularly prominent and the theory is grounded in socioeconomic conditions. • Mass media are perceived as part of the ideological structure which legitimates capitalism. • Socialist feminists focus on the ways in which gender has been constructed through images and language, semiological analysis.	• Investigates the effects of a patriarchal system on the lives of women and children. • Research into the media has concentrated on pornography and the (s)exploitation of women and children by the sex industry (which includes sex-tourism and trafficking). • At its extreme, radical feminism demands separatism at all levels.

Strategies		
• Improvement of occupational opportunities for women in media industries. • Disseminating research findings to journalists and broadcasters to raise awareness.	• Reform of mainstream media industries while creating a separate media structure for women.	• Women-only communication production systems.

Evaluation

✓ Feminist theory has examined inequalities within media industries which show that few women make it to top posts.

✓ Glass ceiling effect is still largely in place.

✓ They have analysed the content of the media at both visual and ideological levels to show how stereotypical assumptions of gender relations still predominate.

✓ They have uncovered the exploitation of women and children by the pornography industries.

✗ Apart from socialist feminists, they tend to underplay factors of class, ethnicity, age and sexuality.

✗ Feminism has tended to focus on white middle-class women and make assumptions about working-class women as passive audiences manipulated by the media (especially in relation to women's magazines).

OTHER RELEVANT THEORIES

Interactionist	Pluralist	New Right
• Confusing term as few media researchers would regard themselves specifically as 'interactionist'. • Taken to include audience research and ethnographic studies of media industries. • News production process used as illustration of the ways negotiation takes place within a newsroom to construct the news. • Tends to be associated with left-wing critique.	• Market-model of media industries. Audience are important as media consumers who influence the output of the media. • Owners compete for large audiences so must take their views into account. • No conspiracy between government and media owners. • No ideological bias as a whole range of views and ideas are presented to the public. • Access to the media is available for competing interest groups.	• Not so much a school of thought but a collection of political ideas prevalent since early 1980s. • Issues of ownership and censorship are of most concern. • Free-market position on regulation. • State should prevent monopolies and encourage competition to enable audience choice. • Takes a moralistic position on censorship of sexual scenes, violence and swearing on TV.

Evaluation
→ **Interactionism** is not a coherent theoretical framework to understand the mass media.
→ **Pluralism** is useful in examining audience selection but less so for the structural position of media industries.
→ **New Right** – again not a body of theory but specific positions on aspects of the media.

5. AUDIENCES AND EFFECTS MODELS

Arguments and evidence	Criticisms

1920s

1930s

1960s

MEDIA-CENTRIC
- **Hypodermic Syringe Model** (1920s–date) assumes that audiences can be manipulated by media messages. Classic example = *War of the Worlds* radio broadcast, Orson Welles (1938).
- **Observational Learning and Behaviourism:** studies showed short-term effects – usually anti-social. E. G. Bandura et al., 'Bobo Doll' experiments 1960s.

✗ Payne Fund Studies (1920s) showed considerable diversity of audience response.

✗ Whether listeners were convinced by the broadcast was related to different social factors.

✗ Experimental methods used in this research are not transferable to real-life situations.

1950s

1960s

1970s

ACTIVE AUDIENCES (1)
- **Two-Step Flow Model (1950s)** assumes an indirect link between media and main audience through opinion leaders. These had specific characteristics which influenced others.
- **Uses and Gratifications (1960s)** saw audience as more active – having needs which were met by media: diversion, personal relationships, personal identity and surveillance.
- **Reinforcement Theory (1970s)** = what we do with the media not what do they do to us (Halloran). Assumes we use media within a set of other social relationships. So media messages can be tested out in relevant situations depending upon the individual or group.

✗ There is no method for determining opinion leaders. There is no explanation as to why they should be active audience members and the rest of the audience passive. Also no reason for just a two-step model – it could be multi-stage.

✗ Although a move towards an active and differentiated audience, but limited by idea of 'rational' choice in media use.

✗ Problem in recognising which texts will be used by whom and how. Can only make this judgment after the event.

✗ Audiences tend to be undifferentiated by gender, ethnicity, class etc.

1970s

1980s

1990s

ACTIVE AUDIENCES (2)
- **Cultivation Analysis (1970s-date)** traces a more long-term effect. Examines media content especially representations and violence. Makes connections between amount viewed and impact of viewing. Heavy viewers take 'mainstream' position; fearful of 'mean' world and supportive of more law and order (Gerbner et al: Violence Profile).
- **Reception Analysis (1980s–date)** sees audiences as media literate, negotiating texts and interacting with media. Children are seen as being as sophisticated as adults and as differentiated. (Hall, Morley, Buckingham).

✗ Methodological problems – no real sense of polysemic messages. Also, attitudes arise from early socialisation experiences not just TV viewing. Too difficult to separate media influences from other social factors?

✗ The approach may confuse cultural competencies with cultural capital. Concentrates on pleasures of the media at the expense of the structures of the media.

6. MORAL PANICS

DEFINITION: A condition, episode, person or group emerges to become defined as a threat to societal values and interests; its nature is defined in a stylised and stereotypical fashion by the mass media; the moral barricades are staffed by editors, bishops, politicians and other 'right-thinking people'; socially accredited experts pronounce their diagnoses and solutions; ways of coping are evolved or (more often) resorted to (Cohen 1972).

PROGRESS OF A MORAL PANIC

A small group of people commits a deviant act

The media report the story as an issue of interest; problem group is identified

Media search for similar stories – sensationalise and exaggerate occurrence of event

Original group becomes marginalised. Identified as folk-devils – a threat to social order

More deviance occurs as those identified react to media coverage – self-fulfilling prophecy

Moral panic – people are aware of the group and concerned for increase in law and order

Greater social control is exerted – politicians, police and magistrates respond by introducing harsher measures to control deviants.
New legislation is introduced.

Characteristics of moral panics	Theories of moral panics	Examples of moral panics
Concern • There must be awareness that group's behaviour will have negative consequences for other people. • Public concern is generated – may be shown through opinion polls and media coverage. **Hostility** • Increased hostility directed at the group (via media). • Group becomes a 'folk-devil' and division opens between them and us. **Consensus** • Widespread acceptance that the group poses real threat. • Not necessarily nationwide consensus, but large enough. **Disproportionality** • Societal reaction is out of proportion to threat posed – fed by sensationalised media reporting. • Often statistics given to show extent of problem.	**Grassroots model** • Moral panic starts when the public becomes concerned about an issue or group. • Rejects the idea that elite groups generate panic, but that it comes from among the people around the threat. **Elite-engineered model** • Elite groups deliberately create fear and panic to divert attention away from other, more serious structural problems. • Mainly associated with Marxist viewpoint (moral panic seen as weapon of social control). **Interest-group model** • Most popular approach. Does not accept elite manipulation, but focuses on middle-level groups such as professionals. • Advancing a moral cause enhances the status of the professional groups involved. • In any moral panic we need to ask who benefits from the concern and ensuing legislation.	**Heroin and crack cocaine distribution in USA in late 1980s** • Response to concern expressed by neighbourhoods involved was passing of anti-drug legislation in 1986 and 1988. **Mugging panic of 1970s** • Reaction to street crime was out of proportion to actual threat to society. • Hall et al. (1978) saw issue as diversionary tactic generated by politicians and media professionals to hide real crisis within capitalist system. **Satanic child abuse (1980s)** • Social workers gained in two ways: 1. Enhancement of their status as professionals 2. Increased funding, as public demand to fight increasing numbers of such abuse cases involved additional state funding.

7. SCREENED VIOLENCE

Case studies where links made between screened violence and audience effects:

⮡ James Bulger murder by two young boys linked to video nasties especially *Child's Play 3*

⮡ Killing of step-mother and half-sister by 15 yr. old Nathan Martinez linked to *Natural Born Killers*

⮡ Killings of school children by fellow students e.g. *'Trenchcoat Mafia'* linked to Internet and music

✗ No substantial evidence in any case for conclusive effects of media violence.

✗ With every dramatic case of violence moral entrepreneurs try to make causal links with media and behaviour.

- **Hypodermic Syringe Model**
- **Observational Learning Model**
- **Stimulation Effects Model**

- Assumes that audiences are passive, easily manipulated especially by powerful influences. Introduction of cinema gave rise to concerns over effects.
- Follows from power of propaganda, e.g. reaction to *War of the Worlds* radio broadcast 1938.
  - ✗ Challenged by Cantril – not all listeners reacted.

EXPLANATIONS ASSUMING MEDIA HAVE DIRECT EFFECTS

Media-centric approaches assume mass media are most significant influences on individual's behaviour.

- Assumes direct effect either short-term or long-term
- Eg. Bobo Doll experiments (Bandura et al.)
- Also evidence for long-term anti-social effects in USA on men who watched TV violence as young boys (Huesman et al.)

- Argued that media arouses aggression in audience and enhances possibility of them acting out violence.
- Catharsis theory argues opposite case. Screened violence makes people less likely to act out aggressively.

- **Reinforcement Theory**
- **Uses & Gratifications Model**
- **Reception Analysis**

- Mainly from ethnographic studies, assumes audience members are active interpreters of texts (Morley, Buckingham).
- Importance lies with reception and interpretation of messages by individuals, but audience subjectivities affect interpretations.
- Children not homogeneous but divided by age, gender, ethnicity, class and educational backgrounds. So we cannot talk of 'children as audiences'.
- Media literacy prevents media manipulation.

EXPLANATIONS CHALLENGING DIRECT EFFECTS

Audience-centred approaches assume that media exists within a context of other social relationships.

- Gives agency to audience members – they are active in their reception of media messages (Halloran 1970s onwards).
- Delinquency is a factor in viewing habits of adolescent boys.
- Recent follow-up shows offenders choose specific programmes relating to relevance and meaningfulness of their own situations.

- Since 1960s has been idea that audiences are not simply passive but look to have needs met by media.
- Selective exposure – choose specific medium.
- Selective perception – each has own interpretation of what they perceive message is.
- Selective retention – information and messages are forgotten.

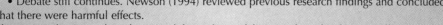

- Debate still continues. Newson (1994) reviewed previous research findings and concluded that there were harmful effects.
- Glasgow Media Group has also joined the violence debate on the side of (some) effects.
- So much depends on ideological standpoint of researchers.

8. NEWS-MAKING PROCESSES

News
- Not a neutral, objective reality but a social construction.
- News needs the media to exist – it is an ideological construct which means some events have more importance than others and we should pay attention to them.
- TV news considered more truthful than newspapers as people do not see it as the result of highly selective, editing process.

News values
- Items are subjected to filtering process to be accepted or discarded as newsworthy.
- Criteria involve practical as well as social factors:
  a) practical = timing and available space for item
  b) social = a framework or pattern of newsworthiness.
- News values = negativity, immediacy, unexpectedness, cultural relevance, clarity, predictability, visibility, elite persons and nations, personalisation and composition.

News sources
- Marxist and hegemonic theorists argue that these are homogeneous – mainly official sources from government, police, experts in the field.
- Pluralists say there is heterogeneity – a diversity of sources from the public to government voices.
- Feminists would argue that they are also mainly male with malestream views.

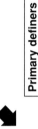

NEWS-MAKING PROCESSES
Inferential structures
News values
Agenda setting
Gatekeeping
Primary definers
Moral panics

Primary definers
- These define the interpretation of the news event for the audience.
- Event occurs, media arrive, spokesperson interviewed who becomes primary definer.
- Oppositional views are then set against this position.
- Inferential structure is set in place and difficult to shift.
- Limit is set on further discussion.

Post-modernist
- The idea of fixed ideologies is redundant.
- News discourse is part of the construction of social realities – therefore impossible to separate one from the other.
- Discourses of what constitutes 'good copy' create opportunities for some stories and closes down others.

Examples of research
- Glasgow Media Group (1976–98): Studies include content analysis of news reporting, Child sexual abuse; AIDS; Africa, mental illness.
- Hall et al., mugging and moral panic (1978).

News construction and ideological bias
- *Marxist* = yes, dominant ideology as part of ideological state apparatus.
- *Hegemonic* = yes, it is formed by the world view of media professionals who are mainly middle-class white men.
- *Pluralist* = no, there is a wide range of view presented.
- *Feminist* = yes, women are marginalised within the news-making process.

- **Agenda setting** = those items deemed newsworthy to become part of the news broadcast or newspaper.
- **Gatekeeping** = the system whereby items are kept out of the news/newspapers by editors, politicians etc.
- **Inferential structures** = a hegemonic term used to signify the way media professionals learn what makes good news stories, TV etc. It is assumed that the socialisation of media professionals attunes them to these taken-for-granted 'structures'.

9. POLITICS AND THE MEDIA

NATION

→ Nation is largest unit audiences asked to identify with.
→ Cultural signifiers – Union Jack, landscapes, the Queen, music, food.
→ Relational devices – use of fictive 'we' in news broadcasts as in 'We, the people of Britain...'
→ Propaganda used in times of war to misinform nation of reality of situation, e.g.

We	They
Suppress	Eliminate
Neutralise	Kill
Dig in	Cower in their trenches
Our missiles are like Luke Skywalker zapping Darth Vader	Their missiles are ageing duds
We precision bomb	They fire wildly at anything in the skies

Political propaganda in peace-time is confined to election campaigns or the politically partisan press.

ROLE OF MEDIA IN A DEMOCRACY

Hegemonic approach
• Ideological bias in news-reporting.
• Not just a reflection of public opinion but can create a framework for ways of thinking about issues.
• Powerful have privileged access to media so their views tend to be represented.
• Media tend to adopt similar positions.

Pluralist approach
• Wide range of media means wide range of opinions.
• Bias occurs but audience are selective and make choices and interpretations.
• Censorship is limited and free speech is upheld.
• Anyone can set up their own newspaper.
• Media play an important watchdog role on government.

MEDIA AND ELECTIONS

Voting intentions of the readers of national press (1992)

(%)	Conservative	Labour	Liberal
Daily Telegraph	71	13	15
Daily Mail	66	17	15
Daily Express	61	19	13
Sun	39	48	10
Mirror	19	59	10
Guardian	12	59	22

Newspaper articles with positive bias to a major party (1997)

Newspaper	Pro-Tory	Pro-Lab
The Times	28	22
Guardian	20	19
Daily Telegraph	22	21
Sun	35	35
Mirror	18	50
Daily Express	32	12
Daily Mail	32	12

PACKAGING POLITICS

• Usefulness of TV seen as an electioneering vehicle.
• After 1959, competition between BBC and ITV meant broadcasters' attitudes to politicians changed.
• 1964 BBC2 on air to produce serious programmes – including political programming.
• Since then PMs and MPs have become TV personalities and politics revolves around personalities of party leaders.
• Growing professionalism in presentation of politics – sound bites, walkabouts, spin-doctored statements, photo-opportunities = marketing of politics and politicians.
• Vast increase in money spent on campaigns and public relations by major parties.
• Influence of new technology = parties have Internet websites, e-mail, pagers, etc.

POST-MODERN APPROACH

• Links with politics and popular culture – Tony Blair, PM on popular chat shows.
• Politics taken less seriously. Political analysis reduced to sound bites.
• Presentation and style become more significant than policies and position.

10. REPRESENTATION OF GENDER

Liberal Feminists: see differences between sex and gender

- Content analysis of television including adverts from 1970s onwards to examine appearances and roles of men and women: (Dominick & Rauch (1972), Gill (1988); Meehan (1983); Gallagher (1980) etc).
- Mulvey (1975): male gaze; women viewed from male point of view. Follows earlier work of Berger who argued that men act and women appear. Similar to 'white eye' of viewing black and ethnic minorities from white perspective.
- Tuchman (1978) argues that limited roles and representation of women in the media is a form of symbolic annihilation.

Marxist

- Media presents interests of capitalism as normal, natural.
- Patriarchy is also reinforced by media.
- Women shown 'women's lives' which justify and support female oppression and exploitation.
- Change in representations of men can be seen as extending consumerism to men.

1980s onwards

- Research still being done by content analysis – some changes have taken place. More women in occupational roles; increasing numbers of women appearing on TV – but still no evidence of gender stereotyping.
- Under-representation of women still evident in the 1990s, especially in advertisements.
- Beauty myth involves body as project – assumption that women's bodies are 'work in progress' to be constantly worked on to stay young, attractive and sensual (Wolf 1990).
- However, this is now the case for men too. Masculine imagery of beautiful bodies now currency in ads and glossy magazines. Pressure on young men to aspire to this standard.

MARGINALISATION

- **Radical feminism:** concentrates on pornographic and violent representations of women. Argues that women must make their own media if situation is to be improved.
- **Marxist feminism:** not really involved with representation of such – more concerned with structure of media organisations. Again need for women to be involved in making media products – local, community media become important here.
- **Ideology:** images of men and women represent contemporary relations of power. Hegemonic view is that women are marginalised into domestic/family and romantic drama and sexually objectified.

H
E
G
E
M
O
N
Y

Gender liminality

- Some changes in TV gender representations including Mulder and Scully in *The X-Files*: Mulder demonstrates typically feminine characteristics of intuition, irrationality, belief while Scully is scientific, rational, level headed and sceptical (Jones, 1999).

Post-modern view

- More fluidity and flexibility in representations of gender which reflects changes in wider society.
- Women's magazines and emphasis on independence and sexual freedom (McRobbie, 1996).

STEREOTYPING

Effects

- Gender bias in representations does not necessarily mean audiences are affected.
- Possibility of popular culture being used by women to resist patriarchy.
- But increase in eating disorders among young women and men *might* be related to body imagery.
- Cultivation analysis assumes ideas of gender are cumulative so ideal bodily images become accepted as desirable over time.

11. REPRESENTATIONS OF ETHNICITY

Ethnicity and media representation – general points

- Ethnic minorities are not homogeneous, they are groups of people sharing a common background, present position or future.
- There is no necessary relationship to skin colour although much of the media research has concentrated on black, Chinese and Asian representations.

✗ Symbolic annihilation can be used in this context as well as with women and the media.

✓ In TV and cinema there are now more positive representations and role models for ethnic minority audiences.

Ethnicity and television (the past)

- Three types of representations of Afro-Caribbeans in TV drama:
  1) native
  2) slave and
  3) entertainer (Hall, 1982).
- Ethnicity is viewed through the 'white eye' and interpreted through the 'grammar of race' as legacy of colonial heritage.
- Imagery and themes show relationships of subordination and domination; stereotypes grouped around superior/inferior peoples; ethnic characters described in relation to naturalistic assumptions.
- Use of ethnic minority actors to play aliens in TV science-fiction exemplifies the 'otherness' of the ethnic minority character (Jones & Jones, 1996: 'Technoprimitives').

Third World Representation

- Concern for charitable events, causes and relief, Band Aid, Live Aid, telethons etc.
- Portrayal of Third World is as zone of disaster, poverty and famine = in need of our aid.
- No discussion given of capitalist structural relationships, only of people who cannot help themselves.
- Coverage is selective and arbitrary so that endorsement of one cause is at expense of another.

✓ Many charities now are very sensitive to photography they use, to give truer reflection of that society.

STEREOTYPING ⬍ **HEGEMONY** ⬍ **MARGINALISATION**

Race and the press

- Hartmann & Husband (1970s) found that press contributed to negative stereotyping of ethnic minorities. This reinforced existing attitudes.
- Van Dijk (1991): news stories are based around tensions and threats, e.g. negative context of ethnic minority news issues.
- Mugging and moral panics – black youth in 1970s seen as threat. Contradictions within capitalism led to need for a scapegoat = black mugger/street criminal. Hall et al. (1978) see this as creation of a moral panic – example of hegemonic control to divide working-class into white and black.

Ethnicity and television (the present)

- Many examples of specific broadcasting for ethnic audiences – both Asian and Afro-Caribbean (especially Channel 4).
- Examples of mainstream TV programmes focused on ethnic minority actors (*Goodness Gracious Me*) and UK films such as *Bhaji on the Beach*; *My Beautiful Laundrette*; *Sammy & Rosie Gets Laid*.
- Soap operas increasingly include ethnic minority characters and sub-plots which are less stereotyped than previously (*EastEnders*).
- Still little evidence of ethnic minorities in higher echelons of the broadcasting companies.

12. REPRESENTATIONS OF AGE AND SOCIAL CLASS

REPRESENTATION OF AGE

Childhood

→ **In past**, children seen as underdeveloped adults who developed from simplicity → complexity; irrationality → rationality; childhood → adulthood.

→ **Now**, childhood seen as social construction = diversity of representation.

→ Innumerable cultures of childhood – not all represented by media.

→ Children use media in identity construction.

→ Move from TV patronising children to reflecting children's view.

→ Heterogeneity of children as media audiences: subjectivities based on
- gender
- personal experience
- ethnicity
- education
- social class
- nationality
- region

→ Children as potential consumers – targets of advertisers and film merchandising

Youth

→ **In past**, adolescents viewed as potentially dangerous, especially male working-class youth became focus for concern of middle-class moral entrepreneurs.

→ Fears expressed that they would be influenced by cinema in anti-social ways.

→ **Now**, adolescents often seen as problematic, especially within youth sub-cultures. Still male working-class and black youth.

→ Representations reflect fears. Moral panics began over Mods and Rockers and have followed many youth groups, e.g. punks, skinheads, rave culture.

→ Focus on use of drug: Ecstasy panic, now alcohol.

→ Youth magazines reflect focal concerns of youth = sex, fashion, drinking.

→ Media concentration on 'Youthism'.

Ageing

→ Old age seen as undesirable.

→ Gender differences as women encouraged to remain youthful whilst elderly men still portrayed as sexual partners to younger women in Hollywood films.

→ Over sixties on TV: males seen as world leaders, politicians, experts, judges etc. Soaps were dominated by middle-aged and elderly, but recently focus on younger characters; sitcoms portray elderly as feeble, difficult, forgetful etc. Limited ads for older groups.

→ New move to present more positive images as UK ages and older groups have disposable incomes.

REPRESENTATION OF SOCIAL CLASS

Upper Class

→ Social construction of Royal Family – presented as 'like us' and 'not at all like us':

Familiar
- On-going soap (before death of Diana)
- Working mothers
- Narrativisation of their lives
- 'Hello' magazine portrayals

Different
- Royal events – ceremonials
- Representatives of the nation
- Immense wealth – not scrutinised

→ TV fixated on historical costume drama of kings and queens – cannibalises history

→ Nostalgic representations of upper-class = ideological maintenance of class relations (e.g. *Brideshead Revisited*; *Emma*; *Sense & Sensibility*: *Pride & Prejudice* and Merchant–Ivory productions).

Middle and working class

→ In general middle class over-represented on TV and working class under-represented.

→ In TV dramas, apart from soaps, professional families predominate.

→ In cinema, professional and upper-class more likely to be represented.

→ Glamorous lifestyles are focused on rather than perceived impoverishment of working-class lives.

→ Non-fictional representations see middle class as sources of authority – experts, scientists, politicians etc. – whereas working-class more often seen as troublesome especially where trade unionism is involved.

→ Poor families portrayed as having themselves to blame or as 'welfare scroungers'.

→ From a Neo-Marxist position, media act against counter-hegemonic groups in order to maintain ideological dominance of elite groups.

13. NEW TECHNOLOGY

SATELLITE TELEVISION	DIGITAL AND CABLE TELEVISION	INTERNET
• 1982: News International bought major share in Sky TV. • 1990: News International merged with British Satellite Broadcasting – BSkyB. • Two major players in satellite ownership: Rupert Murdoch (half-share of BSkyB, Chair of Fox TV, and News International) and Ted Turner (Cable News Network – CNN). • Satellite company does not usually provide programming, but leases to supplying company. • By 1995 UK homes with satellite/cable = 4.5 million.	• Digital TV is predicted to change face of TV. • Will have effects on ownership and control – News International is already a big player in provision of digital decoders and programming itself. • Current cable systems carry around 50 channels but likelihood of several hundreds eventually. • Viewers have to subscribe and pay extra for special programmed events. • Cable has not been as successful in the USA as was anticipated.	• Initially part of USA military project during Cold War, it was set up as a military communications system which would theoretically survive a nuclear war. • Quickly adopted by academics and its use spread through the universities. • In 1980s National Science Foundation (NSF) developed NSFnet linking five university super-computers. • Administration of the Internet passed from military to NSF. • Unforeseen use of Internet facilities now in everyday life: World Wide Web is a global multimedia library used within schools; at work in most enterprises; at home for shopping; general information and even as a dating facility.

SOCIAL IMPACT OF NEW TECHNOLOGY

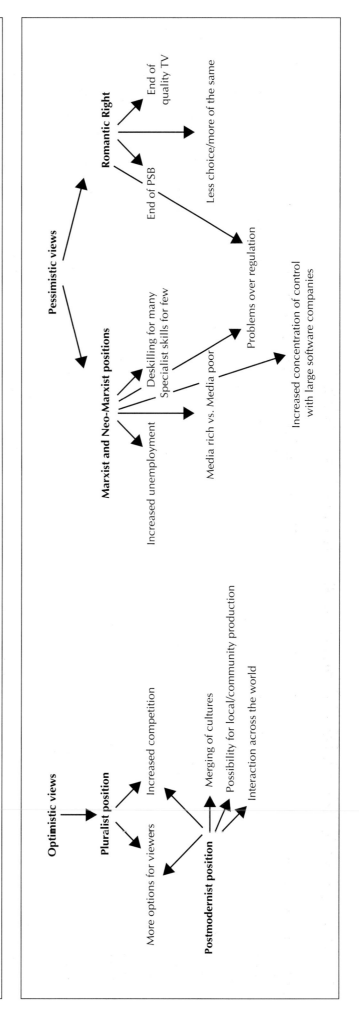

Mass media 61

14. GLOBALISATION

DEVELOPMENT OF GLOBALISATION
- Global nature of capital and rise of global markets.
- Global movement of people around the world.
- Increasing importance of information technology in production, consumption and leisure.
- Awareness of environmental issues with global consequences.
- Political issues stretching beyond the nation state.

Aspects of globalisation
- **Economic** – intensification of economic competition around production, distribution and consumption of goods and services.
- **Political** – attack on nation state and nationalism but also strengthening of national boundaries and increased nationalism.
- **Cultural** – consequences of globalisation on local cultures. Growth of transnational corporations.

Globalisation and culture
- Revolution in communication systems: satellite TV; cable TV; Internet communication.
- Consequences for size of audiences and concentration of media ownership.
- Consequences, too, for relationships with Third World countries – cultural imperialism and McDonaldisation.

GLOBALISATION AND CULTURAL IMPERIALISM
Cultural imperialism = promotion of western culture as superior to that of non-western cultures.
Media imperialism = Process where ownership, structure, distribution and/or content of media in any one country are subject to strong external pressures from another country or countries. A one-way process.

Advantages	Disadvantages
• Possibility of national boundaries dissolving as world becomes 'global village'.	• From a Marxist perspective it exports ideology of consumerism and capitalism to Third World.
• World is becoming media-saturated. We witness world events simultaneously as a global audience (e.g. Demolition of Berlin Wall).	• World is becoming media-saturated. World events become spectacles so we do not differentiate between them.
• Functionalists would see people connected into global communities of interest and value commitment.	• Widens the gulf between media-rich and media-poor. International communication has followed flow of power from West to rest of world.
• Third World countries are themselves becoming involved in production, especially of information hardware. Some countries successfully producing own media content.	• Undermines indigenous cultures by imposing American media products. Creates an information imbalance between nations.

A GLOBAL MEDIA CULTURE?

A global media culture will have values of:
- free market
- consumerism
- individualism
- commercialism.

Research needed to see if this is the case.

YES

- More homogenised culture – seen in global consumption of products of Trans National Corporations.

- Cultural factors seen as more significant than political or economic in producing global culture.

NO

- International media environment much more complex than this.
- Assumes a direct effects model of audience behaviour.

- Increasing amount of resistance to global culture.
- Hybridity of cultures = mixing of cultural styles to produce something unique.

15. SYNOPTIC OVERVIEW

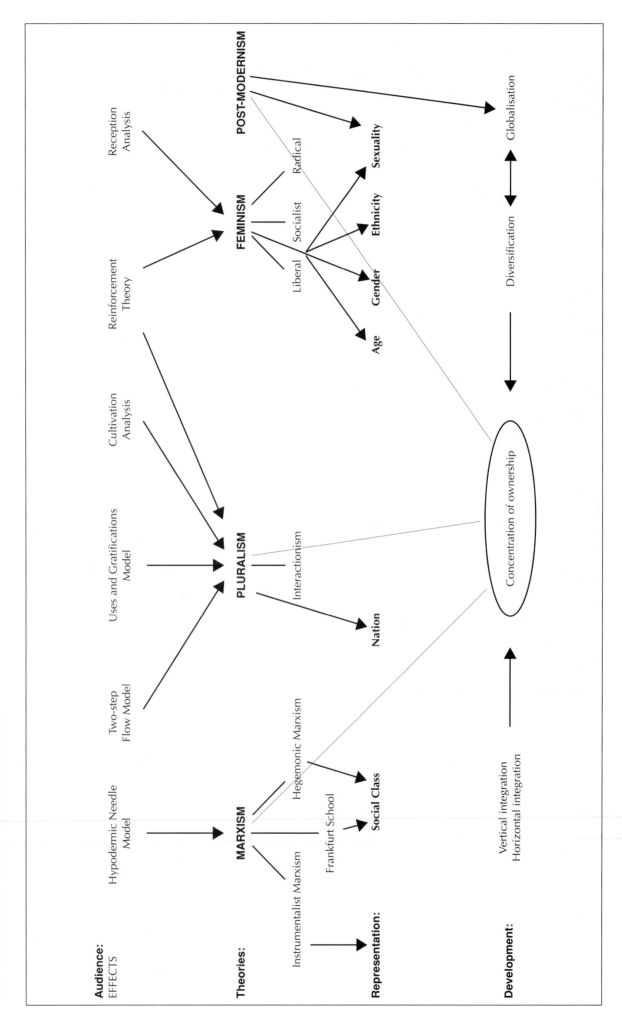

1. EDUCATION AS AN AGENT OF SECONDARY SOCIALISATION

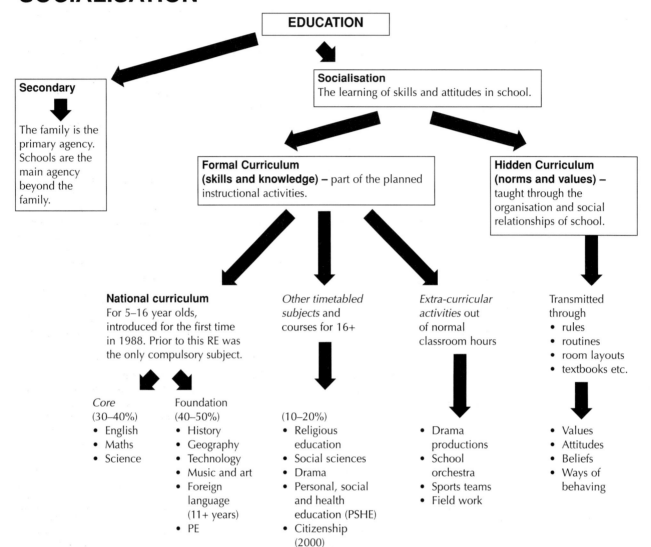

EDUCATION

Secondary

The family is the primary agency. Schools are the main agency beyond the family.

Socialisation
The learning of skills and attitudes in school.

Formal Curriculum (skills and knowledge) – part of the planned instructional activities.

Hidden Curriculum (norms and values) – taught through the organisation and social relationships of school.

National curriculum
For 5–16 year olds, introduced for the first time in 1988. Prior to this RE was the only compulsory subject.

Other timetabled subjects and courses for 16+

Extra-curricular activities out of normal classroom hours

Transmitted through
• rules
• routines
• room layouts
• textbooks etc.

Core (30–40%)
• English
• Maths
• Science

Foundation (40–50%)
• History
• Geography
• Technology
• Music and art
• Foreign language (11+ years)
• PE

(10–20%)
• Religious education
• Social sciences
• Drama
• Personal, social and health education (PSHE)
• Citizenship (2000)

• Drama productions
• School orchestra
• Sports teams
• Field work

• Values
• Attitudes
• Beliefs
• Ways of behaving

THEORIES APPLIED TO THE CURRICULA OF SCHOOLING

	National curriculum	Formal curriculum	Hidden curriculum
Functionalist	Response to changing circumstances in which the needs of the economy are paramount.	There is a consensus on the selection and organisation of knowledge that is necessary for society to function.	Essential for learning the socially appropriate behaviours on which social life depends, it teaches children morals.
Marxist	Government acting in the interests of capitalists has imposed a body of knowledge on everyone and denied children access to subjects that challenge the status quo, e.g. social sciences.	School knowledge is determined by the ruling class and children are assessed and eliminated from the system on their mastery of this material. Official 'knowledge' squeezes out other forms.	Used to pass on ruling class ideology as a means of social control. A feature of the enduring power of capitalism, it is used to establish hegemony amongst the subordinate classes.
Interactionist	Outcome of negotiation processes between teachers, educationalists and politicians in which the group with most power (politicians) had the greatest influence.	Selection is made from a larger body of knowledge i.e. it is socially constructed. It is the interaction between many groups and institutions which affect the outcome.	Important messages and signals are conveyed in interaction processes in the classroom. These are concerned with the 'proper' ways to behave and existing power relationships.

2. ROLE OF EDUCATION IN RELATION TO OTHER SOCIAL SYSTEMS

	POLITICAL SYSTEM		ECONOMIC SYSTEM		SOCIAL STRATIFICATION SYSTEM	
	Political system is democratic and needs education to prepare pupils for citizenship. **Functionalist**	Political system is controlled by the ruling class who use education to hold on to their power. **Marxist**	Economic system requires an expert workforce for efficiency in an advanced society **Functionalist**	Economic system meets the needs of Capitalism for an easily exploited labour force. **Marxist**	Social stratification system is meritocratic and provides social mobility (see **Education 5**) **Functionalist**	Social stratification system is closed and helps reproduce the inequalities of class (see **Education 5**) **Marxist**
SKILLS AND KNOWLEDGE taught through the FORMAL CURRICULUM	Schools provide the skill of literacy necessary for a democracy. Male suffrage came about at the same time as state education, showing the close connection between the two. From 2000, Citizenship will be a compulsory part of National Curriculum.	Education is the most important means of maintaining the ruling class in power. Schools withhold knowledge to achieve this, key thinkers such as Marx, Freud and Darwin are not studied routinely. Democracy is an illusion which is perpetuated by the pretence of a balanced curriculum.	Education is an investment in human capital and the basis for economic growth. General education produces an adaptable and flexible workforce. New vocationalism (see **Education 3**) can be seen as part of the structural differentiation of society.	The curriculum of schools is largely irrelevant to work. Schools prepare pupils for the tedium of work by offering a boring curriculum that crushes creativity and produces compliant workers. Higher-level skills are restricted to a minority.	Schools provide a broad curriculum to allow children to realise their talents. Differentiation of access is based on fair and objective assessment of pupils' abilities. Talent is the prime way that schools allocate pupils to labour markets.	The ruling class defines what counts as knowledge, and the working class are progressively eliminated because of their lack of cultural capital on which they are judged or by self-elimination. The result is that schools reproduce the social hierarchy in society.
NORMS AND VALUES taught through the HIDDEN CURRICULUM **ROLE OF EDUCATION IN RELATION TO OTHER SOCIAL SYSTEMS**	Cohesion and unity are fostered by the teaching of history, this gives a child a national identity and a sense that society is something bigger than herself/ himself. In the USA the raising of the flag starts the day in every classroom. This can be seen as having an important integrative effect on a population of diverse cultures.	Government cannot hold power by force for long so it has to legitimise its rule. Schools do this by teaching loyalty, obedience and respect for authority. The most important weapon for the ruling class is to dominate culture. It does this mainly through the education system.	Schools value and reward individual achievement and hard work, thus fostering the work ethic of industrial society. Habits of good time-keeping, obedience and diligence are taught through the discipline of the school regime.	There is a correspondence between the social relationships of work and school. Pupils are made passive by the rewarding of conformity. Hierarchy is accepted through teacher control. Pupils are motivated by external rewards. Knowledge is fragmented into lessons which limits its potential.	The school acts as a bridge between the family – where particularistic values and ascription dominate – and the wider society where universalistic values are pervasive. Pupils learn that differential rewards are earned for different levels of achievement and this encourages competition. System is seen as 'fair'.	Meritocracy is a myth. It is used by the ruling class to legitimate pre-existing inequalities and make people believe that role allocation is fair. This personalises failure and distracts attention from the inequalities of capitalism which would otherwise be a source of discontent. This results in 'victim-blaming'.

3. NEW VOCATIONALISM

BENEFITS			LIMITATIONS	
Social	**Individual**		**Individual**	**Social**
National policy for...	National Vocational Qualifications – NVQs and GNVQs – to reward practical achievement.	**N**	No work, no benefits for unemployed 16–18 year olds.	New ideology making...
Enterprise encouraged.	Employment opportunities improved.	**E**	Exploits the young by paying low wages.	Education the problem.
Worthwhile to keep young people busy.	Work experience to give realism to learning.	**W**	Work experience already gained from part-time jobs.	Work driven, neglects other skills.
Valuable to learn work disciplines.	Vocationally relevant courses, e.g. TVEI.		Vulnerable young people in hazardous work placements have been injured or killed.	Victim blaming – young people are the problem.
Opportunities for everyone.	Occupations can be tried out for suitability.	**V**	Opportunity for real jobs is lacking.	Organisation divide reinforces academic/ vocational split.
		O		
Core skills developed in problem solving and communication.	Competencies on core skills...	**C**	Controls young by keeping them off the streets.	Cheap labour used to control workforce.
Abolishes status gap between education and training.	Assessed on records of achievement.	**A**	Absence of theoretical knowledge to underpin practical skills.	Academic/vocational divide creates...
TECs deliver training through private enterprise.	Transferable skills, e.g. time keeping.	**T**	Training not provided or of poor quality.	Two-tier system.
Investment in human capital.	Inadequate teaching of basic skills in schools is compensated for.	**I**	Inappropriate skills taught.	Inequality of opportunity between genders and ethnic groups.
Operationally cost effective because it uses industry as the trainers.	Objectives of learning clearly identified.	**O**	Opposition to schemes as they are...	Objectives hidden, e.g. reduced wage levels.
Need for change to provide...	Numeracy gained as a core skill.	**N**	Not popular – school, college or work preferred.	Not marketable to employers.
Appropriately skilled school leavers.	All 16–18 year-olds included.	**A**	Alienating work.	Anti-union by introducing non-union labour at different rates of pay.
Linked to the needs of the economy.	Literacy developed.	**L**	Low-level skills.	Lack of teachers to deliver the technology skills.
Industry provided initiative began with the Labour Party.	IT skills taught.	**I**	Incentives are lacking.	Ideology of work has replaced equality of opportunity.
Standards raised through two-year schemes.	Student-centred learning.	**S**	Strategy lacks appeal.	Subsidy to employers at tax-payers' expense.
Modular courses with more flexibility.	Motivation expected.	**M**	Menial work.	Manipulates the unemployment statistics to give a more favourable picture.

4. SELECTION PROCEDURES IN EDUCATION

	Arguments for	Arguments against
PRIVATE EDUCATION as preparation for a leadership role in the POLITICAL SYSTEM	• Provide small class sizes and a disciplined environment that ensures most children leave with educational qualifications. • Leadership qualities are rare and private schools can foster these talents with an education that will fit people for a political role by character building and public speaking. A high proportion of MPs, cabinet ministers, leaders of industry, the law and media have been to public school and/or Oxbridge.	• An elitist system that perpetuates the cycle of privilege. • Selection is not on merit but on the ability to pay for those with the right family backgrounds. • Operates outdated practices, e.g. fagging, initiation ceremonies and impractical uniforms. • National Curriculum is not compulsory and so a classical education unsuited to a modern technical society can be taught. • Schools have links with Oxbridge colleges, thus ensuring inequality continues into higher education.
SELECTIVE ENTRY into state schools with particular reference to the needs of the ECONOMIC SYSTEM	• The tripartite system 1944–1960s was an efficient way of preparing children for their future roles: 　**Grammar schools** provided academic education for professional and managerial occupations; 　**Technical schools** prepared pupils for skilled jobs; 　**Secondary moderns** gave more practical activities for those who would become semi-skilled and unskilled workers. • In the 1980s **grant-maintained schools** and **city technology colleges** could operate selection and become centres of excellence to produce the workers with the technical and language skills of the future.	• Undermines the principle of equality of opportunity. • Puts 11-year-old children under extreme pressure to be successful. • Creates failures of those children who do not get accepted for the school of their choice. • Produces 'sink' schools from those that do not operate selective entry. • Makes league table comparisons meaningless when only those children with good prospects of academic success will be selected. • Enables middle-class parents to exercise choice, whereas working-class children may have to go to the nearest school to their home.
STREAMING AND SETTING within schools in preparation for position in the SOCIAL STRATIFICATION SYSTEM	• Children are judged by their performance as they will be in a hierarchical society. • Creates a competitive atmosphere that encourages hard work. • Stretches the brightest children whilst allowing the less able to work at their own pace. • Less-able child can taste success by coming top in their group. • Difficult to teach mixed-ability classes so ability grouping within the classroom often occurs. • Necessity in a competitive education system where schools are judged on their position in the league tables.	• Puts labels on children which can produce a self-fulfilling prophecy and an anti-academic sub-culture can develop. • Allocations can result in indirect discrimination, Asian pupils have been put in lower streams than their ability indicated. • The system is inflexible because transfer up the ranking is difficult if the speed or content of work is different. • Lower groups disadvantaged by teachers denying them access to certain kinds of knowledge; emphasis on controlling behaviour rather than teaching; the least experienced teachers being given the less desirable lower groups to teach.

5. REPRODUCTION OR MERITOCRACY?

SOCIAL REPRODUCTION

Structures are created by the activities of individuals and in turn the existence of structures makes actions possible. These structuration processes work to maintain the cohesion of classes from one generation to the next. Most visible at the extremes of the class structure.

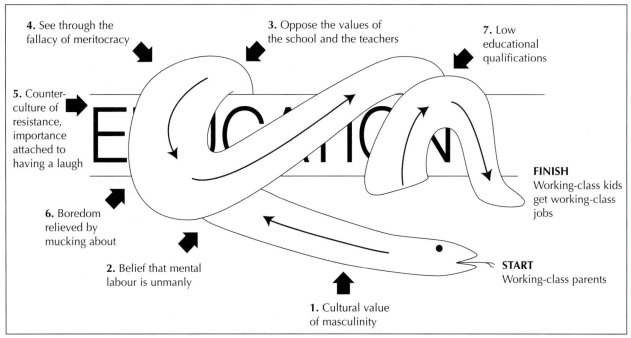

4. See through the fallacy of meritocracy

3. Oppose the values of the school and the teachers

7. Low educational qualifications

5. Counter-culture of resistance, importance attached to having a laugh

FINISH
Working-class kids get working-class jobs

6. Boredom relieved by mucking about

2. Belief that mental labour is unmanly

START
Working-class parents

1. Cultural value of masculinity

(Text based on **Willis**, 'Learning to Labour', 1977)

MERITOCRACY

A social system in which rewards and social position are allocated on ability and achievement rather than ascriptive factors such as class, ethnicity or gender. It operates more obviously in the middle ranges to take people up one status division.

HOW THE LADDER IS ASSUMED TO WORK

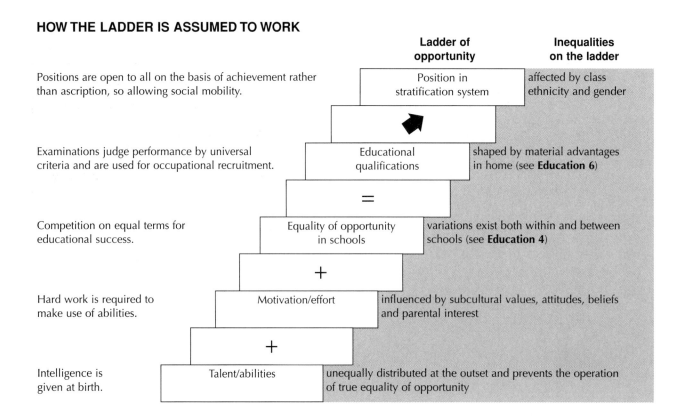

	Ladder of opportunity	Inequalities on the ladder
Positions are open to all on the basis of achievement rather than ascription, so allowing social mobility.	Position in stratification system	affected by class ethnicity and gender
Examinations judge performance by universal criteria and are used for occupational recruitment.	Educational qualifications	shaped by material advantages in home (see **Education 6**)
Competition on equal terms for educational success.	Equality of opportunity in schools	variations exist both within and between schools (see **Education 4**)
Hard work is required to make use of abilities.	Motivation/effort	influenced by subcultural values, attitudes, beliefs and parental interest
Intelligence is given at birth.	Talent/abilities	unequally distributed at the outset and prevents the operation of true equality of opportunity

6. THEORIES OF DIFFERENTIAL ACHIEVEMENT

Arguments and evidence	Criticisms
INDIVIDUAL **A psychological/biological theory** that assumes intelligence is largely innate and can be measured by IQ tests. • Studies of identical twins purported to show the pervasiveness of innate intelligence when twins reared apart from birth had very similar IQs in adulthood.	• It is impossible to measure IQ without an environmental effect, e.g. using language, levels of motivation or well-being. • Tests are sometimes culturally biased by the group who designed the test initially. • Problematic definition of what IQ is measuring. • Possibility of changes in IQ over time. • Burt's (1943) studies of identical twins were discredited when found to be based on false data.
HOME **Subcultural theory** takes a macro perspective and looks for differences in styles of living and socialisation between groups. **Material factors** – books, toys, housing, resources spent on education or to keep children at school. **Cultural factors** – levels of parental interest, values attached to education. **Language** – allows the expression of abstract thought and complex ideas.	• A deterministic theory that implies that the child can do nothing to influence their achievement. • Adopts an implicitly victim-blaming view and reflects prejudice and stereotypes rather than real knowledge. • Does not recognise the possibility of innate differences in children. • Fails to look at the child's experience of school.
SCHOOL **Interactionist theories** take a micro approach that looks at the school processes that are part of the hidden curriculum of schooling. **Teacher – pupil** • Labelling and the self-fulfilling prophecy are used to explain how teacher expectations get translated into educational performance. **School organisation** • Streaming creates anti-academic subcultures as pupils reject the system that has rejected them by labelling them failures. • Processes of differentiation and polarisation occur after streaming. **Pupil strategies** • Examines how the pupils respond to their situation.	• Ignores the macro perspective and so ignores the circumstances in which teaching is carried out, e.g. educational policies and resourcing. • Does not explain where the teachers' definitions of pupils come from and why they are so similar. • Implies that pupils are passive recipients of the labels teachers use, whereas in reality they can respond with a self-refuting prophecy or adopt a variety of pupil strategies that reduce the power of the teacher to control the class or influence learning. • Can be descriptive rather than explaining why one strategy is adopted rather than another.
SOCIETY **Structural conflict theory** examines the political character of educational knowledge and the ways it is controlled. It sets a new agenda in asking and answering new questions. Q. *Who determines the school curriculum?* A. Those with power in society. Q. *What is the content of the school curriculum?* A. It is defined, selected and ranked by those with power to include as valid that which is in their interests. Q. *Is knowledge equally accessible to all pupils?* A. No, high status knowledge is restricted to certain groups.	• Has not been tested with empirical research. • Takes a rather simplistic view of the power structures that operate in education which are as diverse as textbook writers, exam boards, teachers. • Knowledge is socially constructed so no one set of ideas is better than any others. This means the ideas in this box are no more correct than any other explanations on this page.

7. DIFFERENTIAL ACHIEVEMENT AND CLASS

FACTORS EXPLAINING CLASS DIFFERENCES
(see also **Education 6** for general points)

Evidence and argument	Criticism
INDIVIDUAL • The higher IQ of the higher social classes is evidence of innate differences. • Middle-class children consistently gained more places at grammar schools as a result of performance on the 11+ test.	• Cause and effect is being muddled, the relationship is present because of the time spent in education. • The test favoured the middle-class child whose parents could afford to provide coaching and promises of rewards to ensure their children were successful.
HOME **Material** • Lack of books in working-class homes. **Cultural** • Middle-class parents showed more interest in their child's education. • Working-class more fatalistic and placed less value on education as a route to advancement. • Middle-class child-rearing encouraged deferred gratification, self-control and independence. **Language** • Working-class used a restricted code, elaborated code of the middle-class allows more abstract reasoning.	• Patterns are cultural differences not signs of deprivation. • Does not explain middle-class failures or working-class successes. • Visits to school are invalid as a measure of parental interest, working-class parents may not attend for a variety of reasons, e.g. shift working or costs of child-minding. • No search for the underlying cause of the differences found, nor a demonstration of how they link to educational performance. • Tendency to overgeneralise differences at the expense of similarities. • Working-class speech has its own strengths and is not inferior in terms of how it can be used to express ideas.
SCHOOL **Teacher–pupil** • USA counsellors steered working-class boys away from college courses. • A primary school headteacher picked children to sit at tables ranked by family background. • Teachers' conception of ideal pupils came closest to a middle-class pattern of behaviour. **School organisation** • Banding in a comprehensive school was based on primary school recommendations that favoured middle-class pupils. **Pupil strategies** • Middle-class pupils adopted more conformist strategies.	• Teachers' advice to children is a realistic assessment of their potential rather than a stereotyped judgement. • The evidence is largely case-study data that may not warrant generalisation. • Does not take account of strategies adopted with different teachers.
SOCIETY • Ruling class impose their own culture as worthy of being taught in school. Pupils are judged in terms of this body of knowledge and those with more **cultural capital**, i.e. middle-class pupils will be more successful. • There are costs attached to the working class making a choice that would take them out of their class position. • Working-class boys were influenced in their attitude to school by what they perceived as their lack of chances of success.	• Working-class boys were not held back by a lack of cultural capital in the post-war period, evidence was found of education being used to spread cultural capital. • The secondary effects of class position are not more important than the cultural effects of the home. • These findings based on a very small sample of boys, and Willis (1977) accepts without question what the boys tell him.

8. DIFFERENTIAL ACHIEVEMENT AND ETHNIC GROUPS

FACTORS EXPLAINING ETHNIC DIFFERENCES
(see also **Education 6** for evaluation of the theories)

Evidence and argument	Criticism
INDIVIDUAL • In the USA 'blacks score on average 10–15 points lower on IQ tests' (Jensen, 1973). • The differences are said to remain even when environmental factors are controlled for. • Disproportionate number of West Indian boys were in schools for special needs pupils.	• Impossible to remove 200 years of oppression in one generation. • Black undergraduates had culturally induced expectations of failure. When told what their scores would be compared with white students they did less well on the tests. • Placements may have been made on behaviour rather than low intelligence.
HOME **Material** • Amongst Afro-Caribbean there are a large number of one-parent families who use child-minders. **Cultural** • Afro-Caribbean parents lack the understanding of the importance of play and parent-child interaction. • Matrifocal families have a less secure sense of identity. • West Indian family life is turbulent. **Language** • Afro-Caribbean use of patois or Creole. • Asians may not have English as a first language.	• Ethnic minorities are more likely to be working-class. • Explanations are stereotypes with a biased interpretation of culture – Afro-Caribbean parents do have a high regard for education. • Children have a rich verbal culture with the same capacity for complex learning. • A higher proportion of Asian pupils gain GCSE English language than white pupils.
SCHOOL **Teacher–pupil** • Teachers have low expectations of black pupils. • Teachers hold stereotyped views of black children as unacademic but good at sport. • Asians gain less teacher attention and are spoken to in simplistic speech. **School organisation** • Jayleigh School (CRE, 1992) used setting as a barrier to a large number of Asian pupils. • A lack of black teachers as role models. **Pupil strategies** • Racism and bullying on the playground can go unsanctioned.	• Most teachers were actively and sensitively concerned to treat all pupils fairly. • Afro-Caribbean girls were determined to succeed and did despite their double disadvantage. • Schools are developing anti-racist policies.
SOCIETY • White society transmits negative images of black people and this gives children low self-esteem. • The English language contains the images of racism, e.g. 'black' is associated with evil, 'white' with good. • Ethnic minority languages do not have same status as European languages. • The National Curriculum is ethnocentric in the teaching of British history and the requirement for a Christian assembly.	• Afro-Caribbean children do not have low self-esteem. • The idea has been taken to extremes when no negative association is present, e.g. the renaming of blackboard to chalkboard. • These are becoming accepted and taught in school. • Most religious festivals are recognised and celebrated in schools.

9. DIFFERENTIAL ACHIEVEMENT AND GENDER

FACTORS EXPLAINING GENDER DIFFERENCES
(see also **Education 6** for evaluation of the theories)

Evidence and arguments	Criticism
INDIVIDUAL • Girls mature more quickly than boys. • Girls are better on verbal skills, boys on spatial, this may be due to differences in brain lateralisation.	• Differences stressed at the expense of the similarities. • Gendered toys could explain this difference just as well. • Scientific research has tried and failed to show that men have bigger brains than females.
HOME **Material** • Parents have given more resources to the education of their sons. **Cultural** • Sex role socialisation begins from the moment a child is born. • Girls had priorities of marriage and family, this made them place a lower value on education. **Language** • Girls' toys encourage the development of language skills, boys spend less time reading with parents.	• Much of the research is now out of date by trying to explain girls' underachievement. Boys are now the cause for concern. • In addition to parental socialisation media and peer groups play a role from a very early age. • Girls' priorities have changed. • Unisex toys becoming more usual.
SCHOOL **Teacher–pupil** • Girls are praised for appearance and conduct, boys for work, they are treated differently for punishments, jobs, and rewards. • Teachers gave more attention to boys in the classroom. **School organisation** • Use of gendered regimes, e.g. order of names on registers, uniforms, lining up, or seating plans. • Timetabling encourages gendered subject choice. • Traditional gender roles portrayed in reading schemes. **Pupil strategies** • Boys dominate physical space and boys' aggression towards girls is not checked.	• Boys get more attention because they are more likely to require the supervision of the teacher to get on with their work. • Subject choice has opened up for girls. • There is a new generation of books with non-sexist assumptions. • School strategies are boosting girls' achievements (see **Education 10**).
SOCIETY • The school curriculum is gendered, e.g. history and English literature are taught for men, about men. • Science is packaged for boys and given a higher status than arts subjects. • Patriarchal power has restricted girls' access to the full curriculum, e.g. 11+ allocation of places; quotas of females at medical school; Oxford and Cambridge withheld degrees to female students; girls were taught those subjects that would fit them for their role as housewife and mother. • Gendered language, e.g. chairman, mankind etc. is a sign of the continuing power and influence of men.	• Programmes like GIST and WISE (see **Education 10**) attempt to address this inequality. • National Curriculum ensures all children follow the same subjects until the age of 16. • Women have struggled to correct these injustices with some success. • Women's studies bring back some balance by putting women and their contribution into centre stage although these courses generally are only available at higher education.

10. POLICIES FOR UNDER-ACHIEVING GROUPS

THEORY	INDIVIDUAL	HOME	SCHOOL	SOCIETY
Key concept / **Explanation for failure**	• Slow learners. • Children fail because of low ability.	• Deprivation. • Children fail because they are deprived.	• Disadvantage. • Schools fail children.	• Exploitation. • The education system creates and perpetuates failure.
POLICY / **Remedy**	• Education tailored to child's ability.	• Compensatory education and positive discrimination.	• Institutional change.	• Redistribution of power and control.
Class	• Under the tripartite system (see **Education 11**), the 11+ test allocated pupils to one of three types of school, the less academic (usually working-class) went to secondary modern schools. • Streaming and setting (see **Education 4**) places pupils of similar ability in the same teaching group. • Remedial education.	• Educational priority areas (EPA), areas of multiple deprivation identified and additional resources allocated to make up for assumed cultural and language deficits in the home (see **Education 11**). • Involve parents in education by giving them more legal responsibility.	• Comprehensive schools (see **Education 11**) provide the same type of education for children of all social backgrounds, giving them the same opportunity to gain qualifications. • Mixed ability teaching avoids streaming pupils with consequent effects of labelling and self-fulfilling prophecies.	• Suggested abolition of private education (see **Education 4**). • Assisted places scheme (see **Education 11**) gave scholarships to able children to attend private schools (but only a small number of places available).
Ethnic groups	• Disproportionate number of West Indian boys taught in special needs classes.	• Section 11 funding available to primary schools with high proportions of ethnic minorities. • English-as-a-second-language classes.	• Multi-cultural education to encourage respect for other people's culture, e.g. by including the celebration of Divali or a school steel band.	• Voluntary aided status for schools set up by religious communities (but very few schools have been given this status).
Gender	• 11+ allocation of places adjusted girls' marks down on the assumption that boys mature later.	• GIST (Girls Into Science and Technology) to encourage wider participation of girls in male-dominated subjects. • WISE (Women In Science and Engineering).	• Single-sexed schools or classes are an attempt to tackle gender inequality by making the school environment less hostile to girls.	• National Curriculum ensures equal access to the same curriculum. • Sex Discrimination Act. • Women's studies.

11. POLICIES ON EDUCATION 1944–81

POLICY	FAIRNESS AND DEMOCRACY	Criticism	EMPLOYABILITY AND ECONOMIC EFFICIENCY	Criticism
1944 Education (Butler) Act	• Free secondary education for all. • Selection to schools by objective testing at age of 11. • Children receive education suited to their ability. • Parity of esteem between schools. • Eventual raising of school-leaving age.	• Allowed private schools to continue. • Testing favoured middle-classes. • Allocations to grammar schools discriminated against girls. • Regional inequalities in availability of grammar school places. • Unequal funding to the three types of school.	• Tripartite system offered vocational education from the age of 11. • Early selection is efficient as it teaches children only to the level required for their future occupation. • Relates talent to position in economic system.	• Early selection leads to wrong allocations and wastage of talent. • Too few technical schools to meet the needs for skilled workers. • Label of failure and no formal recognition of achievements given to 80% of children.
Comprehensive schools 1965 onwards	• Expected to engage more children in learning through progressive teaching methods. • Offered the same curriculum to all pupils. • Avoided the divisiveness of the tripartite system. • Integration of children with special education needs.	• Inequalities in the catchment area of schools produced schools of different character. • Past status of school, i.e. grammar or secondary modern, affected facilities in school, e.g. labs, libraries and teachers. • Social class divisions continued in friendship patterns.	• Avoids the wastage from early selection. • Provides a broad general education for all pupils with the skills of adaptability for changing workforce needs. • Maximises utilisation of talent in the work force.	• Streaming can create the same labelling as in the tripartite system. • Able children are not stretched and there is a general lowering of standards. • Liberal progressive educational philosophy neglects basic numeracy and literacy in favour of creativity.
Educational Priority Areas 1967	• Compensatory education for schools in deprived areas as measured by levels of unemployment; numbers of free school meals served; numbers of single-parent families, proportion of immigrants. • Additional resources to schools to make up for the deficiencies at home.	• Depended on the local authority applying for extra funding, and some chose not to. • Too little money to make much difference. • Not all children were from deprived homes, and many other children who were equally or more deprived were not included in the scheme.	• Money spent in early years of education is more cost-effective than extending the school-leaving age. • Investing in human potential early in life saves money later, through keeping individuals out of the criminal justice system.	• Benefits only apparent whilst the children were in the scheme, they fell back to previous performance once they had left the EPA school. • Any benefits unevenly spread because of 'hit-and-miss' nature of provision.
Assisted places scheme 1981	• Poorer children could gain access to the private sector of education.	• A smokescreen to give the illusion of openness, it is only available to a small number of children.	• Taps into the abilities of the working-class.	• Money would be more cost-effective if spread around more children.

12. EDUCATION REFORM ACT 1988

POLICY	FAIRNESS AND DEMOCRACY	Criticism	EMPLOYABILITY AND ECONOMIC EFFICIENCY	Criticism
1. National Curriculum	• Gives every child an entitlement to a body of knowledge regardless of where they live or what school they attend. • From 2000, will provide basic instruction in Citizenship and workings of democracy.	• Excludes children at private schools. • Established with too much political control and not enough concern for the needs of the pupils. • Emphasis in Citizenship is on obligations, not rights.	• Intention to raise standards in all schools to make Britain more competitive in Europe. • Puts key skills at the centre of the curriculum and ensures all children study technology.	• Curriculum is not relevant to the interests and abilities of all children of an age group, e.g. Shakespeare plays studied by all 14-year-olds. • Definitions of technology change with political fashion.
2. Standard Attainment Tests (SATs) and league tables	• Gives parents an entitlement to information about the progress of their child and to make informed choices about the schooling of their children. • Identifies children who may require additional help.	• Creates 'sink' schools from which it is difficult to recover. • Information merely reflects the inequalities in the wider society without doing anything to change them.	• Competition is a motivator to improvement. • League tables provide incentive for schools to perform well for their pupils' needs.	• Time and effort wasted by teachers in finding out what they already know. • Administering and marking the tests is expensive. • League tables distract school managements from educating.
3. Grant maintained (Opt-out) schools	• Decision taken by a vote of parents. • Reflects opinion of local community.	• Parents of future pupils not given a voice. • Creates a two-tier system with preferential funding.	• Allows schools to use their budgets more cost-effectively. • Can shift resources to areas of greatest need.	• Schools may choose not to provide some services, e.g. educational psychology because it is too expensive.
4. City technology colleges (CTC)	• Located in inner city deprived areas. • Open to children of all abilities. • Involves local industries in funding education.	• Location of school does not reflect home address of pupil. • Oversubscribed: selection does occur. • Provision is regionally uneven.	• Additional money brought into education by the sponsoring organisation. • Reflects local industry's needs.	• Does not ensure a rational and planned allocation of resources. • State resources needed to top up local investment.
5. Local Management of Schools	• More power to heads and governors in the way a school spends its money.	• Reduces the power of the local authority which has been democratically elected.	• Allows schools to shop around for cheaper goods and services.	• Removes economies of scale that are available to local authorities.
6. Governing bodies	• Gives stronger representation to parents.	• Composition weighted in favour of business interests.	• Unpaid positions so no cost involved. • Local industrialists involved.	• Governors have control over large sums of money but have no contractual accountability.

13. POLITICAL VIEWS ON THE ROLE OF EDUCATION

	LIBERALS	SOCIAL DEMOCRATS	NEW RIGHT
Philosophy	EGALITARIANISM	MERITOCRACY	ELITISM
Focus	• Needs of individuals.	• Needs of society.	• Needs of the economy.
Preferred teaching method	• Progressive, in which the children learn by doing rather than being told, pupil-led curriculum.	• Teacher-directed democratic style. • Whole-class teaching must engage pupils.	• Teacher-centred 'chalk and talk' and use of rote learning of facts.
School organisation	• Mixed-ability teaching groups.	• Streaming, banding and setting (see **Education 4**).	• Separate schools (see **Education 4**).
Economic purpose of education	• Encourage creativity and develop talent to the full so each individual can make their contribution to society.	• A capital investment, since more educated workers are more productive, and society benefits from economic growth.	• Basic literacy and numeracy required by employers. • Vocational training for a disciplined and skilled workforce.
Examples	• Adult education. • Evening classes. • Lifelong learning.	• Free secondary education. • Expansion of higher education. • Open University, open college.	• New Vocationalism (see **Education 3**). • TVEI, CPVE, TECs GNVQ
Social purpose	• Expression of differences. • Promoting tolerance and respect for others.	• Offer the same opportunity to all pupils and thus open up society and diminish class stratification.	• Raise standards. • Parental voice. • Establish respect for traditional authority.
Examples	• Multi-cultural education. • Teacher autonomy in syllabus setting and teacher-controlled assessments.	• Comprehensive schools (see **Education 11**). • Raising of the school-leaving age. • GCSE a common exam at 16.	• Local management of schools, league tables. • National Curriculum. • Grant maintained and CTC schools (see **Education 12**).
Political purpose	• Ability to be able to think critically about the world. • Engage in political activity	• Citizenship and as a means to change society.	• Retain traditional values. • Break the power of local education control.
Examples	• Introduction of social sciences into the curriculum. • Citizenship education. • School Councils.	• Personal, social and health education (PSHE). • Compulsory Citizenship.	• National Curriculum. • Support for private schools and centres of excellence. • Suggestion of a moral curriculum.
Illich's critique of all schooling (1973)	Formal schooling is unnecessary and harmful to both students and society. It is ineffective in teaching specific skills that are better taught by those who use them in everyday life. Schools are repressive and therefore dampen creativity and imagination and produce mindless, conforming students.		

14. EDUCATION AND SOCIAL CHANGE

	OPTIMISTS (Liberals, Social Democrats, Functionalists) change is possible and has occurred.	**PESSIMISTS** (Marxists and some Feminists) change is not possible and has not happened.
Theoretical arguments concerning the possibility of change	• Schools provide equal opportunity so that those with ability can achieve educational qualifications. • Qualifications are increasingly important in determining a person's position in society. • The middle classes have gained all they can from education so any extension of provision will be to the benefit of the working class. • Economic changes in society require high-skilled, well-educated workforce, beyond traditional middle class.	• Change must come from changes to the infrastructure. • The working-class successes are a smokescreen to foster the illusion of fairness. • Educational qualifications merely legitimate the social inequalities that exist, they do not change things. • Credentialisation has occurred, i.e. the more people have qualifications the more they are wanted and the less value they become. • Rate of return on education is higher for white, middle-class males.
Empirical evidence of change to **class** inequalities	• The post-war generation of able working class were able to use education to enter middle class occupations as shown by high rates of upward mobility. • Sons and daughters of the working class are increasingly in non-manual occupations. • Occupational structural changes have encouraged working class into middle class occupations.	• Class chances of entry to grammar schools was heavily in favour of the middle classes and this increased after 1944. • The changing needs of the economy for more non-manual workers produced the mobility rather than any reduction in class inequality. • Private education continues to offer advantages that extend into adult life, it prevents the downward mobility for the less able children of the rich.
Empirical evidence of change to **ethnic minority** inequalities	• Asian pupils are catching up and overtaking white pupils at GCSE. • Afro-Caribbean girls are making significant gains in educational achievement. • High rates of staying on amongst all groups will lead to improved social position.	• This is the result of cultural change rather than the effects of education. • Discrimination and prejudice exist in the labour market and thus limit the extent to which education can bring about social change.
Empirical evidence of change to **gender** inequalities	• Girls have caught up and overtaken boys at GCSE and A level and are now showing more success at undergraduate level. • Access barriers to education have been removed.	• Replaced with a glass ceiling in the workplace. • Gendered subjects still in place. • Female achievement in school is uneven.

15. COMPARATIVE EDUCATIONAL SYSTEMS

	ENGLAND AND WALES PRE-1980	ENGLAND AND WALES POST-1980
Degree of centralisation of provision	*Low*: local variation in types of school and age of transfers. Locus of control is the county – Local Education Authority.	*Growing*: break up of local state system with the introduction of City Technology Colleges and Grant-Maintained Schools and move to central state control.
Control of the curriculum	Religious education only required subject. Teacher autonomy in the classroom.	State control through National Curriculum and testing of children by SATs. Central control of A levels through QCA.
Diversity and choice	Allocation by catchment area, parents had to move house or educate child privately if they did not like their local school.	More parental choice with selective schools and specialisation. Competition between schools for pupils and search for additional funding through sponsorship and commercial activities.
Private schooling	5% of the school age population.	Growth to 7% helped by assisted places scheme (disbanded 1997).
Further Education	Tertiary provision run by Local Education Authorities.	Incorporation of colleges with funding based on student numbers or linked to MSC funding.
Higher Education	Expansion into a binary system in 1960s with polytechnics forming a second tier to meet demographic changes and increased demand.	Further expansion and abolition of binary divide in response to market forces with doubling of student numbers to 30% and increased staff:student ratios as funding per student declined.
HE student funding	Mandatory grants. Fees paid by Local Education Authority.	Replaced by loans and introduction of tuition fees.
Training	Left to private enterprise through apprenticeships. Day-release to FE Colleges.	Government intervention through MSC, later Training Agency, now returned to employer-led bodies through TECs.
Quality controls	Her Majesty's Inspectors (HMIs) infrequent and little power.	Regular Ofsted inspections with powers to take over failing schools and colleges.

	ENGLAND AND WALES	GERMANY
Compulsory schooling	Start early (5 years old). Pre-school education for all 4-year-olds. School-leaving age raised to 16 in 1972.	Later start. Dual system of education and work experience compulsory to 18.
Selection and specialisation	*Early* – 11 years, tripartite, streaming in comprehensives; new Labour support the principle of teaching children in ability groups.	Hierarchical division into three (with only 6% in comprehensive schools).
Structure	Variety (but technical schools were never a viable alternative). Private education growing.	National system with technical schools a powerful rival to grammar schools. Non-existent private sector.
Higher Education	*Elitist* – only available to a minority and costs and debts incurred.	Training allowances, grants and part-time jobs. Remain students until 25 years old.
Participation rates of 16–18	Grown to 75% in full-time education or training.	92% in full-time education or training.
Vocational education	Less highly valued than academic education.	400 trades counted as a profession and require apprenticeship training for the job, i.e. high status.
Social mobility	Sponsored system, parentocracy: Resources + preference = choice.	Contest system: meritocracy Ability + effort = merit.
Spending on education	Growth in spending on education 1980–88 = –1.6%.	Growth in spending on education 1980–88 +4.8%.

6 Wealth, Poverty, and Welfare

1. WEALTH, INCOME, TAXATION, AND REDISTRIBUTION

WEALTH, INCOME AND TAXATION FLOW DIAGRAM

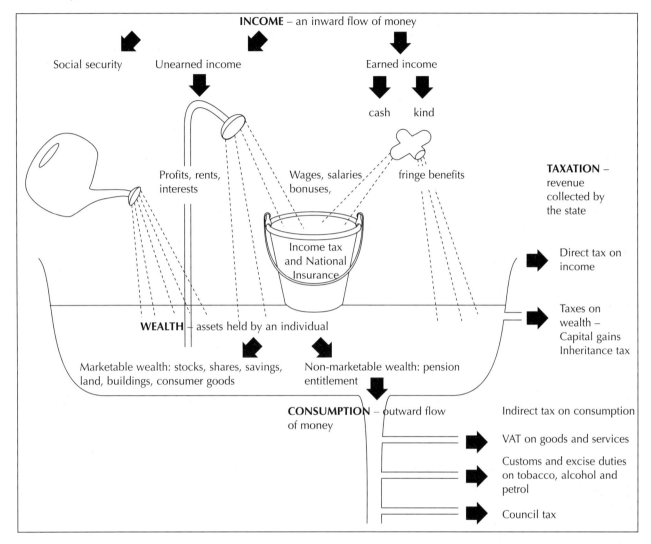

REDISTRIBUTION

Type	Description	Example
Progressive	Rich to poor	Direct taxation funding income support
Regressive	Poor to rich	VAT subsidising mortgage tax relief
Horizontal within income group	From one family type to another on the same income	Single person to families with children, through taxation funding child benefit
Between groups – gender	Women to men, or men to women	Women provide free domestic labour and unequal allocation of scarce resources in some households, e.g. food and personal spending money
Between groups – ethnicity	Black households to white; discrimination against travellers	Black families allocated council housing in least desirable property and areas rather than the most desirable
Life cycle	Working life to non-working life	National insurance and private pension schemes

2. WEALTH AND INCOME INEQUALITIES

	WEALTH	INCOME
Inequalities	**10**% of the population own $$$$$$$$$$ $$$$$$$$$$ $$$$$$$$$$ $$$$$$$$$$ $$$$$$$$$$ **50%** of wealth **50**% of the population own $$$$$$$$ **8%** of wealth	£ £ £ Richest 20% receive **twice** the national average / National average income / Poorest 20% receive **half** the national average
Changes in 20th century	**W** 'Trickle-down effect' Top 1% have a reduced share to the benefit of the top 10%, middle 80% have gained a little, bottom 10% have gained nothing	**I** 'Hour glass' Narrowing of income inequalities to 1980 Widening gap since 1980 Effects of New Labour 1997 onwards?
Explanations	• Redistribution within extended families to a larger number of heirs. • Transfer of assets within families to avoid estate duty. • Increased values of property as result of inflation. • Increased home ownership aided by the sale of council houses. • Wider spread of shareholding as the result of the privatisation of utilities and building societies. • Spread of pension schemes.	**Narrowing** • Benefits boosted the income of the poor. • Taxation depressed income of the rich. **Widening** • Reductions in higher rate taxation. • Increased rates and range of regressive VAT. • Increase in investment income. • High levels of unemployment. • Large salary increases for executives of newly privatised companies. • Reduction in the value of benefits.
Reasons why little change	• No tax on wealth holding as in Europe. • Inheritance tax avoided by passing on wealth 7 years before death. • New shareholders selling shares.	• No legislation to attack positions of privilege, e.g. private education. • New Right philosophy of the market ruled out intervention to reduce inequality.
Problems of measuring (see Wealth 1)	• Different types of wealth which have different levels of power and influence. • Lack of data on wealth because the UK has no wealth tax. • Wealth assessed at death, which is unreliable because the group are older and wealth may have been given away before death. • Concealment of true wealth to avoid tax. • No agreement on what constitutes wealth.	• Varying definitions, e.g. gross, net and disposable after tax and benefits. • Data collected by individual, not household incomes, inequality increased by two or more earners in one family. • Undeclared income. • Some income is received in kind as occupational welfare (see **Wealth 3**). • Grey economy makes accurate collection difficult (see **Work, Organisations and Leisure 2**).

3. WELFARE PLURALISM, AND REDISTRIBUTION

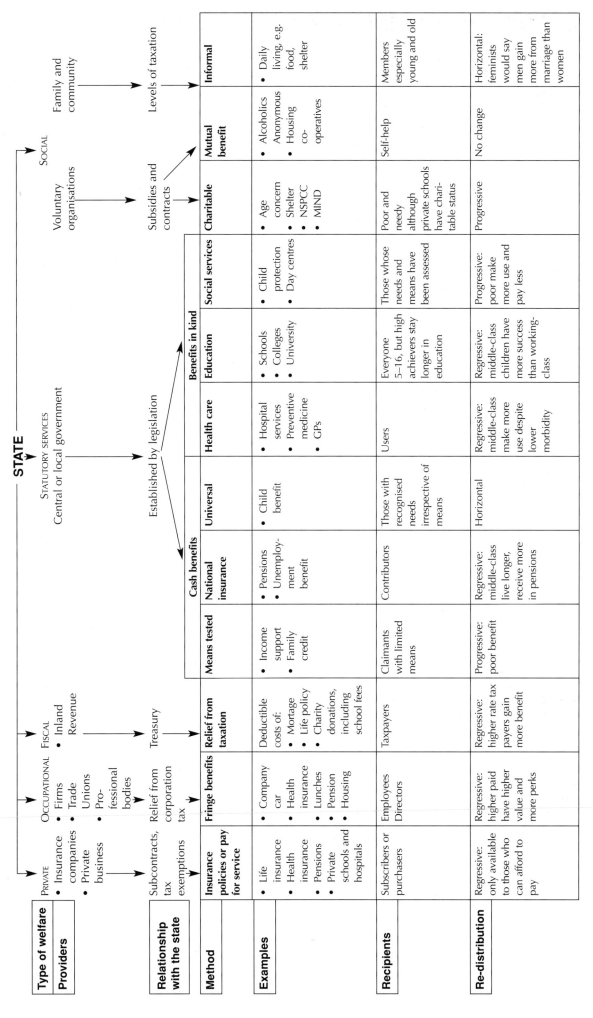

Type of welfare	PRIVATE		OCCUPATIONAL		FISCAL	STATUTORY SERVICES — Central or local government						SOCIAL — Voluntary organisations		Family and community
Providers	• Insurance companies • Private business		• Firms • Trade Unions • Professional bodies		• Inland Revenue	Central or local government						Voluntary organisations		Family and community
Relationship with the state	Subcontracts, tax exemptions		Relief from corporation tax		Treasury	Established by legislation						Subsidies and contracts		Levels of taxation
Method	Insurance policies or pay for service		Fringe benefits		Relief from taxation	Cash benefits			Benefits in kind			Charitable	Mutual benefit	Informal
						Means tested	National insurance	Universal	Health care	Education	Social services			
Examples	• Life insurance • Health insurance • Pensions • Private schools and hospitals		• Company car • Health insurance • Lunches • Pension • Housing		Deductible costs of: • Mortage • Life policy • Charity donations, including school fees	• Income support • Family credit	• Pensions • Unemployment benefit	• Child benefit	• Hospital services • Preventive medicine • GPs	• Schools • Colleges • University	• Child protection • Day centres	• Age concern • Shelter • NSPCC • MIND	• Alcoholics Anonymous • Housing co-operatives	• Daily living, e.g. food, shelter
Recipients	Subscribers or purchasers		Employees Directors		Taxpayers	Claimants with limited means	Contributors	Those with recognised needs irrespective of means	Users	Everyone 5–16, but high achievers stay longer in education	Those whose needs and means have been assessed	Poor and needy although private schools have charitable status	Self-help	Members especially young and old
Re-distribution	Regressive: only available to those who can afford to pay		Regressive: higher paid have higher value and more perks		Regressive: higher rate tax payers gain more benefit	Progressive: poor benefit	Regressive: middle-class live longer, receive more in pensions	Horizontal	Regressive: middle-class make more use despite lower morbidity	Regressive: middle-class children have more success than working-class	Progressive: poor make more use and pay less	Progressive	No change	Horizontal: feminists would say men gain more from marriage than women

STATE

STATUTORY SERVICES

4. WHO SHOULD PROVIDE WELFARE?

PROVIDER	DESCRIPTION	ARGUMENTS FOR	ARGUMENTS AGAINST
Individual and family (informal sector)	Before the 1942–8 welfare reforms this was the most common form of welfare. It continues to provide first line care. It is informal because there are no governmental agencies involved.	✓ Makes parents responsible for their children, e.g. Child Support Agency ✓ Gives people freedom and promotes independence and self-reliance	✗ People may not have the resources to protect themselves against all eventualities ✗ Women can find themselves taking the burden of care ✗ Provision may be patchy or inadequate
Private sector	This is a fast-growing sector and is encouraged by giving contributors tax relief on insurance policies. Organisations emerge which seek to provide welfare functions and produce a profit for their share-holders.	✓ Claims to give a better service and be more efficient than the state so saves money ✓ Treats people as a customer rather than as a recipient ✓ Not perceived as 'charity'	✗ Lack of checks and controls, e.g. mis-selling of pensions ✗ Profit motive could lead to cutting corners ✗ Lack of continuity if the business is closed down
Voluntary sector	An increasingly important sector that has grown as result of the requirement for local authorities to contract out services. Organisations in this sector do not seek to make profits, but often have charitable status.	✓ Can meet highly specialised needs ✓ Fills the gaps in state provision ✓ Most effective when they use a high proportion of unpaid volunteers ✓ Can experiment in new forms of care and act as a pilot for state schemes	✗ May lack security of funding ✗ May lack continuity in service provision ✗ Volunteers may lack training ✗ Unregulated and thus quality of provision varies ✗ Opportunities for exploitation of funds ✗ Recipients may not like 'charity'
State	Either as: **Welfare state** – an attempt to provide for the whole of the population or **State welfare** – providing only for the poor. In one or the other of the above forms the state has been involved since the Poor Law Act 1601. It is currently the largest provider.	✓ Planned and co-ordinated provision ✓ Secure funding and continuity of provision ✓ Can ensure national provision on an equitable basis ✓ No profit motive ✓ Accountable to the government and subject to inspection ✓ Provides equal treatment under the law	✗ Slow in responding to new needs ✗ Bureaucratic insensitivity to individual circumstances ✗ Takes over the role of the family and creates a dependency culture (see **Wealth 6**) ✗ Limits an individual's freedom of choice ✗ Requires high levels of taxation to fund

See also the debate on Community versus Institutional Care (see **Health 13**)

5. POVERTY: DEFINITIONS AND MEASUREMENT

	ABSOLUTE	SUBJECTIVE	RELATIVE
Definition	An insufficiency of the basic necessities of life required for survival. • *Primary absolute* – people do not have the money to buy these necessities. • *Secondary absolute* – people do not have adequate diet, clothing or shelter because of the way money is spent.	A felt poverty that relies on the judgement of the individual concerned. • People feel poor compared with others. • People compare their position to a previous situation they were in. • People compare their position to an imagined 'average' standard of living. • People measure their position to their family's history.	• People have insufficient resources to participate in the customs and conventions of the society in which they live. • Relative deprivation includes factors that are not related to monetary resources, e.g. love, family, health. Relative poverty Relative deprivation
Advantages	✓ Fixed, clear and universal line ✓ Can be used to compare across time and different countries	✓ Recognises the psychological dimension to poverty ✓ Explains why some may not claim benefit	✓ Recognises cultural requirements ✓ Keeps policy-makers alert to deprivation and inequality
Disadvantages	✗ Human needs vary with age, gender, work, climate etc. Therefore a single measure cannot be applied universally ✗ Necessity is itself a relative term ✗ Ignores other forms of deprivation	✗ People's perceptions are infinitely variable; therefore it is impossible to quantify ✗ The rich can feel more poverty than the poor ✗ Psychological dimension difficult to investigate	✗ Can show more poverty in the UK than in India ✗ Economic growth and prosperity can create more poverty ✗ Poverty will only be solved when there is complete equality
People likely to experience poverty	The long-term dependants: • sick and disabled (see **Wealth 9**) • mentally handicapped • long-term unemployed	Those in a crisis: • temporarily unemployed • single-parent family • acutely ill	The life cycle of the low paid: Earning, no dependants Poverty line Childhood Family building Old age
Measurement	• Shopping basket • Income Support (IS) (previously national assistance/supplementary benefit)	• Ask people about their experience of poverty	• Relative income standard • Deprivation index • Essential items
Extent of poverty – research evidence	• 1.5% of surveyed population (Rowntree, 1951) • 8.2 million depend on supplementary benefits (Field, 1988)	• 5+ million considered themselves to be poor. 12+ million said they were poor some of the time, (MORI, 1983).	• 25% of households/16 million people (Townsend, 1989) • 7.5 million (Mack & Lansley, 1985) • 13.7 million below 50% of average income (HMSO, OSS, 1993)
Explanation for poverty	Cultural/behavioural theories (see **Wealth 6**)	Situational constraints (see **Wealth 7**)	Structural theories (see **Wealth 8**)

6. BEHAVIOURAL EXPLANATIONS FOR POVERTY

CULTURE OF POVERTY (Oscar Lewis, 1961)

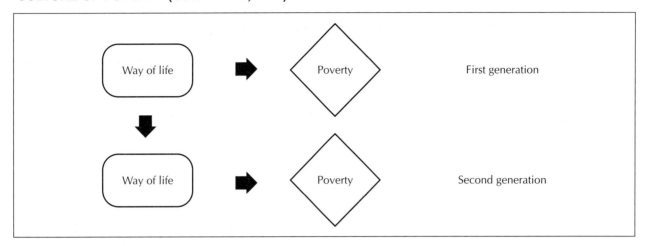

Strengths

✓ Lewis directly observed the peasant cultures of S. America.

✓ He described attitudes of fatalism, apathy, immediate gratification, failure to participate in institutional life.

✓ The theory explains the persistence of poverty by showing how shared values are transmitted from one generation to the next.

✓ The theory shows that poverty has a structure and a rationale, so that policy to alleviate poverty requires a systematic and integrated approach.

✓ Theory led to direct intervention strategies to improve the situation of those in poverty by altering their way of life.

Weaknesses

✗ Cannot generalise to modern Western industrial societies.

✗ Adopts a middle-class perspective with value-laden concepts.

✗ Not all poor have these characteristics – self-help and community organisation are found.

✗ Does not explain the origin of poverty and hence does not look at the structural features of society that produced it.

✗ Used to blame the poor for their situation.

✗ Policies such as Headstart and War on Poverty have not been very successful.

✗ Replication study did not find the same results.

DEPENDENCY CULTURE (Charles Murray (1994), David Marsland (1989), New Right)

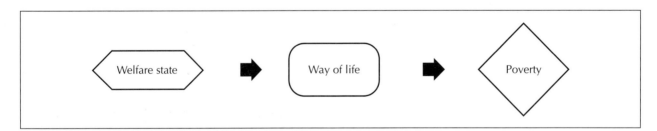

Strengths

✓ Applies the cultural explanation to a modern industrial society by showing how welfare benefits can create a lack of incentives to work.

✓ Suggests there is an underclass of unemployed and single-parent families who are dependent on state welfare.

✓ Suggests the 'Nanny state' has undermined the family's ability to support itself by providing basic needs as free entitlements.

✓ Solution to poverty is to disestablish the welfare state and give communities self-government.

Weaknesses

✗ Revives a moral attitude to poverty and gives the poor a pathological image.

✗ No cut-off point below which people are trapped, rather there is a continuum of poverty to riches.

✗ Welfare benefits are inadequate to support a family and allow poor to participate fully in society.

✗ Creates dependency on other institutions, e.g. the family which cannot cope.

✗ Denies the achievements of the Welfare State in tackling poverty.

7. SITUATIONAL EXPLANATIONS FOR POVERTY

SITUATIONAL CONSTRAINTS (Liebow 1967, Coates and Silburn 1970)

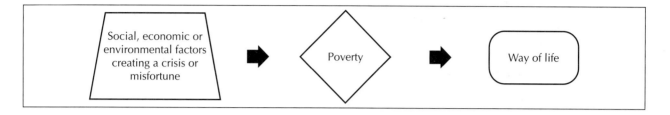

Strengths

✓ The poor have the same norms and values as the rest of society, only their financial situation sets them apart.

✓ Explains behaviour as a response to the circumstances of poverty, e.g. macho culture develops to compensate for poverty.

✓ Identifies a lack of education, unemployment, overcrowded housing as situations that bring people into poverty.

Weaknesses

✗ The poor have their class in common.

✗ People do not change their behaviour when poverty is removed.

✗ Assumes people passively accept the situations they are in.

✗ Not all people thrown into poverty adopt the same way of life.

VICIOUS CYCLE OF DEPRIVATION (Rutter and Madge 1976)

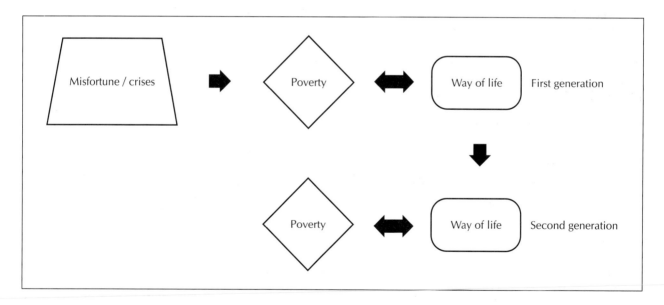

Strengths

✓ Recognises that there is a cultural lag, so even when constraints are removed behaviour may remain unchanged because it is transmitted through socialisation.

✓ Explains the resistance of poverty to intervention programmes and its persistence over time.

Weaknesses

✗ Not all children repeat the pattern of their parents, many disadvantages arise anew in each generation.

✗ Not everyone who experiences misfortunes or crises becomes poor, i.e. the theory ignores structural inequalities.

8. STRUCTURAL EXPLANATIONS FOR POVERTY/INEQUALITY

FUNCTIONALIST THEORY (Parsons 1951, Davis and Moore 1967)

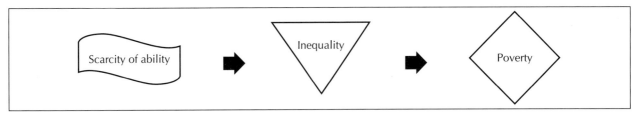

Strengths

✓ Explains the inevitability of poverty, when talent is scarce there will always be some who are poor in relation to others.

✓ Demonstrates that inequality provides the incentives for people to better themselves and achieve their full potential.

✓ Shows that poverty has some positive functions for the middle-class, e.g. providing jobs.

Weaknesses

✗ Used to justify the status quo and lack of political action to help the poor.

✗ Assumes everyone motivated by rational economic considerations.

✗ Does not consider the damaging effects of not being successful.

✗ Assumes high levels of social mobility.

✗ Ignores the dysfunctions of poverty on the poor and society.

MARXIST THEORY (Westergaard and Resler 1976, Kincaid 1979)

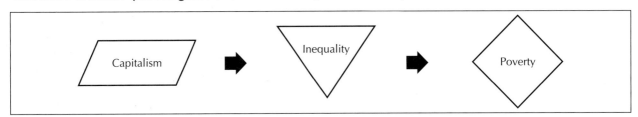

Strengths

✓ Identifies capitalism's concentration of wealth and a low wage sector providing cheap labour as the cause of inequality.

✓ Failure to tackle poverty is explained by the vested interests of the ruling class.

✓ Shows how the focus on the poor distracts attention from the real cause of inequality, i.e. capitalism.

Weaknesses

✗ Does not explain the greater vulnerability of black groups and women to poverty when compared with white middle-class males.

✗ Capitalism has provided the affluence to remove absolute poverty.

✗ Revolutionary solution would not be acceptable to many people.

WEBERIAN THEORY (Townsend 1970)

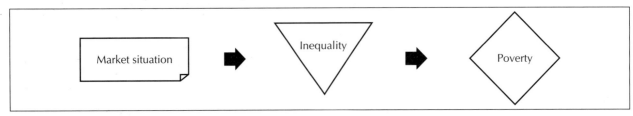

Strengths

✓ Identifies exclusion from the labour market or weak bargaining power as the reason for poverty.

✓ Suggests redistribution by the state to bring greater equality.

Weaknesses

✗ Ignores the power of capitalist interests.

✗ Tendency to blame the victim for their own poverty.

✗ Attempts to redistribute have not worked.

9. EXPLANATIONS FOR POVERTY APPLIED TO VULNERABLE GROUPS

	BEHAVIOURAL	SITUATIONAL	STRUCTURAL
Working-class	• A culture of dependency has produced an underclass, with a preference for immediate gratification. • Patterns of consumption reflect immediate gratification values, rather than planning for future prosperity. • Life-course decisions, reflected in high incidence of single parent families, dilute family resources.	• Have a poor market situation in low skill jobs. • Disadvantaged by unequal educational system. • Working class have few resources to invest in future success. • Low incomes means that it is difficult to support a family, which contradicts the values of masculinity held by working-class men.	• Inequalities are generated by the economic system. • Subject to legal restrictions on the power of the unions. • Taxation system discriminates against the poor, creating a 'poverty trap'. • Poor restricted to the secondary labour market, with part-time, insecure, low-paid jobs predominant.
Ethnic groups	• Larger family sizes. • Language difficulties. • Lower level educational qualifications. • Controversially associated with lower levels of intelligence. • Attachment to traditional ways. • Cultural values may predispose individuals to 'follow in father's/mother's footsteps'.	• Recent arrivals take time to get established. • May come from very poor countries. • Prejudice and discrimination in the job market. • Lack of appropriate education and training.	• Institutional racism in social security benefit rules, e.g. residence requirement to have been resident in UK for 10 of previous 20 years; in housing both public and private sector; jobs market. • Collapse of textile industries where many Pakistanis employed.
Women	• Young girls becoming single parents. • Cultural expectation of home maker. • Over-dependency on males for income. • Role models limited.	• Pregnancy and child care force breaks in work and create dependence. • Carers of disabled and elderly dependants. • Career paths traditionally linked to low wages.	• Patriarchal society creates dependence with unequal access to work and benefits. • Unequal distribution of household resources can produce hidden poverty among women.
Elderly	• Less adaptable. • Failure to make provision for retirement. • Reluctance to claim benefit entitlements.	• Insufficient resources during working life to make provision for retirement.	• Forced retirement. • Fixed income undermined by inflation. • Inadequate state pensions pitched at subsistence needs.
Northern regions	• Unwillingness to move to jobs in south. • Attachment to particular style of life. • Regional pride.	• Lack of job opportunities for relevant skills. • House prices in south discourage movement.	• Shift in economic base from manufacturing to service sector has created unemployment.
Disabled	• Inability to work. • Limitations on physical and/or mental abilities. • Psychology of dependency.	• Additional costs associated with the disability, e.g. mobility or dietary requirements. • Discrimination in the labour market.	• Society makes the disabled handicapped by restricting access thus limiting opportunities to contribute.

10. INNER CITY AND DEPRIVATION

> Focus on Inner City or Zone of Transition or Ghettos

WHY IS THERE SO MUCH DEPRIVATION IN INNER CITIES?

De-urbanisation (see **World Sociology 8**) has affected inner cities more than other zones. Inner cities have always been a magnet for immigrant groups because of low-cost housing, but also because of low-paid job opportunities.

- Jobs in manufacturing in inner cities have declined and those that remain are vulnerable to low wage competition from overseas.
- Road improvements aided flight from the cities, leaving behind the most economically weak.
- Housing stocks decline as best public housing is bought through 'right-to-buy' and maintenance not kept up.
- Social disorganisation increases as inner cities hold concentrations of the elderly, immigrants, single-parent families, lumpenproletariat, unemployed, the ill, the homeless and the generally disadvantaged. This process of concentration is known as 'hyperghettoization' (Wacquant 1989).

EFFECTS OF DE-URBANISATION ON INNER CITIES

• Poverty	• Living on Social Security	• High crime rates	• High suicide rate
• Drug culture	• Feelings of deprivation	• Lack of amenities	• Hostile policing
• Ill-health	• Premature death	• Vandalised environment	• High divorce rate

A NOTE OF CAUTION

Inner cities are not just geographical areas. They are social and economic localities subject to processes of change. Forces affecting inner cities are not only negative, that is, leading to intensification of deprivation, but are two-way with factors alleviating poverty and misery. Groups other than the poor inhabit inner cities.

OTHER SOCIAL GROUPS IN INNER CITIES

Inner cities are mosaics, not just ghettos. There are three other important social groups who inhabit inner cities:

Cosmopolites (Gans, 1968)	Urban upper class	Urban middle class
• Groups such as students, artists, gays, intellectuals, literary figures. • May be poor but are not disadvantaged. • City is meaningful because it provides background for activities. • Part of global cultural scene.	Very wealthy, keep housing in both rural and urban settings. Town houses often located near inner cities. But separated from inner city areas by psychological and physical barriers. 'Gated communities'.	• As house prices rise in capital, gentrification occurs. • Middle class buy up property once preserve of working class. • Changes character of inner city. • Services follow money as transformation occurs.

EFFECTS OF GENTRIFICATION AND URBAN REDEVELOPMENT ON ORIGINAL INHABITANTS OF INNER CITY

Positive effects	Negative effects
✓ Revitalisation of previously derelict property e.g. Docklands in London.	✗ Local interests suffer and concerns about intrusion - lack of democratic accountability.
✓ Brings new employment opportunities to blighted areas.	✗ New jobs limited and low paid.
✓ Breaks cycle of deprivation (Marsland).	✗ Original inhabitants don't have skills to take advantage of any high-paid work.
✓ Creates new cultural opportunities.	✗ Locals priced out of affordable housing, so children have to move away.
✓ New infrastructure created (roads, tube) to meet needs of new inhabitants for mobility to places of work.	✗ Increases resentment of locals as confronted at first hand with what they have not got.
✓ Claim that wealth trickles down from new to original community.	

11. TWENTIETH-CENTURY WELFARE

1900	LEGISLATION	SOCIAL/ECONOMIC CONTEXT	POLITICAL CONTEXT
1899–1902 1906 1907 1908 **1910**	School meals. School medical. Pensions for over 70 years old.	Rowntree's study of York – 33% in poverty. Move away from Victorian system and beginnings of modern welfare state with benefits as a right of citizenship.	Recruits to Boer war found to be unfit for service. Liberal reforms of Lloyd George.
1911 1914–18 **1920**	National Insurance Act – compulsory health and unemployment insurance for workers in selected industries.	No cover for the family.	WW1, 4 out of 9 conscripts unfit for service.
1922 **1930**		Mass unemployment undermines the insurance principle as 2 million in receipt of poor relief, thus showing the inadequacy of the existing provisions.	
1932 1936 1939 **1940**		Rowntree's second survey showed 18% in poverty.	WW2 provided the national identity and common purpose necessary for the establishment of the welfare state.
1942 1944 1945 1946 1948 **1950**	Beveridge Report. Butler Education Act. Family Allowance. New Towns Act. National Assistance Act. NHS Act.	Poor Law abolished. Rowntree's 3rd survey – 1.5% in poverty.	Labour government introduced the post war reforms as a collectivist policy to give universal rights to citizens.
    1960		Period of growth and prosperity, poverty believed to have been eradicated amongst all but the old.	Political consensus on the principles of the welfare state during a period of economic growth and full employment.
1961 1966 **1970**	Introduction of graduated pensions. Introduction of earnings related benefits. Family income supplement introduced.	Abel-Smith & Townsend rediscover poverty caused by low pay. Greater selectivity and means testing introduced to target benefits on poor and save money.	
1974 1977 **1980**	Finer Report – benefits targeted on one-parent families. Capital Transfer Tax introduced. Child benefit replaced family allowance and child tax allowances.	Townsend – 'Poverty in the UK', deprivation index – 23% of households in poverty. Decarceration and community care for the elderly and mentally ill.	
1981 1986 1988 **1990**	Earnings related benefits abolished. Inheritance tax replaced CTT. School leavers excluded from social security benefits. Social fund introduced to provide loans rather than grants for essential items.	7 million people dependent on supplementary benefits. Erosion of the welfare state through privatisation and cuts in benefits.	Thatcherism – anti collectivist free market principles – control of inflation takes priority over reducing unemployment. Encouragement to welfare pluralism.
1991 1993 1997 **2000**	NHS reforms introduced competition and increased powers for managers. Child support agency set up to enforce contributions from absent parents.	Single mothers targeted for welfare to work.	Crisis in welfare spending and new consensus that society cannot afford the welfare state. New Labour pursuing similar policies to previous Conservative government.

Wealth, Poverty, and Welfare 89

12. PRINCIPLES UNDERLYING DELIVERY OF WELFARE

PRINCIPLE	For	Against
SELECTIVITY – benefits only given to those whose income and wealth fall below a minimum level	✓ Ensures that only those in need receive help. ✓ Encourages responsibility for own welfare. ✓ Discourages dependence on the state. ✓ Targeting concentrates resources where they are most needed. ✓ Fills the gaps left by a market mechanism by providing safety net cover below which no one is supposed to fall. ✓ Provides for people's needs on the basis of their means, e.g. income support and free school meals. ✓ Reduces taxation levels for society as a whole.	✗ Requires means testing with loss of dignity and privacy and stigmatises benefit recipients. ✗ Targeting leads to double standards of care and greater social divisions and inequality. ✗ Creates a poverty trap that leaves people just above the poverty line worse off than those on benefits, this can be a disincentive to work. ✗ Means testing creates rules and regulations which can be abused. ✗ Ignorance of entitlements and deterrent effect of bureaucracy can mean low take-up of benefits. ✗ Creates social exclusion and is socially divisive. ✗ Increased bureaucracy to 'police' claimants.
SOCIAL INSURANCE – pools the risks of the population so that everyone contributes in proportion to their ability to pay rather than in proportion to their chance of needing help	✓ Benefits linked to occupation through the payment of a National Insurance stamp. ✓ Family plays a key part in welfare. ✓ Social insurance contributions provide entitlement to benefit without means testing. ✓ Benefits can be quite generous if earnings related contributions and benefits is adopted. ✓ Gives citizenship rights and makes for a socially inclusive society.	✗ Assumes that people will be employed most of the time to make the required contributions. ✗ Men treated as full citizens, women as wives and mothers. ✗ Assumes that everyone is part of a nuclear family with a male breadwinner whose contributions give entitlement to the whole family, this ignores the needs of single parents and young, single people. ✗ Not a 'true' insurance system – benefits paid from current taxation.
UNIVERSALITY – comprehensive benefits that treat people in the same way because they have a particular need (health, education and child benefit) and meet these needs without reference to a person's means	✓ High standards of services because it has to meet the needs of the rich as well as the poor. ✓ Represents a society committed to welfare with a responsibility to fellow citizens. ✓ Benefits are not stigmatised so there is high take-up. ✓ Avoids the poverty trap. ✓ Gives equal access to welfare. ✓ Bureaucracy minimised by not having a means test. ✓ Treats people equally on the basis of need.	✗ Requires high rates of taxation to fund and this can reduce incentives to work. ✗ Prevents freedom of choice in welfare spending. ✗ Provides too little for those who do need help. ✗ Wasteful because it provides for people who do not need state help. ✗ Has no impact on the inequality in society generated by market forces. ✗ Can create a 'culture of dependency'.

13. MODELS OF WELFARE

	RESIDUAL	INDUSTRIAL ACHIEVEMENT	INSTITUTIONAL REDISTRIBUTIVE
Type of poverty	Absolute	Subjective	Relative
Concern for	• Long term dependants	• Those in crisis who are deserving of help	• Those that are less well off than the rest
Assumed cause	• **Culture of poverty/Dependency culture (see Wealth 6)**	• **Situational constraints (see Wealth 7)**	• **Structural inequalities (see Wealth 8)**
Immediate solution	• Help the **few** who cannot meet their basic needs	• Help the **deserving** over the crisis period	• Provide **everyone** with the socially approved goods
Help given short term (see Wealth 11)	• **Selectively** by means testing	• Benefits based on **social insurance** contributions	• **Universal benefits** for recognised needs
Longer term solution	• Encourage people to take **responsibility** for their own welfare	• Work towards a society where the differences between people are seen as **fair**	• **Progressive redistribution** to a more equal society
Help given longer term	• Allow family to provide for itself by lower tax and **choices of welfare**	• Intervention to create **equality of opportunity**	• Increased taxation of the rich and **reallocation of resources** according to need
Government involvement	• **Minimal** and declining, help only for those that are incapable of looking after themselves	• Will always be **required** as there will be crises beyond an individual's control	• Only the state can **counteract the inequalities** created by capitalism and industrialisation
Desired society	• **Unequal**, where people have the freedom to choose to buy their own welfare services	• **Unequal**, but the differences between people are accepted as legitimate	• **Equal**, in which people's welfare is met according to need not money
How poverty is solved	• **Competition** encourages hard work, which in turn leads to a strong economy with low unemployment and little absolute poverty	• **Protection** against the crises which cause felt poverty and removal of inequalities which are unfair	• In an **equal society** there will be no relative poverty
Attitude to helping the poor	• **Charitable** or paternalistic towards those who cannot work	• Earned **entitlement** and citizenship rights	• Social **right**
View of the welfare state	• **Wasteful** and makes people lazy and dependent, money better spent on industry to help economic growth	• **Essential** duty of an advanced industrial society to meet needs that cannot be met by market forces	• Increasingly important as economic growth generates more need, money spent on the welfare state **helps growth**
Political philosophy	Market liberals/laissez-faire	Social Democrats Meritocracy	Socialist Egalitarian

14. SUCCESSES AND FAILURES OF THE WELFARE STATE

	SUCCESSES	FAILURES
To combat ABSOLUTE POVERTY (Residual model)	✓ Social security provides a safety net of protection to prevent people falling into poverty. ✓ Social fund and higher education finance teaches people to take responsibility for their own welfare by providing loans rather than grants. ✓ Treats the poor on the same terms as everyone else by requiring people to choose how to spend for their welfare needs. ✓ Allows the community and family to show altruism by caring.	✗ Benefits are insufficient and falling in value so they are failing to lift people out of poverty. ✗ Loans can drive people further into poverty and charging for services acts as a deterrent to the poor. ✗ People cannot budget without money and benefits fail to bridge the poverty gap. ✗ Groups who are stigmatised by society may not have their needs met, e.g. AIDS sufferers, homeless.
To combat SUBJECTIVE POVERTY (Industrial achievement model)	✓ Beveridge's plan was designed to cover the five giant evils (**W**ant, **I**gnorance, **S**qualor, **I**dleness, and **D**isease). ✓ Offered security, by providing comprehensive cover from 'cradle to grave' for as long as was necessary. ✓ Collective provision ensures everyone is covered. ✓ Focus on 'crisis points' in life-course.	✗ Problems of poor housing and poor job prospects have not disappeared, and unemployment benefit only lasts for 6 months. ✗ Many benefits have been removed or have become means tested, e.g. maternity grant. ✗ Addition of occupational and private welfare has introduced inequalities.
To combat RELATIVE POVERTY (Institutional redistributive model)	✓ The least well off receive the most benefits from the social security system. ✓ Health and education are free universal services covering essential needs. ✓ Direct taxation is progressive. ✓ Incomes became more equal after the war (see **Wealth 2**). ✓ Wealth has become less concentrated in the hands of the top 1% of wealth holders. ✓ Serves to incorporate the least well-off into capitalism. ✓ Creates a consensus of welfarism, with agreement on basic provision across political divisions.	✗ Middle-classes stay longer in education; use the health service more (see **Health 3**); gain more from state pensions because they live longer than the working-classes. ✗ Growth of private and occupational welfare with state support has increased inequality in provision. ✗ Increasing dependence on indirect tax which is regressive. ✗ Incomes have become more unequal since 1980 (see **Wealth 2**). ✗ Wealth is still heavily concentrated in the hands of the top 10 % (see **Wealth 2**). ✗ Degree of redistribution is open to political interference and ideological manipulation.

15. THREE VIEWS OF THE WELFARE STATE

	FUNCTIONALIST	FEMINIST	MARXIST
Role in the structure of society	• Part of the web of interdependencies that helps the *integration* of society by building social solidarity. • Has positive function of alleviating worst of poverty.	• Underpins *patriarchal structures* by assuming the traditional family model is a reality, e.g. married women opting out of National Insurance contributions.	• Part of the superstructure of society brought about by the *needs of a capitalist infra structure*. • Helps to reduce poverty of the proletariat and thus make it less likely they will rebel against capitalism.
Reasons for the welfare state	• New needs are generated by industrial societies and *structural differentiation* occurs as the family cannot meet all the needs of a complex society.	• Maintains the status quo and supports the *interests of men*, e.g. restrictions on women working in certain occupations protecting the jobs for men.	• A requirement of capitalism for a *productive workforce* (educated and healthy). • Forestalls revolution.
Assessment of the welfare state	✓ Major historic change has eliminated the worst excesses of capitalism, and shows that capitalism can serve democratic ends by meeting social needs.	✗ Limited: the state assumes that the care of the sick, disabled and elderly will be undertaken by women.	✗ Very limited as it does nothing to change the social conditions of inequality or to attack the position of the privileged and wealthy.
Effect on poverty	✓ Absolute poverty has been controlled and there is some movement to tackle relative poverty through redistribution. ✓ Basic needs for education and health are met, leading to efficient society.	✗ The welfare state has built in female dependency on men and hence female poverty, e.g. social security rules prevent cohabiting women claiming benefits in their own right because they are assumed to be supported by the male partners.	✗ Poverty continues to exist because it is in the interests of the ruling class, any attempts to remove poverty would destabilize the capitalist economic structure. ✗ The rich have benefited from the redistributive effects of the welfare state.
As a social control agency	✓ An adaptive mechanism for social survival, promoting order by giving a sense of national pride and identity.	✗ By failing to provide adequate child care women are forced into a domestic role, and restricted to access to labour market.	✗ The modern equivalent of religion acting as an opiate hindering progress to revolution.
As a mechanism for social justice	✗ Not intended to reduce inequality. ✓ The means by which those at the top of the hierarchy can exercise responsibility for the welfare of those below them.	✗ Equal Pay Act and Sex Discrimination Act have had little impact in practice. ✗ Creates injustice by employing women in subordinate low-paid welfare occupations and as unpaid carers.	✗ Fails to tackle the source of injustice which is the capitalist system itself. ✗ Legitimates inequality by making it seem to be the result of individual failings.

16. SOCIAL POLICY AND THE CITY

NEW RIGHT

- Reduce public spending on deprived areas, because no work
- Reduce role of local government by creating semi-private agencies to fund development
- Reduce government regulations on business to allow them to grow
- Shift from social programmes to wealth-creating ones
- Give tax breaks to business in city.

Criticisms

- ✗ Allows speculation rather than development
- ✗ Undermines local democracy
- ✗ Trickle-down can't operate
- ✗ Essentially social control theory

NEO-MARXIST

- Should focus less on urban forces which shape the city and more on capitalism as a whole.
- 'Collective consumption' – services provided by the state to keep workforce able – acts as class control, both materially and ideologically.
- Urban planning is used by government to make environment conducive to profit-making.
- Urban planning also used to control population through ghettos and segregated areas.

Criticisms

- ✗ Collective consumption is vague
- ✗ Treats state as monolithic unit
- ✗ Conspiracy theory

NEO-WEBERIANS

Need to look at roles of 'urban managers' when analysing social policy towards inner city.

e.g. planners = public; building societies = private; architects = public and private

- These impose own goals on inhabitants of cities, without living with consequences.
- Business people important urban managers because investment decisions affect level of employment in locality.
- Politicians, both national and local, also affect the city, through taxation levels, environmental legislation, planning regulations etc.
- Urban managers act as gate-keepers to valuable resources such as good housing loans, welfare, amenities etc.
- Communities respond with own organisations of 'citizenship as a whole' who act in own interests.

Criticisms

- ✗ 'Citizenship as a whole' is a vague term, and does not examine operations of many local groups
- ✗ Suggests a sense of powerlessness in the face of urban managers

ENVIRONMENTAL APPROACH

- Looks at inner city in wider context of economic and social environment within which it exists
- Looks at effects of wider government policies in affecting inner city, e.g. use of tax breaks for out-of-town industrial developments adversely affected job prospects in inner city.
- Community Development Projects badly administered and did not address real problems.
- CDPs don't alleviate poverty but control the poor.
- Solution was to integrate all levels of policy in multi-agency approach.

Criticisms

- ✗ Short-lived approach because of 1979 Tory election victory.

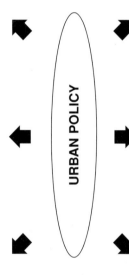

URBAN POLICY

AREA-BASED APPROACHES

- Dominant in 1960s and 1970s
- Based on premise that poverty breeds fatalistic attitude among poor
- Adopted positive discrimination
- Used resources to try and break cycle of poverty
- Designated inner city as special zone for action and improvement.

Criticisms

- ✗ Focusing on inner city misses poverty elsewhere in city and rural areas
- ✗ Tends to 'blame the victim' in citing fatalistic attitudes, which is adaption to poverty, not cause of it
- ✗ Policy often based on implicit patronising and racist assumptions about inhabitants of ghetto, e.g. 'lazy immigrant' etc.

NEW LABOUR

- Amalgamation of area-based and environmental schemes, with private provision (partnerships) included.
- Action Zones are focus for multi-agency resourcing.

17. COMPARATIVE WELFARE SYSTEMS

CAPITALIST WELFARE SYSTEMS

Esping–Anderson's Three worlds of welfare	Welfare states The state assumes responsibility for providing a wide range of welfare benefits for all its citizens		State welfare The state helps only the poor
Country	**Sweden**	**Germany**	**USA**
Degree of decommodification (i.e. the extent to which welfare is independent of the market)	High – universal state welfare as a right. But incomplete decommodification – some loss of income when sick.	Medium – assumes that the family wage of the male worker will provide for welfare together with benefits linked to occupation	Low – market welfare (e.g. health care is bought and sold) is the mechanism for all but the very poor
Principles of social policy	SOCIAL DEMOCRATIC – equality and social solidarity (c.f. institutional redistributive model).	CONSERVATIVE – preservation of existing social order and loyalty to state (c.f. industrial achievement model).	LIBERAL – individualistic self-reliance (c.f. residual model).
Consequences for post-industrial employment	'Good' public sector jobs in welfare work and low unemployment. A strong labour movement that has kept up the level of wages.	Low expansion of service jobs; employment based on manufacturing industry which provides diminishing opportunities, hence growing unemployment	Dual labour market – 'good' private sector jobs with associated welfare benefits and low-paid employment without benefits
Consequences for social divisions	Strong gender division. Private sector male workers and public sector female workers.	Division between employed guarding their jobs and unemployed outsiders mainly foreigners.	Inequality – concentration of women and blacks in 'bad' jobs but equal opportunities programmes.
Changes brought by global competition and economic problems	Pressure on government to cut state spending. Privatisation of state companies and the introduction of the market mechanism into state services.	Shed labour through early retirement and redundancy puts a strain on state finances. Loss of confidence in ability of the state to deliver so people resort to private provision.	Cut welfare spending further to remove the disincentives to work of the poverty trap. Forces unemployed into low paid work and turns unemployment into a problem of poverty.

EVALUATION OF MODEL

- ✓ original and comprehensive model
- ✓ broadened the study of social policy to issues of employment and stratification
- ✓ used a statistical and historical analysis
- ✗ static model of welfare
- ✗ clusters around three types may not be justified
- ✗ does not easily take account of the British model
- ✗ ignores women's decommodified labour

CONVERGENCE?

Japanization of welfare
1. Increasing international competition puts pressure on old industrial societies to cut costs of state welfare.
2. Capital moves to lower cost and safer places. This means any country adopting expensive welfare policies and hence judged to be less competitive is likely to see capital removed.
3. Tiger economies of the east do not have welfare states on European model, but adopt company welfare that encourages a high level of commitment and high productivity as well as giving control over workers.

7 Work, Organisations, and Leisure
1. WORK AND NON-WORK

Although work and leisure are on a continuum, the boundaries between them and the intervening categories are blurred, because they are socially constructed.

There is no hard-and-fast definition of work. It will vary according to society and across time. In industrial societies, work is usually associated with some sort of compulsion and with being paid. However, certain types of work have strong echoes of leisure time in them, such as jobs where interest and enjoyment are involved (e.g. 'a love of cricket').

WORK

Complication 1
Is housework work?
(compulsion, no pay)

Complication 2
If work is so enjoyable, is it still work?
(pay, less compulsion)

Complication 3
Does doing the garden count as work?
(no pay, some compulsion)

Complication 4
If an employed gardener enjoys work, is it work?

Work-related time

Includes all the activities which are necessary for a person to get to work and perform effectively, i.e. travel to and from work, but might also involve some 'working at home'. The boundary between work and work-related time is a confused one and will vary over time and according to culture.

Complication 1
When most 'work' was carried out at home, what did work-related time consist of? Preparing food?

Complication 2
Is having the boss for dinner at home, work, work-related time or leisure?

Non-work obligations

These are all the activities for which we are not paid, but which we feel compelled to do. The main example here would be housework, but there are also social obligations such as assisting with the wider family, attending religious services, if we are spiritual, or social events which we feel obliged to attend.

Complication 1
Is helping the family, leisure or a non-work obligation?

Complication 2
Are social events always in our leisure time, or sometimes a bind?

Leisure

Sometimes known as 'free time', this is the area of choice, where activities are undertaken, not because we are paid to do them, but because they are enjoyable and we choose them. For example, most sport is carried out as a leisure activity, as are hobbies, holidays etc. Leisure is distinct from other activities in its individual freedom.

Complication 1
Can leisure be truly free, when we have to pay money to pursue it?

Complication 3
Are social events always in our leisure time, or sometimes a bind?

Complication 4
Do some people not like housework and choose to do it at their leisure?

LEISURE

2. TYPES OF ECONOMY

Legally regulated

Outside the home

FORMAL ECONOMY

Formal employment

✓ Traditional area for 'earning a living"	✗ Declining employment in manufacturing
✓ Involves employer and employees	✗ Site of conflict between employers and employees
✓ Regulated by law, e.g. minimum wage	✗ Law biased towards employers?
✓ Wages or salaries paid for effort	✗ Returns for effort can be unbalanced
✓ Employer has rights in organising workforce	✗ Workforce can resist employer's instructions
✓ Connection to tax system	✗ Taxes can be evaded by both workers and employers
✓ Usually conducted at place of work	✗ New technology means more working from home

Homeworking

✓ Work sub-contracted to workers at home	✗ Work usually on piece rates fixed by employer
✓ Convenient for workers with young families	✗ Often exploits low-income and lone-parent families
✓ Often used by workers to supplement income	✗ Returns often very poor
✓ Saves employers heating and premises costs	✗ Shifts costs to workers who are already poorly paid
✓ Home becomes a workplace	✗ Health and safety issues?
✓ Eliminates travel needs	✗ Leads to isolation of worker

Domestic economy

✓ Otherwise known as housework	✗ Mainly done by women
✓ Large amounts of money spent here	✗ Creates obstacle to females entering paid work
✓ Enables the reproduction of labour	✗ Women workers also take on domestic duties
✓ Is concerned with 'emotional labour'	✗ Often at the expense of women
✓ Can also be waged labour, though mainly not	✗ Exploitation of women by unpaid work
✓ Makes large contribution to economy	✗ Contribution not recognised by state
✓ Has production and consumption implications	✗ Poor domestic households are socially excluded

Communal economy

✓ Exchange of services in locality	✗ Exchange is not regulated and may be imbalanced
✓ Non-cash economy	✗ Does not contribute towards society's costs through taxes
✓ Baby-sitting circles prime example	
✓ Often involves DIY	✗ Can merge into the grey economy
✓ Creates bonds of civility in locality	✗ Large unregulated sector
✓ Often based on family relationships	✗ Can also create disputes about value
	✗ Isolated individuals may be marginalised

Grey economy

✓ Elements of formal and informal	✗ Balance is important for protecting workers
✓ Boundaries often unclear	✗ Boundaries often shift as state investigates
✓ Includes 'twilight working' and second jobs	✗ Supplements low incomes and creates standard of living
✓ Declaration of income often a personal choice	
✓ Keeps costs low	✗ Much tax evasion is petty and seen as 'fair game'
	✗ Keeps wages low

Black economy

✓ Allows unofficial employment	✗ Open to exploitation, e.g. of illegal immigrants
✓ Opportunities for return to formal economy?	✗ Limited training means few links to formal employment
✓ Associated with industries such as construction	✗ Increasingly investigated by tax authorities
✓ Work is hidden from the state	✗ Often uses young or marginal (most vulnerable)
✓ Sometimes called the 'underground economy'	✗ Can be dangerous work, because unregulated

INFORMAL ECONOMY

Unregulated

Aspects of illegality

Blurred boundaries Home

Outside the home

3. OCCUPATIONAL STRUCTURES AND LABOUR MARKETS

CONTEMPORARY OCCUPATIONAL STRUCTURES

Hierarchies of control will disappear and be replaced with networks organised into a 'web of enterprise'. Vertical divisions will be replaced by horizontal co-operative networks of talent – management of ideas not of people.

Occupational structures will become more fluid, as new entrepreneurs with innovative ideas make their way into the market-place. Design and creativity will become the valuable assets to the information age enterprise. Barriers to mobility will become transparent.

Manufacturing has declined in the industrialised West, as production has shifted to lower wage areas of the world. Increased employment opportunities emerge in the service and information sectors of the Western economies, with the result that there is a shift in the occupational structure upwards. Increasingly, manufacturing accounts for a declining proportion of the wealth of the West, as service industries, especially those concerned with the manipulation of information, increase. Demand for skilled non-manual labour has increased, most notably in the computing and ICT industries. Non-industrial functions are also affected by the growth in new technologies, as government becomes more efficient in both delivering services to its citizens and in the potential for controlling them. Ownership of wealth-creating industries has diversified to a limited extent as greater share ownership developed during the 1980s. The growth in white-collar occupations is accompanied by an increasing feminisation of the workforce, as physical strength is replaced by the manipulation of knowledge as the desired skill for wealth creation. There has also been an increase in the proportion of the workforce officially classified as self-employed. The transition to an occupational structure based on knowledge has been accompanied by structural unemployment, sometimes as very high levels.

Middle managers become subject to de-layering as their functions are replaced by machines. Loss of status results.

Divisions between workers, office-workers and managers will become blurred, as all seek to make enterprise successful and develop their own portfolios of skills.

Claimed that there is an end to the 'age of the machine', and a start to the 'age of information', in which traditional hierarchies will break down under the impact of technological change.

White-collar work becomes routinised and job security disappears for middle-class workers and professionals.

As flexible working increases, the numbers directly employed by a firm will decrease, as non-core functions are franchised out to the lowest cost. There will only be a core of workers in a firm, primarily workers by brain, not brawn.

Workers at all levels of the firm will be working 'smarter not harder', as new technologies impact. While there will be fewer permanent jobs around, workers will be able to command better money, if they have the skills which employers need to function competitively.

TRADITIONAL OCCUPATIONAL STRUCTURES

Access to the top of the occupational hierarchy was limited and relied on personal contact or elite education in the private sector. Individual entrepreneurs were able to force their way to the top, if they had drive and energy.

Individual entrepreneurs were always vulnerable to changes in fashion or to their own folly, but those at the top of the occupational structure also included the professions, who were used to life-long careers in stable relatively well-paid occupations, such as medicine or the law. This sector of the occupational structure was often linked to the entrepreneurs but also provided some opposition to them, especially through the power of ideas. In the end, structural changes affected these professionals also.

Ownership of the means of production was the defining characteristic of those at the top of the occupational structure. Inheritance was thus a key element in perpetuating the occupational hierarchy.

Based on a strong manufacturing sector, the bulk of the workforce was engaged in routine manual work, often in large production units. They were 'serviced' by a relatively small number of office-workers and middle management personnel, who had high status and greater economic rewards. Industrial production was owned and controlled by a relatively small number of individuals, either personally or through shareholding which was relatively concentrated. Surplus value was extracted through taxation to provide the non-industrial functions of society, such as state bureaucracy, education, the military etc. Occupational structure was therefore hierarchical, with status, power and wealth concentrated at the top. The law established the rights of property often at the expense of individual workers.

The market for white-collar workers was limited to those with strong educational backgrounds. As literacy increased, white-collar work became more accessible.

White-collar workers were separated from manual workers by higher salaries and detailed status divisions, which defined a 'pecking order'.

The large-scale nature of much of industry encouraged workers to organise into trade unions to struggle to improve wages and conditions. Many workers were also politically active.

While many lower-class jobs were hazardous, they did offer some security of employment as long as the worker obeyed the employer.

Control over workers was exercised economically but also socially and politically, through rigid status hierarchies, which separated the classes.

4. POST-INDUSTRIALISM AND POST-FORDISM

Criticisms of post-industrial society thesis

- ✗ Great transformation is ideology, not fact

- ✗ Product of Cold War, in which the end of communism was predicted

- ✗ Majority of workers have never been manual

- ✗ Extent of service economy has been exaggerated

- ✗ Many service jobs are not knowledge-driven

- ✗ White-collar work has been routinised, not transformed

- ✗ Underlying ownership remains the same

- ✗ Capitalism still driven by need for profit

- ✗ Workers' interest in firm still alienative

- ✗ Dilution of ownership is a myth – utilities only

- ✗ Old rigidities of class remain

POST-INDUSTRIAL SOCIETY THESIS

- Nature of work is changing.
- Move from physical labour to mental labour at core of industrial activity, e.g. move towards a service economy, where most work is not manual.
- Workplaces need to become more co-operative to be competitive.
- 'Great transformation' taking place in nature of economic activity.
- Capitalism moving towards more democratic forms.
- Impact of emphasis on knowledge will be at all levels of work.
- Changes impact on the nature of class divisions in society.
- Profit is not only motivation for capitalists, but will treat workers more fairly.
- Concentration of ownership will be diluted, as stakeholding grows.
- New forms of ownership and control will emerge.

Alternative thesis – deindustrialisation

Rather than the 'Great transformation' to a knowledge-driven industry, Western capitalism has experienced the destruction of manufacturing as production has moved to low-wage economies. In the place of manufacturing, poorly paid service industries have emerged. The service sector is thus not some leading edge of greater prosperity, but the spread of Taylorism to a previously untouched section of the labour market. Rather, than a 'high-wage, high skill' economy, the effects of globalisation have been to create a 'low skill, low wage' economy for the majority of workers. Production in the meantime has shifted east to the Pacific Rim. The 'typical' occupation of the post-Fordist economy is not the computer operator but serving in a fast food outlet.

Key Concepts

- Fordism, neo-Fordism, post-Fordism
- Flexible specialisation
- Disorganised capitalism
- Just-in-time technologies
- Flexible firm
- Networking

QUESTION:
ARE WE UNDERGOING A SECOND INDUSTRIAL REVOLUTION?

Key Concepts

- Service economy
- Convergence
- End of ideology
- Knowledge society
- Deskilling
- Scientific management
- Human relations

Fordism

Describes the organisation of mass production.
Car plants of Ford are exemplars.
Produces standardised product at affordable prices for mass market.
Work is divided into small, repetitive actions, carried out in sequence along a track.
Workers are primarily semi-skilled or unskilled.
Contrasts with craft-working where workers have training in skills.
Managements are hierarchical and controlling of workforce.
Relations with workers oppositional, with conflict.
Strong trade unions.

POST-FORDISM

- ✓ Describes flexible production modes of work.

- ✓ Products are diverse and aimed at niche markets, not mass.

- ✓ Workers contribute to production according to skills.

- ✓ Need for constant retraining as technologies advance.

- ✓ Products are geared to quality not quantity.

- ✓ Control is dispersed throughout workforce.

- ✓ Workers are involved in decisions and committed to the firm.

- ✓ Relations co-operative.

- ✓ Hierarchies dissolve.

Criticisms of Post-Fordism

- ✗ Flexibility is used in different ways (numbers of workers, tasks etc.)

- ✗ Flexibility actually means short-term, temporary employment

- ✗ Is actually 'neo-Fordism' – new ways of intensifying exploitation

- ✗ Disorganised capitalism means little regulation of employers and work

- ✗ Overstates the dominance of Fordism in 20th century

- ✗ Flexible working is only apparent in a small number of firms

- ✗ Relationships characterised by indifference, not cooperation.

5. GLOBAL CHANGES AND WORK

GLOBAL FACTOR

It has always been recognised by sociologists that there is a global dimension to social change. While the classical sociologists tended to focus on national economies, they did so with an eye to the global situation. Often this took the form of the comparative method, in which two or more societies were compared to establish similarities and differences, but there was also a much wider dimension in their work. The classical sociologists were concerned with the transformations which industrialisation had effected in the world as a whole. For example, Marx argued that the world mission of capitalism was a progressive one, in that it undermined traditional and feudal social relations, which were based on servitude. It was the historic mission of capitalism to destroy these relations throughout the world and thus lay the foundations for the future of communism. Weber had a more pessimistic, if also global view, in seeing the iron cage of bureaucracy triumphing everywhere as rationalisation and modernity conquered tradition and religion.

Is globalisation different?

| Whereas the Industrial Revolution took a long time to transform the world, the effects of globalisation have been relatively swift and all-encompassing, rather than slow and sporadic. | The scale of global connections is greater than anything that has been seen before and thus it is different. | Globalisation affects both production and consumption. It is not just a different way of producing things, but a global culture is also established. |

FEATURES OF GLOBALISATION AND THE IMPACT ON WORK

Feature	Description	Impact on work
New international division of labour	Manufacturing of goods increasingly moved to low-wage economies of the South, e.g. Taiwan. Countries in the North focus on information-rich industries with high levels of skill.	Manual work under threat in the North. Where it remains it is squeezed by low wages paid in other countries, so that real wages for the working class fall. Non-manual workers expected to exercise higher levels of skill.
Global culture	Proliferation of the mass media leads to emergence of a similar culture, often based on American products, throughout the world.	Cultural products form an increasing proportion of wealth creation. Production has to be geared to global tastes and work is aimed at satisfying global needs.
Multinationals	Industry increasingly dominated by organisations with a global reach, so that they are no longer constrained by the nation-state. The search for profit becomes intensified throughout the world.	Decisions about location of work increasingly taken by multinationals on the basis of profitability, rather than investment in communities or populations. Shifts in production frequent.
Global financial markets	Deregulation of capital and electronic commerce 24 hours a day throughout the world means that economies are subject to virtually irresistible forces from time to time. 'You cannot buck the market'.	Lifelong careers disappear, as events in far reaches of the world impact on individual's job security. Local economies are subject to global financial movements, beyond their control.

Criticisms of globalisation

✗ Degree of global interconnection has been exaggerated. While trading contacts have increased enormously, the rate of increase is much the same as previous eras.

✗ Shift to the South also impacts on the South, as workers ask for higher wages there.

✗ Financial crisis of the South in late 1990s shows the mythical nature of much globalisation theory.

✗ Global financial markets are still concentrated in the West and most profits flow towards the industrialised world.

✗ The nation-state continues to control activities of the multinational in many ways.

✗ International regulation of the multinational corporations (MNCs) has also increased.

✗ Continued importance of the military and political institutions of the nation-state suggest that local factors are more important than global ones.

6. MOTIVATIONS TO WORK

WHY DO PEOPLE WORK?
Two Broad Responses

Instrumental theories		Self-actualising theories
Focus here is on the need to earn money to support self and family. Involvement in work is therefore calculative, that is, enough effort will be given to maximise income at minimum cost to self. Work is not a 'central life interest', but only a means to an end. Workers gain only extrinsic satisfaction from the job itself, keeping main pleasure outside work.	*Difference is often based on class position;* ← *W/class* *M/class* →	Workers engage in work because it is a source of personal satisfaction to them. Work provides self-esteem and pleasure and constitutes a 'central life interest'. The income generated is welcomed, but involvement in work is moral, not instrumental, and work gives intrinsic satisfaction.

WHAT IS THE MOTIVATION BEHIND THESE IDEAS?

Often routine and boring, there is no pleasure in the day-to-day grind of hard labour.	**Experience of work itself**	Having some control over varied work, which is challenging and holds the worker's interest.
Manual work is seen in society as having low status and little worth. Consumption is seen as more important than engagement in work.	**Broad ideologies**	A 'culture of engagement' exists amongst some workers, where 'staying late at work', is the norm. Commitment to work is seen as praiseworthy.
Working-class culture seen as hedonistic and 'living for the day' with little long-term planning.	**Sub-cultural values**	Work defines the moral worth of individuals, with a strong work ethic as a central value.

MAIN VARIATIONS

Taylorism (1911) • Assumes a rational economic worker. • Worker will work harder if given a financial incentive. • Controlling workers minutely allows piecework. • Production maximised when workers controlled.	**Herzberg (1957)** • Workers need non-financial motivation to work harder. • Job content crucial factor in motivation. • Workers need achievement, recognition, responsibility. • Job enlargement – key to better economic performance.
Likert (1967) • Adapts Taylorist principles to whole organisation. • Human beings are just a form of capital. • Need a rigorous science of management. • Incentives primarily economic in driving enterprise.	**Maslow's Hierarchy of Need (1954)** • Workers need more than just money to perform. • 5 levels of need from money to self-actualisation. • Work needs to engage workers at all levels, if possible. • Production maximised when all needs met.
Goldthorpe and Lockwood (1968) • Rising wages have led to the 'affluent worker'. • Affluent workers develop instrumentalist, not collectivist ideas. • Affluent workers interested mainly in money. • Incentives work best when financial.	**Argyris (1972)** • Always conflict between organisation and individual. • Conflict frustrates self-actualisation. • Solution is group decision-making on the factory floor. • Creates opportunity for involvement and an incentive.

Criticisms of work motivation theories
✗ Work motivation theorists give appearance of being concerned about workers, but it is production they are interested in
✗ Early subordination of worker by employers had virtue of being an honest and open exploitation
✗ Function as ideologies, in that they justify extreme control of workers in workplace by reference to need for productivity
✗ Job enlargement and self-actualisation are thus techniques of control, not liberating devices to make work nicer
✗ Attempts to implement job enlargement techniques few in number and not very successful over sustained period
✗ Where job enlargement techniques are implemented, they arise out of concerns of management in times of falling productivity, not from needs of workers

AN ATTEMPT AT SYNTHESIS

Wahba and House (1981) argued that work behaviour can be predicted on the basis of what the individual worker expects to gain by following the organisation's rules and producing maximum output. Workers hope to gain both monetary rewards and satisfaction in their tasks. This **Expectancy theory** gives equal weight to instrumental and self-actualising influences, arguing that where the reality in either area does not match up to worker's expectation, then effort will be curtailed.

MARX AND ALIENATION

Marx's basic argument

That the increased division of labour, combined with the institutions of capitalist production, mainly the concentration of ownership in the hands of the few, leads to increased alienation amongst the industrial workforce. Alienation also extends to other social classes in society, through the impersonality of the system.

Factors in the development of alienation

1. Mechanisation takes the skill out of work, so that active satisfaction become passive resentment.
2. Specialisation reduces tasks to monotony and leads to feeling that life is controlled by impersonal forces over which workers have no control.
3. Because of property relationships, workers do not own their tools or the product which they create, which belongs to a distant capitalist.
4. Workers sell labour for a wage, and are thus exploited to squeeze profits from the fruits of their labours.
5. Worker's material needs are satisfied by work, but not the 'whole man', as work becomes separated from other relationships and leads to isolation.

Anti-alienation arguments

1. That people seek self-actualisation in work and capitalism allows them to achieve it.
2. That individuals do not seek self-actualisation, but income from work and this is satisfied through capitalism.
3. That work deprivation exists, but it is not that important for workers, who see work only as a tool for survival, a means to an end.

An Anti-Marxist Empirical Study

Blauner (1964) argued that alienation was the result of technological organisation, rather than a matter of ownership. Feelings of alienation emerged from the condition of large-scale production in an assembly-line, but were weaker in other forms of industry.

Pro-alienation arguments

1. That most sociologists accept the elements of alienation exist: powerlessness, meaninglessness, self-estrangement, isolation, normlessness.
2. That white-collar work is just as alienating as manual work.
3. That individual capitalists are alienated by a system which they also cannot control.

A Pro-Marxist Empirical Study

Braverman (1974) argued that the alienating conditions of manual work were extended to office work, which increasingly came to resemble the factory floor. The central part of this process was the deskilling of previously skilled work.

FRUSTRATION THEORY

Where incentives other than monetary reward do not feature, it is argued that frustration at work can appear and take a number of pathological forms:

• aggression, against other workers or management
• resignation, the feeling of not being bothered
• fixation, resistance to all change
• labour turnover, as workers 'vote' with their feet
• absenteeism, illicit days off, when there is nothing really wrong
• conflict, over wages and conditions.

These effects can be at the individual or the collective level. In the case of collective action, this might be unorganised and spontaneous, where trade unions are not involved, or organised and planned where they are. Sickness accounts for most interruptions to production, rather than industrial action.

BALDAMUS AND TRACTION

Though the division of labour creates boring, routinised tasks for most manual workers, these need not, of themselves, be tedious. The rhythm of repetitive work can create 'traction' – a sense of enjoyment from being pulled along by the tempos involved in production. These tempos may be the speed of the machines, the intervals between processes, or the series of operations carried out by the individual worker.

DURKHEIM AND ANOMIE

Society was based on more than just a contractual relationship between individuals, had a moral dimension too. The division of labour was thus not just a means of dividing people into efficient work units, but was also a way of organising individuals with each other, so that a higher standard of living could be produced and integration of the individual into society achieved. The result was organic solidarity, an interdependence of individuals that creates a sense of participation in a common enterprise. The effect of a division of labour was beneficial to individuals except where a state of anomie existed.

Where the division of labour did not match the distribution of talent, dissatisfaction rather than satisfaction at work might occur.

Satisfaction at work ———— Dissatisfaction at work

8. TECHNOLOGY AND WORK

TECHNOLOGICAL DETERMINISM

The idea that technology (machines and how they are organised) leads directly to certain types of structures and to specific attitudes held by workers, that is, technology is the determinant of organisations and ideas.

Technology does affect work in a number of obvious ways: the physical exertion required, the pace of work, the level of skill required, the possibilities of interaction with others.

Effects on attitudes

Self-actualisation is central concept. Whyte (1955) argued that technology determines the degree of self-actualisation and thus attitudes to work and the way workers felt about the wider world.

Sayles (1963) argued that the technology determined the type of work group which evolved, identifying four groups:
- apathetic (unskilled and unorganised)
- erratic (unskilled but organised)
- strategic (skilled and organised);
- conservative (highly skilled but unorganised).

Blauner (1964) differentiated types of technology in his 'Inverted U-curve theory'. Early technologies such as craft work had highly skilled artisans making individual products. More modern production technologies took the form of large-scale assembly-lines making mass products, with little control for the worker. Process and automated industries allowed a greater control for the worker. Alienation thus was low in craft, high in assembly-line, low in process technologies. The implication was that industry would become less alienating as it computerised.

Effects on structures

Socio-technical system is central concept. Tavistock Institute (1950s) argues that the technological demands of work place limits on the type of work organisation possible.

Burns and Stalker (1966) argued that technological change introduced new forms of work organisation – from mechanistic (hierarchical, strict divisions, tight control) to organismic (networks, divisions according to contribution, control on the shop floor).

Woodward (1965) argued that production systems were on a continuum from simple to highly complex depending on type of technology used. Unit and small batch technologies had a non-bureaucratic management structure with a limited span of control. Large batch and mass production technologies led to complex hierarchies of management, organised bureaucratically with tight control of workers. Process production reverted to leaner organisation structures, with fewer managers and shop floor control.

M a i n

s t u d i e s

Criticisms about TDs

✗ Critics take technological determinist arguments to an extreme. TDs do not argue that technology is the *only* factor.

✗ Clearly, technology does have an impact on work. It is the extent to which it does which is important.

✗ Workers do see different technological systems in various ways.

✗ There are systematic differences in both structure and attitudes in different work situations. Technology is likely to figure.

✗ The relationship between technology and attitudes and structures does not stand up to the empirical evidence. Processes of new technologies are much more varied than Blauner or Woodward suggests.

✗ Technological determinists ignore the effects of other factors, such as size of the firm or managerial choice, in affecting both attitudes and structure.

✗ Ignores the issue of relations of property in alienation.

✗ It is arguable whether more complex technologies are more or less alienating.

A COMBINED APPROACH FROM THE MARXIST BRAVERMAN

Braverman (1974) argued that the introduction of new technologies by management had the intention of increasing control over both workplace organisation and attitudes of workers, with the aim of maximising profits. Scientific Management was the technique used to self-consciously introduce tighter control, take the skill out of work, to establish a management monopoly over knowledge of the labour process and to separate manual from mental labour. The technologies introduced were the result of a decision by management to take control away from the workforce – a sort of intentional technological determinism. The effect was to alienate increasing sections of the workforce as Taylorist principles were extended to white-collar workers and even lower management.

Arguments in favour

✓ Critics take technological determinist arguments to an extreme. TDs do not argue that technology is the *only* factor.

✓ Clearly, technology does have an impact on work. It is the extent to which it does which is important.

✓ Workers do see different technological systems in various ways.

✓ There are systematic differences in both structure and attitudes in different work situations. Technology is likely to figure.

Criticisms of Braverman

✗ Intentions of management are complex and cannot be reduced to a simple dimension of control. It is a 'reading in'.

✗ Ignores workers' resistance to Taylorism.

✗ New technologies not just introduced to effect control but to cut costs directly by improving product or making savings.

✗ It is overly determinist and ignores examples of where management has attempted to make work interesting, e.g. in post-modern organisations.

9. AUTOMATION

CYBERNATION THEORY	Criticisms
• Computerisation is a radical break from previous mechanisation and constitutes a 'new industrial revolution'. • The pace of technological change is accelerating. • This is demonstrated by continuing high levels of unemployment.	✗ Extent of computerisation is exaggerated, as no industry has yet become fully automated, and claims to the contrary are just science fiction. ✗ Rate of technological innovation is only slightly higher than previously. ✗ Unemployment is caused by structural not technological factors.

Claimed effects for the automation of industrial processes on work

• Less physical exertion needed • Fewer workers needed • More workers needed • Pacing of work determined by computers	• Higher levels of skill needed by workforce • Greater team work needed • Greater isolation of workers • Reduced specialisation

NB. Some of these claims are contradictory, so what evidence exists of the effects?

Effect on employment	*Effects on working week*	*Effects on hierarchies*
Jobs are clearly lost (typists?) but others are created by automation. Problem is that those who lose out are unlikely to be retrained for the new jobs, so there is a 'generational effect' on employment. Micro-electronics accelerates job losses because they are so cheap to use in place of costly labour and obsolete capital equipment.	Little evidence that automation cuts the working week and leads to a 'new age of leisure'. It increases shift working and takes away 'normal' leisure times. Leads to increase in shop hours (?) as superstores respond to new arrangements with 24-hour shopping.	Certain grades, such as clerical workers, are reduced in size, but also importance and power is centralised in top management and computer technicians. Some evidence of a de-layering of hierarchies, as some functions become redundant.

Effect of automation on workers' consciousness

Theories begin with Marx and the idea that consciousness (awareness of interest and of place in the social world) is a product of the workplace, and of the technology employed, in the context of capitalist property relations. Two approaches emerged from this argument:

1. Anti-Marxist – technological determinists such as Blauner and Woodward, who stress the importance of technology at the expense of property relations.	**2. Neo-Marxist** – historical materialists, such as Mallet and Naville, who stress property relations, at the expense of technological issues.

Effects of automation on workplace

• Highly differentiated career structures develop which motivates workers to 'get on'. • Moves towards smaller industrial units and away from the large factories of assembly-line production. • Basic work unit becomes a small team rather than individual isolated workers. • Distinction between manual and non-manual work becomes blurred. • Increased profitability of firm enables them to move to a 'welfare' concept of employment instead of an exploitative one. • Workers develop status consciousness with little interest in trade unions.	• Workers only objectively integrated into work because their high wages are dependent on overall profitability of firm. • Skills become highly specialised with little value in the general market-place. Workers are thus stuck with the firm that trained them. • Automation leads to the final rupture between worker and product. • Increased unsocial hours of work through need to keep machines constantly running to pay back the investment in costly equipment. • Hierarchies of control exposed as unnecessary for the technology to run effectively and are challenged by workers.

Automation creates a New Working Class

Because automated technologies re-aggregate the division of labour, work becomes more interesting to the workers and they develop a commitment to the industrial enterprise. The workers are thus *integrated* back into capitalism through the introduction of computerised technologies, because they find enjoyment in work and gain greater control over their own work.	Because automated technologies intensify the exploitation of workers, work becomes more *alienating* and conflict between employers and employees increases. The workers dislike the shift work associated with continually running automated industries and find the work to be routinised and dull. These alienating conditions spread through all levels of the workforce, so even office workers lose control.

All these theories are ultimately technological determinist. Effects of automation are not independent, but exist in context of managers' decisions about work, the culture and attitudes of workers towards these changes and wider social movements connected to the impact of technology on our lives.

10. INDUSTRIAL CONFLICT

FUNCTIONALISM

Systems theory and pragmatism

✓ Based on concept of fairness
✓ Firms represent unity of interest
✓ Conflict seen as pathological
✓ Believes in a value consensus
✓ Legitimises managers' powers
✓ Management has competence
✓ Management has power
✓ Balance of interests

Unitary theory

✓ Firm is like a family
✓ Common purpose
✓ Loyalty of workers

Criticisms of functionalist theories

✗ One-sided in support for legitimacy of management
✗ Value consensus is asserted rather than shown
✗ Common purpose between workers and bosses cannot be assumed – real differences exist
✗ Does not accept trade unions as legitimate, but as disruptive
✗ Conflict is seen as pathological rather than an expression of grievance

N.B. There are some similarities between functionalist and pluralist conceptions

Criticism of Pluralism

✗ Assumes legitimacy of management actions most times
✗ Assumes that all have survival of the firm at heart
✗ Denies legitimacy of workers' desire to overthrow system
✗ Assumes a working consensus of values, does not demonstrate it
✗ Seeks to modify aspirations of workers for different ways of organising industry
✗ Ignores imbalance of power between workers and bosses

Pluralist theory

✓ Firm is like a miniature democratic state, with different interests.
✓ Industrial relations are negotiated between competing interests.
✓ All members have an interest in the survival of the firm overall.
✓ Antagonistic co-operation is the norm between workers and bosses.
✓ Conflict only as far as is compatible with the survival of enterprise.
✓ Trade unions have legitimate but limited role of play.
✓ Industrial relations always a matter of compromise between parties.

PLURALISM

MARXISM

Neo-Marxist theories

✓ Must look at context of capitalism for conflict.
✓ Worker–employer contract is not free, but unequal.
✓ Employers' power in conflict is greater.
✓ Employers can call upon vast ideological resources, and in the last analysis force, to defend interests.
✓ State intervenes to protect property and lay limits to workers' (and employers') actions.
✓ Conflict is institutionalised, so that relatively little strike action actually happens.

Criticisms of Marxist approaches

✗ Over-stresses power of employers to control
✗ Assumes a 'conspiracy' of interests between state and employers
✗ Pessimistic about ability of workers to effect change

N.B There are similarities between Neo-Marxism and Action theories

Criticism of action approaches

✗ Ignores structural factors in conflict
✗ Focus on workers' conceptions ignores where such ideas come from
✗ Assumes that processes of conflict end up in state of stability
✗ Sometimes defines workers' interest in narrow economic terms

Action (processual) approach

✓ Conflict is result of interaction between management and workers.
✓ Management and workers command their own resources.
✓ Management try to implement policy.
✓ Workers defend own conceptions of workmanship and control over work.

ACTION THEORY

Focus on strikes (1): difficulties in definition

International comparisons:
- Countries collect data in different ways.
- Definitions of when a work stoppage is a strike differ
- Reporting rules differ.

National statistics:
- Hard to separate strikes and lock-outs.
- Managers reluctant to declare a strike because want to resume production quickly.

The act of defining a strike is a social process emerging from the interaction between managers and workers. It is not always an obvious event, even to those involved.

Forms of industrial conflict

	Organised	Unorganised
Individual	Grievance procedure	Industrial sabotage
Collective	Official strikes	Mass absenteeism

Forms of collective action

Go-slow	Deliberate slowing down
Work-to-rule	Following rules rigidly
Unofficial strike	No union backing
Official strike	With union backing

Striking is seldom undertaken lightly, but is often the tactic of last resort when grievances have not been addressed through usual channels.

Focus on strikes (2): Factors explaining strike-proneness

Communication failure	Where poor communications hinder the expression of grievance
Community integration	The more integrated a work community the greater the incidence of striking
Technological levels	More complex technologies lead to low strike rates
Culture	Different societies approach strikes and striking with different attitudes

Work, Organisations, and Leisure 105

11. GENDER, ETHNICITY, AND THE WORKPLACE

POSITION IN WORKPLACE

Though the structural location of women as members of the workforce has undergone substantial change since 1945, there are still areas of disadvantage to be identified.

- More women work in paid employment than before.
- More married women than ever before work.
- Women with children also work, but less involved.
- Women more likely to have part-time work.
- Women more likely to have temporary employment.
- On average, women get paid less than equivalent men.
- Certain kinds of 'caring' jobs are seen as female work.
- Women get promoted less than men.
- Women are less likely at the higher reaches of firms.

TRADITIONAL EXPLANATIONS FOR SEGREGATION

Functionalist explanations
✓ Women's role primarily concerned with family, so should not work
✓ Women by nature equipped for home life
✓ Men need to be 'breadwinners' to 'civilise' them, otherwise are useless
✓ Inequality thus gives men a role in society
✗ Sexist to assume women are naturally home-makers, rather than workers
✗ Legitimate inequality by reference to bestiality of men

Exchange theory
✓ Most women content to be home-makers
✓ Women balance costs of going to work against benefits of staying at home and decide to stay
✓ Many women do not prize independence but security
✓ Thus accept less income for stability
✗ Over-rational view of decision not to enter paid employment but remain at home
✗ Many women do not have the choice

Conflict theory
✓ Subordinate position of women at work reflects position at home, and physical prowess of men
✓ Sexual attractiveness is used as a measure of women at work
✓ Ideology of domesticity serves to divide men from women and distract from the class struggle
✗ Sees women's position only in relation to men
✗ Biological determinist in view of male and female nature

MORE RECENT EXPLANATIONS

Dual systems theory
✓ Patriarchy and capitalism both operate against women in work
✓ Exclusionary strategies (not letting women work) have given way to segregationist strategies (keeping women in different work)
✓ Capitalism needs women as an easily dismissable workforce
✓ Capitalism needs women to keep wages down
✓ Men benefit from this situation
✗ Conspiracy theory
✗ Women increasing part of work force
✗ Men increasingly less so

Choice theory
✓ Men and women have different attitudes to work
✓ Women are less committed to work than men
✓ Women often choose to remain looking after children
✓ Childcare is not a major reason to prevent women working
✗ Ignores structures within which women's choices made
✗ Assumes that women are committed and uncommitted to work at different stages in life
✗ Over-simplifies women's position

Gender Differences in the Workplace

Ethnic Differences in the Workplace

The location of ethnic minorities in the workplace is complicated, particularly because it is difficult to separate out gender effects from ethnic effects, i.e. the 'nesting' of disadvantage makes the issue complex. However, clear inequalities do exist.

- There are differences in employment involvement between women from different ethnic groups.
- Segregation occurs in types of jobs, as well as levels.
- In higher paid jobs, ethnic minorities are under-represented.
- Ethnic minority workers more likely to be in temporary employment.
- Black (Afro-Caribbean) workers are less likely to gain promotion.
- Nursing is staffed heavily by ethnic minority workers.
- Pay levels for ethnic minorities are, on average, lower than for white workers.

Assimilationist theory
✓ Temporary situation of discrimination
✓ Ethnic minorities will gradually 'catch up' with the rest of population
✓ As long as they adopt indigenous ways of behaving
✓ Will be gradual equalisation of pay and location
✗ Implicitly racist assumptions operate
✗ Though progress made, inequalities still large scale in pay and location
✗ Degrades ethnic minority culture

Discrimination theory
✓ Position of recent immigrants is the problem
✓ Ethnic minorities inhabit margins of society
✓ Host society does discriminate in multitude of ways
✓ Legal redress will lead to equalisation
✗ Not all ethnic minorities are recent immigrants or on the margins of society
✗ Ignores institutionalised discrimination in favour of individualistic explanation
✗ Legal remedies have had a limited effect on the extent of inequality at work

Conflict theory
✓ Capitalism benefits from division within the working class
✓ Ethnic differences are exploited to divide workers
✓ Ideologies of race employed to suggest that ethnic groups take jobs from white workers
✓ Pay segregation feeds resentment and keeps ethnic minorities out of trade unions
✗ Based on a conspiracy theory of capitalism
✗ Ignores cross ethnic co-operation
✗ Downplays trade union efforts to recruit ethnic workers

Dual labour market
✓ Two labour markets exist in economy
✓ Secondary market has disproportionate ethnic minority component
✓ Dual market largely the result of recruitment decisions
✓ Racist attitudes influence composition
✗ Degree of segregation exaggerated
✗ Racist attitudes assumed not shown
✗ Hides gender element

Reserve army thesis
✓ Distinctive group in working class
✓ Used by capitalism when it suits economy
✓ Discarded in bad times
✓ Immigration is result of need for reserves of labour
✓ Divided from white working class by racist ideologies
✗ While racism exists, is hard to prove it is systematic
✗ Based on conspiracy view of capitalism
✗ Not all ethnic minorities are in secondary market

12: UNEMPLOYMENT

Difficulties in measuring unemployment

Definitions:
1. Not always easy to identify who is unemployed and who is not.
2. Not always easy to identify when an individual actually becomes officially unemployed.
3. Different interest groups have different definitions of unemployment beyond the official ones.

Categories:
1. Disputes over those who take early retirement.
2. Those invalided out of work sometimes count as unemployed and sometimes not.
3. Domestic labourers (housewives) not counted as unemployed or employed – grey category.

Politics:
1. Level of unemployment is controversial political issue between parties.
2. Ways of defining and counting unemployed open to political interference.
3. Even official figures have more than one way of defining unemployed, which leads to different totals.

Counting:
1. Not everyone who leaves work registers as unemployed.
2. Some registered as unemployed work in the black economy.
3. Some legitimate claimants refused registration on technicalities.

Difficulties experienced by the unemployed

Finance:
1. Low levels of household income result, with implications for standard of living.
2. Problems with mortgage repayments may lead to repossession of the family home.
3. Lack of ready cash impacts upon long-term prospects of whole family.

Social contacts:
1. Can lead to isolation, as the unemployed cannot contribute as fully as those in work.
2. Reduces the options of the unemployed and their families to take part in a variety of social activities.
3. Work is a main source of friends and acquaintances.

Physical capabilities:
1. Unemployed are likely to have lower levels of fitness than the employed.
2. Are more likely to suffer from long-term health problems.
3. Are less likely to develop skills and competence which are of value to potential employers.

Mental capabilities:
1. More likely to suffer from depression as a consequence of being out of work.
2. May lose central plank of an individual's identity by not being in work.
3. Can lead to mental illness and psychological problems and even to higher rates of suicide.

Implications
Official figures of unemployment are socially negotiated through a complex political and statistical process, because they have political consequences. They do not reflect 'real' levels of unemployment

Types of unemployment

Cyclical	Related to economic cycle
Structural	Changes in skills base in industry
Frictional	Short-term changes in job

Implications
Loss of job can be devastating for individuals and their families, moving through shock, to distress and eventually resignation, in which unemployed become less able to reintegrate into work without assistance.

EXPLANATIONS OF UNEMPLOYMENT AND VARIATIONS IN ITS INCIDENCE

Technological changes	Advances in technology have resulted in job losses in those industries most open to new machinery.	✓ Machines do replace jobs ✓ Technological change accelerating as are job losses	✗ Technology creates jobs not just loses them ✗ Job losses result of decisions not machines
Globalisation	Manufacturing moved to low wage countries of Pacific Rim.	✓ Growth in manufacturing in developing world apparent ✓ Decline in industry in West	✗ West moving towards high skill economies ✗ Collapse of Pacific Rim
Failure of the market	Left to itself the market does not provide full employment, as shown in 1930s.	✓ Market forces result in long-term mass unemployment ✓ Governments create jobs	✗ Government jobs are not wealth-producing jobs ✗ Less interference would free enterprise
New Right	Government intervention increases unemployment because of its tendency to tax business.	✓ Reduced taxation stimulates employment ✓ Less regulation allows growth in employment	✗ Market forces lead to increase in unemployment ✗ Monetarism loses jobs

13. ORGANISATIONS

Developments in Weber's theory

A. Informal organisations
- Formal aspects do not cover all the activities in bureaucracies.
- What actually goes on influenced by informal contacts and procedures.

B. Goal theory
- Organisations needs goals to keep them focused on purpose.
- Individuals have own goals that clash with organisations.

C. Iron law of oligarchy
- All organisations end up non-democratic and elitist – Michels.
- Interest of leaders always win.
- Challenged by existence of long-term democratic organisations.

D. Total institutions
- Organisations in which inmates spend all their lives.
- Inmates dealt with in batches.
- Focus on individual survival and techniques of adaption.
- Also interactionist here.

Weber developed a functional and formal theory of organisations. Bureaucracy was seen as the most efficient form of administration, because of its potential for organising individuals into a single unit to achieve goals. It provided a legitimate means because its powers were limited by rules.

Ideal type of bureaucracy (Weber)
- Hierarchy of paid officials
- Roles limited by strict rules
- Authority is based on office
- Separation of official and personal
- Constitutes a career for officials
- Officials subject to discipline
- Rules provide blueprint for action

Development in Weber's theory

E. Dysfunctional bureaucracy
- Segregation of roles can lead to alienation of officials and loss of understanding of their place in the operation of the organisation.
- Rules designed for efficiency can become inefficient as circumstances change and they dysfunction.

F. Organismic organisations
(Burns and Stalker)
- Bureaucracy best fitted for conditions of stability. New challenges create potential for disruption of efficiency.
- Networks rather than hierarchies suited to conditions of change.
- Contribution to problem-solving more important than obeying rules.
- Knowledge and power distributed amongst members, not concentrated at top of hierarchy.
- Deals with change of a post-modern society, enabling niche production and meeting individual demand.

INTERACTIONIST

Gouldner and rules
Stresses that rules are always used by individuals in structural positions. Thus, can be deployed in interests of individuals as well as organisation. Rules are thus double-edged sword – they protect individuals who are subject to them, as well as control them, e.g. the 'work-to-rule', where rules designed for efficiency can become inefficient if applied to the letter. Need to look at 'situational rules', which operate as 'rules-in-use' rather than official rules of organisation.

Ethnomethodologists and bureaucracy
Bureaucracy does not 'really' exist, but is used as an idea by participants in an organisation to 'account for' their actions. The concept acts as a justification for any course of action chosen by individuals in a bureaucracy. It thus only exists when called upon by participants to legitimate actions. The concept is used as a resource by inhabitants.

Total institutions (Goffman)
Individuals respond to incarceration in many different ways, such as situational withdrawal, rebellion, conversion, colonisation or 'playing it cool'.

MARXIST

The structure of organisations, the technology used and the way it is deployed are designed, not for maximum production of goods, but for control of the workers. This is true whether Taylorist or work enrichment principles are used (Braverman). This has been criticised by Marxist Buraway who argues workers work hard without coercion because ideology of profit-making is accepted as normal and legitimate in capitalist societies. There is no need for strict controls.

Marxists suggest that, for Weber, the efficiency of bureaucracy was in controlling the actions of the lower levels, not the administration of things. The starting point of Marxist approaches is that control of people by those at the top is the prime aim of all organisations.

POST-MODERNIST

Foucault's disciplinary society
- Focus on organisations in post-modern society is the body and its activity.
- Control is achieved through surveillance of all.
- Awareness of surveillance by society leads to self-surveillance.
- Where individuals police their own actions whether being watched or not.
- Computerisation of records allows for extension of surveillance in large organisations and social life generally.

✓ Details growth of many disciplinary techniques

✓ Focuses on individual's body

✗ Depends on a conspiracy-type approach

McDonaldisation (Ritzer) against post-modernism
- McDonald's fast food chain stands as exemplar for modernist living.
- Consumers subject to strict rationalisation of product.
- Products standardised, not customised, and choice is limited if global.
- Physical space used to control actions of customers in predictable ways.

✓ McDonaldist ideas spread widely and in global context

✓ Driven by profit motive and advertising rather than customer

✗ Understates importance of choice in society

✗ Overstresses impact of McDonaldist production principles

14. LEISURE

THE RELATIONSHIP BETWEEN WORK AND LEISURE

	Compensation thesis	Segmentalist approach	Holist approach
Main ideas	Leisure provides compensation for the deficiencies of work that is non-satisfying.	Work and leisure are separate areas of social life, with little similarity or connection between them.	Work and leisure are becoming alike, with work taking on many of the attributes of leisure and vice versa.
Evidence for	✓ Where work is boring, central life interest (Dubin, 1958) is leisure. ✓ Leisure can be controlled where this is not possible at work. ✓ Leisure provides social opportunities denied at work.	✓ Is a class-based difference with upper class more ready to see leisure as extension of work. ✓ Work is seen as a means to leisure by relaxation. ✓ Leisure industry based on distinctiveness from work.	✓ Lunch hour and coffee breaks becoming longer (Meissner, 1971). ✓ Leisure increasingly taken in large organisations. ✓ Some middle-class workers see no distinction between the two.
Evidence against	✗ Assumes that leisure can solve the problems of work. ✗ Ignores connections between type of work and type of leisure pursued (Parker, 1976). ✗ Based on false idea that those alienated at work would not be alienated in leisure also.	✗ Leisure has taken work forms to be efficient. ✗ Much leisure life is based around work colleagues. ✗ Interactions at work have leisure as focus of conversation. ✗ People work hard at leisure pursuits. ✗ Work is seen as pleasurable by many.	✗ Work has taken over leisure time under pressure from global competition. ✗ Much leisure still based on home and family. ✗ When asked, workers do draw distinct lines between the two (Dunkerly, 1976). ✗ Leisure is a central life interest, not work.

ISSUES ASSOCIATED WITH LEISURE

Class, gender and ethnicity
Social class
- Type of leisure activity pursued dependent in part on levels of income, with middle class having more disposable income.
- Income is unequally distributed along social class gradient.
- Thus working class participate less in leisure activities which cost, either membership or clubs or equipment.

Gender
- Leisure is pursued outside of work and non-work obligations, which includes domestic labour.
- Women take the prime responsibility for looking after the home whether they work in paid employment or not.
- Thus, women have less 'free time' to pursue leisure activities than men.
- Women also more fearful of using public space by themselves because of fear of attack or harassment.

Ethnicity
- Segregated leisure emerges where leisure is an expression of cultural identity.
- Music, sport and the arts offer opportunities for cultural expression.

A leisure society? (Dumazedier, 1967)
- Leisure increasingly becoming a focus for people's lives, both in time available and individual central life interest.
- Decline in work through computerisation means a loss of identity through employment and transfer to leisure.
- Leisure becomes increasingly privatised, with decline of public leisure opportunities (fairs, festivals) and growth in home-based entertainment (computer games, television).

Against a leisure society
✗ Though work hours have formally decreased, actual hours worked have increased as a result of pressure to perform well.
✗ Opportunities for leisure decreased by responsibilities in household increasing (self-provisioning through DIY, care of the old and sick, 24-hour shopping).
✗ Leisure time squeezed by more people entering labour market, especially women, with no domestic support.

A leisure industry?
- Industrialisation has freed individuals for many hours in which to pursue leisure activities of their choice.
- Leisure itself has become an industry as many activities controlled by institutions (e.g. media) which are designed primarily to make a profit rather than just provide leisure.
- Leisure itself has become a prime site of profit-making for capitalism and has become a major wealth-creating sector.
- Leisure also performs 'hidden services' for capitalism in terms of legitimation and ideological functions.
- Leisure legitimates social inequalities through the transference of hierarchies from, e.g. sport, into society.
- Leisure also provides a safety valve for talented lower class youths who can achieve status and income through participation in leisure as an employment activity.
- Sport and entertainment are central culture industries.

Globalisation of leisure?
- Leisure now concerned with construction of identities and lifestyles, drawing on global possibilities for playing.
- Masculine identities often constructed in relation to sport and physical prowess, but without violence of folk sport.
- Entering an era of post-tourism, where there are no authentic foreign travel experiences, just packages of simulated opportunities prepared in advance for masses.
- Communications are now global and instantaneous, bringing opportunities for leisure to us 24 hours a day, e.g. via internet.
- Cultural products now have 'global reach', e.g. produce of the world has transformed cuisine in our kitchens.
- Global leisure becoming dominated by huge conglomerations of multi-media empires, e.g. Murdoch.
- Debate is whether these mean homogenising leisure (e.g. music) or whether this brings local interests to a global audience.
- No area of world is immune from the 'tourist gaze'.

8 Sociological Methods
1 SOURCES OF DATA

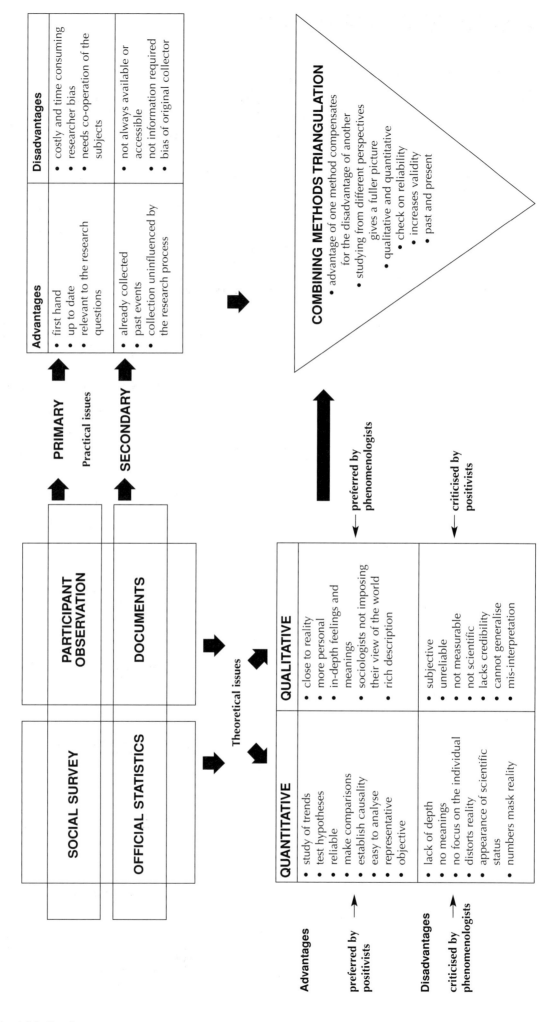

	Advantages	Disadvantages
PRIMARY	• first hand • up to date • relevant to the research questions	• costly and time consuming • researcher bias • needs co-operation of the subjects
SECONDARY	• already collected • past events • collection uninfluenced by the research process	• not always available or accessible • not information required • bias of original collector

Practical issues

COMBINING METHODS TRIANGULATION
• advantage of one method compensates for the disadvantage of another
• studying from different perspectives gives a fuller picture
• qualitative and quantitative
• check on reliability
• increases validity
• past and present

preferred by phenomenologists

criticised by positivists

	SOCIAL SURVEY	PARTICIPANT OBSERVATION
	OFFICIAL STATISTICS	DOCUMENTS

Theoretical issues

	QUANTITATIVE	QUALITATIVE
Advantages **preferred by positivists**	• study of trends • test hypotheses • reliable • make comparisons • establish causality • easy to analyse • representative • objective	• close to reality • more personal • in-depth feelings and meanings • sociologists not imposing their view of the world • rich description
Disadvantages **criticised by phenomenologists**	• lack of depth • no meanings • no focus on the individual • distorts reality • appearance of scientific status • numbers mask reality	• subjective • unreliable • not measurable • not scientific • lacks credibility • cannot generalise • mis-interpretation

2. CHOICE OF METHODS

FACTORS AFFECTING CHOICE

Theoretical assumptions	Practical factors	Ethical issues
• Positivists prefer scientific and quantitative data. • Phenomenologists prefer naturalism and qualitative data. • Feminists prefer personal experience and ethnographic methods that are collaborative and democratic. • Realists prefer combining techniques to discover the unobservable social processes that influence people's activities and the social structure in which they operate.	• purpose of the research, e.g. exploration, description or explanation • nature of the topic • time and money • funding source • size and nature of the study group • access and availability • personal characteristics of the researcher • skills and preference of the researcher • chance and opportunity	• effects on the study group • invasion of privacy • confidentiality/anonymity • deception/misrepresentation • researcher's participation or knowledge of illegal acts • implicit sanctioning of bad behaviour • lack of informed consent

Research method   **Research style**

Choices to be made in selection of method   or

Quantitative   or

Secondary

Registration data

or

Government survey/ Census

Documentary

Primary

Postal questionnaire

or

Structured interview

Survey

Qualitative

Primary

Unstructured interview

or

Participant observation

Ethnographic

Secondary

Personal documents

or

Non-personal documents

Documentary

3. OFFICIAL STATISTICS

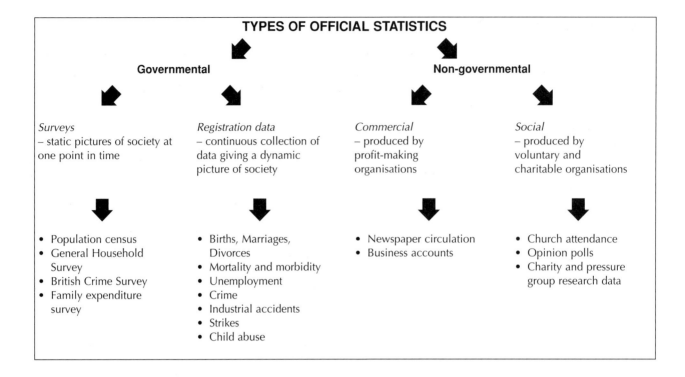

TYPES OF OFFICIAL STATISTICS

Governmental

Surveys
– static pictures of society at one point in time

- Population census
- General Household Survey
- British Crime Survey
- Family expenditure survey

Registration data
– continuous collection of data giving a dynamic picture of society

- Births, Marriages, Divorces
- Mortality and morbidity
- Unemployment
- Crime
- Industrial accidents
- Strikes
- Child abuse

Non-governmental

Commercial
– produced by profit-making organisations

- Newspaper circulation
- Business accounts

Social
– produced by voluntary and charitable organisations

- Church attendance
- Opinion polls
- Charity and pressure group research data

EVALUATION OF OFFICIAL STATISTICS

	Advantages	Disadvantages
Practical	• already collected • past events • collection uninfluenced by research • quick and cheap • easy to analyse • credible source • provides background data • large amount of factual detail	• access may be restricted • required information not available • categories used may not be those required by researcher • definitions may change over time or between societies • bias of the original collector • efficiency of data collection • out of date before publication
Theoretical **Positivists**	• quantitative • large coverage • before and after studies (see **Methods 14**) • trends of social change • comparisons can be made	• hidden figures of unrecorded events • problem of consistent collection, categorisation and reporting
Phenomenologists	• can learn about the producers of the information, e.g. the way coroners make decisions as to whether a death is a suicide	• lack of depth • no purpose or motive for action is given • no focus on the individual • socially constructed • manipulated to suit a particular set of interests

RESEARCH EXAMPLE: **Durkheim**, 'Suicide', 1897 compared suicide statistics from European societies and showed how the most individual of acts was socially patterned by social forces operating outside the individual (see **Crime and Deviance 16**).

4. SECONDARY QUALITATIVE DATA

TYPES AND EXAMPLES OF SECONDARY QUALITATIVE DATA

Studies	Personal, e.g.			Non-personal, e.g.		
	Auto-biography	Letters	Diaries	Media	Records	Other
S. Cohen, *Folk Devils and Moral Panics* (1972)				Local papers	Court reports	
Banks, *Prosperity and Parenthood* (1950)		Queen Victoria to her uncle		Daily paper, *Reynolds News*	Trial of Bradlaugh and Besant	Novels, Trollope and Austen
Willmott & Young, *Family and Kinship in East London* (1962)			Wives asked to keep diaries			
Laslett, *Household and family in past times* (1972)					Parish records	
Thomas & Znaniecki, *The Polish Peasant* (1918)	Statement from one man	764 from Polish immigrants		Polish newspapers	Social work agencies	

EVALUATION OF SECONDARY QUALITATIVE SOURCES

	Advantages	Disadvantages
Practical	• background information • generates ideas for study • cheap and available • used as part of triangulation process • wide range of data available • provides a historical dimension	• may not provide the information required • time-consuming to search for relevant material • motivation for writing may have effects on the content • problems of survival of documents • access and availability may be restricted
Theoretical **Positivists**	• can falsify a theory • provides support for theory • original uninfluenced by the research process	• cannot prove a theory • sources may not be representative • too few examples for statistical analysis
Phenomenologists	• richness and detail • personal documents give meanings and feelings • can study social processes	• understanding the author's meaning • establishing the credibility and authenticity of the source

5. ANALYSING DOCUMENTS

	CONTENT ANALYSIS	THEMATIC ANALYSIS/SEMIOLOGY
Description	A **quantitative**, objective and systematic method for analysing the **frequency of**, or the amount of time and space devoted to certain themes, words or events. It involves creating a list of categories and counting how many times they occur in a given document.	A **qualitative** method which studies the **signs and symbols** in a document to find out the **implicit meanings**, e.g. a dove means more than a white bird, it also symbolises peace. Semiology seeks to discover the motives and meanings underlying the content of a document which have significance beyond its physical existence.
Uses	• **Measures** simple objective aspects of content, e.g. number of swear words on television after 9 p.m. • **Reliable** data • **Unobtrusive** and so does not influence people • **Easy** to find sources of data • Used to **test an hypothesis** • Findings have credibility • **Identifies** issues for further research • Makes **comparisons**	• The **hidden** becomes more apparent • **Uncovers** the ideologies and bias of the producers of the document • Aids a deeper **understanding** of the text • Analyses **advertisements** • Shows the formative **influence** on young people's lives of media sources • Focuses attention on the **symbolic nature** of language and signs
Problems	• **Subjectivity** when defining the categories and allocating the content to the appropriate category • **Time-consuming** (but computers can speed the process) • **Significance** of the document not explained • **Biased** interpretation of the results • **Snapshot** picture only • **Atheoretical** as it merely describes rather than attempts to explain the findings	• Makes **assumptions** about the meaning of the text • **Unreliable** as different researchers may produce very different accounts • **Impossible to falsify** an interpretation • **Worth** of competing interpretations impossible to judge • Assumes the reader is a **passive receiver** of messages • Representations can change, analysis can quickly become **out of date**
Examples of research	• **Glasgow University Media Group** (1976) – television news coverage of industrial relations issues by counting the verbs used to describe the actions of both sides • **Lobban** (1974) – portrayal of gender roles in children's reading schemes • **Tuchman** (1977) – on US television men outnumbered women by 3 to 1	• **McRobbie** (1978) – looked behind the content to identify the ideology of femininity communicated by '*Jackie*' magazine for teenage girls • **Hebdidge** (1979) – examined the music and dress of youth groups and interpreted them as a form of resistance to society • **Williamson** (1978) – Decoding Advertisements

6. PRIMARY SOURCES

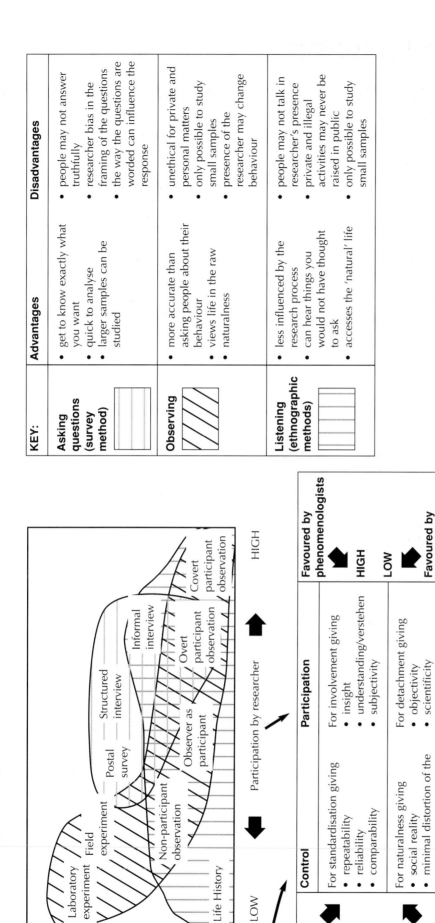

KEY:	Advantages	Disadvantages
Asking questions (survey method)	• get to know exactly what you want • quick to analyse • larger samples can be studied	• people may not answer truthfully • researcher bias in the framing of the questions • the way the questions are worded can influence the response
Observing	• more accurate than asking people about their behaviour • views life in the raw • naturalness	• unethical for private and personal matters • only possible to study small samples • presence of the researcher may change behaviour
Listening (ethnographic methods)	• less influenced by the research process • can hear things you would not have thought to ask • accesses the 'natural' life	• people may not talk in researcher's presence • private and illegal activities may never be raised in public • only possible to study small samples

7. ETHNOGRAPHIC RESEARCH

ETHNOGRAPHY – Researching a way of life using a variety of qualitative methods (including secondary sources where appropriate). The technique originated in anthropology but has been extended and adopted by sociologists to study a variety of social situations.

Social situation	Research examples	Methods		
		Life history	Participant observation	Informal interviews
Individual	Shaw (1930) – 'Jack Roller', a delinquent boy's own life story	Told to Shaw from subject's prison cell		
Collection of individuals	Moraga & Anzaldua (1981) 'Writings by radical women of colour'	A compilation of personal accounts		
Groups	Oscar Lewis (1961) – 'The children of Sanchez', the poor of Mexico and Puerto Rico	Descriptions of their way of life from personal accounts and direct observation		
Institutions	Goffman (1961) – 'Asylums', a study of the patients' and staff's world of mental hospitals		Author became an orderly in a hospital	
Community	Stacey (1960) – 'Banbury', an account of the place and its inhabitants through time		Researchers lived in the town and used key informants	
Anthropology	Malinowski (1954) – 'The Trobriand Islanders', a study of the way a different culture operates		First-hand observations and conversations rather than relying on missionary reports	

COMPARISON AND CONTRAST OF TWO ETHNOGRAPHIC METHODS

Similarities	Differences	
Both the life history and autobiography:	**Life history**	**Autobiography**
provide a useful source of data for sociologists	primary data in the form of an oral or written account of people's lives which they tell to the researcher	secondary data obtained through published works
give a personal account of an individual's life story	complete account of a person's experiences honestly told	account of what the author wants the reader to know
are written by unrepresentative people, so it is impossible to generalise from either account	more likely to be ordinary people	more likely to be important people in political or social life
can be biased in the writing of the account	researcher may lead the subject in a particular direction	writer has a motive for writing which may distort the truthfulness of the account
provide descriptions that help build a picture of social life of the time, place and group of people concerned	view of history, often unavailable in documents and therefore difficult to verify and subject to distortion of memory	particular view of events that may be well documented elsewhere and so can be checked for accuracy
have been criticised for failing to give a theoretical account or any analysis	unjustified, because the account can be organised according to the key dimensions of a person's life; the turning points; or the adaptations	valid, but it was not written for sociological research

8. OBSERVATION

TYPES OF OBSERVATION AND HOW THEY RELATE TO KEY DIMENSIONS

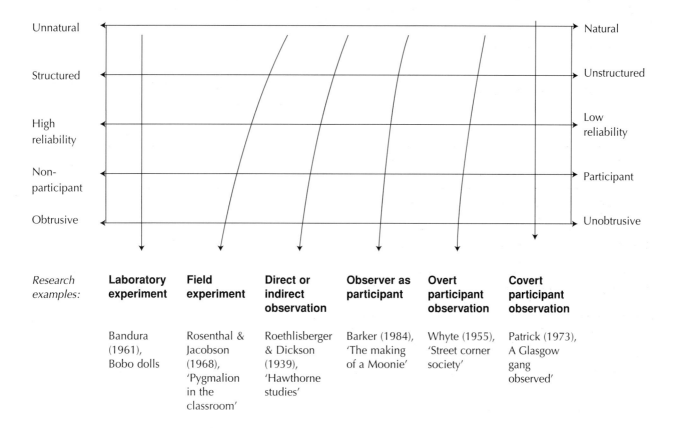

Research examples:	**Laboratory experiment**	**Field experiment**	**Direct or indirect observation**	**Observer as participant**	**Overt participant observation**	**Covert participant observation**
	Bandura (1961), Bobo dolls	Rosenthal & Jacobson (1968), 'Pygmalion in the classroom'	Roethlisberger & Dickson (1939), 'Hawthorne studies'	Barker (1984), 'The making of a Moonie'	Whyte (1955), 'Street corner society'	Patrick (1973), A Glasgow gang observed'

EVALUATION OF EXPERIMENTAL METHODS

	Advantages	Disadvantages
Laboratory	<ul><li>replicable and reliable</li><li>control over the independent variable</li><li>useful for testing hypotheses</li><li>controlled environment: no confounding variables</li><li>can establish cause and effect relationships</li><li>possible to match control and experimental groups on key variables</li><li>reflects natural science methodology</li></ul>	<ul><li>'Hawthorne effect', behaviour changes as the result of the researcher's presence or the knowledge of being the subject of an experiment</li><li>artificial environment</li><li>unrepresentative samples when using volunteers</li><li>ethical issues</li><li>only appropriate for study over short periods</li><li>cannot control for variables outside the experimental environment</li></ul>
Field	<ul><li>results generalisable to the real world</li><li>can cover time spans over a year</li><li>real-life situations in natural settings</li><li>researcher can focus on specific aspects of social life</li><li>can give an element of control of variables</li></ul>	<ul><li>results only applicable to the 'field' studied</li><li>lack of control over confounding variables</li><li>impossible to repeat in the same conditions</li><li>ethical problems of deceit and intervening in people's lives</li></ul>

9. PARTICIPANT OBSERVATION

COMPARISON OF OVERT AND COVERT PARTICIPANT OBSERVATION

	Overt	Covert
Getting in	✓ introductions possible ✗ researcher must be able to fit in and be prepared to play the part ✗ may be refused entry	✓ normal entry channels must be used, e.g. applying for a job or hanging around appropriate places ✗ researcher must be convincing ✗ time consuming
Staying in	✗ sensitivity about when to ask questions ✓ allowed some passivity	✗ cannot ask questions or ask for help ✗ required to participate fully including illegal and deviant activities ✗ may be found out and so have to leave
Getting out	✓ can mark the end of the study period with an occasion to help the transition ✓ can return for follow up or respondent validation	✗ danger of going native ✗ no going back if group find out they have been deceived
Advantages	✓ fewer ethical problems ✓ less dangers ✓ easier to maintain role	✓ less likely to change people's behaviour ✓ only way of studying secret or deviant groups

EVALUATION OF PARTICIPANT OBSERVATION

	Advantages	Disadvantages
Practical	• study of one or a small number of groups • study of secret or deviant groups • cheap for a primary method • appropriate for non-literate societies • possibility of respondent validation • gives direction to future research • amplifies other sources	• getting too involved • ethical problems • difficulty of recording the data • time consuming • requires commitment and skill • potential dangers to the researcher • some groups will be impenetrable hence there are more studies of the weak than the powerful
Theoretical **Positivists**	• provides ideas for hypothesis testing • can be used to falsify a theory • tests the usefulness of wide-ranging theories • background information before more quantitative techniques are used	• unrepresentative groups so cannot generalise • subjective • unrepeatable and unreliable • not quantitative • unlikely to provide causal explanations • focuses on the surface features of social life ignoring the structural features that produced them
Phenomenologists	• puts people at the centre of research to see life as they see it • allows empathetic understanding/verstehen • wide initial focus prevents the researcher being blinded by the assumptions of pre-structured data collection • social reality in a natural setting • small-scale detailed research that is valid • hypotheses emerge from the research process (grounded theory)	• researcher can be misled or misinformed • researcher bias in the interpretation of what is observed • getting in, staying in and getting out (see above)

10. SURVEY RESEARCH

Characteristic and mnemonic	Postal questionnaire	Structured interview	Semi/unstructured interview
QUANTIFICATION	✓ high: especially when fixed choice responses	✓ high: especially when fixed choice responses	✗ low: unless content analysis of transcripts is carried out
EXAMPLE	Brittain (1976),'Teacher opinion on aspects of school life'	Townsend (1979), 'Poverty in the UK'	Oakley (1981), 'From here to maternity'
DESCRIPTION	Pre-prepared questions answered by respondents	As postal questionnaire but asked and recorded by a researcher either face to face or by telephone	Prepared topics brought up in an informal conversational style
PARTICIPATION OF RESEARCHER	✗ limited: only in questionnaire design	✗ limited: can only repeat questions using the same words	✓ high: probing and prompting widely used
RELIABILITY	✓ highest: standardised questions – no interviewer effect	✓ high: standardised questions but some interviewer effect	✗ low: cannot repeat conversation ✗ low: interviewer bias
INTERNAL VALIDITY	✗ low: limited chance to respond in own way ✓ allows time to find accurate information ✓ anonymity may increase the honesty if personal or sensitive information asked for	✗ low: limited chance to answer in own way ✓ less dishonesty in face-to-face situation ✓ spontaneous reply may increase truthfulness	✓ high: interviewee can explain in own words and in more depth ✓ comfortable relationship, more open answers
CONTROL	✓ high: in questions asked and by the use of fixed choice responses	✓ high: over who completes the answers and the order of asking	✗ low: variations in how and when the topics are raised
EXTERNAL VALIDITY	✓ high: large size samples geographically spread ✗ low: large non-response	✓ high: lower non-response ✗ low: small samples less spread than postal questionnaire	✗ low: tends to use small non-random samples
USES	✓ as for quantitative data ✓ factual information ✓ anonymous replies ✓ busy people	✓ as for quantitative data ✓ studying attitudes and emotions ✓ funnelling possible (see **Sociological Methods 11**) ✓ observation check that the person is who they say they are	✓ as for qualitative data ✓ sensitive topics ✓ help in designing a questionnaire by identifying the issues and likely responses
PROBLEMS	✗ unsuitable for people with limited literacy ✗ misunderstanding questions ✗ high non-response introduces bias	✗ interviewer bias ✗ costly and time-consuming	✗ difficult to record ✗ skilled interviewer required ✗ comfortable and quiet place needed ✗ very costly and time-consuming

11. DESIGNING QUESTIONNAIRES

DO have an introduction to explain who is carrying out the study and why.

DO give instructions on how to complete the questionnaire.

DO use funnelling to avoid asking irrelevant questions.

DO have a clear layout for ease of recording and data analysis.

DO use multiple choice answers where more than one answer is possible.

DO use open-ended questions, particularly if you cannot anticipate the answer.

DO use prompts if appropriate.

DO lead the respondent through the questions and ask personal questions last.

DO phrase the questions in the least threatening way.

DO keep all the questions short and simple.

DO NOT make the questionnaire too long, a few relevant questions will give a better response rate.

DO NOT use vague terms that will result in imprecise answers.

DO NOT use technical terms that may not be understood.

DO NOT ask personal or embarrassing questions that may cause offence or lead to untruthful responses.

DO NOT ask leading questions, they will merely produce the answer you expect.

DO NOT use ambiguous terms that have different meanings for different people.

DO NOT make assumptions about behaviour.

DO NOT have insufficient categories that do not provide realistic options.

DO NOT have overlapping categories.

DO NOT ask double questions that require more than one answer.

NEWSPAPER READERSHIP SURVEY

I am an A level Sociology student researching newspaper readership for my coursework project. Please would you help me by answering the following questions by ticking in the appropriate box.

Questions   **Answers**

1. Do you read a daily paper regularly?   ☐ Y ☐ N

2. Have you bought a newspaper today?   ☐ Y ☐ N
   If 'no' go to question 4

3. Was it a broadsheet or tabloid?   ☐ B ☐ T

   If tabloid
   Did you buy it for the page 3 pictures?   ☐ Y ☐ N

4. Do you think tabloids are easier to read because of the size of the pages?   ☐ Y ☐ N

5. Which sections of the paper do you read?   ☐ domestic news   ☐ foreign news   ☐ entertainment   ☐ sport

6. What quality Sunday paper do you read? (e.g. *Times, Telegraph, Observer, Independent*)   Write in ——

7. Do you read the paper at breakfast or in the evening?   ☐ B ☐ E

   Now some questions about yourself

8. Which age group do you come in?   ☐ 15–30 ☐ 30–45   ☐ 45–60 ☐ 60+

9. Are you married or living with a partner?

12. SAMPLING DECISION TREE

Define the group of people you are interested in studying (target population) by setting:
• geographical limits
• age limits
• any other factors

KEY

General population

Target population

QUESTIONS AND ANSWERS

TYPE OF SAMPLE

Is the target population small enough so time and money allow complete coverage?

YES

Census, (all target population covered)

NO

NO

NO

Do you want to be able to generalise to the target population?

Do you want your sample to be typical of the target population?

Purposive e.g. snowball (links between sample units)

YES

YES

Quota (finding people to fit predetermined categories)

or

Do you have a sampling frame of the target population?

NO

Cluster (using everyone in a randomly chosen group)

YES

Is there any order in the sampling frame?

NO

Systematic (selecting at regular intervals)

YES

Do you want to increase the precision of the sample?

YES

Stratified random (division then selection by social characteristics)

NO

Do you want to reduce the geographical spread?

YES

Multi-stage random (selection from selected groups)

NO

Simple random (selection without human bias)

13. SAMPLE DESIGN

Sample	Description	Uses	Problems
Census	Complete coverage of the target population. Held every 10 years. Funded by Government.	✓ accurate findings ✓ full picture ✓ comparison over time	✗ usually costly and time consuming ✗ non-responders reduce representativeness
Snowball	An initial contact is used to provide further contacts. New contacts are used to extend the chain of respondents.	✓ to build a sample of secret groups or those engaged in deviant activities ✓ no sampling frame required	✗ not random so no generalisations can be made ✗ may run out of new names
Quota	The interviewer has a list of characteristics required of the respondents and the number to be interviewed in each category, e.g. class, age, gender.	✓ for market research as a quick way of getting a cross-section of people with the desired characteristics ✓ no sampling frame needed	✗ not random and so generalisations to a wider population should not be made ✗ choice of person relies on judgement of researcher
Cluster	The target population is divided into smaller groups from which random samples are taken. Smaller groups are at the level where an appropriate sampling frame is available.	✓ for large target populations ✓ when there is no sampling frame for the individual units ✓ concentrates the sample in geographical areas saves time and money	✗ reduces representativeness ✗ need a sampling frame for the clusters ✗ can be loss of important targets if not included in cluster
Systematic	Taking every 'nth' name (e.g. every 10th) from a list to produce a sample of the required size.	✓ quick and easy way of obtaining a sample ✓ avoids researcher choice	✗ sampling frame must not be ordered in a way that might produce a biased sample ✗ difficult to generalise
Stratified random	The target population is divided into groups, e.g. age, class, gender, and then random selection is made in the correct proportions for each group.	✓ increases the precision of the sample by making sure certain characteristics of the target population occur in the right numbers ✓ guarantees representation of minority groups	✗ requires knowledge of the characteristics of the target population ✗ finding a sampling frame that provides the information on the stratified characteristics
Multi-stage random	A first sample is selected at random, e.g. of universities, and then a further sample is taken, e.g. of students.	✓ for a large dispersed target population ✓ requires a full sampling frame only for the selected areas	✗ reduces representativeness ✗ compounds sampling error ✗ requires two or more sampling frames
Simple random	Each member of the target population has an equal chance of selection. This is achieved by random selection, i.e. not influenced by the selector, as in a lottery. Use is often made of random number lists generated by computer.	✓ representative of the target population ✓ generalisations can be made ✓ sampling error can be calculated ✓ computers reduce human input	✗ requires accurate up-to-date and complete sampling frame ✗ time-consuming ✗ expensive ✗ sample may be widely dispersed

14. RESEARCH STRATEGIES

Strategy	Description	Illustration	Uses	Problems	Example
Case study	Study of one group or event		✓ insights from atypical cases ✓ as a pilot study ✓ unique historical event ✓ falsify a theory using an extreme case	✗ generalisations cannot be made from a one-off case ✗ lacks a macro perspective and the wider social context	• Ball – Beachside comprehensive (1981)
Comparative method	Two or more groups analysed for similarities and differences		✓ a 'natural experiment' that can establish causality without manipulating the independent variable ✓ fixes similarities and differences	✗ difficult to isolate the independent variable when cases are not sufficiently similar ✗ correlation can be confused with causality	• Durkheim's study of suicide (1897)
Before and after study	Comparison of data from the same group before and after a change	Before / After	✓ assess the effectiveness of legislation or intervention programmes ✓ establishes causality	✗ cannot discount other intervening variables affecting the outcome ✗ subject to external influences	• introduction of mixed ability teaching at Beachside comprehensive (Ball 1981)
Cross-sectional	Representatives taken from a varied population to get a picture of the whole		✓ generalisations can be made to the target population when the sample is chosen randomly ✓ gives snapshot picture	✗ static picture of one point in time which can quickly become out of date ✗ danger of over-generalisation	• Townsend, Poverty in the UK (1979)
Repeated cross-section	As above but comparable samples taken at another point in time		✓ provides a dynamic picture ✓ charts changes ✓ combines comparison with longitudinal	✗ cannot make changes in later studies if comparisons are to be made with the first ✗ expensive	• British Crime Surveys, six surveys between 1982 and 1996
Longitudinal	Same sample of people studied at intervals sometimes from birth into adulthood		✓ data on unrelated areas can reveal associations not anticipated ✓ records changes in behaviour over time ✓ not dependent on memory ✓ provides information on lifecourses of individuals and groups	✗ maintaining co-operation ✗ keeping track of people ✗ conditioning effect from repeated study ✗ unrepresentative over time because of drop-out (attrition rate)	• Douglas, children born in 1946 • Butler and Pringle, 1958 • Butler, 1970

15. VALUES IN SOCIAL RESEARCH

RESEARCH PROCESS	VALUES	EXAMPLE
Choice of topic	• Concerns of the researcher/career interests. • Society's perception of what is a problem. • Researcher's past experiences. • Moral climate of the times.	• Durkheim's (1897) friend had committed suicide. • Underage drinking is a problem; adult consumption of alcohol is not.
Characteristics of the topic	• Theoretical perspective of the researcher. • Social characteristics of researcher.	• Feminists will focus on women, functionalists will look for the useful purposes of institutions.
Funding	• Sponsors of the research will have their own agenda which will determine whether the research gets done. • Sponsors will have view of how research should be carried out.	• ESRC funding agency require applicants to justify their research proposals in terms of policy usefulness, cost effectiveness or potential value.
Methods	• Ethical considerations limit how the subject can be pursued. • Some methods can be seen as intrinsically unethical, where is covert aspect.	• Schofield (1965) did not use postal questionnaires in his survey of young people's sexual behaviour as the range of questions might have corrupted some young people.
Operationalising concepts	• Choice of the indicators to measure a social phenomenon. • Social facts are saturated with a subjective element which affects the meanings people attach to them.	• Townsend (1979) chose non-ownership of a refrigerator as a measure of poverty. • Class, slum, suicide are not neutral terms.
Hypothesis testing	• Questions asked about the data will be influenced by the built-in bias resulting from personal experiences and cultural traditions of the researcher.	• Durkheim ignored the gender differences in suicide rates which did not fit with his theory.
Interpretation of findings	• The way the researcher presents the results. • Researchers make choices as to what is important and what is not important. • Pressure from external sources.	• Do you say the glass is half full or half empty? Becker (1967) said the sociologist should be on the side of the less powerful, i.e. siding with the underdog.
Publication	• Withholding information that might compromise the subjects of the research or contradict the researcher's theory. • Timing of publication to maximise or minimize impact.	• Whyte (1955) used fictitious names and places in 'Street Corner Society'.
Use of results	• Knowledge gives power and to whom this is made available is a political decision.	• Barker (1984) set up the organisation INFORM to give public access to knowledge of new religious movements.

9 Power and Politics

1. THE NATURE OF POWER AND AUTHORITY

POWER

TYPES OF POWER

Political
- Decision-making power through holding public office, not always elected
- Power of voting politicians into public office

Economic
- Ownership of means of production
  - To hire and fire
  - To locate business
- Purchasing power
  - As consumers – to buy or not to buy

Ideological
- Moral power
  - Formal religious authority
  - Informal power of the 'good'
- Populist power
  - Mass media agenda-setting
  - Modelling examples set by the famous

AUTHORITY

Type of Authority	Source of legitimacy	Governance	Examples	A note of caution
Charismatic	Exceptional character of an individual leader, who has qualities of heroism, will or spiritual presence. Force of personality is crucial element in establishing charisma.	By the whim of the leader, decision-making is personal.	Religious societies; Dalai Lama, Ayatollah Khomeini	These distinctions are ideal types, as defined by Weber (1919). They do not exist in the real world in a pure form. Rather, any one society is likely to have a balance of these types of authority, with one dominating. To illustrate, all three forms exist in the role of teacher: personality, history of teachers, office-holding. Which one of these is dominant will depend on contingent circumstances – that is, the context, social and cultural, in which the teacher operates.
Traditional	Established ways of ordering things, so that what has been in the past acts as a model for the present.	By the way things have always been done.	Medieval England; monarchs, the papacy	
Rational-legal	Sanctioned rules of society, which have the force of law. Legitimacy is given to whomever the rules define as in a lawful position to issue orders and expect obedience.	By the rule of law, so that those in authority have the lawful right.	Modern democratic societies; Great Britain, United States.	

OBEDIENCE

Utilitarianism	Coercion	Consensus	Contract
• Positive utilitarianism, where we come together in society to increase co-operatively the goods that we can create. Only by mutual working can we achieve the 'good life'. • Negative utilitarianism, where we come together to restrain our natural passions, which tend towards selfishness.	We obey because the consequence of disobeying is punishment. The system of law and regulation set up in society reflects the interests of powerful groups in society. The use of violence and force to defend these interests is in the nature of all societies. Most citizens must therefore obey from fear.	We obey the state because there is a general agreement in society that this is the most rational way of organising our affairs. Order stems from the value consensus which defines a set of ideas which the majority in society agree are civilised ways of acting.	We enter into a contractual relationship with each other when we enter society, to establish acceptable ways of behaving. These are defined by the law and establish the limits of power. We obey the state because its actions are constrained by the law and it cannot act arbitrarily.
✗ Based on the idea of the state of nature as a war of all against all ✗ Negative view of human nature	✗ Dismisses altruism and goodness in nature ✗ Ignores peaceful ways of organising society	✗ Overestimates agreement in society ✗ Legitimates the status quo	✗ Assumes that all are rational ✗ Ignores law-breaking by the state

2. IDEOLOGY

DEFINITIONS	DOMINANT IDEOLOGY
• Ideologies are sets of ideas that represent the interests of social groups. • Ideologies therefore compete in society for dominance, as they are weapons in the struggle for control over scarce resources. • The competition between ideologies exists both at the level of politics (through competing for the people's vote) and at the level of ideas (through the media, for example).	• When an ideology becomes accepted by the bulk of the population as 'natural' and 'obvious' then it is a dominant ideology. • When an ideology is dominant then the interests of the social group which is represented by that ideology are likely to be fostered in society. • Having a dominant ideology is therefore an important element in the social control of a society.

POLITICAL IDEOLOGIES	SUBTERRANEAN IDEOLOGIES
Political ideologies have traditionally represented the interests of social classes and have taken organisational form in the main political parties. Working class = Labour Middle class = Conservative Segments of classes have their own political ideologies and political organisations. Progressive middle class = Liberal Militant working class = Communist	• No matter how dominant an ideology becomes, its hegemony (control) is never complete. • This is because ideologies represent real social interests and as these change in society, so new ideologies emerge which challenge the legitimacy of the already existing ideologies. • Therefore there is always competition between ideologies in society.

EXAMPLES OF IDEOLOGIES

Capitalist ideology	Socialist ideology
✓ Privileges the ideas of economic freedom ✓ Legitimates the pursuit of profit ✓ Emphasises the important of the individual in society ✓ Emphasises the rights of employers ✓ Opposes any regulation in restraint of trade	✓ Privileges the ideas of equality and fairness ✓ Maintains the right to a decent wage ✓ Emphasises the importance of collective solidarity ✓ Emphasises the rights of trade unions ✓ Opposes absolute rights of employers to hire and fire workers

NEW EMERGENT IDEOLOGIES

As new social movements have emerged in society, so new ideologies are developed to express these interests. These ideologies may take on the organisational form of a political party or not.

Organisational form of a political party	Organisational form not a political party
Green party, which represents the interests of the environmentalist movement.	'Black consciousness', which emerged among the ethnic minorities in Britain and the United States as an expression of their distinct interests.

WAYS IN WHICH MARXIST SOCIOLOGISTS HAVE USED THE CONCEPT OF IDEOLOGY

ALTHUSSER	GRAMSCI	DOMHOFF
A French Marxist, who argued that ideologies had 'relative autonomy', that is an independence from the interests of the ruling class, though, in the long run, ideologies did represent class interests.	An Italian Marxist who stressed the importance of ideologies in creating dependency in the working class, through the establishment of ideological hegemonies.	An American Marxist who saw the 'ideological process' as one of the ways in which a social class can dominate politics even where there was a universal democracy, with the right to vote given to everyone.
Implications	**Implications**	**Implications**
Politicians could make policies that seemed to go against the short-term interests of the ruling class, in order to secure capitalism's long-term survival.	Any fundamental change in society would be a long slow process that involved changing ideas, not just power.	Overthrowing the dominant class in society is very difficult as existing arrangements are largely unchallenged by alternative ideologies.
Criticism	**Criticism**	**Criticism**
✗ It remains an economic determinist theory by insisting that ideologies do represent economic interests in the long run.	✗ The emphasis on the power of ideology is overstated and neglects other aspects such as force and the law.	✗ This is a defeatist view of the potential for change in democratic society and neglects the real progress that has been made.

3. ELITE THEORIES AND PLURALISM

<table>
<tr><td rowspan="4">A N T I - D E M O C R A T I C   T H E O R I E S</td><td></td><td>Who Rules?</td><td>Source of power</td><td>Strengths</td><td>Weaknesses</td><td rowspan="4">E L I T E   T H E O R I E S</td></tr>
<tr><td>Classical elite theory</td><td>Mosca (1939) and Pareto (1902) identified a small ruling group in all societies whether formally democratic or not.</td><td>Those with courage (lions) and those with cunning (foxes) formed a tight organisational unit at the centre of the state.</td><td>✔ Adds a psychological dimension to power
✔ Emphasises short lines of communication amongst elite
✔ Sees control of the few as historical necessity
✔ Sees elite as natural</td><td>✗ Is consciously anti-democratic
✗ Legitimates rule of the few
✗ Cynical view of the elite
✗ Dismisses the masses as unfit to rule</td></tr>
<tr><td>Unitary elite theory</td><td>A single political elite governed the US. Their preferences prevailed in policy-making, even when in conflict with the masses.</td><td>Ability to manipulate resources in varying spheres, but especially control of decision-making and the political sphere.</td><td>✔ Sees policy as result of elite preferences
✔ Emphasises stability of elite rule
✔ Stresses control of access to elite positions by elite</td><td>✗ Does not offer an adequate theory of change
✗ Assumes that personal contact means interests in common
✗ Cynical view of the elite
✗ Conspiracy theory</td></tr>
<tr><td>Radical elite theory</td><td>There were a number of interlocking elites in US called the 'military–industrial complex', who had personal and organisational connections.</td><td>Control over the political bureaucracy, industry and military power, whose leaders had interests in common, and who acted in concert.</td><td>✔ Describes a more complex social reality
✔ Moves beyond political decision-making
✔ Is supported by empirical evidence
✔ Takes military into consideration</td><td>✗ Time-bound, describing 1960s US
✗ Ethno-centric, focusing on America
✗ Empirical evidence not conclusive
✗ No 'processual' dimension, showing how decisions are reached</td></tr>
<tr><td rowspan="3">D E M O C R A T I C   T H E O R I E S</td><td>Elite pluralism</td><td>There are a number of elites who compete for power. Other non-political elites are also important.</td><td>Social elites have status, 'governing elite holds political office', specialised elites have specific knowledge.</td><td>✔ Recognises the influence of different types of elite
✔ Retains the idea of a central elite
✔ More sophisticated</td><td>✗ Not clear why there are only three types of elite
✗ Wants best of both worlds
✗ Neglects masses</td><td rowspan="3">P L U R A L I S T   T H E O R I E S</td></tr>
<tr><td>Community pluralism</td><td>In local communities, there are no elites, rather there are interest groups who make coalitions with each other over specific issues and seek to influence the decision-makers.</td><td>In local communities, power is constantly shifting and the capacity to affect decisions is based on the ability to forge alliances with other groups and lobby effectively.</td><td>✔ Focus on the local community
✔ Strong empirical base
✔ Looks at real campaigns
✔ Accords with commonsense views of politics
✔ Has a processual dimension</td><td>✗ Neglects larger issues of power
✗ Assumes power is only decision-making
✗ Ignores power to prevent issues being raised in first place
✗ Idealised view of local communities
✗ Ethno-centric American view</td></tr>
<tr><td>Classical pluralism</td><td>Decision-making in modern democratic societies is dispersed among many competing interest groups. While some groups may have more power than others no one group's interests are consistently met.</td><td>Power is so dispersed that any interested individual or group can influence decision-making office-holders through campaigning with other groups, aiming at the public or at the decision-makers themselves.</td><td>✔ Chimes with democratic sentiments
✔ Gives due attention to political campaigns
✔ Allows for social change
✔ Gives central role to office-holders who are decision-makers
✔ Asks 'does anybody rule?'</td><td>✗ Ignores inequalities of power
✗ Has simplistic view of power as only decision-making
✗ Assumes all interests are fairly equally represented
✗ Dismisses importance of control of economy as source of power</td></tr>
</table>

4. MARXIST THEORIES OF THE STATE

TRADITIONAL MARXIST THEORY

- Ownership of industry and finance gives political power to bourgeoisie.
- Ruling class acts in politics directly to promote their own interests.
- Lower classes are subject to the power of the ruling class.
- 'The State is but a committee for managing the common affairs of the bourgeoisie'.

Implications

- Revolution is the only way to change society in a fundamental way.
- The power of the bourgeoisie is largely unchallenged in society.
- The relationship between economics and politics is direct, with economics determinant.
- The law is biased against the interests of the working class.

Criticisms

- ✗ Economic determinist theory
- ✗ Relies on conspiracy theory of politics
- ✗ Downplays other important social institutions
- ✗ Has mistaken conception of the way the law operates

STRUCTURAL MARXISM (ALTHUSSER AND POULANTZAS)

- The state has relative autonomy from the bourgeoisie.
- Power can be exercised against the short-term interest of the ruling class, for example in creating a Welfare State.
- Power is exercised always to promote the long-term survival of the capitalist system, e.g. welfarism legitimates capitalism.
- State ideological apparatus promotes capitalist ideology.

Implications

- Working-class interests can be met in part, through political struggle.
- Power operates in sophisticated ways in bourgeois societies.
- Ultimately the interests of the ruling class are protected by political action.
- Ideology is a powerful weapon.

Criticisms

- ✗ Never clear how autonomous political power is from economics
- ✗ Relies on an automatic functioning of institutions in the interests of one class
- ✗ Not clear what the relative importance of ideology is
- ✗ Suggests real social progress is not possible

Repressive state apparatus, ideological hegemony, economic determinism, relative autonomy

HUMANIST MARXISM (GRAMSCI)

- Capitalism establishes its rule through ideological hegemony, that is, the workers accept the ideas of the ruling class as natural and right.
- Power is therefore exercised to manipulate and organise the consent of the masses, which involves some concessions to their interests.
- There is a clear distinction between political power (coercion) and civil power (gaining ideological consent) and the ruling class uses both for its own ends.
- Workers do not accept the ruling class ideology unquestioningly.

Important concepts:
Consciousness, False Consciousness, Dual Consciousness, Ideological State Apparatus

Implications

- Changing society can only be a long-term political goal.
- The battle of ideas is important in changing things.
- There needs to be a 'long war through the institutions'.
- Propaganda work is important.

Criticisms

- ✗ Not clear whether hegemony can be successfully challenged
- ✗ Relative importance of economic and ideological not given
- ✗ Gives too much importance to power of ideas
- ✗ Does not detail how ruling class control ideologies

Comparison of Marxist, Elite and Pluralist Theories of Power

Name of theory	Marxist	Unitary Elite	Pluralism
Who rules?	Ruling class	Power elite	No one (everybody)
Distribution of power	Concentrated	Concentrated	Diffused
Locus of power	Ownership of means of production	Key office-holders	State
Nature of power	Economic power	Institutional power	Political power

5. THEORIES OF THE STATE

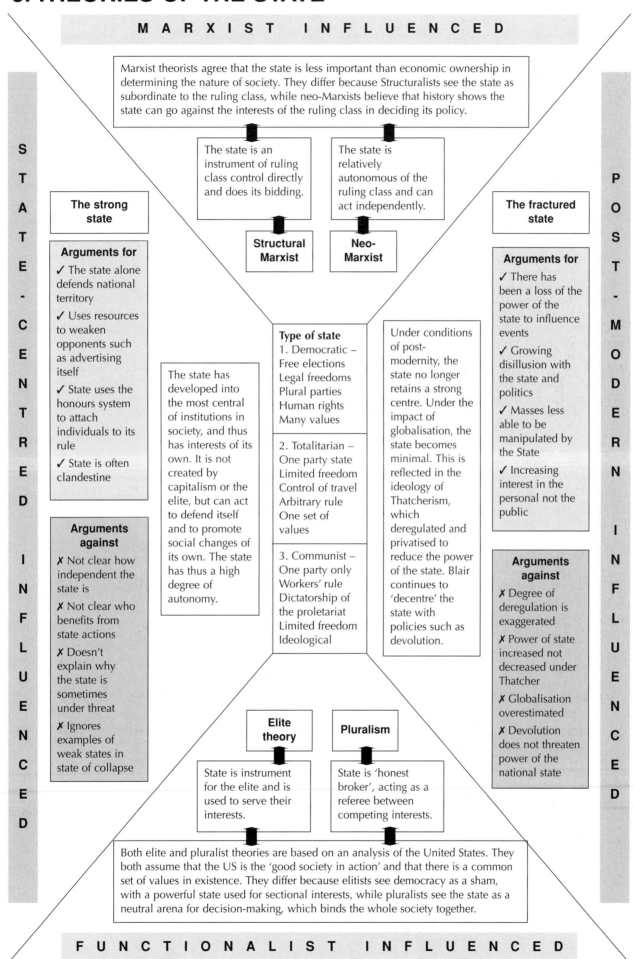

MARXIST INFLUENCED

Marxist theorists agree that the state is less important than economic ownership in determining the nature of society. They differ because Structuralists see the state as subordinate to the ruling class, while neo-Marxists believe that history shows the state can go against the interests of the ruling class in deciding its policy.

The state is an instrument of ruling class control directly and does its bidding.

The state is relatively autonomous of the ruling class and can act independently.

Structural Marxist

Neo-Marxist

The strong state

Arguments for

✓ The state alone defends national territory

✓ Uses resources to weaken opponents such as advertising itself

✓ State uses the honours system to attach individuals to its rule

✓ State is often clandestine

Arguments against

✗ Not clear how independent the state is

✗ Not clear who benefits from state actions

✗ Doesn't explain why the state is sometimes under threat

✗ Ignores examples of weak states in state of collapse

The state has developed into the most central of institutions in society, and thus has interests of its own. It is not created by capitalism or the elite, but can act to defend itself and to promote social changes of its own. The state has thus a high degree of autonomy.

Type of state
1. Democratic –
Free elections
Legal freedoms
Plural parties
Human rights
Many values

2. Totalitarian –
One party state
Limited freedom
Control of travel
Arbitrary rule
One set of values

3. Communist –
One party only
Workers' rule
Dictatorship of the proletariat
Limited freedom
Ideological

Under conditions of post-modernity, the state no longer retains a strong centre. Under the impact of globalisation, the state becomes minimal. This is reflected in the ideology of Thatcherism, which deregulated and privatised to reduce the power of the state. Blair continues to 'decentre' the state with policies such as devolution.

The fractured state

Arguments for

✓ There has been a loss of the power of the state to influence events

✓ Growing disillusion with the state and politics

✓ Masses less able to be manipulated by the State

✓ Increasing interest in the personal not the public

Arguments against

✗ Degree of deregulation is exaggerated

✗ Power of state increased not decreased under Thatcher

✗ Globalisation overestimated

✗ Devolution does not threaten power of the national state

Elite theory

Pluralism

State is instrument for the elite and is used to serve their interests.

State is 'honest broker', acting as a referee between competing interests.

Both elite and pluralist theories are based on an analysis of the United States. They both assume that the US is the 'good society in action' and that there is a common set of values in existence. They differ because elitists see democracy as a sham, with a powerful state used for sectional interests, while pluralists see the state as a neutral arena for decision-making, which binds the whole society together.

STATE-CENTRED INFLUENCED

POST-MODERN INFLUENCED

FUNCTIONALIST INFLUENCED

6. GLOBALISATION AND NATIONALISM

GLOBALISATION AND GOVERANCE

- As economic and environmental problems have become international, nations have increasingly pooled sovereignty to resolve them.
- Increase in the number of intergovernmental organisations, for example NATO, and the EU.
- Growth in world organisations such as the United Nations and the World Trade Organisation.
- World organisations are increasingly taking the lead in solving global political problems.
- Internationally recognised standards of behaviour, such as the Convention on Human Rights, are increasingly incorporated in the laws of nation-states.
- A new 'Cosmopolitan Order' is being created in which no nation has sole jurisdiction over its territory.
- Democratic ideas are being adopted everywhere.
- Growth of the 'cyberstate', in which commercial enterprises, connected by electronic means, are the future world order.

GLOBALISATION AND THE NATION-STATE

- Growth of 'trans-national practices' such as electronic financial dealings, make it difficult for governments to control economies.
- Environmental problems transcend national boundaries and make it difficult for one nation to protect its citizens.
- Global migration has decreased the uniformity of national populations.
- National identities have been undermined by growth of trans-national and regional identities.
- Political decisions are increasingly taken internationally rather than with the nation-state, e.g. the Kosovo situation.
- Activity centrally associated with the nation-state is given over to international structures, e.g. the unified military commands of NATO.
- Individuals are destabilised in a global culture and assert their identity in terms of common humanity.
- Free movement of ideas undermines the 'imagined community' of the nation-state.

Arguments and evidence for globalisation

✓ Electronic communications have increased the flow of information across the globe.

✓ Time and space restrictions on political action have been dissolved as mass communications have become instantaneous.

✓ Nation-states look to international legal systems to arbitrate in situations of dispute.

✓ Political disputes between nations are carried on in front of a world media and care is taken to present a case in a quarrel to the world community.

✓ Ideas of liberal democracy are triumphant everywhere.

Arguments and evidence against globalisation

✗ Extent of globalisation has been overstated.

✗ Global processes have always gone on, such as imperialism.

✗ Global interaction on a large scale is not a recent phenomenon, but the results of long-term historical processes.

✗ Pace of transactions may have increased but this does not create a completely new situation.

✗ Parts of the world remain relatively untouched by global processes.

✗ There has been an increase in the number of nation-states following the collapse of communism.

✗ Areas such as the Balkans demonstrate the continued strength of national feelings.

Conclusion

While the pace of global change has quickened and there has been increasing global political action, the case for globalisation is not yet proven. While many events would support globalisation, fragmentation and localisation can also be evidence against globalisation. Political action has become multi-layered rather than just located at the level of the nation-state. Those layers would include global, regional and local dimensions.

11. CHANGES IN VOTING BEHAVIOUR POST-1979

CONFLICT THEORY

Approach
- Changes in economy important.
- New divisions in society.
- Sectoral cleavages appear.
- New forces of identity emerge.
- Public/private sector split.
- Regional splits.
- Ideological hegemony strong.
- Interests a central concept.

Strengths
- ✓ Recognises new social divisions emerging
- ✓ Retains importance of economic change
- ✓ Retains central role for ideology
- ✓ Establishes north-south divide
- ✓ Links new cleavages to class but recognises their autonomy and potential for division
- ✓ Stresses political policies such as council house sales

Weaknesses
- ✗ Based on 1980s analysis and success of Thatcherism
- ✗ Does not identify the relative importance of new sectoral divisions
- ✗ 1997 election creates difficulty for theory, because of Labour's victory in the South
- ✗ Not clear how identity links to vote for a party

DEALIGNMENT THEORY

Approach
- That the link between class and voting has dissolved, as affluence has increased.
- That there has been a weakening of commitment to specific parties, as political awareness has increased.
- Growth of media and education has made voters more critical of parties.
- Communal bases of class solidarity have been eroded by economic change.
- Increased volatility results from the decline of class and partisan alignment.

Strengths
- ✓ Accounts for recent psephological history
- ✓ Long-term view of voting behaviour
- ✓ Based on analysis of structural and attitudinal changes in GB since 1945
- ✓ Attuned to the zeitgeist of the late 20th century
- ✓ Based on 'end of ideology' theory
- ✓ Links with theories such as convergence, embourgeoisement and post-industrial society

Weaknesses
- ✗ Traditional partisanship never existed anyway
- ✗ Unconditional loyalty of past was a calculation of interest
- ✗ Degree of vote-switching between elections is exaggerated
- ✗ Serves an ideological purpose in seeing class as unimportant
- ✗ Bedrock votes still large

CHANGES TO VOTING BEHAVIOUR WHICH NEED EXPLAINING

Decline of political identification – voters no longer associate strongly with one political party or see themselves as 'Labour' or 'Tory'.

Decline in class as indicator of voting behaviour – electorate less likely to vote along class lines or in class interest.

Greater volatility of voting – voters are much more likely to change votes between elections, so that there is a decline in 'bedrock' support for the two main parties.

Growth in third party support as, successively, the Liberals, the SDP, the Liberal Democrats, the SNP and Plaid Cymru gain support. The share of vote going to Labour and Tory decreases nationally and large swings are recorded at by-elections and in local councils.

Rise of 'frustrated instrumentalism' – voters more likely to vote against a party, than for one.

Increase in sectional influences on vote, such as gender, public sector/private sector etc.

INTERACTIONIST INFLUENCED

Approach
- That politics more important than social class in voting behaviour.
- Class dealignment has not happened.
- Partisan dealignment happens as both main parties lose 'natural' supporters.
- Changes in occupational structure leads to fall in Labour bedrock vote.
- Voters can be moved by ideologies as well as practical instrumental reasons.
- Labour up to 1997 and Tories after were politically unpopular.

Strengths
- ✓ Retains idea that social class is important in influencing votes
- ✓ Stresses political campaigns and ideas as important influences
- ✓ Takes into account some structural changes
- ✓ But focuses on the voters' meanings and intentions rather than social forces
- ✓ Tries not to impose meanings onto voters
- ✓ Does not have a 'model' of society which forces people into false political allegiances

Weaknesses
- ✗ Underplays the importance of structural factors
- ✗ Overemphasises importance of political campaigns
- ✗ Tends to an ahistorical approach
- ✗ Tries to be all things to all people
- ✗ Views voters as both rational and ideologically loyal, but does not explore the balance between them
- ✗ Dismisses income as factor

RATIONAL CHOICE THEORY

Approach
- Consumer model of voting.
- Self-interest main motivation.
- Party loyalty is conditional.
- Voters vote for perceived interest.
- Based on 'clusters' of values.
- Three main clusters – liberal, authoritarian and radical.
- Rational choice.

Strengths
- ✓ Emphasises individual motivation in making choice
- ✓ Makes calculation of interest central to voting
- ✓ Analyses values of individuals and connection to political parties
- ✓ Argues for political campaigning as important process
- ✓ Sees tactical voting as a means of voters making choices

Weaknesses
- ✗ Gives too much rationality to voters
- ✗ Reduces political campaigns to shopping expeditions
- ✗ Dismisses important social factors such as family and socialisation
- ✗ Parties are not just interested in attracting consumers, but have ideological dimension
- ✗ Underplays the resilience of class attitudes
- ✗ Underestimates effect of inequality
- ✗ Leads to spin doctors as central players in politics

12. NEW SOCIAL MOVEMENTS

	OLD SOCIAL MOVEMENTS		NEW SOCIAL MOVEMENTS	
Characteristics	• Also known as 'pressure' or 'interest' groups. • Often based on class or occupational interests. • Concerned with single issues. • Seek to influence political decision-makers through campaigning activity, either aimed at the government or at the public. • Use a variety of techniques to achieve aims. • Media are central focus of their activities. • Attack the state over economic inequality, class struggle and fairness.		• Associated with the rise of new divisions in post-industrial society. • Reflect the interests and identity of groups organised outside of traditional class divisions and who represent challenges to the social order. • Not based on ideologies of class. • Less concerned with material issues; focus on issues of identity and style. • Concerned primarily with individual and group autonomy from the state.	
Categories	**Protective pressure groups** defend the economic and status interests of their members, often against other OSMs.	**Promotional pressure groups** try to change the circumstances they are concerned with, in a positive way.	**Defensive groups**: rights movements seek to establish and defend the rights of sectional interests, human and non-human.	**Offensive groups**: political movements focus on national and international issues, with aim of asserting autonomy for group.
Examples	• Trade unions • Professional associations	• Campaign for Nuclear Disarmament • Greenpeace	• Women, black and gay movements • Environmentalist	• Self-determination movements (Kosovo) • Peace campaigns

> In practice, it is often difficult to distinguish between these categories, both within OSMs and NSMs and between them.

ISSUES TO DO WITH OSMS	ISSUES TO DO WITH NSMS
Role of pressure groups • Number has greatly increased since WW2 • Single issue groups have been largely unsuccessful • Attempts to influence focused on the state • Entryism to political parties failed • Protective groups have more formal relation to government than promotional	**Role of NSMs** • Seen as fundamental challenge to industrialism and militarism • Represent the new politics of identity • Organise groups previously unorganised • Aim to achieve social transformation • Bring the global to the local
Relationship to democracy • Channel political protest in positive way • Act as information givers to government • Important aspect of representation • Provide vehicle for political activity between elections • Can be cutting edge opinion-formers	**Relationship to democracy** • Reflect fragmentation of society and politics • Represent traditionalist sections of society who feel threatened (defensive NSMs) • Represent those who want radical transformation of society towards greater autonomy (offensive NSMs) • Struggle for minority rights
Criticisms of OSMs ✗ Are inherently unrepresentative ✗ Rich OSMs are more influential than the poor ✗ They reflect class differences in membership ✗ Many groups unrepresented by OSMs ✗ Largely uninfluential ✗ Act as a safety valve rather than achieve things	**Criticisms of NSMs** ✗ Often presented as inevitable development – (determinism) ✗ NSMs are not uniform, but diverse in ideology, aims and organisational capability ✗ Too narrow in their composition for effective change ✗ Much activity tries to counter opposing NSMs

THEORETICAL ISSUES – WHY HAVE NSMS EMERGED?

Post-industrial society	Critical theory	Post-modernism
As material needs are satisfied by capitalism, people turn to non-material issues in a post-materialist culture. Here, issues of identity and belonging are more important than 'bread-and-butter' issues. The emergence of NSMs reflects the new economies of a globalised society, which seeks to effect large-scale change through local actions.	The dominance of a commercial attitude, in which everything including relationships is reduced to a commodity, creates a yearning for an authentic identity, behind the false needs of capitalism. The 'commodification of the socio-cultural life-world' is responded to by the emergence of NSMs concerned with the intimate and immediate questions of identity and belonging. They thus represent 'real needs'.	The failure of the Welfare State to offer security in a 'Risk Society' has led to a DIY culture, in which individuals select aspects of identity and consumption with which they wish to identify. NSMs are no more than an expression of individual choice in a consumerist society.

> N.B. Critics argue that NSMs are not coherent enough to pose a threat to the state and class is still the most important factor.

13. URBAN DISORDER

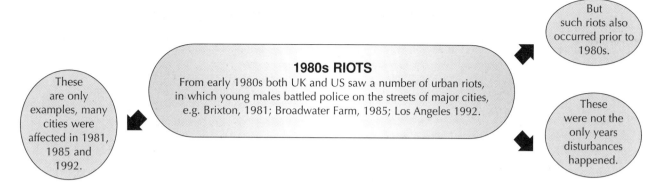

1980s RIOTS
From early 1980s both UK and US saw a number of urban riots, in which young males battled police on the streets of major cities, e.g. Brixton, 1981; Broadwater Farm, 1985; Los Angeles 1992.

These are only examples, many cities were affected in 1981, 1985 and 1992.

But such riots also occurred prior to 1980s.

These were not the only years disturbances happened.

COMMON FEATURES OF RIOTS

1. Though location of centre of riots might differ (inner city or outlying estate) all were areas of high unemployment and deprivation during the recession years of the 1980s and 1990s.
2. Often, but not exclusively, riots involved ethnic minority youths. There was an ethnic dimension to unrest, particularly in US, less so in UK.
3. Conflict with police was major factor in unrest, both leading up to and during the riots.
4. Exclusion issues (both ethnic and non-ethnic) were prominent (e.g. changes in gendered nature of work meant many males excluded from gainful employment in these areas).

DIFFERENCES IN NATURE OF RIOTS (JANOWITZ)

Communal Riots	Commodity Riots
Clashes between rival groups over 'ownership' of urban spaces, often ethnically based and featuring 'white backlash' against expansion of minority areas.	Symbolically represent collective resentment at exclusion from mainstream society, involving bouts of looting and all ethnic groups who are excluded.

LIFE-CYCLE OF THE COMMODITY RIOT

Triggering incident, often involving conflict with police

Crowd develops, tension mounts, police stoned

In extremes, arson and sniping at police follows, until control restored

Windows broken, control breaks down, looting shops

EXPLANATIONS OF URBAN RIOTS

Underlying social conditions	Official explanations	Participant explanations
1. Decline of urban conditions in 1980s, under impact of welfare retreatism, worsened position of already marginalised groups.	1. Scarman Report reported on insecurity and impoverishment of young people in affected areas. They shared aspirations of mainstream but not the means to achieve security.	1. Rioters often seek to explain actions to legitimate them, in terms of injustice and unfairness. Often blame police for precipitating actions by heavy-handedness or discriminatory practice.
2. Concentration of deprivation and greater inequality in specific areas heightens potential for disorder.	2. Copy-catting through media reporting explained spread of riots throughout British cities as young people jumped on rioting band-wagon (but not all of them?).	2. Police and media deny role of grievances in riots, but attribute them to extremists or looters manipulating people for own political or material ends.
3. Leads to 'urban social movements' (Castells) of protest, often disorganised and based on 'consumer' issues.		

14. THE THIRD WAY?

TRADITIONAL CONCEPTIONS OF POLITICS

Support for capitalism (Conservative)		Support for socialism (Old Labour)	
• Free market economy • Lack of regulation of industry • Minimalist state • Free flows of capital • Anti-trade union • Strong defence • Traditional family values • Hostility to public services • Low taxation regime	• Tough on crime • Hostile to welfare • No dependency culture • Nation-state • Loyalty to Crown • NATO • EU as trading organisation • Anti-devolution • Strong local goverment	• State intervention in economy • Regulation of industry • Maximalist state • Exchange controls • Trade union rights • Hostile to defence industry • More permissive attitudes • Hostility to private sector • High taxation regime	• Liberal on crime • Pro-welfare • Equality • Internationalism • Ambivalence to Crown • Ambivalence to NATO • Hostile to EU • Anti-devolution • Strong local government

GIDDENS (1997) AND THE RADICAL CENTRE

Challenges which face late-modern societies	Traditional ideas which no longer meet these challenges
• Globalisation of the economy, so that nation-states can no longer determine their own future path in the world. • A new individualism, in which welfare has removed many of the economic uncertainties of the past. • Changing nature of the family and individual identity, which are more a matter of choice than tradition. • Environmental problems, which cannot be contained within national boundaries, but have international effects.	• The Left–Right division over distribution no longer applies as political issues transcend this dichotomy. • The collectivist response to issues is no longer appropriate with the triumph of the new individualism. • Nuclear family and conceptions of the individual, which are inappropriate where many forms exist. • Faith in science as a solution to problems dissolves as scientists disagree fundamentally on causes and solutions.

COMMUNITARIANISM

Communitarianism rejects the neo-liberalism associated with Thatcherism and the collectivist state-directed socialism of Old Labour. Communitarianism calls for a restoration of a moral community in society, in which individuals commit themselves to intermediary structures such as the local community, the family and school. It rejects the idea that 'there is no such thing as society', but also stresses individual responsibility, rather than the rights of the individual. A central idea is that of 'social inclusion', in which each individual is encouraged to take part in the welfare of everyone, through work and active citizenship. There is an acceptance of the importance of capitalism, but communitarianism seeks to move beyond the amoral concern with the individual at the expense of society and to re-engage citizens with the social. Third way politics is thus concerned with managing the challenges of late modern capitalism, while retaining a concern with social justice and social cohesion.

Key concepts of the Third Way	Key policies of the Third Way
• Social exclusion • Welfare to work • Tough on the causes of crime • No rights without responsibilities • Positive welfare	• Education and Health Action Zones • 'Education, Education, Education' • Retraining programmes for unemployed • Remove right to jury trial for some cases • Target benefits on needy and stamp out fraud

Criticisms of the Third Way

✗ New Labour has moved to the right and stolen many Thatcherite policies	✗ Hostile to non-traditional families
✗ New Labour has not moved far enough and 'high tax' Labour is still there	✗ Hostile to claimants
✗ Extent of globalisation has been much exaggerated	✗ More to do with spin than reality
✗ Moralistic and victim-blaming approach to social problems	✗ Third way is 'no way'

15. DEMOCRACY

VERSIONS OF DEMOCRACY

Emphasis on	Rule of the people	Rule by the people	Rule for the people
Type of democracy	Direct (participatory) democracy	Representative democracy	Communist democracy
Description	Participation by all eligible individuals in decision-making in a public assembly of citizens	Citizens elect MPs from a selection of parties to represent their views in decision-making	Comrades vote for delegates from a one-party list to toe the party line in Congress
Examples	Classical Athens	Great Britain	Soviet Union
Claimed advantages	✓ Everyone gets a say ✓ Policy reflects majority opinion ✓ Encourages loyalty to the state ✓ Public discussions	✓ Fair and open system ✓ Creates strong government ✓ Citizens feel involved ✓ Politics done by 'experts'	✓ Eliminates bourgeoisie ✓ Strong government ✓ Party vanguard rules ✓ 'Expressive' of workers
Problems	✗ Easily manipulated ✗ Not all inhabitants eligible ✗ Can lead to anarchy ✗ Conflict leads to division	✗ Uninvolved between elections ✗ Parties more important ✗ 'Elective dictatorship' ✗ Open to corruption	✗ Not truly democratic ✗ Cronyism ✗ New party elite ✗ Little loyalty to state

THEORIES OF DEMOCRACY

	Classical democratic theory	Democratic elitism	Group theory of democracy
Description	An idealistic view of democracy, it argues that there is no such thing as 'real' democracy existing in the world, but that people should continually strive to achieve it. Basic premise is that democratic control should extend as far as possible to all social areas, and in particular to economic enterprises. Only by workers controlling their workplaces can real democracy be established.	A realist view of democracy, it argues that elections are where different elites compete for the people's vote. Democracy is thus a limited arrangement to allow the intermittent involvement of the people in the political process. Democracy is defined as a method not as an ideal or a principle to keep the people quiet.	A functional view of democracy, it argues that democratic participation is most likely in groups which stand between the soulless, remote state and the individual. Thus, democracy exists where intermediate groups such as family, factory or community are strong.
Origin	Influenced by Marxist, radical and conflict theory, and strongly by idealism, it appears most strongly in liberation struggles.	Influenced by classical elite theories, it appears most strongly in authoritarian societies.	Influenced by pluralist and functionalist theories, it is strongest in the US.
Problems	✗ Too idealistic to be achievable ✗ Owners never give up power to workers ✗ People too busy to control ✗ Can be manipulated	✗ Too elitist to be democratic ✗ Dismisses interest of masses ✗ Patronising ✗ Conspiracy theory	✗ Has never existed anywhere ✗ Pessimistic view of state ✗ Optimistic view of groups ✗ Used to support fascism

Marxist critique of democracy
Democracy is a sham, designed to pull the wool over the people's eyes and give them the semblance of control. The reality is that powerful economic forces manipulate the democratic system for their own ends. Behind the façade of democratic rule, the ruling class control the system through manipulation of the media and by force if necessary. A main tactic is the use of the media to create false consciousness amongst workers, to create the illusion of control.

THE PROBLEMS AND THE IDEAL

Real gains have been made in pushing forward democratic control of society and this process is the result of struggle by the masses. While not perfect, the promise of democracy is one that people are prepared to die for in conflict with oppressive and authoritarian forces.

Elitist critique of democracy
All systems, whether formally democratic or not, are controlled by a small group in the key institutional positions of society. Their internal lines of communication and location within the institutions of power enable them to manipulate the masses and ensure that the system operates to their advantage. A main tactic is to prevent issues that might benefit workers ever being raised in the first place (third face of power).

16. DEVELOPMENTS AROUND THE TURN OF THE TWENTIETH CENTURY

DEVELOPMENTS IN THE CONCEPTION OF POWER

The disciplinary society

Societies have developed new ways of organising and controlling their populations to avoid the use of coercion. The growth of disciplinary regimes in specialist institutions has acted as a model for the spread of power into everyday life, in a mundane and barely noticed way. Science has been an important aspect of the growth of 'capillary power' as it classifies populations into categories, so that they are more easily controlled. Ultimately, individuals act as if they were always being watched by those in authority – a system of self-surveillance.

Implication: individuals are subject to increasing powerlessness as they limit their own actions.
Critique: the processes of self-surveillance in everyday life are not made clear.

Language and power

Language itself is seen as an important aspect of power, as individuals engage in 'language-games' as they interact with each other. Institutions shape and thus limit the way individuals are able to exercise language power, by defining what is acceptable through the establishment of discourse.

Implication: all interactions are exchanges of power, with individuals constantly seeking to gain advantage over others through their language games.
Critique: offers a very cynical view of human interactions, dismissing altruism as ultimately selfish.

Knowledge as power

Knowledge has been reduced to the condition of a commodity. Its relation to truth has been dissolved, because meta-narratives no longer hold in post-modern conditions. What becomes defined as knowledge is a product of the exercise as power, because to control knowledge is to control resources.

Implication: controlling knowledge gives an individual power, so that education is a key social process for the creation and possession of wealth.
Critique: religious and other meta-narratives continue to survive and thrive in post-modernity.

DEVELOPMENTS IN THE CONCEPT OF CITIZENSHIP

Traditional concepts of citizenship have been concerned with the balance of rights and obligations that the citizen owes to the political unit of which she or he is a member. This is complicated in the case of Great Britain as the inhabitants are technically subjects of the Crown rather than citizens of the country.

As subjects of the Crown, individuals owe an absolute duty of obedience to the Monarch, and any rights are given at the pleasure of the ruler. The emphasis is thus on *individual duty*.

During the 20th century, individual rights were established in law, which established expectations for the citizen to receive a certain amount of security within a state. These rights were increasingly defined by international standards of human rights and were greatly influenced by the horrors of the Holocaust, where the state systematically slaughtered its citizens who were deemed hostile to the state. The emphasis became one of *rights*.

In reaction to what was seen as a 'whinger's culture', in which citizens loudly claimed their rights but gave up any responsibility, the New Right in the 1980s promoted the idea of the 'active citizen'. This was a citizen who was engaged with the community and offered something back to society rather than just taking from it. The emphasis returned to *duty*.

With the advent of the Labour government in the 1990s, a new conception of citizenship was advanced – that is, that citizenship had to be learned (in school mainly) and consisted of a balance of rights and responsibilities. This was a vision of the 'stake-holder society', in which citizens were active with others because they felt a part of society and were not marginalised from it. This was an attempt to strike a *balance between rights and obligations*.

> This debate is important because it attempts to explore the connection between society and the individual.

DEVELOPMENTS IN CONCEPTIONS OF THE STATE

A non-democratic future?

The growing autonomy of the state

As the state continues to grow it increasingly takes on importance as an institution, independent of other social groups in society.
It develops interests of its own, and, as the most powerful institution, is able to defend those interests against the encroachment of others.

Implication: 'Rule by the people' no longer has any reality.
Critique: the state does have limits, legal and moral, on the exercise of power in democracies.

The growth of 'the silent minorities'

As the power of the state increases, the majority of people become disillusioned and uninterested in party politics. Powerless to change things, they turn away from power and participating in political processes.

Implication: political participation will continue to decline.
Critique: on important political questions, the electorate does turn out and vote in large numbers.

The state in decline

The growth of New Right ideas

New Right ideology provides the framework for the politics of the 1990s, with its view that the growth of the state has led to the creation of 'welfare dependency', so that democracies can no longer afford the cost of the welfare burden being raised through taxes.

Implication: the state should be cut back to its minimum function.
Critique: abandoning the welfare state serves the interest of the rich against the poor and represents an ideological movement.

The growth of post-modern ideas

As the nation-state is increasingly constrained by global events, the ability of any single state to control its citizens' destinies is limited. As such, Western capitalism is reverting to political arrangements reminiscent of medieval times.

Implication: the legitimacy of the state as a protector of the people will be weakened.
Critique: the extent of global influences is exaggerated – societies are internationalising, not globalising, with the state still powerful.

DEVELOPMENTS IN SOCIOLOGICAL THEORY OF POLITICS: POST-MODERNISM

Post-modernism offers a contrast to modernity. Modernity is seen as characterised by certainty, science and the search for fundamental truth and unity. Post-modernity is seen as uncertain, fractured and rejecting of all ideologies or anything which suggests an underlying truth.

Post-modern politics	Criticisms of post-modern politics
Features of post-modern politics	
✓ A complex pluralistic democracy exists in which no group holds power.	✗ Power still retained mainly by a small group of society.
✓ A rejection of the politics of totalities, in which the state or ethnic group is seen as the focus of loyalty for the citizens. Rather, difference is celebrated.	✗ The state claims powerful loyalty from those it seeks to include, for example, Serbia in the 1990s claimed a 'totality' over all Serbs.
✓ A rejection of the role of the state as protecting 'us' from 'them'.	✗ Ethnic and other differences are still important, e.g. Israel and the Arabs.
✓ No strong centralised state.	✗ State still very strong.
✓ Importance of the politics of identity and the privileging of ethnicity.	✗ Class politics is still important, not just ethnic identity.
✓ Politics is made by individuals and not imposed upon them.	✗ Institutions can still impinge on individual decisions, e.g. road-building.
✓ Risk becomes a central political issue, e.g. over-exposure to BSE or GM crops.	✗ We no longer trust the experts who establish the discourses of risk.
✓ Individuals make political decisions, not on basis of knowledge, but on trust.	✗ Usually we are let down!

10 Religion

1. BELIEF SYSTEMS – RELIGION, SCIENCE, AND MAGIC

A belief system refers to ideas which we hold to be right and true; those ideas offer guidelines on behaviour and justifcations for that behaviour. Three factors interact to maintain that belief system (Polyani, 1958):
1. A 'circularity of ideas' where every single idea is explained in relation to another within the same system. If an idea or belief is challenged, it is defended by reference to another idea or belief.
2. Supporting explanations for difficult situations; if an idea is seen not to work, there will be a reason to explain it (this is the case with anomalies in science which are initially rejected).
3. No alternative belief system is acceptable. A Marxist would not accept any other proposition to explain social inequalities.

LINKS BETWEEN RELIGION, SCIENCE, AND MAGIC AS DIFFERENT VARIETIES OF BELIEF SYSTEM

Religion	Science	Magic
• Differences between exclusivist and inclusivist definitions. • Definitions which make explicit reference to god/s or supranatural beings are *exclusivist* definitions, e.g. used by Wilson (1966). • Those who speak of belief, but without reference to god/s are *inclusivist*, e.g. as used by Durkheim. Can include belief systems such as psychoanalysis, Buddhism, positive thinking and even communism. • Berger (1969): religion forms a 'sacred canopy' – an overarching framework of meanings that gives special significance to the social world.	• **Positivists**: Science is based on the application of theory to phenomena. Hunches and assumptions are tested under controlled conditions using the hypothetico-deductive methodology. Objectivity of scientist; discovery of laws governing natural phenomena (Popper, 1959). • Kuhn (1962) sees community of scientists as less than objective with their use of paradigmatic science as 'normal science'. Anomalies eventually are taken seriously and an anomic state of uncertainty arises until revolutionary science takes over which eventually becomes normal science, and the process starts again. ✓ So science has characteristics of a belief system.	• Magic is the belief that it is possible to influence events through the use of potions and rituals. It has no church and no collective ceremonies binding populations together. There may be some rituals, but they are not all-encompassing and are often practised by individuals. • People may turn to magic to change their luck or to take revenge on someone who has harmed them. • Azande of Sudan had widespread belief in magic and the poison oracle. However, high status individuals (the princes) were exempt from accusations of magic and each had their own oracle.
Types of religions	**Scientific realists**	**Science and magic**
Supernaturalism – found in small, pre-literate societies; a force that can be part of an individual like hunting skills. *Animism* – spirits which reside in people or natural objects. *Totemism* – reveres totemic objects, and often symbolises clans. In our society, flags and football emblems may become totemic. *Theism* – belief in god/s who intervene in individuals' lives. Can be monotheistic (one god) or polytheistic (several gods), as were the religions of ancient Greece and Rome.	✓ Pose a challenge to earlier positivists by emphasising need to examine surface and underlying realities of society. ✓ Opposed to 'empiricism' which is not based on theoretical frameworks, but purely on empirical observations. ✓ They require construction of models which take into account observable phenomena together with underlying generative mechanisms. ✓ Differ from interpretivists by emphasis on deeper structures.	• Levi-Strauss (1962) argued that there are links between scientific thought and so-called 'primitive thought'. • Both are based on deep structures, classification systems and are characterised by forms of rationality. • Levi-Strauss challenges Malinowski (1954) on totemism as he says it uses the same categories of thought as modern individuals. 'Savage mind' uses vast complex classificatory system. Telling of myths shows use of technique of analogy.

DEFINITIONS

2. RELIGION AS A CONSERVATIVE FORCE

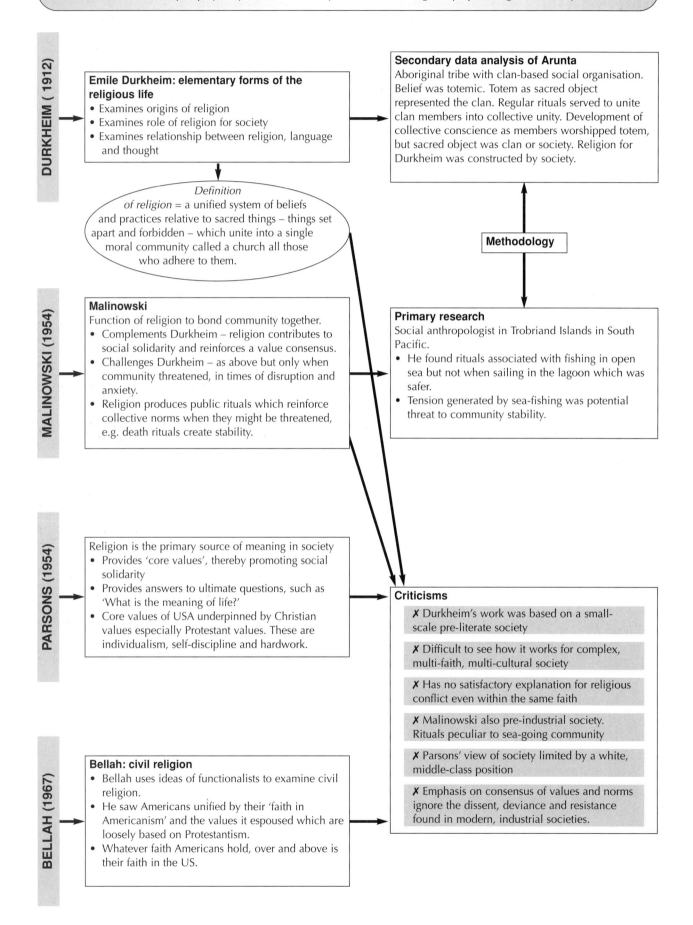

FUNCTIONALISM
A function is the part played by an element of a system in maintaining and perpetuating the whole system.

DURKHEIM (1912)

Emile Durkheim: elementary forms of the religious life
- Examines origins of religion
- Examines role of religion for society
- Examines relationship between religion, language and thought

Definition of religion = a unified system of beliefs and practices relative to sacred things – things set apart and forbidden – which unite into a single moral community called a church all those who adhere to them.

Secondary data analysis of Arunta
Aboriginal tribe with clan-based social organisation. Belief was totemic. Totem as sacred object represented the clan. Regular rituals served to unite clan members into collective unity. Development of collective conscience as members worshipped totem, but sacred object was clan or society. Religion for Durkheim was constructed by society.

Methodology

MALINOWSKI (1954)

Malinowski
Function of religion to bond community together.
- Complements Durkheim – religion contributes to social solidarity and reinforces a value consensus.
- Challenges Durkheim – as above but only when community threatened, in times of disruption and anxiety.
- Religion produces public rituals which reinforce collective norms when they might be threatened, e.g. death rituals create stability.

Primary research
Social anthropologist in Trobriand Islands in South Pacific.
- He found rituals associated with fishing in open sea but not when sailing in the lagoon which was safer.
- Tension generated by sea-fishing was potential threat to community stability.

PARSONS (1954)

Religion is the primary source of meaning in society
- Provides 'core values', thereby promoting social solidarity
- Provides answers to ultimate questions, such as 'What is the meaning of life?'
- Core values of USA underpinned by Christian values especially Protestant values. These are individualism, self-discipline and hardwork.

Criticisms

✗ Durkheim's work was based on a small-scale pre-literate society

✗ Difficult to see how it works for complex, multi-faith, multi-cultural society

✗ Has no satisfactory explanation for religious conflict even within the same faith

✗ Malinowski also pre-industrial society. Rituals peculiar to sea-going community

✗ Parsons' view of society limited by a white, middle-class position

✗ Emphasis on consensus of values and norms ignore the dissent, deviance and resistance found in modern, industrial societies.

BELLAH (1967)

Bellah: civil religion
- Bellah uses ideas of functionalists to examine civil religion.
- He saw Americans unified by their 'faith in Americanism' and the values it espoused which are loosely based on Protestantism.
- Whatever faith Americans hold, over and above is their faith in the US.

3. RELIGION AS A CONSERVATIVE FORCE: MARXISM

CLASSICAL MARXISM	NEO-MARXISM
• Religion closely linked to alienation: 'it is the sigh of the oppressed creature, the sentiment of a heartless world and the soul of soulless conditions'. • Religion acts as a social opium – it is a form of self-delusion that obscures reality and offers temporary comfort from the oppression within capitalism. • Provides hope of life hereafter for those suffering in this world, but hides the real causes of their suffering. • Prevents any revolutionary spirit because people threatened with eternal damnation. It is therefore, an important social control agent. • Traditional religious thought was simply a distortion of real class relations dividing people. Therefore, it had an important ideological function.	• Neo-Marxists take a materialist position common to traditional Marxists, but are often more interested in cultural struggle and the role of ideology. Maduro (1982) sees religion having relative autonomy from economic base. • Turner sees strong links with the economy and religion, but is more interested in the ways religion controls sexuality, especially as it relates to inheritance of property and property rights. • Under feudalism, religion played an important role for ruling class. The legitimation of marriage ensured that inheritance was to legal heirs – primogeniture. Remaining sons might be sent to monasteries. • Turner argues that there are two ideological positions – for bourgeoisie and proletariat – so that each class is bonded together by a specific ideology producing individual class solidarity.

Criticisms

✗ **Even traditional views contentious** Engels (1984) himself saw early Christian sects as radical challenge to authority of Roman law. Also saw early Christianity as a form of early socialism even though it placed salvation after death not in this life.

✗ **No single or dominant ideology** Turner (1983) argues that there are two ideological positions – for bourgeoisie and proletariat – so that each class is bonded together by a specific ideology.

✗ **No single or dominant ideology** Assumption of a dominant ideology presumes people are easily manipulated and have no ability to reason for themselves.

Criticisms

✗ **Liberation theology** This shows that religion can act for change of a radical and political kind as with radical movements in Nicaragua, but theory still credits mass of population with little independent action.

✗ **Rise of Islamic fundamentalism** challenges idea of religion as non-change agent. Although Islamic fundamentalism revolutionised societies some observers see it as repressive and reactionary.

✗ Little evidence to show that working-class have ever been especially religious in UK and thus have not been duped by religion.

Strengths

✓ Important links made between infrastructure and superstructure and nature of legitimation.

✓ Evidence in support:

• Caste system legitimated social stratification within Hindu society.
• In USA today, the New Christian Right are a large movement supporting reactionary legislation; but they are opposed to divorce law reform, women's rights for abortion, gay rights etc.
• Also, in Latin America Roman Catholic church supports right-wing regimes.

Strengths

✓ Links with important movements of underprivileged groups like Martin Luther King's movement and civil rights legislation.

✓ Sometimes revolutionary movements use religion to gain support. To be successful the people need:

• to be religious
• the religion has to be capable of being turned against the powerful
• clergy and revolutionaries need to have close contact.

4. RELIGION AS AN AGENT FOR SOCIAL CHANGE

THE PROTESTANT ETHIC AND THE SPIRIT OF CAPITALISM

- In this study Weber demonstrates that religion has relative autonomy from the economic base.
- His work has been taken to show that religion can influence social change.

Weber uses **Verstehen sociology** – what was it like to be a Calvinist? Weber uses *interpretive understanding*. He takes the imagined position of the Calvinist.

- He produces an historical analysis of the development of Western capitalism.
- Accepts Marx's main arguments, but emphasises the rationality of this form of capitalism which separates it from other forms.
- He sees this as emerging from a particular type of Protestant belief – Calvinism – as in countries which demonstrated Western capitalism the entrepreneurs and skilled artisans were Calvinists.

What is the 'spirit of capitalism?'
The pursuit of profit and forever renewed profit, together with the application of calculation and rational book-keeping.

What are the characteristics of Calvinism?
1. Predestination with no possibility of discovering whether they were saved.
2. A transcendental god who was incapable of being understood by mere humans.
3. Work was a 'calling' and had to be done for the greater glory of God.
4. Life was to be simple and ascetic. No frivolity or pleasure, no conspicuous consumption, as wasting money and time meant a challenge to God.

- So Weber links a particular kind of religious belief with a type of economic behaviour.
- The link is not causal, but an 'elective affinity' – it is this point which has given rise to criticisms against Weber as historians assume he was demonstrating causality.

Criticisms

✗ Sombart (1907) criticised the historical validity of Weber's description of the values of the Calvinists.

✗ Some critics show that not all countries that were Calvinist developed a system of Western capitalism. For example, Switzerland, Hungary, Scotland and part of Holland.

✗ Kautsky (1953) argued that capitalism preceded Calvinism not the other way around. He said that the successful capitalists used Calvinism and Protestantism to justify their social positions.

Counter arguments

✓ Weber argued that rationality was an unintended consequence of a set of religious ideas.

✓ Although some Calvinist countries did not develop Western capitalism, it does not lead us to reject the argument as Weber argued that there was no necessary relationship between the two – every society would have to be analysed empirically.

✓ There is an ongoing debate between supporters and challengers as to whether Protestantism or capitalism developed first.

Application of Protestant ethic

There are two main areas to which the Protestant ethic can be applied in contemporary society:

- *Public sphere* – work and workaholics. Increased pressure on professional and managerial workers to stay long hours at work, fearing being seen by bosses as shirking responsibilities if they arrive or leave on time. Also seen as a growing problem for professional women who wish to have children.
- *Private sphere* – sex and performance. Increased pressure on individuals to 'perform' and an industry of advisers and sex therapists can be called upon to help. Women's magazines emphasise the importance of sex at the expense of romance (Jones, 1996).

5. CHURCH, DENOMINATION, SECT, AND CULT

CHURCH: a large organisation where membership is ascribed. Sometimes closely related to the state, like the Roman Catholic church in the Middle Ages, it does not reject the wider society. In some societies it claims authority over the population, whereas in other countries it coexists with other faiths. Members tend to be conformists accepting the norms and values of society. Weber saw it as a 'trust foundation for supernatural ends'.

DENOMINATION: this organisation lies midway between the church and sect. Unlike the church it does not expect universal domination and can co-exist peacefully with other denominations and churches. Generally, members accept the wider society, but there is more emphasis on individual choice and consent. Usually membership is chosen by the individual and is a more personal phenomenon.

SECT: this is smaller than the first two, more personally focused and non-bureaucratic. Sects reject wider society and membership is chosen by adults. Each sect offers a personal path to salvation.

CULT: the smallest religious group, often seen as more radical than a sect but in reality difficult to distinguish. Sometimes linked to quasi-religious groups such as believers in UFOs. There may be no commitment demands on members so likely to be short-lived.

RELIGIOUS ORGANISATIONS (IDEAL TYPES)

Characteristics	Church	Denomination	Sect	
Attitude to wider society	Domination: wants worldwide control	Compromise with society and makes no attempt at domination	Rejection of values and way of life	
Attitude of wider society	Fashionable, many members of elite groups belong	Fashionable or neglected	Ostracised – in some cases sects have been persecuted and forced into exile	**Ideal Types**
Attitude towards other religious groups	Intolerant, although increasingly have to accept them	Tolerant, usually have to co-exist with other religious organisations	Intolerant. They assume that only they have the true path to salvation	These are heuristic devices that can be used
Attitude towards members	Concentration on global domination not individuals	Ideological influence	Ideological and social influence over members	to measure the relevant
Type of membership	Obligatory, therefore large, ascribed	Voluntary, but often given at birth	Voluntary, but assumption that children will accept the faith	criteria of specific
Basis of membership	No membership requirements other than ritualistic ones	Loose formal membership requirements	Experiential and often very strict rules of commitment – ascetic	religious groups
Social background of members	All inclusive, but leaders are wealthy and powerful. Includes 'both the just and the unjust.'	Middle-class and some working-class	Typically deprived, but forms of relative deprivation can include middle classes	in order to see how far
Scope	International	International	Local, but some have much wider scope	they fit
Internal organisation	Bureaucratic	Bureaucratic	Often charismatic, problems arise when leader leaves/dies.	

Criticisms
✗ The criteria are not really suited to non-Christian faiths
✗ They do not fit all Christian organisations either
✗ There is no clear pattern to show how an organisation, such as a sect, moves to become a denomination or a church

6. SECTS AND CULTS

> **Reasons for the rise of sects (Weber):**
> - *Marginality* – generally arose from poor and disprivileged. The sect offers a *theodicy of disprivilege* which justifies its disadvantage in this world by offering honour and reward in the next.
> - *Relative deprivation* – this helps to explain the appeal to more privileged groups who may feel relative deprivation of a spiritual or ethical kind.
> - *Social change* – sects arise in times of rapid social change especially during high immigration, industrialisation.

	Wilson's Typology of types of sects (based on response of the New Religious Movement (NRM) to the world)	Wilson's Typology of characteristics of sects (based on central characteristics)
W I L S O N	1. *Conversionist:* evangelical/fundamentalists who see world as evil, therefore need to be saved. Examples: Pentecostals, Salvation Army, Charismatics. 2. *Revolutionist or Adventist:* they see the end of the world or a second coming. Tend to be millenarian so believe in Armageddon followed by the 'new' world. Examples: Jehovah's Witnesses, Mormons. 3. *Introversionist:* as name implies they withdraw from rest of society, usually form communities away from society where they live a life of spirituality. Examples: Amish, Mennonites. These groups are similar to the Utopian groups who also founded new communities often based on egalitarian principles. 4. *Manipulationist* or cults of success: they offer a set of secret teachings or ritual practices which will bring success in this world. Sometimes known as Gnostic because they provide a gnosis (arcane knowledge) to members. Examples: Scientologists, Rosicrucians. 5. *Thaumaturgical:* they offer 'miracles' or 'magical healing' from spiritual sources which are taught to members. Examples: Theosophy, Spiritualism. 6. *Reformist:* desire change in society, but not of a radical or revolutionary nature, may be close to Introversionists. Examples: Quakers.	1. *Voluntariness:* in the beginning membership was voluntary, although children are born into membership in many cases. 2. *Exclusivity:* based on membership being exclusive. Some sects require considerable individual allegiance and personal commitment. Often demonstrated by donation of material wealth. 3. *Merit:* some sects want evidence of commitment or spiritual experience for membership to be allowed to continue. Failure might mean expulsion, especially in the more strict sects. Commitment is more than just attendance at services. 4. *Self-identification:* this is even greater for sectarian membership as an individual is a sect member before anything else. Thus the sect members are admonished to live according to the rules of the sect and their conscience. Some restrict contact with non-members, even relatives. 5. *Elite status:* this means being one of the Elect or one of the Chosen. Gives enhanced personal status to individuals. 6. *Legitimation:* there are sets of ideological values which serve to legitimate and so maintain the life of the sect for its followers.

	Wallis's Typology of sects (based on sect's relationship with the rest of society)
W A L L I S	1. *World affirming:* these are often referred to as cults as they are not really organisations, but loose collections of like-thinking individuals. They may lack any theology, church or ritual. Not rejecting the values of the world they emphasise ways of gaining personal achievement and worldly success. Membership is not central to the life of the individual and does not impinge greatly on them. Examples: Transcendental Meditation, sannyasin (followers of Bhagwan Shree Rajneesh). 2. *World accommodating:* these accept the world, but tend to ignore it and concentrate on spiritual matters. Often splinter groups from established faiths, they seek to restore spiritual purity to religion. Members do not need to separate themselves from the rest of society to pursue their faith. Examples: Neo-Pentecostals who believe they have the gifts of the spirit such as speaking in tongues (glossolalia). 3. *World rejecting:* these groups reject the world as evil and corrupt. Commitment is strictly observed and devotees have to sever ties with family and friends. Some are millenarian and introversionist. Examples: People's Temple led by Jim Jones where some 900 followers took part in a mass 'suicide'. The Moonies also fit this category as do the Branch Davidians, led by David Koresh, and the Children of God, led by David Berg.

Criticisms

✗ As with all classifications they are categorisations not explanations

✗ They do not apply to non-Christian sects and can be accused of being ethnocentric

✗ The categories are not mutually exclusive so one organisation may fit several categories

✓ They allow us to see overlaps between Wilson's categories and those of Wallis so we can examine the appeal and relationship of these sects to society at the same time.

7. NEW SOCIAL MOVEMENT AND NEW RELIGIOUS MOVEMENTS

NEW SOCIAL MOVEMENTS (NSMS) DIVIDE INTO TWO DISTINCT GROUPS:

Social issue groups	Social values groups
These groups are sub-divided into two: 1. Those who defend the natural and social environment against threat. Issues include protection of rain forests, anti-nuclear power, etc. New Age travellers often associated with this group. 2. Those who are involved in promoting social and civil rights to disadvantaged groups. Among those groups would be the women's movement, gay and black rights groups.	• These groups usually propose an alternative set of values challenging the dominant order, which is seen as racist, patriarchal, materialist or technocratic. • The new values include active participation, personal development, collective responsibility = post-materialist values. ✗ However, some critics see them as hedonistic, irresponsible, subversive and repressive and too politically correct.
Organisational structure of NSMs: • Anti-hierarchical and anti-bureaucratic • Full membership participation	• Low levels of officialdom • Small scale and fragmentary

NEW RELIGIOUS MOVEMENTS (NRMS)

Social issue groups	Social values groups
• NSMs and (NRMs) have been seen as separate until recently. Eder (1990) argues for links between environmentalism and NRMs /'Green politics is possibly replacing socialism as the first genuinely modern form of religion.' • NRMs recurrent within history of Christianity – many are actually old RMs. • Wilson (1992) sees typical characteristics as: salvation, elitism and scepticism, mobility and therapy, fervour, discipline and rational organisation.	

Functions of NRMs
• *Integrative*: some sects and cults are seen as bringing alienated youth back into mainstream culture, often away from a drug-related culture.
• *Disintegrative*: break down norms and promote social change. Some cults have been perceived as dangerous and legal action has been taken against them, e.g. banning prominent Scientologists from entry into Britain.
• *Socio-cultural transformation*: during the 1960s, some commentators see the counter-culture potentially promoting peace and harmony.
• *Irrelevance*: marginality of NRMs and largely irrelevant to wider societal changes. Numbers are small and do not balance the declining numbers from the established churches.

Some sects and cults demonstrate that these functions may overlap or occur at different times in the lifecycle of NRMs. Some movements may be seen as important at one time in history, but lose their relevance as time goes by.

Formation of NRMs	Criticisms of NRMs
Two stages in formation: 1. production of new ideas 2. getting the new idea accepted. *Three Models of NRMs:* 1. psychopathology model (leaders have a mental illness of some description) 2. entrepreneur model (leaders desire to make money out of converts) 3. evolution model (cults evolve by the interactions of like-minded individuals).	✗ Politically often on the right ✗ Inward-looking ✗ Divisive of religion – can be seen as evidence of secularisation process ✗ Secretive ✗ More concerned with appearance than actual substance ✗ Can be seen as exploiting the vulnerable ✗ Recruitment tactics sometimes suspect (e.g. 'flirty fishing')

8. WOMEN AND FAITH

CHURCHES AND WOMEN
In 1991, in Britain and Northern Ireland, almost two-thirds of frequent (Christian) church attenders were women, but not until 1992, after considerable pressure, did the Church of England decide to ordain women, although they still cannot be bishops. Roman Catholic church still opposes ordination of women as priests.

(marginal letters: C H U R C H)

SECTS AND WOMEN
Weber saw reasons for appeal of religion to women → sects appeal to underprivileged and women are underprivileged in all societies. Participation gives women power and status.
Women have been involved in religious movements since the Middle Ages. In 19th century several sects were initiated by women: Madame Blavatsky and Annie Besant set up Theosophy; Ellen White set up the Seventh Day Adventists; Mary Baker Eddy founded Christian Science and the Fox sisters began the Spiritualist movement. Ann Lee founded the Shakers.

(marginal letters: S E C T)

NEW AGE AND WOMEN
This movement attracts more women than men. Bruce (1995) argues that it divides along gender lines as men are more attracted to parapsychology and esoteric knowledge whereas women are more interested in healing, alternative therapies and spirituality. This includes New Science which challenges conventional science and medicine, emphasising herbal and homoeopathic remedies for illness; New Ecology (linked with eco-feminism) concerned with green issues and animal rights, and New Spirituality which includes ideas on reincarnation, aromatherapy and massage.

(marginal letters: N E W A G E)

WOMEN AND ISLAM
Western view of women under Islam tends to be stereotypical or prejudicial. However, many Islamic scholars see Islam as egalitarian. Butler (1995) found approval from young Moslem women for their faith, specifically as a defining point for identity, but concern was expressed over patriarchal attitudes within the Islamic community. 'Cultures are man's invention.' Some saw Islamic communities in Britain as in process of change.

(marginal letters: I S L A M)

Women and social control
- Religion seen as a source of social opium to control women.
- Control over women's bodies by labelling some as deviant.
- Denying female sexuality as a threat to social order (seen as evil desire).
- Religion underpinned by patriarchal ideology especially· around the desirability of family.

Women and fundamentalism
Fundamentalism has negative effect on women, challenging new-found freedoms:
- Conservative fundamentalism asserts traditional social and religious values.
- Radical fundamentalism rejects corrupt forms of religion and wants to return to traditionalism.
- Role of women assumed to be familial – they play vital part in reproducing the moral and religious community – but this involves acceptance of patriarchal ideology.

FEMINISM AND FAITH

Familism and sexuality
- Simone de Beauvoir saw Christianity as oppressing women. The legitimation of marriage by the Church further subjected women to male domination.
- Feminism links familism, religion and the control of women's sexuality.
- Foucault argued that women's sexuality became an object of scientific (Freudian) investigation seen as being in need of control by men.

Women and the C of E
- Changes towards acceptance of female priests.
- Changes in liturgy towards more women-friendly language.

Witchcraft (can be adapted to take a feminist analysis)
- Medieval witch-hunts focused on marginalised women who were seen as a burden on villagers.
- Again seen as fear of female sexuality and power.
- Where women used healing and medicinal powers, they were scapegoated by new medical knowledge monopolised by men.

9. ETHNICITY AND FAITH

In a multi-faith society religion can serve several functions:

→ a support mechanism for those with a shared culture
→ a possible means of assimilation into society
→ cultural identity preserving value commitments and a sense of belonging.

✗ Much of early sociology of religion concentrated on Christian faith, so can be accused of ethnocentrism. Western societies have become increasingly multi-faith.

Christianity and ethnicity

→ Membership of Baptist and Pentecostal churches mainly African or Afro-Caribbean.
→ Evangelical churches are among the fastest growing denominations which have opened 1900 churches since 1980. Baptists have opened 439 and Pentecostalists 419. Unclear how many of these are ethnic minority churches.

Implications of a multi-faith society

- Relationship between religion and culture and identity. This has been researched, especially with identities of young Muslim women in UK and the place of Islam in the creation of their personal identity.
- Differential levels of commitment. Muslim, Hindu and Sikh communities are markedly more religious than host society.
- Possible that closer family and community bonds create social pressure to conform to faith.
- Assimilation and integration.
- Simple assimilation unlikely and far from inevitable, but integration may also generate hostilities.
- 'Culture clash' – dated term and relevance limited to possible conflict between laws and religious sensibilities.
- Some faiths may find the challenges from the newly-won freedoms for women and homosexuals difficult to embrace.
- Setting up of schools for Islamic children, especially girls, grounded in Islamic rather than secular education.
- Emphasis on pluralism, cultural and religious diversity. However, Fatwah against Salman Rushdie illustrates tensions which have emerged.
- Ecumenicalism – potential for association between the various faiths in the future.

NON-CHRISTIAN RELIGIONS

Judaism

→ Dates from 1000BC in the Middle-East.
→ Monotheistic and demands strict adherence to moral code.
→ In 1948 State of Israel declared, Judaism became official faith.
→ Holy Book is Torah which is interpreted by the Rabbi or religious leader.
→ Sabbath is kept holy.
→ In 1996 there were 350 synagogues in Britain, over half in London.
→ Population has remained fairly static since 1960s.

Islam

→ Belief in one god, Allah. Mohammed is the last and greatest prophet. Holy book is the Qur'an.
→ By 2000, Muslims will number more than Methodists and Baptists in combined membership.
→ Private Muslim schools are single-sex and provide an Islamic education mainly but not exclusively for girls.
→ In 1996 there were 600 mosques in Britain.

Sikhism

→ Sikh community well established by 1970.
→ Many Sikhs came from the Punjab, East Africa and other British colonies.
→ Approximately 400,000 Sikhs in UK.
→ Sikhs have ten spiritual masters led by Guru Nanak Dev.
→ Monotheistic, but one god called by many names.
→ Orthodox Sikhs wear 5 'K's – long hair, hair comb to symbolise spirituality, steel bracelet, long undergarment for modesty and a dagger to symbolise readiness to fight.

Buddhism, Confucianism, Taoism

→ Buddhism – objective of Buddhist to reach Nirvana by series of reincarnations. Major influence in Far East. China, Japan, Korea, Sri Lanka.
→ Confucianism – Chinese faith which follows teachings of Confucius. Based on inner harmony of nature and veneration of ancestors.
→ Taoism – stresses meditation and non-violence to attain higher life.

Hinduism

→ Polytheistic faith; belief in Dharma, a universal which applies to each individual's life-stage and status.
→ No single holy book but reliance on several religious sources. Belief in reincarnation.
→ Population in UK is 400,000 approx. of whom 70% are Gujarati.
→ In 1996 there were 120 temples in Britain.

10. RELIGION AND POLITICS

Functionalists and most Marxists argue that established religions are politically conservative and function to inhibit or block social change. However some movements have had considerable political significance. In fact there are similarities between political and religious ideologies:
- both require adherence to a set of beliefs
- both serve to justify the interests of some groups over others.

CHURCHES AND POLITICS

→ Christian and Muslim churches have tended to support the establishment.
→ Churches are encouraged to play a conservative role to attract a large congregation so glossing over internal conflicts within their community.
→ Church's role to maintain stability largely hidden except in times of crisis (as Tsar Nicholas II was supported by Russian Orthodox Church in 1917 during Russian Revolution).
→ Roman Catholic Church – traditionally opposed to liberal reforms (contraception, divorce, abortion) but Liberation Theology rose against right-wing governments in Latin America.

SECTS AND POLITICS

→ *Sects* generally oppose the state. Some can play active political role, others not. Wilson (1992) sees Conversionists as most involved with politics and Introversionists as least involved.
→ Not all sects involved in right-wing politics. *Methodism* has strong historical links with Socialism and the emergence of the Labour Party.
→ *Cargo Cults* in Melanesia and Polynesia were hostile to European colonialists. Many leaders who emerged within these Cargo Cults became important as political leaders during independence of the islands.
→ *Rastafarianism*, based on the teachings of Marcus Garvey, was also opposed to colonial rule. Emphasis on black homeland of Ethiopia, not West Indies. Babylon (oppressive, white society and its institutions) will one day be overthrown and black population will become truly liberated.
→ *Black Civil Rights Movement* in USA in 1960s was supported by ideology of Martin Luther King and Black Power Movement supported by Malcolm X and the Black Muslims.
→ *Televangelists* in USA – popular and politically conservative. Active in 1970s and supportive of Reaganite politics in 1980s.

RELIGION, POLITICS AND NATIONALISM

→ *Northern Ireland* is clear example of religion and nationalism being linked. The Catholic faith has traditionally been Republican or Irish Nationalist, while Protestantism is linked with Loyalist politics and Great Britain.
→ *Poland:* many Poles remained loyal to Catholicism throughout communism as they saw it as part of their national identity. This link to Catholicism was particularly noticeable when Pope John Paul II, a Polish cardinal, was appointed in 1978.
→ *C of E and the Establishment.* The Anglican Church is the established church in England and the head is the reigning monarch of the time. This dates back to Henry VII who had set up a national Anglican church by 1536 thus denying the Pope any power over Church of England. There are bishops who sit in the House of Lords which gives weight to political pronouncements of the church. Some may be critical of the state (e. g. *Faith in the City* 1985 which highlighted the problems of the inner cities and angered Margaret Thatcher's government). At any national event of state significance such as Memorial Sunday we can see the ranks of the Establishment together, the Royal Family, representatives of parliament, leaders of the armed services and heads of the church.

CIVIL RELIGION

→ 'Civil religion' refers to non-religious events which generate loyalty and express a national sentiment in similar ways to religious ceremonies. Used by Bellah (1967) in examining American society. Shared traditions such as Thanksgiving, although not specifically religious, draws allegiance from Americans as it is traditional and unify the nation.
→ Even international sports events such as the Olympic Games and the World Cup can be seen to do this as fans pledge allegiance to their national teams.

11. SECULARISATION 1

INDICATORS OF SECULARISATION AND ASSOCIATED PROBLEMS

Definitions of secularisation	Problems and issues
• *Decline of religion:* where the previously accepted beliefs, rituals and practices lose their symbolic significance.	✗ From what date can such a decline be measured? Wilson sees it as 19th century, but we could start in 16th or even 4th century BC.
• *Conformity with this world:* where the orientation of new religious movements become oriented to this world rather than the next, e.g. manipulationist sects.	✗ This is very difficult to measure and to date – similar to the criticism above.
• *Disengagement:* the established church loses its prominence and its place *vis-à-vis* the state. Other social institutions take over the previous functions of the church such as social services and media.	✗ This is slightly easier to measure. It is possible to examine the place of religion in political life; how much religious practice takes place in schools; how far has social welfare taken over church social work.
• *Transposition of religious beliefs and institutions:* where what was regarded as grounded in divine power becomes seen as the creation of individuals.	✗ Again it is difficult to demonstrate that secular belief systems actually derived from religious beliefs.
• *Desacrilisation of the world:* where scientific and rational explanations take precedence over religious faith. This includes the rise of rationality, the development of an anti-emotional logical ethic and the rise of science and technology.	✗ There is little evidence that individuals give up religious thinking completely, e.g. the rise in alternative therapies like Feng Shui and the subterranean theologies such as superstition, belief in UFOs etc.
• *From a sacred to a secular society:* where a society moves from reliance on religion in promoting social solidarity towards a more complex situation where religion takes a place in a competitive market of beliefs and ideas.	✗ This is the modernity thesis that as societies progress the need for religious thinking lessens. Fundamentalism in USA and Iran has been a major challenge to this argument.

These are the categories created by Shiner (1967) and other sociologists of religion have used others. To simplify the debate which is probably one of the most complex of all sociological debates, we could divide the factors into objective and subjective factors. **Objective factors** are those which are capable of being measured; **subjective factors** relate to the beliefs individuals may hold in what may be seen as a 'secular' society.

Objective factors
• Religious participation – statistics for USA and UK • Disengagement – church and state relationship • Structural differentiation – changed functions • Religious pluralism – place of church against competing ideas, faiths etc. • Fundamentalism – a challenge to decline?

Subjective factors
Secularisation of consciousness • religion in the personal sphere • religion as a commodity • New Age faiths

12. SECULARISATION 2

MODERNITY AND SECULARISATION

Early theorists like Comte, Durkheim, Marx and Weber predicted that religion would inevitably decline as the process of modernisation got underway and societies would come to depend more and more on scientific and rational explanations at the expense of religious explanations.

The debate about secularisation is ongoing. Some sociologists see it as the most significant development in the sociology of religion while others see it as an illusion or a myth. Wilson and Bruce support the thesis; Hadden, Stark, Martin all oppose it.

SIGNIFICANT FACTORS IN THE DEBATE

Religion:

to make sense of secularisation, we need to decide what definition of religion is being used.

✔ An exclusivist definition will link with secularisation as it focuses upon belief in god/s.

✗ However, an inclusivist definition which includes all kinds of belief systems under religion, will not link so easily to secularisation as alternatives will replace religion.

Context:

✔ Different countries demonstrate different levels of participation.

✔ In USA attendance at church is high, in UK it's low, but each may mean secularisation is occurring.

✗ Little evidence of secularisation outside the Western world; focus mainly on Europe.

✗ Islamic countries show the highest level of participation and commitment to faith.

✗ New Religious Movements (see **Religion 7**)

- Wilson sees them as marginal, ephemeral and trivial in relation to individuals.
- Numerically they do not account for decline from established churches, although they may affect small number of people deeply.
- New Age movement seen as more of pastime or hobby than serious religious commitment.

✗ Fundamentalism (see **Religion 13**)

A major threat to the thesis:
- it demonstrates deep (increasing?) religious commitment
- it is embedded in traditionalism rather than modernism
- it has taken hold in societies which were seen as previously secular or secularising.

✗ Conclusions (difficult to make as so many different threads)

- Multi-faith society like UK has to encompass different levels of commitment and participation.
- Public and personal spheres are very separate.
- Science cannot answer questions of ultimate meaning – individuals without faith send 'arrow prayers' at times of anxiety.
- Religion as a commodity among many others – people shop for God.
- Post-modernism – place of religion may be part of personal identity make-up. A matter of choice.

Problem of individual faith

✗ Strength of belief hard to determine.

✗ May be formal adherence rather than personal commitment.

✗ Challenge from scientific belief.

13. FUNDAMENTALISM

A **fundamentalist movement** is one that challenges progress and refers its adherents back to the original scriptures as Holy Writ. Fundamentalism has been evident within Christianity, Islam and Judaism.

CHARACTERISTICS OF FUNDAMENTALISM
- Emerges out of traditional cultures which have been undisturbed for many generations.
- Threats to the faith generate insecurity which may be addressed by a specific leader.
- Group reactions make use of selective retrieval of evidence from scriptures – which gives authority to the new position.
- An 'us and them' mentality develops.
- Even though set against modernity, fundamentalism often utilises modern technology.

NEW CHRISTIAN RIGHT (NCR) – USA
- This has been highly significant in American politics, especially during Reagan's presidential term of office.
- Some commentators were concerned at the number of millenarians who were given high office during the 1980s. Although nothing seems to have developed as a result of this, it was thought that belief in the Second Coming would mean little emphasis on peace-keeping especially in the Middle East.
- NCR followers have been instrumental in challenging liberal reforms such as divorce legislation, abortion law reform, gay rights and civil liberties for black and other minority groups.
- It was not until 1967 that the Butler Act was repealed which forbade the teaching of evolution in place of the Creation story.
- The American Civil Liberties Union took the case to court on scientific grounds and won the case.
- NCR is politically very conservative and has developed as a result of several factors:
1. a perceived threat from federal government into local affairs bringing liberal ideas into traditionally conservative communities
2. increasing demand from minority groups for equal rights
3. economic rise of the southern states and increasing affluence of southerners
4. rise of the televangelists which helped to promote fundamentalist principles across the USA.
- Pray TV: religious channels prospered from the 1960s to the 1980s in the USA funded by evangelical sects, e.g. Pat Robertson's Christian Broadcasting Network. These channels spoke to previously marginalised groups. Preaching by TV pioneered psychological techniques of developing intimate relationships with audiences. Audiences have been estimated at around 15 million, but numbers declined in the 1980s with marked saturation. Sex and fraud scandals involving the leaders also affected audiences.
- 1990s have seen a revival in televangelism because of Internet communication and the continued personal appeal of the sects.

ISLAMIC FUNDAMENTALISM
- Shi'ism has been the official form of Islam since the 16th century. The 'Iranian Revolution', started in 1979, has been seen as a challenge to Western secularisation.
- Persia was a westernised state under the Shah who had introduced several liberal reforms including land reforms, emancipation of women and the introduction of secular education.
- In 1978/9 the Shah was deposed, exiled and an exiled priest living in Paris was called back to lead the new Iranian Islamic state. Led by Ayatollah Khomeini, the new state reversed the previous trend of liberalisation and reintroduced Islamic law according to the Qur'an.
- Educational segregation by gender became the norm and many women were punished for going out in public insufficiently veiled. Adulterers were to be stoned and practising homosexuals were to be executed.
- The fundamentalist process is still incomplete with conflicts continuing between Radicals, Conservatives and Pragmatists. The Radicals wish to export the revolution across the world; the Conservatives wish to concentrate the revolution within Iran, and the Pragmatists want to liberalise and open Iran to foreign investment and trade (Zubaida, 1996).

Salman Rushdie and the *Satanic Verses*
The book published in 1988 met criticism from British Muslims for blasphemy. Bhiku Parekh argued that the press created something of a moral panic over the book and exacerbated the Muslim response. In 1989 Ayatollah Khomeini imposed a fatwah on Rushdie, a death sentence to be carried out by any Muslim, which lasted for ten years.

Implications of fundamentalism
NCR and Islamic Fundamentalism demonstrate that there is no inevitability in the relationship between secularisation and an increasingly industrialised state.

14. RELIGION AND CIVIL RELIGION

Functionalists view religion as promoting social solidarity in society
BUT

✗ Solidarity argument seems to work best for small, less complex societies

✗ Today many societies are pluralistic = multi-faith, multi-ethnic, multi-cultural

✗ Religion may serve to provoke conflict, e.g. Northern Ireland, former Yugoslavia, Palestine and India

CONCEPT OF CIVIL RELIGION AS ALTERNATIVE?

Bellah (1965) used concept to apply to USA where different faiths held same 'secular' values, e.g. loyalty to nation-state, symbolic value of USA flag and national ceremonies like Fourth of July. **BUT** the concept may be no longer relevant. Examples of civil religion in Britain have been Coronations, Royal Anniversaries and Memorial days. Another recent example was the **death and funeral of Diana, Princess of Wales**. This was seen by many as a day of mourning where the whole nation was 'in grief'.

The way we structure experiences of grief and mourning are culturally specific, related to: 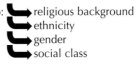 religious background
ethnicity
gender
social class

Factors affecting 'modern' grief and mourning
• Move towards a secular view of death
• Values of Protestant ethic
• Scientific explanations rather than religious ones
• Culture not religion shapes grieving process and dictates the nature of the loss
• Culture also dictates the opportunities for public mourning.

Media construction of grief
Some argue that the media manipulated the national sentiments at the time of Princess Diana's death, but others see the occasion as having taken even the media by surprise. There was almost blanket media coverage of her life and death – she became a public possession: 'the people's princess', and 'the queen of people's hearts'.

Public reaction – the death of an icon
• Untimeliness and unexpectedness added to tragedy.
• Diana's life followed avidly by journalists and paparazzi.
• Affirmation of belonging through shared sense of loss.
• Diana as 'ordinary' and 'extraordinary' in her many different roles.
• Post-modernist view of Diana as a 'hyperreal' persona created by the press and by her own manipulation of the press.
• A secular event transposed into the spiritual domain.

Personal reaction – death of a loved one
• Reaction affected by individual bereavement.
• An opportunity to grieve publicly over a personal loss.
• Fear of not being seen to share the grief demonstrated by others.
• A sense of 'being there' at a memorable media occasion.
• Some evidence that marginalised were deeply affected – ethnic minorities, gays, and women who saw Diana as having shared many of the emotional problems they had experienced.

Significance of Diana's funeral for religion
• Provided an opportunity to re-establish a sense of personal identity and belonging to community.
• Whether authentic or constructed, Diana's death connected her with millions of individuals at a level previously unimagined.
• That the funeral functioned as a civil religious event would be accepted by functionalist and Marxists and challenged by post-modernists. The debate remains open.

15. SYNOPTIC OVERVIEW

CULT	→	SECT	→	DENOMINATION	→	CHURCH	→	SECT	→	CULT

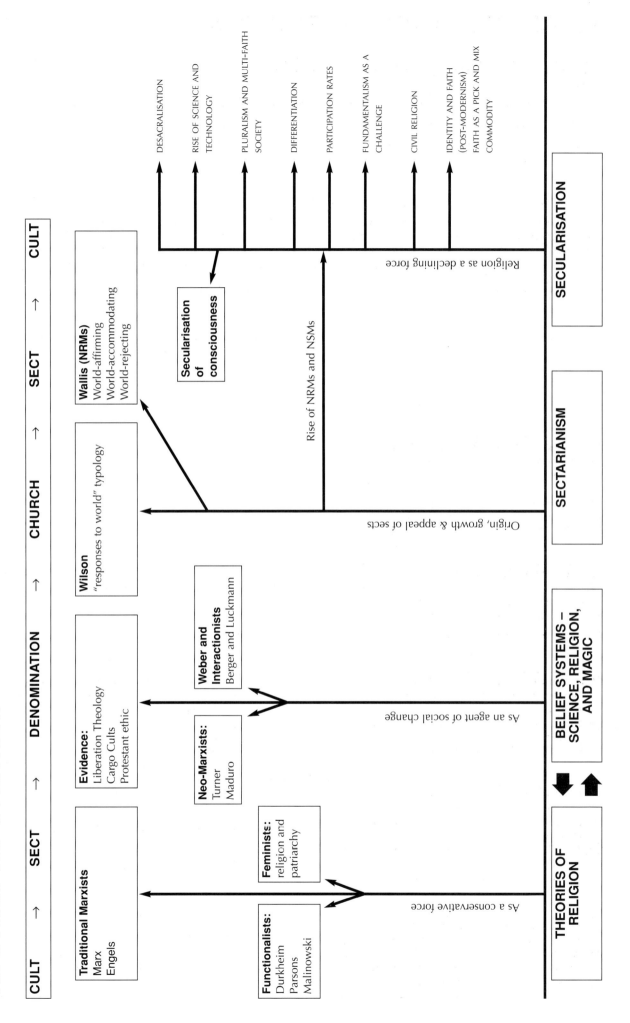

Traditional Marxists
Marx
Engels

Functionalists:
Durkheim
Parsons
Malinowski

Feminists:
religion and patriarchy

Neo-Marxists:
Turner
Maduro

Evidence:
Liberation Theology
Cargo Cults
Protestant ethic

Weber and Interactionists
Berger and Luckmann

Wilson
"responses to world" typology

Wallis (NRMs)
World-affirming
World-accommodating
World-rejecting

Secularisation of consciousness

As a conservative force

As an agent of social change

Origin, growth & appeal of sects

Rise of NRMs and NSMs

Religion as a declining force

DESACRALISATION

RISE OF SCIENCE AND TECHNOLOGY

PLURALISM AND MULTI-FAITH SOCIETY

DIFFERENTIATION

PARTICIPATION RATES

FUNDAMENTALISM AS A CHALLENGE

CIVIL RELIGION

IDENTITY AND FAITH (POST-MODERNISM)

FAITH AS A PICK AND MIX COMMODITY

THEORIES OF RELIGION

BELIEF SYSTEMS – SCIENCE, RELIGION, AND MAGIC

SECTARIANISM

SECULARISATION

11 World Sociology

1. CLASSICAL SOCIOLOGISTS AND THE GREAT TRANSFORMATION

THEORY OF CAPITALISM

Main Theorist	Karl Marx, writing in second half of 19th century
Others	Lenin, Saint-Simon, Bukharin
Description of Theory	Industrialisation is the product of historical forces, in which the struggle between social classes results in revolutionary change. The emergence of capitalism represents the highest achievement of humanity so far and is impelled by the search for maximum profit. Relationships between developed and less developed parts of the worlds are shaped by capitalist relations of production and the need for capitalism to secure raw materials and markets for the goods produced.
Positive developments in society	• Historic mission of capitalism to destroy feudalism throughout the world • Capitalism represents greater productivity and wealth for a small minority in society • Capitalism inevitably gives way to communism – 'from each according to ability, to each according to need', which represents highest achievement
Negative developments in society	• Intensification of exploitation by capitalist class leads to immiseration of proletariat • Development is uneven, both between social classes and parts of the world • Short-term suffering results as societies move from feudal to capitalist and capitalist to communist
Criticisms of theory	✗ Deterministic, seeing all societies moving towards a communist end-state ✗ Over-emphasises the importance of economics in the process of social change ✗ Ignores the role of individuals in the making of history, by emphasising structures ✗ Ignores differences between societies which might lead to different ways of progressing

THEORIES OF INDUSTRIAL SOCIETY

Main Theorist	Emile Durkheim, writing at start of 20th century	Max Weber, writing in early part of 20th century
Others	Herbert Spencer, Auguste Comte	Raymond Aron, David McLelland
Description of Theory	Industrialisation is the result of evolutionary change in society, in which social formations become ever more complex and productive. Progress is thus linear towards a fixed end-state that can be identified as Western societies, the most developed nations in the world. Less developed societies need to follow the example of the West if they are to make progress through industrialisation. The West represents the most advanced human society morally.	Industrialisation is the result of changing ideas and the choices made by individuals, represented by those Calvinists whose Protestant calling led to patterns of behaviour favourable to capital accumulation. Modern societies are thus characterised by increasing rationalisation and bureaucratisation, in which social life is increasingly subject to scientific processes. Less well developed societies need to cultivate certain attitudes in order to make progress.
Positive developments in society	• Complex division of labour enables a more productive economy in which all may share • Interdependence in society creates a mutuality on which solidarity and stability is based • Slow pace of change allows the preservation of the best of the past with the best of the future and allows the happiness of the greatest number	• Rationality allows for the scientific solution of social problems and economic prosperity • A more tolerant and liberal society is likely to result from the pluralism of modern living • Innovation – a central feature of industrialised societies – introduces new pleasures and experiences for the majority population
Negative developments in society	• Dislocation may occur as societies move towards the fixed end-state, leading to unrest • Possibility of state of anomie resulting from the destruction of traditional norms and communities • Acquisitive individualism may be over-dominant so that solidarity is undermined by selfish egoism	• Bureaucracy may result in an 'iron cage', which stifles individuality and innovation • Over-rational societies lose their 'myths, charm and poetry' and become less than human • Potential for control of individual heightened by products of industrialisation
Criticisms of theory	✗ Over-optimistic in its view of social development, seeing modern societies as 'good' ✗ Overestimates the destruction of traditional forms in society and ignores ability to adapt ✗ Ethnocentric view of the world seeing the West as the natural end-state for developing societies ✗ Plays down the different starting points for and varying cultures of societies that are industrialising, which means they end up different	✗ Overstresses the rationality of modern societies, ignoring many non-rational aspects that survive ✗ Overemphasises the importance of ideas in creating social change and ignores structural factors ✗ Gives primacy to religious ideas in creating development without showing if held strongly ✗ Underestimates the degree of individuality and freedom which developed societies offer their citizens, despite bureaucracies

Modernisation Theory
Neo-Liberal and New Right Theories
Social Action Theories

Dependency Theory
Under-development Theory
World Systems Theory

2. MODERNISATION THEORY

Unilinear and teleological theory – moving in one direction towards a fixed end-state, which is liberal capitalist democracy.

• Undeveloped • Mechanical solidarity • Gemeinschaft • Agriculture • Traditional authority	Is based on the contrast between sets of simplistic dualisms, in which undeveloped societies represent a lower state of civilisation. The theory assumes that, because developed societies have higher rates of production, they are 'superior' to less developed, who aspire to become like the developed.	• Developed • Organic solidarity • Gesellschaft • Industrial • Rational authority

Criticism of Structural–Functionalist Approach

✗ Dualisms too sharply drawn – developed societies retain many traditional features

✗ Economic development not always accompanied by democracy

✗ Was ethnocentric in view of undeveloped world as lacking in some respect

✗ Reduced development to simple technical problem, ignoring history

HISTORICAL CONTEXT
- Emerged from the success of the Marshall Plan after WW2, which successfully reconstructed countries of Western Europe as liberal democracies, industrialised and capitalist.
- Stood in contrast to the Soviet bloc during the Cold War of the 1950s to 1980s, which offered an alternative path to development to nations emerging from colonialism.
- Modernisation theory was tinged with ideological assumptions of capitalist and colonial ideology.

Criticisms of Rostow

✗ Transposes experience of US to the rest of the world

✗ Overemphasises economic factors and ignores political, moral and social forces

✗ Ignores historical context of undeveloped countries, who, unlike US, do have more developed economies to take account of

✗ Sees any alternative roads to development as pathological – that is leading to destruction

✗ Ignores trading arrangements of modern world which act against development

STRUCTURAL–FUNCTIONALIST EXPLANATIONS
- Associated with Parson (1966), and drawn from work of Radcliffe-Brown (1930) and Malinowski (1922), there was a strong concern for stability and integration.
- Assumption that economic development was inevitably associated with liberal political democracy.
- Was a deficit model of development, i.e. identify what the undeveloped world lacks, inject it and development would proceed.
- Based on traditional/modernity dichotomy.

 FEATURES

ROSTOW'S FIVE STAGES OF DEVELOPMENT (1963)
1. Traditional society – agricultural, low levels of technology.
2. Pre-conditions for take-off – reorganisation of agriculture, building infrastructures, accumulating surplus capital.
3. Take-off – technological developments in leading sectors, capital investment.
4. Maturity – diversification of industry, increasing investment.
5. Developed society – high consumption and growth of service sector.

MODERNISATION THEORY'S EXPLANATIONS FOR THIRD WORLD POVERTY

Too many people	Not enough capital	Too few entrepreneurs
Undeveloped societies' populations are increasing too fast so that funds for development are diverted into survival. Need for birth control programmes to limit growth.	Undeveloped societies do not produce enough surplus capital to fund their own development. Need investment by West to generate critical mass to take-off.	People in undeveloped countries lack sufficient enterprise to create sectors of development. Need to have a psychological boost of 'need-achievement' to take-off.
✗ Ignores fact that most consumption of resources carried out in West, not Third World.	✗ Bit like saying Third World is poor because it is poor – a tautology.	✗ Stereotypes of the 'lazy' colonial lie behind this, denying the hard work of Third World populations.

Criticisms of Modernisation theory as a whole

✗ Eurocentric, based on a colonial mythology, which is ultimately racist.

✗ Lumps all third world countries into the same category of 'undeveloped'.

✗ Ignores history of imperialism which shaped third world.

✗ Assumes that third world can just repeat the experience of West.

✗ Assumes that 'traditional' features of third world are natural and not imported by colonisers.

✗ Distorts the West's own history of development.

3. DEPENDENCY THEORY

Metropolis
Used to describe the outposts of developed societies in the under-developed world, usually found in cities.

REACTION AGAINST MODERNISATION THEORY, LED BY FRANK (1967)
Two basic differences:
1. Need to look at relationships between developed and undeveloped world, not just at national societies.
2. Lack of development in third world (TW) is not a natural state, but a product of relationships between developed and less developed societies.

Satellites
Used to describe the less developed parts of under-developed societies, usually found in agricultural hinterland.

UNDER-DEVELOPMENT

The central concept of Dependency theory, which describes the process whereby TW countries were systematically exploited by the imperial powers of the West, so that, not only were they prevented from industrialising to any significant degree, but also any advanced sectors of their economies were restricted and constrained. The result was that colonised countries were worse off in terms of development at the end of the imperial period. Moreover, this process of under-development continues through the way the relationships between the West and the poor countries of the world are organised. Lack of development is not an earlier stage of development but is the result of development in the First World (FW).

HOW IS UNDER-DEVELOPMENT ACHIEVED?

First World causes the decapitalisation of the poor countries of the world, as the former systematically arranges trading relationships in their own favour. The result is that capital is shifted from the TW to the FW, reducing the TW to satellite status, while retaining centres of the metropolis, usually in the capital cities and other quasi-industrial centres. Surplus from agricultural activity is attracted to the metropolitan centres and then expatriated to the FW, through the processes of trading.

THREE STAGES IN EXPLOITATION

Early colonialism
Expropriation by plunder – imperialists took what they wanted by force and sent it directly back to metropolis.

Settled colonialism
Expropriation by destruction of indigenous industry and forced acceptance of FW goods. Capital investment in infrastructure to ease exploitation.

Post-colonialism
Terms of trade favour the West, which uses aid as device for continued exploitation of TW. Capital investment is linked to ability to export profits directly back to FW.

End result of under-development is **DEPENDENCY**, that is the TW is made to be reliant on the FW for survival, in terms of industrial goods, for technologies (rarely the most advanced), for capital and for aid in times of crisis. Role of military and the ruling class in TW countries is important in defining the relationships between FW and TW.

Criticisms of Dependency theory

✗ Not clear what is actually meant by 'dependent'. E.g. Canada is dependent on US capital but is not a TW country.

✗ Assumes that there is a uniform pattern of dependency, when degree and form of dependence varies over time and between different countries.

✗ 'Balance of dependence' is not solely determined by economic relations, but by political events also.

✗ Implies that dependency is a permanent state, when history suggests that there can be development in TW societies.

✗ Ignores socialist exploitation of TW, by focusing on capitalism only.

✗ TW often accepts capitalist ideology willingly.

✗ Plays down role of FW in breaking down feudal relationships in TW and allowing capitalist penetration which does permit some development.

✗ Not clear how mechanism of under-development operates and surpluses expatriated.

Strengths of dependency theory

✓ Emphasises processes of trade and economics over political and ideological relationships.

✓ Recognises the legacy of colonialism and its impact on present relationships in the world.

✓ Avoids the optimistic conclusions of modernisation theory.

✓ Focuses on 'realpolitik' of relationships between TW and FW.

✓ Identifies the complexity of relations between FW and TW through recognising FW enclaves in the TW.

✓ Seeks a dynamic explanation of world relationships.

✓ Offers an historical overview of relationships between FW and TW.

✓ Based on realistic assessment of motivation of capitalist enterprises.

4. CONTEMPORARY THEORIES OF INDUSTRIAL SOCIETY

NEO-LIBERAL THEORY OF DEVELOPMENT
- Emerges from the writings of New Right theorists, influential in the governments of Thatcher and Reagan.
- Emphasises the primacy of the market in development policies, and argues against the role of government.
- Influential in international agencies concerned with development such as the World Bank and IMF.
- Points to the increased flow of private capital, especially banks, in the flow of funds to TW countries.
- Blockages to development result from government intervention (corruption and diverting funds).
- Development flows from opening up trade with other countries, not from any other government policy.

Critics of the New Right argue:
- ✗ No evidence that New Right solutions work
- ✗ Leads to great inequality in TW societies
- ✗ Free trade policies benefit FW, not TW

Neo-liberal theory (Lal) argues that
1. any barriers to trade, such as tariffs and protectionist policies, distort market prices, and lead to unproductive economic practices and higher prices
2. state intervention usually leads to monopolies and lack of competition, which also leads to higher prices
3. competition is central to development because it encourages innovation and leads to lower prices in the long run.

NEWLY INDUSTRIALISING COUNTRIES (NICS) PROVIDE MODELS
- Some TW countries provided a model for the development of the rest of the South, e.g. Tiger economies (Singapore, Hong Kong, South Korea, Taiwan).
- They had adopted sound economic policies that had liberalised trade and removed tariff barriers.
- They had reduced the role of government to ensuring a stable economic and political environment.
- They focused on Export-Oriented Industrialisation (EOI), that is, producing goods for the export market, which generated income from abroad for re-investment in industrial projects at home (Vidler).

Advantages of neo-liberal theory
- ✓ Seemed to lead to trouble-free development.
- ✓ Showed that development could take place in relationships with FW countries.
- ✓ Offered a model of development based on Japan rather than FW.
- ✓ Acknowledged that TW did not have to follow example of the West.
- ✓ Drew attention to blockages to development in TW countries themselves.
- ✓ Avoided distortions in markets due to government regulation of trade.

Criticisms of neo-liberal theory
- ✗ Based on low wage economies, so that exploitation of workers was main reason for success.
- ✗ Shift of production to TW meant loss of manufacturing jobs and lower worker wages in FW.
- ✗ Success often based on authoritarian anti-democratic regimes which, in long run, were unstable.
- ✗ Not every other society could copy the NICs as there was only so much trade possible in world.
- ✗ NICs face increasing global pressure to open up domestic markets to FW goods and face stiffening competition from more efficient FW production technologies.

THE CRASH
Over-extension in the NICs led to currency collapse and economic ruin for many Tiger economies in 1997. Political instability followed and subsequently renewed state intervention through global agencies.

5. NEW DEVELOPMENTS IN THEORY OF CAPITALIST SOCIETY

MAINSTREAM MARXISM

THEORY OF UNEQUAL EXCHANGE (KIDRON, 1975)
- Emerged from Dependency theory.
- Stressed that movement of capital to core countries occurred because of unequal trade relations.
- Meant that core goods sold for more than they should and periphery for less.
- Allowed higher wages in core than in periphery.
- Core working class, not periphery were most exploited, even though had higher wages, because they were more intensely exploited.

MODE OF PRODUCTION THEORY (LACLAU, 1971)
- Critical of Frank's emphasis on market relations.
- Same mode of production (capitalism) can be articulated (appear) in many forms.
- Thus diversity in global economy can be explained by different articulations to suit local conditions.
- x There are so many articulations as to make the idea of a single mode of production impossible.

HISTORICAL MISSION THEORY (WARREN, 1980)
- Capitalism is fulfilling its world role in destroying feudal relationships in periphery countries.

Marxist critiques
- x There is no necessary connection between development and under-development, or systems of global exploitation.
- x Development of core economies was not made possible by exploitation of the periphery, but by exploitation of its own proletariat.
- x Focusing on world systems ignores the importance of national class relations both core and periphery.

WORLD-SYSTEM THEORY (WALLERSTEIN, 1975)
- Grew out of, but in opposition to under-development theory of Frank.
- Like Frank, insists on long-term historical view of development.
- Unlike Frank, argues that there is a world economic system, which is independent of relations between nation-states.
- World divided by 1640 into core, semi-periphery and periphery states.
- Core countries have a global reach made possible by existence of a world economy.
- Stresses the primacy of ownership in establishing global reach.
- Division of labour should be seen as an international phenomenon.
- Semi-periphery are exploited and exploit, so preventing unity amongst the exploited.
- There is no such thing as 'national development' because progress is globally generated.
- However, integration of the local periphery economy into the world-system means that capital is 'patriated' to the core.
- Local accumulation of capital is difficult.
- United action by international working class is unlikely because of differences in conditions.
- Strength of the core arises from its ability to extract surplus value from the whole world economy, not just from semi-periphery and periphery states.
- Insistent that world-system exists as an independent social reality, which impinges on ability of individual nations to control their own destiny.

NEO-MARXISM

POST-MARXIST (LACLAU AND MOUFFE, 1985)
- Development emerges from radical democracies emerging in periphery.
- x Not precise about how radical democracies differ from liberal democracies.

MODES OF DOMINATION (MOUZELIS, 1986)
- Mainstream Marxism ignores role of military in many periphery countries.
- Military have own interests independent of capitalists.
- x Unclear what the relations between a mode of production and a mode of domination are.

REGULATION SCHOOL (LIPIETZ, 1987)
- To survive, capitalism has developed 'periphery Fordism' in relocating to cheaper wage economies of the South.
- x Fordism delivers high wages in North, so why not in the South?

Non-Marxist critiques
- x Category of 'semi-periphery' includes many different societies with little in common most of the time.
- x Is deterministic and ignores the part played by active human agents such as government personnel, entrepreneurs etc.
- x Ignores important cultural forces that influence development – Bauer (1991) of the New Right argues for ethnicity as a factor.
- x Implies that the core countries are a 'model' for development and that the periphery are somehow distortions of this model.

6. EDUCATION, ENVIRONMENT, AND DEVELOPMENT

EDUCATION

Education is seen as an aspect of development. Need for a highly skilled workforce identified as main factor in 'take-off'. Post-WW2, developing world placed many resources into education, building more schools, training more teachers and aiming to keep children in school longer with significant increases in numbers who went to university or higher education, especially vocational.

Functions of education in developing societies	Dysfunctions of education in developing societies
✓ To provide sufficient numbers of people with technical, managerial and entrepreneurial skills to assist the process of development.	✗ Growth in availability of education did not ensure quality, with great strain placed on existing systems.
✓ To instil appropriate attitudes and values among masses to assist development process.	✗ Curricula were not always appropriately balanced, with ideology often substituting for technical learning.
✓ To inculcate approved ideology of the newly independent states of the Third World.	✗ Poverty meant that those with most to gain were often absent because of domestic pressures or need to contribute to household upkeep.
✓ To assist nation-building in societies where there were often class, caste, ethnic and regional divisions.	✗ Financial costs to society of large population in school is enormous and comes under pressure in crisis.
	✗ Qualification inflation develops as more graduates are produced than can be employed in top jobs.

BUT **education** remains extremely popular amongst the people, because it opens up employment opportunities, allows migration away from tradition-bound environments, is a source of mobility, especially for women and other oppressed groups, and is often seen as a human right.

Effects of education on rural areas
- Critics of mass education argue that main effect is to draw the brightest and most entrepreneurial away from rural areas towards the cities and thus contribute to overurbanisation.
- Supporters say they often return to revitalise countryside.

Two perspectives on education and development
Human capital – sees investment in education as central to development, and an alternative to money capital.
Cultural imperialism – sees content of education as reinforcing imperial ideas of dependency.

ENVIRONMENT

Approaches to the environment and development

Neo-liberal approach	Environmental approach	Structuralist approach
Include costs to the environment in calculating benefits and losses of development.	Need radical rethink of what development is, to focus on small-scale improvements which don't harm environment.	Need to solve debt crisis of TW (result of structure of global economy), which is cause of environmental harm, because capitalism sets global agenda.
Criticisms	**Criticisms**	**Criticisms**
✗ It could be calculated that it was beneficial in money terms to pollute environment	✗ Small-scale change may not sustain population growth in TW	✗ Reduces cause of environmental harm to single factor – debt and global capitalism
✗ Societies which cost pollution will lose out in the market place to those who do not include pollution costs in production	✗ Tends to a minimalist and 'zero growth' option which does not meet aspirations of people	✗ Implies that, left to its own devices, TW would not pollute or deplete, but engage in sustainable development (see **World Sociology 15**)

Development and the environment issues

Traditional areas of concern			Problems with this focus
Deforestation of rain forest	Endangered species	Loss of usable land	Implies that most environmental damage is done by TW, in 'dash for growth', and ignores FW's contribution to global pollution problems.
Pesticide use	Drought	Pollution	

SUSTAINABLE DEVELOPMENT
Conflict between industrialisation and care of the environment seen as a natural outcome of the drive for growth in developing areas of the world. Population growth is seen as one of biggest threats to the environment in the Third World. Sustainable development seeks to meet the needs of the present population without degrading or depleting resources to the extent that future generations will suffer. Critics argue that this doesn't go much beyond a slogan, which does not really say how to achieve it.

7. WOMEN, HEALTH, AND DEVELOPMENT

WOMEN

Measures of gender inequality in development

Gender-related development index (GDI)	Gender empowerment Index (GEI)
Measures life expectancy, educational level, in terms of years in school, literacy level and income satisfaction, taking into account gender as a variable.	Measures levels of participation in decision-making, both political and economic, at both local and national levels.

Both attempt to quantify the differences between men and women, but whereas the GDI shows some improvement in satisfaction of basic economic and educational needs in many developing societies, the GEI indicates that there has been much less progress in the empowerment of women.

Issues of concern in gender and development

- Unequal levels of abortion of female foetuses
- Lower pay for female workers than for male counterparts
- Incidence of dowry deaths in traditional societies
- Unequal 'burden of development' falls on women
- Lower life expectancy in some countries, e.g. India and Pakistan
- Exploitation of female labour by FW corporations wanting docility

Burden of development

- ✗ Women work longer hours than men in developing world.
- ✗ Women continue to take major responsibility for raising family.
- ✗ Female children seen as source of income to family.

Advantages of development

- ✓ Improved educational levels.
- ✓ Greater potential for independence economically.
- ✓ In revolutionary societies women are equals in struggle.

Feminist perspectives on development

Radical feminist	Socialist feminist
Development reinforces patriarchal relations as FW companies reproduce traditional gender roles by employment policies. Any improvement in life of women because FW companies want productive workers.	Revolutionary political ideologies of socialism offer a way forward for women as they struggle with men to achieve justice and freedom. Improvements for women will emerge from class struggle.

HEALTH

Sources of threats to health of TW countries

1. Poverty – main reason for ill-health of citizens and early deaths.
2. Lack of knowledge – about health risks and sources of infection.
3. FW drug companies – using TW as dumping ground for less safe treatments and drugs controlled in FW, e.g. thalidomide.
4. Other FW companies – unsafe industrial operations allowed to continue, e.g. Bhopal disaster.
5. Lack of medical personnel, especially doctors and basic carers.

Perspectives on health and development

Modernisation theory (Rostow, 1963)	Marxist theory (Navarro, 1976)
Good health provision is a necessary part of development and a sign of a developed society. Importation of FW medical procedures is needed for a healthy workforce. So, the influence of FW medicine on TW is beneficial.	Too much attention is paid in TW to high-tech medical procedures and not enough to basic health provision. Too many TW doctors migrate to FW in search of better income and do not serve basic health needs of their countries.

Issues of concern in health and development

- Inequality of health provision between different parts of TW population.
- World-threatening diseases making first appearance in TW countries.
- Incidence of AIDS endemic in parts of Africa and other parts of the TW.
- Organs for sale for transplantation to FW recipients by TW citizens.
- Dumping of First World (FW) medicines on TW citizens, for profit.
- Inappropriate use of FW products by TW mothers (baby milk).

Health as an indicator of development

Examples of health indices

Several welfare indicators have been used, e.g. Morris's 'physical quality of life index (PQLI)', which included level of infant mortality and life expectancy, as well as level of literacy.

Advantages of using indices

- ✓ Reflect life-and-death factors
- ✓ Can be compared statistically across different countries
- ✓ Represent real factors in people's lives
- ✓ Reflect social not just economic reality

Disadvantages of using indices

- ✗ Narrow in their view of development
- ✗ Treat each indicator as having equal worth
- ✗ Ignore other important social indicators or society's well-being
- ✗ Not easy to collect accurate statistics in some countries

8. FROM RURAL TO URBAN – NATURAL HISTORY OF DEVELOPMENT

RURAL AREAS
Mistake to see rural areas as timeless and unchanging. Are subject to similar social and economic processes as urban areas. Rural areas are dynamic and changing.

Ways in which rural areas have changed

- Prior to WW2, land-owners rented out land to farmers. Post-WW2, land was bought up by those who farmed it. This can be seen as the 'capitalisation' of farming.
- Countryside has been protected from urban intrusion by law and planning regulations.
- Profit need has led to changing environment, e.g. disappearance of hedgerows.
- Lack of availability of affordable housing is biggest issue facing low-income farm workers.

- Rural areas integrated into mainstream society through social policies such as education, welfare state, health service etc.
- Countryside eroded by intrusion of motorway network and urban spill.
- Growth of agribusiness has undermined independent farmers and created uniformity in look of countryside.
- Loss of working population, especially young, to urban areas threatens long-term stability of rural areas.

Industrialisation and imperialism
Development of large concentrations of population speeded up by Industrial Revolution and demand for labour. Growth of imperial centres such as London (Metropolitan capital) were linked to development of colonial capitals and regional cities, especially ports in Empire. Growth fuelled by trade.

URBANISATION

Associated processes
1. De-urbanisation – loss of population from cities into rural areas
2. Suburbanisation – growth of outlying housing areas
3. New Town development – creation of new smaller urban spaces

Global cities
As cities grow and rural areas are squeezed, rural and urban towns merge and become like one location. 'Urban sprawl' means extension of size but retention of units within the larger location. With new technologies linking urban spaces electronically, Jonathan Friedman (1994) argues that there is only one world city which is the site of cultural, economic and political power. The 'command cities' are London, Tokyo and New York. Transnational Corporations (see **World Sociology 13**) are located there, if anywhere.

MEGALOPOLIS

SOCIAL PROCESS IN THE GROWTH OF CITIES

DECENTRALISATION

Reasons for decentralisation
1. Loss of urban employment, linked to decline of labour-intensive industries, accelerated by new technologies that make location less important in production.
2. Global competition in manufacturing puts premium on technology, not labour, for most productive output.
3. New transport facilities allowed increase in commuters, who can easily travel to work
4. Over-crowding and high land prices in cities supported flight to suburbs and new urban locations such as New Towns and Garden Cities

GENTRIFICATION
Seen as a part of the revitalisation of urban areas from 1980s onwards:
- Movement of affluent back to cities
- Usually associated with the regeneration of previously unpopular locations
- Often associated with private and public development of prized locations which had been in decline e.g. waterfronts, riversides etc.
- Refurbishments of older, larger properties, bought up cheaply.

  ✗ Often at expense of poorer inhabitants of location who are priced out of their homes.

  ✗ Creates two-tier society, with the rich living next to low wage workers who service their needs e.g. for cleaners.

Suburban and New Town myths

✗ That there was similar lifestyle in most suburbs – but Gans (1968) showed that there was a wide variety.

✗ That locality was key factor in determining lifestyle – but social class and stage in life-cycle were more important.

✗ That New Towns were overspill housing for all segments of the working class – but it was skilled workers who migrated to New Towns, leaving unskilled working-class in inner city areas (see **World Sociology 9**).

9. APPROACHES TO URBAN SOCIOLOGY

THEORIES OF URBAN DEVELOPMENT

	Description	Strengths	Weaknesses
Evolutionary approach	Cities develop in much the same way, as natural progression of society.	✓ Has dynamic view ✓ Emphasises gradual change	✗ Treats all cities as similar ✗ What is natural?
Restructuring capital	Firms seek to maximise profits by locating capital in most exploitable locations – sometimes cities, sometimes not. Workforce is factor.	✓ New spatial division of labour ✓ Accounts for differences between cities	✗ Treats workforce as all the same ✗ Firms not always located just for profit
Second-circuit theory	Land and buildings are seen as commodities. When capital is idle urban buildings are invested in, but they are 'let go' when capital is needed.	✓ Explains 'building booms' ✓ Has dynamic understanding	✗ Economic determinist ✗ Little supporting evidence
New international division of labour	Capitalist firms are able to divert capital to periphery where there is low-cost labour and weak unions.	✓ Global perspective on development ✓ Explains de-urbanisation	✗ Firms not as mobile as this ✗ Localities resist relocations
Californian School	Post-Fordism (see **Work, Organisations, and Leisure 4**) allows innovative products to be sub-contracted and production fragmented. This impacts on urban environment.	✓ Takes in technological developments ✓ Recognises post-modern condition	✗ Economically based – ignores social factors ✗ Ignores role of state

PERSPECTIVES ON URBAN ISSUES

	Description	Strengths	Weaknesses
Neo-Weberians	Rejected traditional conservative approach, in light of 'urban crisis'. Look to market and dynamics of capitalism to explain urban issues, such as housing. Examined role of planning as integral part of market.	✓ Overturned complacent view of urban issues ✓ Focused on practical issues such as housing ✓ Emphasised central role of law in regulating cities	✗ Did not take corporate interests into account ✗ Tends to deal with city in isolated fashion ✗ Could be vague on remedies for urban crisis
Neo-Marxists	Extends traditional Marxist concern with class conflict to examine other social group's struggles for social justice. This approach also called political economy.	✓ Avoided economic determinism of crude type ✓ Involved in empowerment politics ✓ Drew in new constituencies	✗ Often subordinated interests of minority groups to class interests ✗ Still economic determinist, giving primacy to ownership as factor in cities
New Right	Urban areas worked better if left to market forces. Public choice theory argued that public goods should be subject to same rational calculations as private goods. State should take back seat in planning and regulating cities.	✓ Attuned to anti-state feeling of 1980s ✓ Privileged individual in operation of cities ✓ Attacked welfarism as distortion of market ✓ Stressed rationality of public planning decisions	✗ Welfarism supported many poor families ✗ Ignores distortion of markets through inherited wealth ✗ Dismissed safety net which state provides for urban poor ✗ Too much faith in unfettered market

10. URBANISATION AND DEVELOPMENT

MODERNISATION THEORY

- Urbanisation – central process for development of economies.
- Cities represent nucleus for the cultural penetration of modernising elements.
- Key cultural values needed for development grow in cities.
- Development occurs when habits of cities diffuse outwards to the rural hinterland

Importance of urbanisation	Cultural values in rural and urban areas	
• Cities act as beacons for the rural population because they represent higher standard of living. • Cities offer opportunities to people, not available in countryside. • Cities exhibit a different 'spirit' to the traditional ways of rural areas.	**Countryside**	**Cities**
	Fatalism (acceptance) Home-centred action Particularism (family) Few contacts with outside	Activism (challenge) Career-oriented action Individualism (self) Media opens up rest of world

Modernising characteristics of cities (Hoselitz)	Key factor is that people in cities are 'open to innovation' compared to traditional lifestyle of rural areas.
• Universalism in occupational placement (not reliant on family to get jobs, but need qualifications). • Roles are highly specific and division of labour complex, so that people are mutually dependent. • Elites oriented towards economic goals rather than religious or social goals, i.e. non-traditional.	**Criticisms** ✗ Ethnocentric, based on view of FW cities ✗ Deterministic, seeing culture as only factor ✗ Not specified how diffusion from cities happens

URBAN–RURAL CONTINUUM

- Rural society is one type of lifestyle and urban society another.
- Development is shift from dominance of rural lifestyle to urban one.
- Proposes series of dualisms (mechanistic/organic solidarity, Gemeinschaft/Gesellschaft) in which 'developed' one of the pair mainly found in cities.
- Development can be measured by the degree to which society is urbanised by calculating the density of social relations in urban areas.

Strengths	Weaknesses
✓ Emphasises differences between city and rural living	✗ Is more descriptive than analytical about move to cities
✓ Focuses on social relations in cities, not just size	✗ Assumes that increasing concentration leads to urban way of life
✓ Draws on traditional notions of importance of cities in development process	✗ Ignores negative aspects of urban concentration

DUAL ECONOMY THESIS

- In TW, rural society is separate from urban centres.
- Rural areas inhabit different economic reality from urban centres, which are more technically advanced.
- Effectively two economies in TW societies – urban and rural with little connection between them.
- Caused by colonial policies that developed urban areas at expense of rural ones.

Strengths	Weaknesses
✓ Allows for separate analysis of urban and rural areas	✗ Unrealistic to separate out the urban areas
✓ Locates stage of development in history of colonialism	✗ Divides TW societies into progressive and backward sectors
✓ Recognises different problems in each	✗ Assumes cultural unity but economic difference as a norm of TW

DEPENDENCY THEORY

- Reality of TW cities not like model of modernisation theory.
- Impact of colonialism crucial to understanding TW cities.
- Crucial feature of TW cities is 'over-urbanisation'.

Life in TW Cities	Over-urbanisation
• Majority lead life of insecurity not opportunity. • Contain opposites of great wealth and poverty. • Defining feature of TW city is the 'barridos' (shanty towns). **Effects of colonialism on TW cities** • Many different types of city developed under colonialism. • Had 'settler' towns, administrative centres, commercial etc. • Cities isolated from surrounds seen as a 'home from home' by colonisers. • Urban development concentrated in port-based 'capitals'.	• Cities are vital link between FW and TW hinterland, acting as the metropolis outpost in the periphery. • Growth often result of forced migration of peasants. • Market of cities is overseas not local, so a 'comprador' bourgeoisie grows up with interests in FW. **Criticisms** ✗ Ignores local elites' desire for local control ✗ Role of cities in exploitation unclear ✗ Doesn't recognise advances made in TW city conditions

11. STRATEGIES FOR DEVELOPMENT

THEORIES OF INDUSTRIAL SOCIETY

'Injections' attempted

- Capital (often tied to individual projects)
- Need-achievement for entrepreneurial spirit through educational programmes
- Aid for infrastructure programmes, such as roads, dams, power projects
- Direct capital investment in TW enterprises, often in partnership with Trans-National Corporations
- Capital investment in agricultural programmes, such as cash crops, e.g. cocoa in Ghana
- Investment in 'Green Revolution', such as development of new strains of crops to produce larger yields (GM controversy).

Description of strategies	Strengths	Weaknesses
• Based on the idea that TW 'lacked' things which FW had to make them 'developed'. • Solution to TW lack of development was to 'inject' appropriate amounts of that which was lacking. • Crucial notion was 'development programme' involving international agencies like World Bank or individual donor countries of FW. • Concept of 'Aid' was therefore an important component of development.	✓ Drew on success of the post-war Marshall Plan that successfully regenerated European economies ✓ Offered straightforward solution to TW societies ✓ Emphasised relationships between TW and FW strategies for development ✓ Did have some success in some areas	✗ Economist in essence, seeing capital injection as trigger for development ✗ Social programmes (education) subordinated to economic targets ✗ Corruption of some TW elites who siphoned off capital into own pockets ✗ Development programmes geared to FW not TW needs ✗ Limited progress made

THEORIES OF CAPITALISM

'Go-it-alone' strategies attempted

- Building on traditional methods to push forward development (Tanzania's Pan-African socialism)
- Large-scale nationalisation of FW companies to control own economy, such as attempted by radical military regimes in Latin America
- Appropriation of indigenous capitalists assets to fund development, e.g. expulsion of Ugandan Asians
- Revolutionary seizure of power, such as Cuba or Nicaragua
- Cutting off ties with outside world, e.g. Communist Albania.

Description of strategies	Strengths	Weaknesses
• Based on idea that underdevelopment of TW is product of relations with FW. • Solution internally is for TW countries to make radical break with the past, finding own 'roads to development'. • Solution externally is to break off contact with exploiters of the capitalist FW and gain control over own destiny. • Build relationships with other TW countries to develop a 'third way'.	✓ Based on understanding economic relations between FW and TW ✓ Offered a 'third way' between capitalism and communism ✓ Appealed to nationalistic TW elites coming out of colonialism ✓ Land reform programmes popular amongst poorer sections ✓ Some progress made where own ideas pursued	✗ Land reform met massive resistance from the wealthy ✗ Implies violence as legitimate means to make progress ✗ Difficult for TW countries to isolate themselves in increasingly global economy ✗ Hostility of FW to 'revolutionary' schemes of development ✗ Essentially economist, ignoring political and ideological factors

Conclusion

Both strategies seem to have failed and the Newly Industrialising Countries offered alternative until their crash in the 1990s.

12. AID AND DEVELOPMENT

TYPES OF AID

Bilateral aid	Multilateral aid	Non-governmental aid
Direct contributions from a single country to another, often linked to treaties, both economic and political.	Indirect contributions through international organisations such as World Bank or IMF, mostly given as loans, not gifts	Often charitable, but sometimes individual donations, associated with relief for disaster or specific projects.

POSITIVE VIEW OF AID

Modernisation theorists see aid as central to development process, as a mechanism for providing TW with the capital they lack for infrastructure and other projects. Both grants or loans are seen positively because they provide what the TW lacks. Based on a deficit model of TW.

NEGATIVE VIEWS OF AID

Marxist perspective (Hayter, 1985)	Social Democratic perspective (Hartmann and Boyce, 1980)	New Right perspective (Bauer, 1971)
• Aid is a form of 'imperialism by the back door'. • Aid is used to dominate economic and political affairs of TW. • Aid does not help recipients as much as it helps FW sponsors, especially transnational corporations (TNCs). • Aid often linked to arms.	• Many aid projects focus on large-scale technological developments. • Does not take account of local needs and conditions. • Results in inappropriate projects which cause more harm than good. • Leads to inefficient deployment of resources.	Aid creates a dependency culture of TW on FW. Lack of capital result of TW rich not saving to invest but consuming. Aid subsidises this spending rather than development. Aid becomes seen as a 'right' when disaster falls, rather than a safety net, e.g. Montserrat.
Criticisms	**Criticisms**	**Criticisms**
✗ Ignores moral imperative of FW politicians to help poorest countries ✗ Ignores altruism of charitable campaigns	✗ Plays down beneficial effects of projects, e.g. High Aswan dam (Egypt) ✗ FW expertise important for development projects	✗ Ultimately a moral position based on pessimistic view of human nature ✗ Result is that poor suffer needlessly as aid is denied ✗ Ignores inequalities imposed by international finance system

PROBLEMS WITH AID DONATIONS

Problem	Solutions
1. Most aid is not 'free' or given as charity, but comes with various strings attached. In particular, majority of aid is in form of loans rather than gifts, and creates a burden of debt for many TW countries. Re-payments on these loans can absorb a good proportion of the GNP of the poorest countries.	• Reschedule TW debts, so that the burden on the poorest is eased BUT who decides on schedule? • Moratorium on debts to give breathing space to TW BUT for how long and with what purpose? • Debt cancellation to permanently relieve poor BUT would it encourage 'fecklessness'?
2. Most aid is tied to specific projects and comes with requirements which 'aid' the FW not the Third, e.g. recipients may be required to purchase donor country's goods, or use technical experts from donor countries rather than indigenous skilled labour.	• Repackage aid projects to encourage use of TW skilled labour BUT is this available? • Uncouple aid and purchasing requirements BUT would this reduce incentives for donors?
3. Aid is used as a political weapon by FW to encourage 'friendly' regimes, e.g. Cold War, when aid was given to authoritarian military regimes (in packages which included purchase of arms) if they were anti-Communist.	• Make aid independent of political relations BUT what would induce FW to contribute? • Give a 'moral dimension' to foreign and aid policies BUT difficult to maintain with *realpolitik*?
4. International agencies given great influence over domestic economic policies of recipients and have interests of 'shareholders' at heart, not TW poor, when imposing policies.	• No-strings' aid BUT would private and corporate donors give without some protection? • Give social dimension to imposed policies BUT agencies run by economists, not charity workers?

13. DEATH OF COMMUNISM / DEATH OF THE THIRD WORLD?

DEATH OF COMMUNISM

Consequences of death of Communism
1. Collapse of support for radical regimes, e.g. Libya, Cuba.
2. Undermining of socialism as alternative to capitalism.
3. Disintegration of countries into ethnic states.
4. Liberalisation of former Communist economies.
5. Hardship for people as societies transform.
6. Emergence of ethnic cleansing in Europe.

Problems faced by Communist societies

Economic	Political	Ethnic
• Agriculture in crisis as collectivisation not able to deliver stable supplies of food. • Heavy industry inefficient and subsidised. • Soviets had cosmonauts but queues for basic goods. • Growth in black economy (see Work and Leisure 2). • Guarantee of full employment meant overstaffing industry.	• Centralisation meant decision-making slow. • Cold War gave military great influence. • Gap between idea of proletarian plenty and empty shelves. • Demands for greater involvement of civil society in decision-making. • Glasnost and perestroika opened up space for political opposition.	• Resurgence in ethnic and religious identity. • Demands for autonomy on basis of culture, language, history or ethnicity. • Balkanisation of multi-ethnic states once control lifted. • Historical ethnic rivalries were suppressed not eliminated.

Importance of Communism in world sociology
• Represented an alternative model of development to newly independent countries of TW.
• Engaged in competition with capitalist West for global domination (Cold War).
• Ideological alternative to capitalism with stress on proletarian interests.
• Leading Communist country of Soviet Union dominated Eastern Europe.
• Soviet Union was nuclear power and influential in many parts of underdeveloped world.
• Operated a one-party state as opposed to pluralist democracies.

DEATH OF THIRD WORLD?

Definitions and problems
1. First World = Industrialised West
2. Second World = Industrialised Communist states
3. Third World = non-industrialised South BUT

✗ Divisions were often arbitrary and not always clear which category any single society belonged in.

✗ Division into three implied a separateness to each category, when increasingly the world was inter-connected in myriad ways.

✗ Concept of 'Third World' had ideological dimension in that it was used as a way of uniting disparate and poor societies to try and establish better terms of trade and economic conditions for all of them.

Rise of the Newly Industrialising Countries (NICs) (Fukuyama, 1993)
• Claim that emergence of strong industrialised sectors in 'traditional' Third World meant that concept was no longer useful as analytical tool.
• Parts of Latin America, and the 'Asian Tiger' economies had phenomenal industrial growth during 1980s.
• Adoption of free market policies was argued to be the cause of this growth.
• Government role limited to establishing stable political environment for economy, even where it involved repression, e.g. Pinochet's Chile.

Problems with NICs
1. Often based on exploitation, e.g. low wages, which leads to long-term unrest.
2. Urban bias and neglect of countryside.
3. Environmental damage in 'dash for growth'.
4. Democratic deficit of authoritarian and often corrupt regimes.
5. Progress vulnerable to changes in world economy – hence the crash.

Has this led to the death of the Third World?

✓ Global markets mean all societies are now part of world economy

✓ Strength of capitalism globally means 'Third Worldism' always doomed

✓ Growing diversity of countries means that categorising becomes more problematic as some less developed societies make progress

✗ Collapse of NIC economies in crash of 1990s show flimsy nature of economic miracles associated with them

✗ Collapse of communism thrown many Second World societies into Third World

14. ASPECTS OF GLOBALISATION

BASIC ARGUMENT

That the world is undergoing a radical transformation as technology, especially the new technologies of communication, change relationships between elements of the world in hitherto unknown ways. The end-result is that social life is lived in the context of global developments, rather than just national or local events. What individuals do has global consequences (for example, patterns of consumption in one part of the world impact upon economies elsewhere) and events in the rest of the world impact upon our own lives (e.g. the effect of global warming on our weather systems).

Three dimensions to globalisation

1. *Economic* – capitalism operates in a global context and transformations occur in areas of finance, production and work (see **Work, Organisation, and Leisure 5**).
2. *Politics* – carried on increasingly at an international level with consequences for the nation-state (see **World Sociology 16**).
3. *Culture* – consumption has a global aspect, as ideologies, fashions, art, music, etc, gain world-wide audiences through new media technologies, e.g. Internet.

Three key concepts

1. *Disembedding* – social relations are taken out of the immediate local context and situated in the global.
2. *Space-time distanciation* – process whereby space and time become compressed so that global events are experienced immediately through the media and commodities become distanced from their points of origin (e.g. pizza as global 'Italian' phenomenon).
3. *Localisation* – these processes allow ethnic, linguistic, cultural, economic and life-style groups to emerge as significant examples of individual identity.

Finance and globalisation

$ International money markets become divorced from national locations.

$ Technologies allow fast flow of capital 24 hours a day, regardless of location – there is always a financial market open somewhere.

$ This flow of capital is largely unregulated and arguably uncontrollable – 'you can't buck the market'.

$ Growth of credit in global market-place increases power of private individuals (e.g. George Soros).

$ Global markets have unforeseen consequences for control of national economies (e.g. 'Black Wednesday').

$ Banks no longer control financial markets – those who work in Exchanges in major cities have the power.

$ Money now divorced from productive capacity of a nation and exists in a global context.

Environment and globalisation

• Consumer conduct on global level has consequences for environment.

• Increased sensitivity to environmental issues on global scale.

• World has become an 'imagined community' in which all suffer/benefit from other's actions.

• 'Global community' encompasses non-human elements such as animals and plants.

• Global tourism is factor in threats to environment.

• Nature has become a 'subject' not an object, seen as having potential for life (Gaia).

• Slogan of the Greens – 'think global, act local'.

• Pollution has international dimension and action must be common to be effective.

• Nation-states need to co-operate with own citizens and other nations to protect environment.

Culture and globalisation

• Media industries organised on a global basis, with fewer national interests (e.g. Rupert Murdoch).

• Symbolic forms of culture transmitted worldwide and have global resonance.

• How symbols received and deployed is result of local actors using them for own purposes.

• Governments no longer have monopoly on information – global networks allow exchange of information without regulation.

• New media create 'virtual communities' unrestricted by space or time.

• Images of global media help construct identities both locally (e.g. ethnic identity) and globally (cosmopolitan identity).

• Much global media output is American in origin, but does not mean 'cultural imperialism' as 'readings' of the text varies according to locality.

National identity and Globalisation

See **World Sociology 16**.

Criticisms

✗ Assumes that identification with global dimension by individuals is real, when little evidence that people 'think globally'

✗ Degree of co-operation to tackle environmental threats is limited to pious wishful thinking

✗ Governments continually seeking to control media output, individually or internationally

✗ Media organisations subject to local regulation, even if global in scope

✗ Banks still powerful players in international money markets

✗ Credit still controlled in some localities

15. ENVIRONMENTALISM

Environmental Issues

- Global warming
- Loss of rain forest
- Acid rain
- Loss of habitat
- Loss of species

Aspects Polluted

Water supply = pesticides
Air = carbon dioxide
Soil = erosion of land
Locales = rubbish in landfills

FUNCTIONAL APPROACH

- Basic human ability to impose will on nature should be exercised.
- Values of conspicuous consumption shape our attitudes towards nature.
- Environmental problems need inter-dependent solutions from all participants if they are to be effective.

| ✓ Optimistic about solutions to problems | ✗ Sees few limits to growth that cannot be solved |
| ✓ Emphasises co-operative endeavour to solve them | ✗ Tends to ethnocentric view of problems |

CONFLICT APPROACH

- Environmental issues emerge from activities mainly of rich and powerful, who control national and global green agendas.
- When the powerful break environmental laws, tend to be ignored.
- Corporate crime (see **Crime and Deviance 12**) on environment punished leniently.

| ✓ Focuses on the main polluters not the victims | ✗ Underplays ordinary polluters like car owners |
| ✓ Draws attention to inequality in dealing with offenders | ✗ Discounts legal protections which have partly worked |

CULTURAL ECOLOGY APPROACH

- Examines how culture shapes environment, but also how environment shapes culture.
- Cultural expectations such as religious beliefs often have environmental logic, e.g. prohibition of pork in hot countries has medical basis.
- Cultural factors affect way that people interact with environment, e.g. New Age beliefs and vegetarianism.

| ✓ Stresses interrelationships | ✗ In complex societies, relationship not direct |
| ✓ Importance of beliefs and ideas | ✗ Ignores inequality – poor suffer most |

MARXIST APPROACHES

- Capitalism itself is greatest threat to environment because of its relentless search for profit at any cost.
- 'Environmental racism' – hazards are disproportionately located near the poor.
- Planned obsolescence ensures waste in production of goods.
- Rich consume disproportionate amount of world's resources.

| ✓ Highlights imbalances | ✗ Shift to TW pollution |
| ✓ Focuses on global processes | ✗ Capitalism has long-term agenda |

APPROACHES TO ENVIRONMENT

KEY CONCEPT

Sustainable development: The 'Holy Grail' of environmentalism, this is where growth is achieved at a rate which will not deplete natural resources faster than alternatives are found. Energy is crucial here, because non-replaceable sources of fuel will eventually run out and will need to be replaced by renewable sources. Another aspect of this is to reduce waste in development, so we maximise resources.

KEY CONCEPT

Biodiversity: Refers to the variation in species and habitats which is essential for long-term survival. Loss of plants and animals affects resources and genetic inheritance of Earth. Biodiversity gives access to natural remedies.

16. GLOBALISATION AND THE NATION-STATE

MULTI-NATIONAL CORPORATIONS BECOME TNCs (TRANS-NATIONAL CORPORATIONS)

Modernisation theory	Dependency theory
• Sees role of industrial firms with more than one centre of operations (MNCs) as good for development. • MNCs invest in developing world, bringing work and contributing to GDP of undeveloped nations.	• Sees role of MNCs as negative, exploiting TW workers and acting as agents of metropolis. • Most profits made in TW patriated to home base of MNC legally or through dubious accounting.

MNCs grow in order to compete in a global market-place, by acquiring other firms and amalgamating with corporations regardless of national boundaries. They lose their 'centres of operation' and operate on a global basis with little regard for any national interest, whether FW or TW. Result is that TNCs owe no allegiance to any stage, only to their own shareholders, who themselves have a global profile. It is drive for profit, not national interest, which governs their decision-making.

GROWTH OF INTERNATIONAL AGENCIES

Governmental	Quasi-governmental and others
• Governance of globe being transferred to transnational agencies such as United Nations or NATO (e.g. Kosovo). • Increasing political co-operation on regional basis (e.g. European Union). • Global issues determined by global conferences (e.g. Rio conference on environment). • Security and other cross-border issues routinely organised across national boundaries.	• Conflict resolution handled by international courts. • Adherence to Declaration of Human Rights policed by international agencies. • Aid and charity agencies organised internationally. • Sport and culture organised on global basis (e.g. Olympics). • Economic issues dealt with by international bodies (e.g. World Trade Organisation).

IMPACT ON THE NATION-STATE AND NATIONAL IDENTITY

1. Undermining nation-state
- Changes nature of citizenship, so that identities can extend beyond the national, into imagined communities of global community or virtual communities of cyberspace.
- Undermines ability of nation-state to determine own future. State has to take into account interests of partners and neighbours if it is to operate effectively.
- Foreign policy increasingly a collective process, involving other nation-states and international organisations.
- Produces a global consumer culture, in which goods and services are universal, regardless of location.
- Adherence to international standards of human rights – limits legal sanctions of nation-state.
- Loss of sovereignty by acceptance of international courts' jurisdiction.

2. Limited impact on nation-state
- National identities still strong.
- National interests still determine policy.
- Adherence to international standards provisional not absolute.

3. Strengthens national identities
- Globalisation encourages 'break-away' ethnicity,' as old empires crumble.
- Small nations can operate globally as well as large ones.
- Localisation encourages devolution of powers to lowest denominator (subsidiarity).

APPROACHES TO GLOBALISATION AND NATIONAL IDENTITY

1. Realist
- Dominant players on international scene remain the nation-state.
- Not globalisation but internationalisation.
- Inter-state relations still most important dimension.
- Emphasis remains firmly on nation-state.

2. Neo-Marxist
- Global dimension is a capitalist world-order.
- International relations characterised by inequality not co-operation.
- International agencies reflect interests of dominant capitalist nations.
- Emphasis remains firmly on class relations, on a global scale.

3. Liberal-pluralism
- Recognises importance of human rights and environment as issues for global action.
- Stresses importance of international agencies in dealing with cross-national issues.
- Emphasis is on the international aspects of a global politics.
- National identity remains important in context of increasing global profiles.

17. COLONIALISM, GLOBALISATION, AND ETHNICITY

BASIC NOTIONS ABOUT RACE

1. Ideologies of race were forged in an era of colonialism in which Western nations invaded and conquered large tracts of the world, seeing this as the 'white man's mission'.
2. Basic tactic of imperial powers was divide and rule, so that subordinates did not see interests in common together and challenge colonial rulers with a united front.
3. Colonial powers racialised colonies by establishing hierarchies of ethnic groups, often by importing migrant workers of a different ethnic group from indigenous peoples, e.g. Fiji had influx of Indian workers on plantations.
4. Hierarchies reflected ideological notions of superiority and inferiority often linked to religion, but usually expressed through crude stereotypes and name-calling.
5. Ideologies acted as legitimation for colonial rule, in which indigenous peoples were denied their past history and characterised as children who needed the guidance of the colonial 'father', because they were unable to rule themselves.
6. These ideologies still powerful in sections of the post-imperial power's population and take form of racism, in which ethnic minorities, especially non-whites, are seen as being innately inferior.

POST-COLONIAL MIGRATIONS

1. Following WW2, labour shortages in the post-imperial nations prompted recruitment of ethnic populations from former and still existing colonies to take up slack.
2. Economic migrants from former colonies moved to the imperial nations in search of better economic prospects and expecting a welcome, especially those who had fought in WW2.
3. This led to reaction by imperial powers who increasingly restricted immigration, imposing laws which discriminated against non-white populations.
4. Post-1970 European Union legislation makes it easier for citizens of EU to live in another EU country and obtain employment there.
5. Barriers to immigration now at European borders not just national ones.
6. Migration can also be triggered by political unrest or ethnic cleansing.

EFFECTS OF MIGRATION ON NATIONAL IDENTITY

Two-fold response:

1. 'Laager' response (i.e. form a defensive circle)
- Increase in ethnic minority population leads to negative reaction among indigenous population.
- Calls for limitation of entry to ethnic minorities.
- Made worse by globalisation, which is seen as threat to national identity.
- Ethnic minorities seen as visible aspect of the threat ('defensive exclusiveness').
- Tebbit's 'cricket test' (who do you support) represents fear of difference.

  BUT ✗ implicitly racist

2. Embracing diversity response
- Celebration of difference as enrichment.
- Stress on cultural benefits of diversity.
- Integration of ethnic culture into 'way of life' – cuisine, carnival etc.
- Rediscovery of indigenous ethnic identity – Scottishness, Welshness.

  BUT ✗ don't embrace all aspects of culture e.g. arranged marriage

ETHNIC MINORITY RESPONSES TO IDENTITY ISSUES

Three-fold response:

1. Assimilationist
- Keep head down and try to get along.
- Adopt indigenous characteristics where possible.
- Passive in face of racism.

  BUT ✗ rejected by second-generation ethnic minorities ('Uncle Tomism')

2. Black Nationalism
- Black is beautiful as slogan.
- Emphasises separateness from indigenous population and other ethnic minorities.
- Black becomes a political category with its own agenda.
- Challenges racism directly.

  BUT ✗ often masculinist and homophobic

3. New ethnicities
- Draws on many cultures to express identity – is eclectic.
- Emphasises being Black and British.
- Fluid notion of identity.

  BUT ✗ means uncertainty in identity

18. SYNOPTIC OVERIVEW

STRATEGIES FOR DEVELOPMENT

Theory of industrial society

Theory of capitalism

- Time of colonial administration
- Forging of ideologies of racism
- Development in colonies limited
- Under-development

Modernisation theory

Technology

Entrepreneurs

Capital

Free markets

Under-development

Satellite and metropolis

Dependency theory

Patriation of capital

Core, semi-periphery and periphery

Capitalist relations

World Systems theory

Marxist theories

Interrelationships on world scale

Aid

NICs

Neo-liberal theory

Death of communism

End of nation-state?

Globalisation theory

Culture, finance, environment

Transnational corporations

Common issues
- Women
- Health
- Urbanisation
- Environment

Time Line

Pre-WW2 – Time of the Empires | 1945–1969/70s | 1970s–1980s | 1990s

12 Sociological Theories

1. POSITIVISM AND ANTI-POSITIVISM

> These concepts are very important as they influence the approaches
> sociologists take and the methodology they engage

POSITIVISM	ANTI-POSITIVISM
• Developed by social philosophers Saint-Simon and Comte. • Comte was originator of positivist approach to social sciences. He saw a hierarchy of sciences with sociology at the top. • Positivists assume sociological explanations should be like those of natural sciences and sociologists should use logic, methods and procedures of natural science. • More recently associated with structuralist approaches in sociology.	• Developed from work of Weber and early Chicago School – Dewey (1953), Cooley (1902), Thomas (1909) & Mead (1934). • Weber's 'verstehen' sociology emphasised the meaning of social action as understood by the social actors involved. • Mead emphasised the concept of Self in understanding social action. • Associated with interpretivist approaches to sociology.
Assumptions → Social reality is an objective entity capable of being measured. → Sociologists can uncover the nature of social reality by using scientific methods. → As with the natural world, social behaviour is governed by underlying causal laws and is therefore, predictable. → By systematic observation of causal relationships between social phenomena, social laws can be revealed. • An example of the discovery of causal laws can be seen in Durkheim's work on suicide where he showed that the laws of moral regulation and social integration affected an individual's likelihood of suicide.	**Assumptions** → Subject matter of sociology is fundamentally different from that of natural sciences. → Subjective consciousness of individuals cannot be quantified. → No possibility of gaining understanding of social action via scientific methods. → Meanings are the most important aspect of interaction and these need to be understood by sociologists using qualitative methods. → There are no causal laws governing social behaviour. • An example of this approach can be seen in Goffman's work on total institutions where he showed how inmates construct practices to 'make out' in the institution.
Sociological approaches Functionalism, Marxism	**Sociological approaches** Phenomenology, Social Action, Symbolic Interactionism, Feminism, Phenomenological Marxism, Weberian Sociology
Evaluation ✓ Supports the debate that sociology can be seen as a scientific discipline. ✓ Allows us to examine the nature of external constraints. ✗ Individuals have subjective consciousness and are not easily predictable. ✗ Does not allow for the possibility of examining the meaning of social actions. ✗ There is more than one social reality – all dependent on people's perceptions.	**Evaluation** ✓ Allows us to see that individuals perceive social reality in different ways. ✓ Gives agency to individuals – they are not seen as simply manipulated by external forces. ✗ Methods used tend to be unsystematic and rely on subjectivity of researcher. ✗ Fails to examine effect of structured relationships on individuals (e.g. power differentials). ✗ Undervalues the extent to which society is structured.

2. PERSPECTIVES

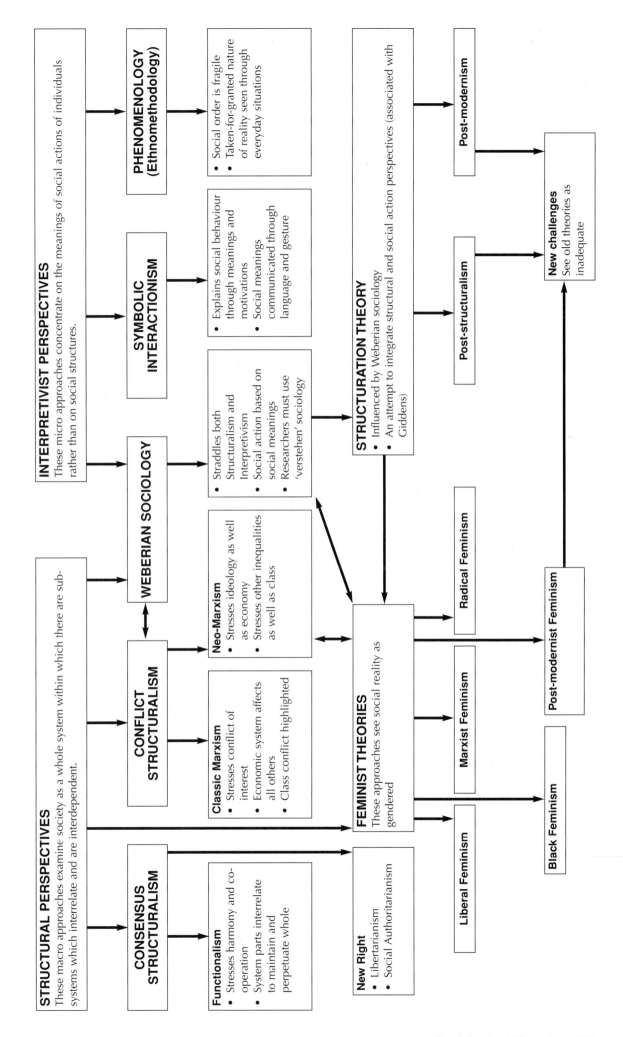

STRUCTURAL PERSPECTIVES
These macro approaches examine society as a whole system within which there are sub-systems which interrelate and are interdependent.

CONSENSUS STRUCTURALISM

Functionalism
- Stresses harmony and co-operation
- System parts interrelate to maintain and perpetuate whole

CONFLICT STRUCTURALISM

Classic Marxism
- Stresses conflict of interest
- Economic system affects all others
- Class conflict highlighted

Neo-Marxism
- Stresses ideology as well as economy
- Stresses other inequalities as well as class

WEBERIAN SOCIOLOGY

INTERPRETIVIST PERSPECTIVES
These micro approaches concentrate on the meanings of social actions of individuals rather than on social structures.

- Straddles both Structuralism and Interpretivism
- Social action based on social meanings
- Researchers must use 'verstehen' sociology

SYMBOLIC INTERACTIONISM
- Explains social behaviour through meanings and motivations
- Social meanings communicated through language and gesture

PHENOMENOLOGY (Ethnomethodology)
- Social order is fragile
- Taken-for-granted nature of reality seen through everyday situations

STRUCTURATION THEORY
- Influenced by Weberian sociology
- An attempt to integrate structural and social action perspectives (associated with Giddens)

Post-modernism

Post-structuralism

New challenges
See old theories as inadequate

New Right
- Libertarianism
- Social Authoritarianism

FEMINIST THEORIES
These approaches see social reality as gendered

Liberal Feminism

Marxist Feminism

Radical Feminism

Black Feminism

Post-modernist Feminism

3. STRUCTURALIST THEORIES (CONSENSUS): FUNCTIONALISM

BASIC ASSUMPTIONS

- Not a school of thought as such, but a set of shared assumptions. Developed from 19th century social anthropology. Main proponents: Radcliffe-Brown, Spencer, Durkheim and later, Parsons and Merton.
- A macro approach, which sees society as a whole system made up of interrelated parts or sub-systems. Each of these functions to maintain and perpetuate the whole society.
- Organic analogy – society operates like a living organism with parts that are interdependent. Change occurring in one part will produce changes in the others.
- Some parts may become diseased and this can contaminate the rest (e.g. too much crime in a society will be disabling).
- Every society has needs which are met by four major sub-systems: economic, political, kinship and cultural systems.
- System is integrated harmoniously because of a fundamental acceptance of a consensus of values by members of the society. Interdependence is maintained through the division of labour.
- Individuals become social through the process of socialisation where shared values, norms and beliefs are transmitted.
- Conflict exists but is minimal because people accept the inevitability and necessity of inequality, based as it is on different levels of talent and ability.
- Social change occurs slowly and in an evolutionary way, as shifts in the consensus takes place.

EVALUATION

Strengths

✓ Parsonian functionalism was the first major attempt to produce a grand theory of society.

✓ It allows for the examination of the functions of 'strange' rituals which superficially seem to be redundant.

✓ It demonstrates the links between the major social institutions, e.g. family, education and the economy.

Limitations

✗ Overemphasises the harmonious nature of society; fails to examine power differentials.

✗ Teleological – tries to explain the origins of a social institution by its functions. Religion functions to promote social solidarity, so society must have a need for religion to perform this role.

✗ It provides an inadequate explanation of social change – assuming it is mainly evolutionary.

✗ Seen as a politically conservative position by emphasising the status quo and failing to see the social disadvantage some groups suffer.

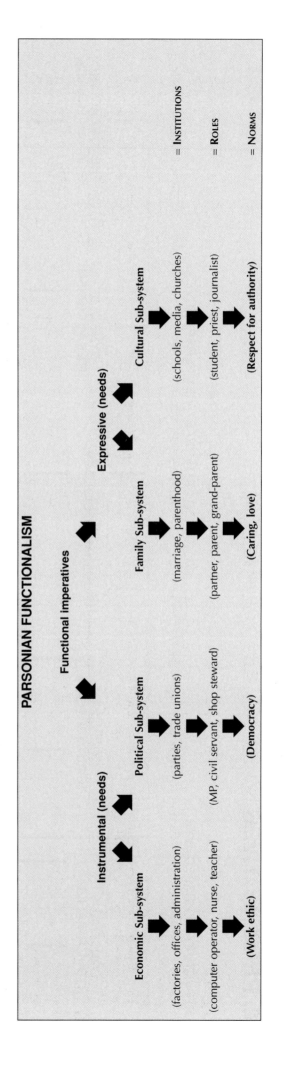

PARSONIAN FUNCTIONALISM

4. SOME APPLICATIONS OF FUNCTIONALISM

FAMILY	DEVIANCE	EDUCATION	RELIGION

• Two basic functions of the family:
  1. primary socialisation
  2. stabilisation of adult roles
• Family + industrialisation: march of progress theorists assume pre-industrial society characterised by extended family whereas nuclear family best fits modern society (Parsons, 1956).
• Symmetrical family thesis: as industrialisation proceeds nuclear family becomes more democratic (Young & Willmott, 1975).
• Scapegoated child used as means of uniting family (Bell & Vogel, 1968).
	• Durkheimian view = deviance and crime seen as necessary and inevitable for society.
	• Deviance tests usefulness of norms and laws and reinforces collective consciousness.
	• Concept of anomie demonstrates deviant adaptations to disjuncture between goals and means (Merton, 1968).
	• Sub-cultural theories examine reasons for working-class males' involvement in deviant sub-cultures: focal concerns; differential opportunity structures; differential association; rejection of middle-class values; drift into deviance.
		• Education system examined in relation to family and economy.
		• Examines the contribution of the education system, especially training, to meeting needs of whole society.
		• Economic function: responds to demand for a skilled labour force. Selection and role allocation functions ensure that most suitable candidates reach appropriate situations in occupational system.
		• Socialisation: societal values transmitted via schooling. Difference between manifest (intended) and latent (unintended) functions – similar to official and hidden curricula.
			• Studies originate with 19th century social anthropology which examined what role religious ceremonies provided for the community.
			• Religion seen as integrative force – helps to generate the collective consciousness.
			• Durkheim (1982): origin of religion as force for social solidarity.
			• Malinowski (1984): religion offers comfort and solace at times of stress.
			• Parsons (1959): religion promotes the value consensus, social order and social meaning.

Evaluation ✗ Historians dispute march of progress thesis – little evidence of extended families in pre-industrial society – in fact more likely to be a product of an industrialising society. ✗ Does not take into account diversity of family types. ✗ Does not account for the 'dark side of family life'.	**Evaluation** ✗ Assumes crime statistics are accurate – so concentrate on explanations for working-class deviance. ✗ Ignores women and middle-class crimes. ✗ Fails to examine law-making processes and who benefits from legal system.	**Evaluation** ✗ Emphasis on integrative role of schooling rather than ideological role. ✗ Sees underachievement as result of inadequate home background or lack of ability. ✗ Ignores class-related inequalities.	**Evaluation** ✗ Does not account for social conflicts generated by religious differences. ✗ Assumes statistical evidence can be used unproblematically. ✗ Makes interpretations of individuals' belief but fails to check these with individuals concerned.

5. STRUCTURALIST THEORIES (CONFLICT): MARXISM

BASIC ASSUMPTIONS

- A structuralist approach which, unlike functionalism, sees societies characterised by conflicts of interest.
- Marxist analysis is based on historical materialism – all societies can be characterised by the nature of their mode of production.
- Society is divided into, the infrastructure and the superstructure thus:

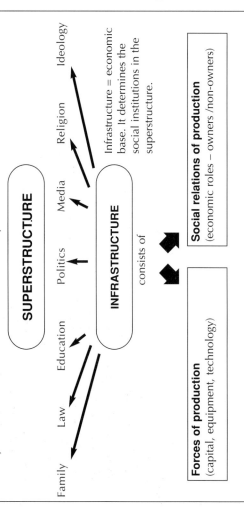

SUPERSTRUCTURE

Family   Law   Education   Politics   Media   Religion   Ideology

INFRASTRUCTURE

Infrastructure = economic base. It determines the social institutions in the superstructure.

consists of

Forces of production
(capital, equipment, technology)

Social relations of production
(economic roles – owners /non-owners)

- Although Marxism can be applied to all historical periods, Marx concentrated on the development and eventual overthrow of the capitalist system.
- Social institutions in the superstructure serve to legitimate the power generated by the social relations of production. In capitalist society the owners are the bourgeoisie and the workers, the proletariat.
- Those who own the means of production also have their power reinforced by the ideologies within education, the family, media, religion, law etc.
- Social change is inevitable and generated by conflicts between interest groups (social classes).
- Revolution is an inevitable process of historical change as the subject classes gain consciousness of their oppressed position.
- Neo-Marxism retains an emphasis on the economic base of society but examines the role of ideology in maintaining the power of the ruling class. In Gramsci's view the ruling class could only rule by winning the consent of the subject class.

EVALUATION

Strengths

- ✓ A structuralist approach which links the major social institutions.
- ✓ Marxism has been a major influence on other social theories such as Weberian sociology and feminism.
- ✓ Emphasis on the important economic dimension of society.
- ✓ Attempts to link the structural elements of society with the consciousness of the individual. Individuals may form an objective social class by way of their similar situation in the social structure, but they must gain awareness of this shared position before they can take action.
- ✓ Accounts for revolutionary upheaval as societies go through large-scale change.

Limitations

- ✗ Functionalists criticise the approach for overemphasising conflict when it is evident that there has to be harmony and shared values for social order without coercion to be possible.
- ✗ With its emphasis on the economic base, it is seen as overly deterministic. Weber argued that elements in the superstructure could have relative autonomy in particular historical situations (e.g. influence of religion on the work ethic).
- ✗ Classic Marxism has ignored role of women in society – this analysis has been taken up by later Marxist feminists.
- ✗ With the recent changes in the Soviet Union and the eastern bloc countries it looks as though Marxist theory is no longer viable.
- ✗ Society does not always operate in the interests of the ruling class.
- ✗ Relationship between infrastructure and infrastructure is not proven. It is unclear how economic base determines the superstructure, relying on assertion.
- ✗ Criticised by post-modernists for being 'meta-narrative' – an attempt to explain the whole society by reference to a single cause – economics.

6. SOME APPLICATIONS OF MARXISM

FAMILY	DEVIANCE	EDUCATION	RELIGION
• Development of the family through historical stages based on the mode of production of that time. • As part of the superstructure the family is determined by the economic base. • It acts as an agent of social control reproducing labour power and the social relations of production. • It becomes a haven from an alienating world and thus inhibits revolution. • Domestic division of labour necessary for capitalism. Women as unpaid domestic labourers form a reserve army of workers as and when the economy demands. • Families as units of consumption perpetuate capitalist system.	• Law, police and judiciary are seen as part of superstructure. • Emphasis on law creation process and ensuring benefits to ruling interest groups. • Range of approaches: → Examination of white-collar crimes and the ideological role of law. → Examination of ideological and repressive state apparatuses. → New Criminology linked Marxist and interactionist approaches. → New Left Realism examined (black) working-class street crime from socialist perspective. → Examination of role of media in deviancy amplification – moral panics over drugs and mugging.	• Education system seen as part of superstructure transmitting ruling class ideology to new generation. • Education system is seen as closely aligned to economic system as education prepares new workforce for a class-based society. • Cultural reproduction role of education again legitimates class divisions. • Education not seen as meritocratic. • Range of studies: → Examination of working-class males at school and work. → Correspondence theory of education – school parallels aspects of work-life to prepare students for work. → Examination of effects of 'New vocationalism'.	• Religion seen as playing important ideological role in reinforcing false consciousness. • Religion is opiate of the people as it offers comfort and solace. Whilst people have religious faith they can never be free. • Religion veils the real oppression (of capitalism) by offering hope for eternal life. • Believers must remain humble and accepting of their situation in order to gain rewards in the next life. • Neo-Marxists have challenged the idea of the power of religion and see other elements of society as having taken over its role.
Evaluation ✗ Assumption that the nuclear family is typical – no account taken of diversity. ✗ No real account taken of family life under modern non-capitalist economies. ✗ Marxist feminists have had to take up the analysis of women in the family which was previously ignored. ✗ No account taken of individuals choosing family relationships based on love and commitment.	**Evaluation** ✗ Tendency to overemphasise structure at expense of individual agency. ✗ Tendency to side with offenders against authority and/or victims. ✗ Overlooks the degree of consensus over laws amongst public. ✗ Over-emphasis on coercion and violence.	**Evaluation** ✗ Education system not as closely linked historically to economy as assumed by Marxists. ✗ Highly selective in empirical evidence. Some studies seen as polemical. ✗ Ignores role of education as social control agent in non-capitalist societies. ✗ Ignores potential of education as ladder of success for working-class.	**Evaluation** ✗ Insufficient allowance given for relative autonomy of religion in social change – Weberian critique. ✗ Fails to examine the way religion integrates individuals and gives meaning to their lives. ✗ Neo-Marxists have examined role of religion as change agent (Liberation Theology). This challenges classic Marxism.

7. CONFLICT STRUCTURALISM: FEMINISM

The various branches of feminism have some shared basic assumptions:

- Sociology was previously a 'malestream' discipline which largely ignored the role of women.
- Even today feminism is seen as biased whereas malestream sociology is seen as value-free.
- Gender relationships are based on power inequalities.
- Feminism tends to reject biological or functionalist explanations of gender based on naturalistic assumptions.

RADICAL FEMINISM

- Seen as most extreme position as it emphasises oppressive nature of patriarchy.
- Male supremacy oppresses women – demonstrated in violence against women.
- Necessary for separatist movements, especially lesbian separatism.
- Equality possible if biological motherhood ceases (cybernetics).

Evaluation

- ✗ Highly selective view of society.
- ✗ Ignores choices women make to live with men.
- ✓ Exposes dark side of family life and sexploitation of women and children.

MARXIST FEMINISM/FEMINIST MARXISM

- Women's oppression is a result of class inequality in exploitative societies.
- Women as domestic labourers provide cheap labour for economy and reproduce social relations of production.
- Feminist Marxists examine role of ideology within patriarchal societies.

Evaluation

- ✗ Ignores domestic labour of men and increasing female economic independence.
- ✗ Ignores oppressed role of women in socialist societies.
- ✓ Links structure to individual lives.

LIBERAL FEMINISM

- Concerned with legal restrictions on women and gender inequality in society.
- Assumption that once legislation was changed then equal opportunities would prevail.

Evaluation

- ✗ Overemphasis on individual prejudice at expense of structural inequalities.
- ✗ Fails to address why inequalities persist apart from through socialisation process.
- ✗ First approach to examine systematically the gendered nature of social inequality.

BLACK FEMINISM

- Arose from concerns of black women that they had been ignored by 'white feminists'.
- Black women face two forms of oppression: racism of white society as well as patriarchal exploitation.
- Ending capitalism will not end either of these two forms of oppression.

Evaluation

- ✗ Exposed colour-blind nature of mainstream sociology.
- ✓ Possibly ignores commonalities with white feminists.

POST-MODERN FEMINISM

- Challenges assumptions around gender identities and 'compulsory heterosexuality'.
- Individuals have on offer a vast range of femininities and masculinities constructed through language and discourse.
- There are no fixed certainties about gender or sexual identity.

Evaluation

- ✗ In rejecting meta-narratives, then feminism too should go.
- ✓ Does highlight the fluid and flexible nature of gender identity.

BRANCHES OF FEMINISM

8. NEW RIGHT

- This is the name given to a set of ideas which influenced the political right in recent years.
- Prominent in the 1980s and 1990s under Thatcherite politics in the UK and Reaganism in the USA.
- Two sets of seemingly contradictory ideas: libertarianism and social authoritarianism (neo-classical or free-market economics and traditionally conservative values relating to family and morality).

LIBERTARIANISM

Economics

- The **free market** is essential in producing affluence and political freedom.
- **Privatisation** of previously nationalised industries encouraged competition and wider share-holding so that more people would feel part of the 'enterprise culture'.

Welfare

- **Culture of dependency theory** assumes that the poor need to take responsibility for their situation and to become less dependent on the welfare state.
- The Thatcher government condemned the 'nanny state' for stifling initiative and creating dependency in claimants. This issue was a major focus of political conflict in the 1980s and early 1990s.
- Dependency generates more poverty and unemployment. Individuals should be encouraged to find work rather than remain on benefits.
- **Concept of 'underclass'** became widely used to describe those on welfare benefits. This underclass was a class beneath the working class and was characterised by crime, persistent unemployment, family instability, especially that generated by lone parents and drug abuse (Charles Murray's ideas (1984) were transposed from USA society to the UK).

SOCIAL AUTHORITARIANISM

Law

- Enhancement of **law and order** to control those who refuse to accept society's codes.

Morality

- **Moral regeneration** was seen as necessary so that traditional values could be restored.
- **Family values** – the traditional 'Victorian' image of the middle-class family was emphasised – a nuclear family which was economically self-sufficient and had a strong sense of morality.
- **Lone-parent families** were demonised by politicians and held responsible for most of the contemporary social problems, especially those posed by working-class males (much of the political concern was around the increasing cost to the state of these families).
- **Education** – traditional ideas were reintroduced and parental choice encouraged even where it meant private education was endorsed.
- **'Marketisation' of schools** was encouraged as schools had to face increasing competition for pupils. Freedom from central and local government allowed schools to determine how their budgets were to be allocated.
- **Religion** – this is seen as having a profound effect on society. A decline in moral values is the result of a decline in the importance placed on religion in society. Religious education was encouraged in all schools as well as daily acts of worship.

Evaluation

✓ Can be used as a challenge to Marxism especially after fall of communist economies.

Strengths

✓ Can be used to assess the development of the 'enterprise culture'.

✓ Stresses individual freedom.

Weaknesses

✗ Not a coherent social theory.

✗ Too aligned to a political position to be objective.

Comment

NB. Some of the ideas of the New Right have been appropriated by New Labour and are reflected in rough 'law-and-order' policies.

9. INTERPRETIVISM

PHENOMENOLOGY/ETHNOMETHODOLOGY

Basic assumptions
- Originated from phenomenology of Husserl and Weber.
- Social reality must be studied from actor's perspective.
- Social reality is fragile and tentative and constantly being realised by individuals.
- Social order depends on the 'taken-for-granted' which, if challenged, generates anxiety and discomfort.
- Task of ethnomethodology to uncover the everyday assumptions that make social order possible.
- Language is infinitely ambiguous.
- Individuals have to 'gloss' the meaning of words by taking for granted that they share a perspective with the speaker.

Examples in research
- Experimental interventions into everyday situations challenge the taken-for-granted assumptions (Garfinkel's students had to behave as guests in their own homes).
- Discourse analysis – examining the words and phrases in everyday speech.

Limitations
- ✗ Failure to recognise and/or explain structural constraints on individuals.
- ✗ Failure to examine why some groups have power to label others.
- ✗ Self-fulfilling prophecy can be seen to be over-deterministic.
- ✗ Ethnomethodology provides interesting insights but does not interrogate origins of shared meanings.

SYMBOLIC INTERACTIONISM

Basic assumptions
- Social reality is a social construction.
- Individuals define situations, interpret and negotiate in social interaction.
- Social meanings are generated through interaction based on a universe of discourse.
- Language and gestures convey meaning.
- Use of concept of self which consists of 'I' and 'me'. Individuals are conscious and self-reflexive and can modify action on basis of previous experience, i.e. 'looking-glass self'.
- Dramaturgical metaphor, i.e. use of role, role-play, stage, presentation of self.
- Labelling is a powerful control mechanism used by those in authority.

Examples in research
- Examination of deviant groups challenging official definitions, e.g. mental patients, prisoners, youths. Labelling process.
- Examination of presentation of self in everyday life demonstrates diversity of individual personae.

Strengths
- ✓ The various approaches share the importance to sociology of understanding social meanings in social interaction.
- ✓ Individuals have agency and are not simply passive recipients of social forces.
- ✓ Allows us to understand the constructed nature of social reality.

WEBERIAN TRADITION

Use of ideal type
- An heuristic device used as a measurement against social reality.
- Can only ever be an approximation of the reality it characterises.

Ideal types of social action
- Rational action – towards goal achievement
- Value-rational action – non-instrumental
- Traditional action – habitual/routine
- Affectual action – emotional

Verstehen sociology
- Interpretive understanding of social action as perceived by social actors involved.
- Empathic understanding – seeing the world from perspective of social actor.

Examples in research
Protestant Ethic and the Spirit of Capitalism (1930) Weber takes position of Calvinist faced with terrible uncertainty of salvation. Then discovers elective affinity between religion and work.

10. SOME APPLICATIONS OF INTERPRETIVISM

WEBERIAN SOCIOLOGY

Religion
- The clearest example of interpretative understanding is in Weber's work on the *Protestant Ethic and the Spirit of Capitalism* (1930).
- In order to make sense of the relationship between rationality and Western capitalism, he takes the position of the Calvinist believer.
- The Calvinist had to work in a calling, be frugal, accept predestination and be faced with the uncertainty of not knowing whether or not he was saved.
  - Weber's methodology was totally appropriate at the level of meaning – only by putting himself in the position of the Calvinists could he make sense of their faith and work.

Weber's work has been influential on the consequent development of interpretivist sociology, especially Symbolic Interactionism and Ethnomethodology

SYMBOLIC INTERACTIONISM (SI)	ETHNOMETHODOLOGY
Deviance - This is an area well-visited by symbolic interactionists. - SI challenges the adequacy of crime statistics on which most functionalist and Marxist explanations are based. - Lemert (1989) demonstrated the differences between primary and secondary deviance. - Goffman (1991) looked at the coping strategies and meaning systems of inmates of total institutions. - Becker (1973) examined 'outsiders' and the labelling process which maintains a distance between them and 'respectable' members of society. - Young (1977) examined the relationship between outsiders and the amplification of deviance by media and agents of social control. **Education** - Labelling has been an important concept for empirical research: → Becker (1951) outlined the teacher's view of the 'ideal student' (this framework has been used in research on teachers' perceptions of Afro-Caribbean students). → Rist (1977) examined the kindergarten year to show how early labelling 'sticks' with the child during their primary schooling. → Fuller (1980) has challenged the perspective by studying the resistance of Afro-Caribbean girls to negative labelling. → Although there are many problems with the research, Rosenthal and Jacobson's work (1968) on the self-fulfilling prophecy has shown the influence of teacher expectations on children's achievements.	**Deviance** - Atkinson (1977) outlined the mechanisms that coroners use in decisions on suicide. - Cicourel (1976) examined the negotiation processes between young offenders and the judiciary. - Sacks (1984) analysed the 'search for help' of potential suicide victims with relatives and help-agencies. **Everyday life** - Garfinkel (1967) used disruptive 'breaching' experiments to test for common-sense assumptions and the underlying rules of social interaction (most of these experiments involved college students). - Conversational analysis – Sacks has analysed the rules and structure of conversations to demonstrate the ways people manage conversations. **Education** - Garfinkel's work can be used here to demonstrate how students make sense of the responses of college counsellors to their questions. In this case the counsellors were not authentic and gave random answers to the students' questions. **Work** - Zimmerman (1971) studied behaviour of staff in a US state bureaucracy in relation to official rules. Staff used rules flexibly but justified their behaviour as if the flexibility actually created a better sense of order. This is a useful challenge to the idea that rules govern behaviour in a bureaucracy.

11. STRUCTURATION, POST-STRUCTURALIST, AND POST-MODERN THEORIES

STRUCTURATION

- Giddens (1987) attempts to combine the sociology of structure with social action approaches.
- Individuals are 'knowledgeable agents' who construct their own theories which then motivate their actions.
- These actions are restricted by structural conditions which limit their actions, but structures also enable actions to take place – this is the 'duality of structure'.
- Example 1: **Language** acts as a structure limiting what we can actually say, but without language we could not enter into communication and negotiation. New words are generated through social action so that the structure itself is subject to change.
- Example 2: **Power** can be seen as enabling as well as restricting social action. It also cannot exist without social action. Resources are divided into allocative (raw materials like land and technology) and authoritative resources (systems of power and authority). Neither of these types of resources can exist unless human action turns them into resources.

Evaluation

- ✓ Instead of separating structure from action, Giddens attempts to demonstrate the interplay between the two (interestingly this is a legacy of both Weber and Parsons).
- ✓ Giddens makes links between the individual and global social processes.
- ✗ Giddens underplays the importance of structures and the nature of the restraint they produce.
- ✗ His emphasis on individuals constructing the world assumes that if only they made different choices the world would be changed at will.
- ✗ He does not account for the fact that some groups have greater choice than others.

POST-STRUCTURALISM

- Mainly associated with the work of Lacan, Derrida and Foucault who are not sociologists themselves but have influenced recent sociological thought.
- Much of their work has concentrated on language and discourse. **Language** is seen as a constraining structure and our understanding of the world is provided for us by the language which predates us and which we learn through socialisation.
- Foucault is interested in the exercise of power involved in the creation and use of a language. Ways of talking and thinking about the world is a form of knowledge or **discourse.**
- An individual's identity is constituted by discourse and in different historical periods there are different discourses but they are always related to power.
- Foucault has analysed the history of medicine, madness, sexuality, punishment and the body in relation to discourses and, therefore, to institutional/power arrangements.

Evaluation

- ✓ Foucault (1972) has made an important contribution to our understanding of the construction of individuality.
- ✓ Foucault's work on discipline has relevance in understanding increased levels of surveillance in contemporary society.
- ✗ Some Marxists argue that post-structuralism ignores the importance of the sources of power which are part of the organisation of capital.
- ✗ Concept of power is vague – not interrogated closely.
- ✗ Some feminists are concerned that the 'real' impact of structures on women's lives is abandoned here.

POST-MODERNISM

- Mainly associated with the work of Baudrillard, Lyotard and Jameson.
- Relativist position which assumes that all accounts of reality have equal validity. No single theory can have special access to truth.
- Decline of grand theories or metanarratives as each is inadequate as a complete view of the world.
- Application of post-modernism has been to art, culture and architecture generally but is increasingly being applied to other aspects of social life like the family.
- Importance of mass media, especially advertising so that reality and media representations of reality merge (Baudrillard (1983) + Simulacra: mass media).
- Not all post-modernists have abandoned modernism completely. Jameson (1984) still uses a capitalist framework in his analysis of modern society.
- Post-modernist feminists use post-modernist approach to deconstruct mythologies created by patriarchy.

Evaluation

- ✓ Post-modernism has attempted to deal with new cultural developments which have taken place at the end of the 20th century.
- ✓ Helps to understand the increasing complexity of individual identity.
- ✗ Like the Frankfurt School, it assumes a passive, manipulated audience.
- ✗ It overemphasises the place of the mass media in social life – it ignores the role of social relationships and the use people make of media and media technology.
- ✗ If all metanarratives are abandoned, then that must make post-modernism redundant as well.

12. POST-MODERN APPROACHES TO THE CITY

ARCHITECTURE

In modern cities, function determined appearance, but in post-modern cities, appearance and style dominant. Façades no longer signal what goes on inside. Theming is central concept of post-modern architecture, such as themed shopping malls. Building design borrows from many styles of architecture all within same structure. There is no sense of unity. Cities compete to provide architectural looks to centres.

Emphasis on 'playfulness'.

ECONOMY

Modernist cities based on manufacturing and consumption of goods. Post-modern cities based on production and consumption of culture. This links the post-modern city to global urban terrains through new communication technologies.

✗ Manufacturing still exists in cities.

BOUNDARIES

In modernist cities, zones were established in which specialised functions took place. In post-modern cities, boundaries blur and activities are dispersed throughout the whole city. Activities concerned with symbolic economy.

✗ New boundaries between haves and have-nots appear.

TOURISM

Tourism becomes important aspect of post-modern city. Modern cities concerned with work, while post-modern cities concerned with leisure. Links made to the global city through TNCs creating similar habitats all over.

✗ Tourism restricted to those with surplus income.

FRAGMENTATION

Modern cities had sense of unity. Post-modern cities fragmented and privatised. Concern with surveillance and restricting access in parts of the city affect those who inhabit the space. Public space neglected as financial limits of public spending reached.

✗ Increased surveillance at odds with claim to openness.

APPLICATION: POST-MODERN APPROACHES TO THE CITY

13. SPACE AND BODIES

SPACE

Changes in conceptions of space
- Traditionally space been defined by boundaries – identifiable limits.
- Space linked to social position and power, e.g. larger office denotes higher position in hierarchy.
- Space signals social characteristics, e.g. where you live implies things about you.
- Space also signifies physical power, e.g. way that motor transport has shaped urban locations.
- Space becoming less bounded, e.g. where we work is no longer constrained by specific location.
- Conceptions of space expanding to the global.
- Cyberspace is important dimension of postmodern social space.

Space is gendered
- Men and women have different experiences of public spaces.
- Men and women have different relationships to private domestic spaces.
- Women-only space is rarer than men-only.
- Space designed by men more often than women, even in private areas.

Space as liberation and containment
- While cities may be threatening they are also areas of pleasure for women as well as men.
- Space often organised to restrict groups and individuals, e.g. CCTV, access to buildings.
- Space is arena for play.

BODIES

Bodies are socially constructed
- Gender identities are embodied in people with certain physical characteristics.
- Conceptions of body size and shape are socially determined in complex inter-play between media images, ideologies, fashion and physical shapes.
- Reproductive capacity of female bodies has profound social effects, e.g. for conceptions of who should nurture young.

Bodies are controlled and disciplined (Foucault)
- Described as anatomo-politics of the body, which sees the body as a capable 'machine' with abilities and usefulness for others and society.
- While controls may be physical, can also be non-material, as social control is achieved less through coercion and more through manipulation of the mind.
- Disciplinary regimes of prisons translated into everyday life through schooling, work etc. which seek to shape the actions of the body in socially useful ways.
- Medical practice categorises bodies in particular ways to divide populations into controllable sections and channel bodily energy, e.g. sexuality, into specific socially acceptable forms.

Bodies are stereotyped and labelled
- Disabled are invisible in sociological analysis because society tends to have negative images of them, and few sociologists are themselves disabled.
- Disabled are seen in particular way by society which defines them as less able rather than differently abled.
- Laws designed to protect disabled often flouted because of cost involved in meeting needs.

Reasons why the body emerged as a sociological concern
- Feminists reject masculine control of bodies by medical profession.
- Ageing population has increased awareness of ageing and dying.
- AIDS and 'new' diseases increased interest in pathology of the body.
- Technology has opened up space for body with, e.g., reproductive technologies.
- Growth of cult of the body through media interest in youth and stars.
- Health and body 'fascism' become popular as healthy living encouraged.

14. THE NATURE OF SCIENCE

> Whether sociology as a discipline is scientific depends on what we take 'scientific' to mean.
> The following approaches have differing perceptions of the nature of science.

APPROACHES	NATURE OF SCIENCE
Positivism	• Natural science is based on the hypothetico-deductive method. • Science searches for cause and effect relationships between phenomena and the laws which govern such relationships. • Scientists can be totally objective and value-free. • Data collected is reliable and quantitative. • Data is objective and factual – not contaminated by social factors. • Scientific knowledge is both cumulative and falsifiable (Popper). • End-result is generalisable theory – applicable to similar situations at all times.
Interpretivism	• Scientific method is appropriate to natural phenomena. • It cannot be applied to individuals in social action. • Positivism cannot expose the less tangible aspects of existence, e.g. spirituality.
Kuhn (1970)	• Science is not a cumulative body of knowledge. • Scientists work within a given scientific community using a shared paradigm (a taken-for-granted set of assumptions and techniques of research). • 'Normal science' is the normative state but is inevitably challenged by anomalies which eventually give rise to an anomic situation and a 'scientific revolution'.
Kaplan (1964)	• **Reconstructed logics** = methods and procedures scientists claim to use. **Logics in use** = what actually takes place in scientific research (possibility of phenomena being dismissed as 'artefacts' if they do not fit the pre-existing theoretical assumptions). • Scientists do not work in a 'positivistic' way.
Marxism	• Science is not value-free but responds to demands of capitalism – profit and ideology. • Scientific research is dominated by competition, the profit motive, and ideological justification of the interests of powerful groups. • Funding by capitalist firms is central to scientific research.
Feminism	• Science is a patriarchal institution. • Most scientists are male and the scientific establishment emphasises 'male' values of rationality and logic. • Scientists have sought to justify the social inferiority of women by recourse to ideologically based research. • Science prioritises aspects of society which are of more benefit to men – e.g. space exploration.
Realism	• Realists see science as an attempt to explain causal relationships in terms of underlying (unobservable) structures, mechanisms and processes. • Difference between **open** and **closed** systems in natural science (Sayer, 1984). • Within closed systems variables can be controlled and measured, e.g. chemistry and physics. • Open systems cannot control all variables and prediction levels are uncertain, e.g. medicine, meteorology and seismology. • Realism accepts that there are limits to what science can explain.

15. SOCIOLOGY AS A SCIENTIFIC DISCIPLINE

APPROACHES	YES/NO	SOCIOLOGY AS A SCIENCE	PROBLEMS WITH APPROACHES
Positivism	Yes	• **Comte and Durkheim** = sociology was a positivistic science. • Sociology is the examination of social facts. • Use of methods of the natural sciences allowed social scientists to look for causation and the natural laws governing social behaviour.	• **Durkheim** used what is now recognised as a realist approach in his analysis of suicide by examining meanings of religious/family membership etc. as well as structural factors.
	No	• **Popper** – sociology is not scientific because, for example, Marxist theory cannot be falsified.	• Popperian assumptions have been challenged by more recent philosophy of science.
Interpretivism	No	• Subject matter of sociology is fundamentally different from that of natural sciences. Cannot be studied using controlled observation. • Individuals have consciousness and free will and are not passive. Motivation and meaning must be taken into account to gain a true understanding of social action. • Official statistics do not present a true picture.	• Interactionist research methods can be as systematic as more quantitative methods, e.g. coding schedules for secondary data and clear guidelines on conducting participant observation. • Observers can remain as objective as those using positivistic methods.
Kuhn	No	• Sociology is not scientific as it has no single paradigm shared by all sociologists. • It is pre-paradigmatic.	• **Kuhn** has overestimated the amount of consensus between natural scientists. Fails to examine competitive nature of scientific community. • Many sciences are multi-paradigmatic.
Kaplan	Yes	• Sociology can be seen to operate reconstructed logics and logics in use, so is as scientific or as unscientific as the natural sciences.	• Reconstructed logics in sociology depend on the subjective interpretation of meaning.
Marxism	Yes	• **Marx** claimed that his theory of the development of capitalism was scientific as it was testable to a degree (law of capital).	• If Marxism is testable, then it has not been proven so by events. • Marxism is also an ideological approach. • Claim to epistemological privilege ('Marxism know the truth') is unsustainable.
	No	• Positivistic sociology may claim to be scientific but is merely an ideological approach.	
Feminism	No	• Sociology must produce interpretative understandings using in-depth methods. • Sociologists should be able to relate to respondents and gain their trust, even reciprocate with information etc. (Oakley).	• Some feminists argue that research should use all available methods but care should be taken to avoid sexist attitudes and assumptions.
Realism	Yes	• Similarities between sociology and other sciences. • Both concerned with observable phenomena and the (invisible) underlying structures and processes. • Both have to accept limitations to what they are able to explain.	• Realist theories cannot be tested as they are not in a positivistic sense testable. • Realism wants the best of both worlds – to be 'scientific' and to access meaning.

16. SOCIOLOGY AND VALUE FREEDOM

VALUE FREEDOM

The idea that researcher's beliefs and desires should not enter the research and prejudice the results. It is a central part of the positivist approach to research.

SOCIOLOGY CAN BE VALUE-FREE	SOCIOLOGY CANNOT BE VALUE-FREE
Positivism • As this approach sees sociology as scientific, then it must also be value-free as researchers are detached from their research and their results can be verified against other social facts. **Weber** • Weber accepts a scientific approach generally, but as he stresses the uniqueness of historical events, he rejects the possibility of social laws governing behaviour. • Individuals view the world from a value-laden perspective so the value position of the sociologist will affect the actual choice of what will be investigated. This is value-relevance. • The selection of a research area will frequently reflect contemporary issues and concerns. • Once the topic has been selected, then the research must be carried out objectively. • It is even possible for sociologists to take values as a topic of investigation to see how they change over time.	**Gunnar Myrdal** • Objectivity is an ideal to strive for but is unachievable. • All scientists are prone to bias but more so in social science because social scientists are part of the subject matter they study. • Sociologists should make their value position clear when they present their findings. **Interpretivists** • The idea of sociology as a social enterprise possibly being value-free is inconceivable. • To choose a subject of study is to express a value position. **Gouldner** • Sociologists actually commit themselves to domain assumptions and these affect their perceptions. • Facts cannot be separated from values in research. **Becker** • Anti-value freedom. • He believes that social researchers should declare 'whose side they are on'. This is likely to be the anti-establishment side aligned with the 'underdog'.

LEFT   **Whose side are we on?**   RIGHT

Marxism
• Examines social inequalities and conflicts of interests.
• Theoretically and politically committed to revolutionary change – left-wing.

Functionalism
• Supports status quo is against revolutionary change.
• Does not interrogate power interests so ideologically conservative.

Feminism
Ideological differences between the various approaches:

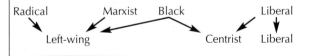

Radical   Marxist   Black   Liberal

Left-wing   Centrist   Liberal

New Right
• Committed to disestablishment of welfare state.
• Sees poverty as fault of individuals.
• For traditional morality and more control over disruptive elements.

Values and research
1. Funding of project – might create obligations to funding body – possible bias.
2. Choice of topic – affected by value-relevance.
3. Choice of method = level of involvement of researcher = some methods have greater/lower levels of personal involvement – possible bias.
4. Interpretation of data = effect of sociological community – schools of thought create different perspectives for sociologists. Data interpreted within certain frameworks.
5. Dissemination – to whom and where will also involve values. A study on a deviant group might be helpful to the establishment and detrimental to the interests of the group studied.

17. CONCEPTS

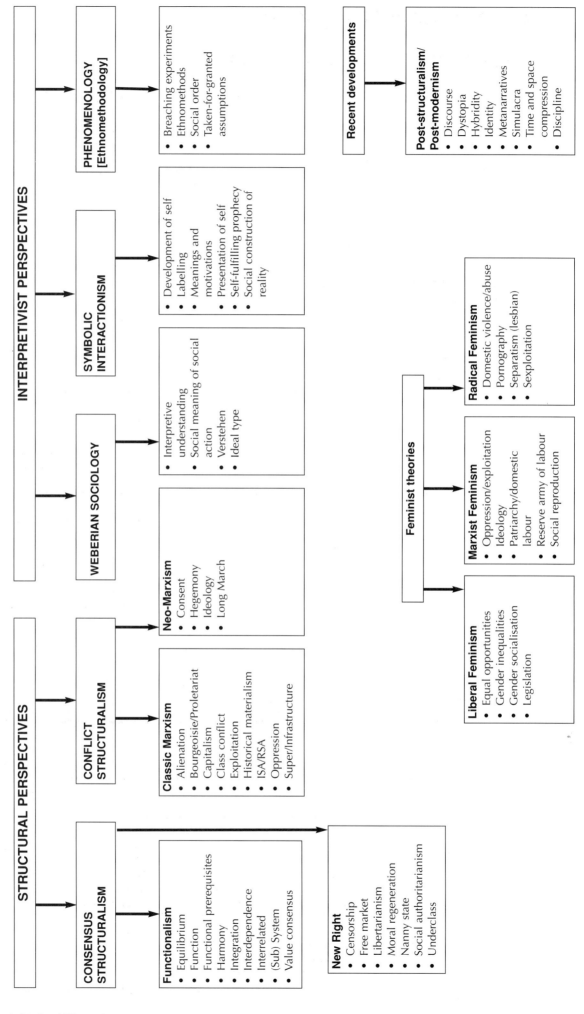

STRUCTURAL PERSPECTIVES

INTERPRETIVIST PERSPECTIVES

CONSENSUS STRUCTURALISM

CONFLICT STRUCTURALISM

WEBERIAN SOCIOLOGY

SYMBOLIC INTERACTIONISM

PHENOMENOLOGY [Ethnomethodology]

- Breaching experiments
- Ethnomethods
- Social order
- Taken-for-granted assumptions

Recent developments

Post-structuralism/ Post-modernism
- Discourse
- Dystopia
- Hybridity
- Identity
- Metanarratives
- Simulacra
- Time and space compression
- Discipline

- Development of self
- Labelling
- Meanings and motivations
- Presentation of self
- Self-fulfilling prophecy
- Social construction of reality

- Interpretive understanding
- Social meaning of social action
- Verstehen
- Ideal type

Neo-Marxism
- Consent
- Hegemony
- Ideology
- Long March

Classic Marxism
- Alienation
- Bourgeoisie/Proletariat
- Capitalism
- Class conflict
- Exploitation
- Historical materialism
- ISA/RSA
- Oppression
- Super/Infrastructure

Functionalism
- Equilibrium
- Function
- Functional prerequisites
- Harmony
- Integration
- Interdependence
- Interrelated
- (Sub) System
- Value consensus

New Right
- Censorship
- Free market
- Libertarianism
- Moral regeneration
- Nanny state
- Social authoritarianism
- Underclass

Feminist theories

Radical Feminism
- Domestic violence/abuse
- Pornography
- Separatism (lesbian)
- Sexploitation

Marxist Feminism
- Oppression/exploitation
- Ideology
- Patriarchy/domestic labour
- Reserve army of labour
- Social reproduction

Liberal Feminism
- Equal opportunities
- Gender inequalities
- Gender socialisation
- Legislation

13 Crime and Deviance

1. NATURE OF THE CONCEPTS

CRIME – behaviour which breaks the laws of a particular society, and could result in action being taken by formal agencies of social control, e.g.
- taking goods from a shop without paying
- child abduction.

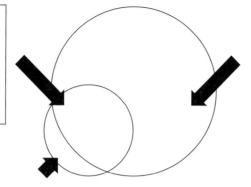

DEVIANCE – behaviour which goes against the dominant social norms of a specific society or group, and causes some form of critical reaction or disapproval, e.g.
- talking to plants in the garden
- cross-dressing.

CRIME NOT DEVIANCE – actions which, despite breaking the law, are so common or accepted that they are not subject to informal sanctions, e.g.
- driving at 40 mph in a built-up area
- making personal telephone calls at work without permission.

ILLUSTRATION OF THE RELATIVITY OF CRIME AND DEVIANCE

Variations	Examples of crime	Examples of deviance
Time • No longer in UK • New to UK	• Abortion, homosexual activity for 18–21 year olds • Stalking	• Body piercing • Smoking in public areas
Societal • Accepted in UK but not somewhere else • Accepted elsewhere but not in UK	• Alcohol consumption (Saudi Arabia) • Euthanasia (Holland)	• Wearing of miniskirts (Iran) • Spitting in public places (China)
• Context	• Taking someone's life may be tolerated in self-defence	• Belching at a formal dinner, not with a group of friends
• Person	• No sexual relationship with your patient (if doctor) or pupil (if teacher)	• Drunken child, not drunken man
• Place	• Punching on football terraces, not in boxing ring	• Topless on cricket pitch, not in sauna

A CONTINUUM OF CRIME AND DEVIANCE

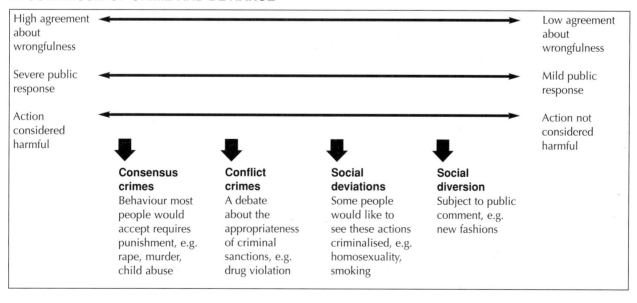

High agreement about wrongfulness ⟷ Low agreement about wrongfulness

Severe public response ⟷ Mild public response

Action considered harmful ⟷ Action not considered harmful

Consensus crimes
Behaviour most people would accept requires punishment, e.g. rape, murder, child abuse

Conflict crimes
A debate about the appropriateness of criminal sanctions, e.g. drug violation

Social deviations
Some people would like to see these actions criminalised, e.g. homosexuality, smoking

Social diversion
Subject to public comment, e.g. new fashions

2. CRIME STATISTICS

GROWTH IN CRIMES KNOWN TO POLICE

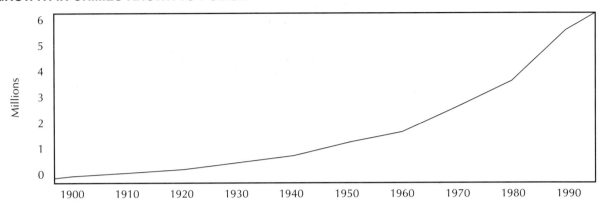

RECORDED AND HIDDEN CRIMES

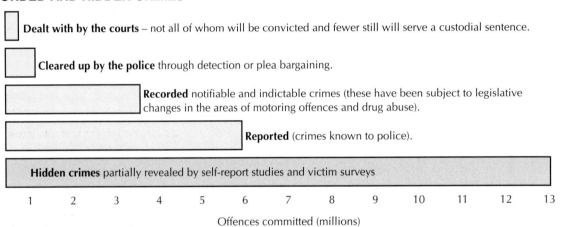

Dealt with by the courts – not all of whom will be convicted and fewer still will serve a custodial sentence.

Cleared up by the police through detection or plea bargaining.

Recorded notifiable and indictable crimes (these have been subject to legislative changes in the areas of motoring offences and drug abuse).

Reported (crimes known to police).

Hidden crimes partially revealed by self-report studies and victim surveys

Offences committed (millions)

CHARACTERISTICS OF KNOWN OFFENDERS

Characteristic	Pattern
Age	Mainly young involved in vehicle crimes and drug-related offences.
Class	Mainly working-class for burglary, street offences. Middle class – fraudulent business activities, violation of health and safety laws, tax evasion.
Gender	Predominantly male. Women for less serious offences, e.g. shoplifting and prostitution, but gap between the two is narrowing.
Ethnicity	Higher proportion of ethnic groups as offenders and victims. Drug offences common among Afro-Caribbean.

NOTIFIABLE OFFENCES (relative proportions)

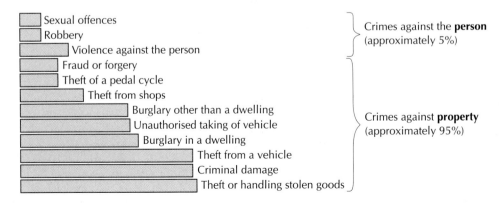

3. SOCIAL CONSTRUCTION OF STATISTICS

FACTORS INFLUENCING THE PROCESS	STAGES IN THE PRODUCTION OF CRIME STATISTICS	ILLUSTRATIONS FROM WHITE-COLLAR CRIMES (i.e. crimes by non-manual workers in the course of their occupation)
• Victims • Witnesses • Where the offence was committed, e.g. subject to police surveillance • Nature of offence	**Observation of the offence**	• Victims may be unaware • Paper or computer fraud not readily observed • Police cannot routinely patrol private organisations
• Perceived seriousness • Faith in the police • Fear of reprisals • Availability of telephone • Requirement for insurance • Embarrassment of victim • Changes to the law • Failure of victim to perceive themselves as such	**Reporting**	• Crimes seen as clever rather than bad • Employees may fear loss of job by reporting superiors • Employer and employee may be beneficiaries • Sacking rather than criminal process • Preference for informal sanctions • Offence seen as trivial
• Priorities/crackdown • Workload/chance of clear-up • Social status of complainant • Interpretation of the law	**Recording by the police**	• Low chance of clear-up • Expensive in time and labour to investigate • Difficult to investigate
• Availability of officers • Sensitivity and moral values of public	**Follow-up**	• Handled by other agencies, e.g. Inland Revenue, Health and Safety officers
• Police methods • New technology • Stereotypes of criminals • Informants	**Arrest**	• Easy to remove evidence, e.g. wipe the computer or destroy the paperwork • Lack of police expertise in this field
• Police discretion to caution or let off with warning • Perceived threat posed by suspect • Plea bargaining	**Prosecutions**	• Suspect takes ill-health retirement • Lack of forensic evidence • Does not fit police stereotype of a criminal
• Quality of legal representation • Trial by jury • Nature of charges	**Convictions**	• Complexity of case makes it easy to confuse the jury • Defendant has the means to buy the best legal advice
• Previous record • Judge's discretion • Public opinion • Media interest	**Sentencing**	• Assumed to have already suffered loss of status and income • Judge shows empathy for person of the same social background • Lack of social reaction to crime

4. NON-SOCIOLOGICAL EXPLANATIONS

	DESCRIPTION	EVALUATION
BIOLOGICAL	**Lombroso – Evolutionary Theory (1876)** Discovered physical characteristics that were the outward sign of inborn criminal traits found in earlier life forms, e.g. large jaws, acute eyesight and love of orgies! Key concept used was atavism: that is, criminality was typical of less-developed humans.	✓ Made detailed measurements of prisoners in Italian jails and compared with a control group of soldiers ✗ Used unrepresentative samples ✗ Even if there is an association between physique and criminal conviction this is not evidence of causation
	Klinefelter's Syndrome (1960) Additional Y chromosome makes people aggressive and this results in criminal behaviour.	✓ Condition found to be very common in the prison population ✗ Cannot explain non-violent criminals
	Glueck (1950) Delinquents are twice as likely to have a mesomorphic (stocky and powerful) build. Physical build and temperament are inherited and affect response to the stresses of life.	✓ Seems to fit stereotypical 'criminal' type ✗ Based on institutionalised delinquents ✗ Build is not found to be significant when social class factors held constant
PSYCHOLOGICAL	**Pre-menstrual tension (PMT)** Stress caused by menstruation can make women act irrationally and so they cannot be held responsible for their actions. 80% of all female crime occurs around the period of menstruation.	✓ Accepted as defence plea ✗ Fits the male stereotype of the female criminal ✗ Implies that women are not responsible for their actions most of the time
	Eysenck – personality theory (1977) Criminality is an inherited characteristic like personality and intelligence. The neurotic extrovert is less easily conditionable and hence more prone to criminality because the individual takes longer to learn the rules of society.	✓ Personality tests of prisoners showed a higher proportion of neurotic extroverts than in the population as a whole ✗ Tests may be measuring the effects of imprisonment not the cause ✗ Ignores the fact that convicted criminals are an unrepresentative sample of criminals
	Bowlby – maternal deprivation (1965) A mother provides emotional security for the growing child, without this intimate relationship the child will show psychopathic personality (i.e. shows no guilt, fails to respond to punishment).	✓ Based on the biographical details of 44 juvenile thieves ✗ Fails to take account of other variables that could explain this association, e.g. poverty ✗ Many exceptions to the pattern
ALL	**Non-sociological theories** • Attempt to explain crime scientifically • Treat all crime as a homogeneous category • Search for a single explanation.	✗ Fail to explain the social patterns of crime ✗ Ignore social factors ✗ Assume it is possible to distinguish between criminals and non-criminals ✗ Unlikely to find one explanation for all varieties of crime ✗ Offer incomplete and partial explanations

5. FUNCTIONALIST THEORIES

DURKHEIM – CRIME AND SOCIAL ORDER (1938)

High levels of crime are dysfunctional and destabilise society but some crime is necessary as it helps the social system survive. Hence it is:

Functional	Inevitable	Normal
• Boundaries of acceptable behaviour are made known by the arrest of those who transgress. • Strengthens bonds between people and reaffirms values when they are drawn together by horrific crimes. • Public opinion on crimes shows whether the law needs to be changed. • Law and crime form one of most distinct of boundaries in modernity.	It is impossible for everyone to be equally committed to the norms and rules of society. Even in a society of saints a distinction would be made between what is acceptable and unacceptable behaviour. Because there are differences between people, naturally occurring, there are bound to be those who step over the boundary of lawful behaviour.	There is no society where there is no crime. Abnormal levels of crime occur in times of social upheaval when the power of the collective conscience is weakened and a state of **anomie** develops as people look after their own interests rather than respecting their neighbours. Individualism is therefore a source of crime.

Evaluation

✓ Shows the useful purpose served by crime

✓ Offers an explanation that recognises a social dimension to crime

✓ Explains the reason for unhealthy levels of crime which could be altered by social engineering

✓ Does not explain crime by reference to 'sick' individuals

✗ Does not explain individual motivations and why only some people commit crime

✗ Assumes harmony and that the law reflects the interests and views of the majority, hence ignores issues of power

✗ Over-emphasis on degree of consensus in society

✗ Pessimistic view of control of crime

MERTON – SOCIAL STRUCTURE AND ANOMIE (1949)

Deviance occurs when there is an attachment to the goals but not the means for everyone to achieve.

Mode of adaptation	Institutional means	Cultural goals	Description
Conformist, e.g. law-abiding	✓	✓	• Works hard to achieve success and wealth
Innovator, e.g. criminal	✗	✓	• Gains wealth by illegitimate means
Ritualist, e.g. bureaucrats	✓	✗	• Abides by the rules but scales down the goals
Retreatist, e.g. drug-users	✗	✗	• Rejects both by dropping out of society
Rebel, e.g. terrorists/ freedom fighters	✗ (✓)	✗ (✓)	• Rejects both but replaces with own goals and means

Evaluation

✓ Shows how the social structure causes a strain to deviance

✓ Provided a stimulus for sub-cultural theories

✓ Explains how classes are socialised in different ways to create different types of deviance

✓ Emphasised that the majority reaction is conformity

✗ Assumes a consensus on goals

✗ Fails to explain why some conform and others do not

✗ Ignores different illegal opportunities

✗ Does not explain non-utilitarian crime

✗ Reflects American Dream ideology

✗ Does not explain why some individuals become innovators and others retreatists, or rebels, or ritualists.

6. ECOLOGICAL THEORIES

CONCENTRIC ZONE THEORY (ERNEST BURGESS, 1927)
- Cities spread out in successive circles or zones.
- Each zone has distinctive style of life.
- Zone of transition was area of social disorganisation.
- Central Business District had distinctive 'feel'.
- Residential and dormitory zones on outskirts.

THEORY OF HUMAN ECOLOGY (ROBERT E. PARK, 1922)
- Fascinated by ebb and flow of urban life – its sheer speed.
- City like organism with life of its own.
- Propelled by tension between individual's need for freedom and society's need for social control.
- Strongest seize more favourable urban locations.
- Each area develops own way of life.

URBANISM AS A WAY OF LIFE (LOUIS WIRTH, 1938)
- Cities are the distinctive feature of modern life.
- Characterised by:

Size – grow into distinct neighbourhoods

Density – large numbers mean less meaningful contact

Heterogeneity – becomes fluid mass with few rigid class distinctions.

CHICAGO SCHOOL

WHY CHICAGO?
- fast growing
- heavy industry
- waves of immigration
- constant state of flux

Criticisms of Burgess's model

✗ While some socio-spatial studies confirmed model of concentric rings, others did not.

✗ Over-simplified view as cities are more complex than series of rings.

✗ Treated city in isolation, as single organism, unrelated to wider economic, social and political processes.

✗ Took social divisions for granted, ignoring factors which force some people to live in slums and others in desirable neighbourhoods.

✗ Ultimately descriptive rather than analytical, as does not explore fully reasons why zones develop as they do.

✗ Had ideological commitment to capitalist economics, which took for granted.

✗ Saw distribution of housing as somehow 'natural'.

Criticisms of Wirth's approach

✗ Had pessimistic view of urban life, seeing it as empty emotionally.

✗ Psychologically suspect in seeing city dwellers as nervy and irritable.

✗ Used Chicago as model, but it was not typical of cities at the time.

✗ Deterministic in its view of culture, seeing it as determining the way that urban people lived their lives.

✗ Over-emphasised the potential of voluntary groups to overcome the isolation of urban living.

✗ Stereotypes urban dwellers.

Commuter zone

Residential zone

Central business district

Working-class homes

Zone of transition

Concentric zones

Conclusion
Underlying these approaches is the position that there are distinct differences between urban and rural ways of life, and that the move from the rural to the urban has meant a loss to society of something precious, to gain something which is not quite fully human. See **Stratification 7**.

7. SUB-CULTURAL THEORIES

	STATUS FRUSTRATION (A. Cohen, 1955)	OPPORTUNITY STRUCTURES (Cloward & Ohlin, 1961)	LOWER CLASS CULTURE (Miller, 1962)
Type of sub-culture	Reactive i.e. each generation responds to their situation/opportunities		Independent sub-culture i.e. the values are passed down from one generation to the next
Description	Working-class boys that are denied status in the education system from their position in lower streams, invert the values of society and gain status from their peers by acting according to the opposite values, e.g. • politeness → rudeness • respect for others' property → vandalism • restrained actions → unrestrained actions	Three forms of deviant sub-culture exist with different access opportunities: 1. criminal (stable working-class communities with a career structure in crime) 2. conflict (lack of criminal career but violent gangs) 3. retreatist sub-cultures (double failures who turn to drugs).	A set of focal concerns guides the behaviour that leads the young into delinquency: • Fate – little can be done to change your life • Excitement – a search for cheap thrills • Autonomy – resent authority • Smartness – an ability to con others • Toughness – displays of masculine powers • Trouble – acceptance of violence
Positive evaluation	✓ Explains negative acts of vandalism ✓ Shows that deviance is rational ✓ Shows that deviance is learned in peer groups ✓ Relates deviance to need for status	✓ Shows the importance of illegitimate opportunity structures ✓ Recognises different types of youth sub-culture ✓ Emphasises access to legitimate means	✓ Describes a true independent sub-culture ✓ Shows the importance of socialisation of family and peers ✓ Relates deviance to the real social conditions of the city
Negative evaluation	✗ Does not recognise the fun and kicks that the young may get from breaking the law ✗ No evidence of status frustration among East End youth	✗ No evidence for the hierarchy of sub-cultures described ✗ Overlaps and interrelationships between each sub-culture	✗ Exaggerates the difference in values between classes ✗ Adopts a middle-class perspective ✗ Tends to generalise working-class youth

All three theories	
✓ Explain male, working-class and youthful deviance ✓ See deviance as the result of a collective response ✓ Recognise the social origins of deviance ✓ Focus on socio-cultural factors	✗ Do not explain female, middle-class and middle-age crimes ✗ Overly deterministic, i.e. give no recognition to the free choices of the deviant ✗ Assume moral consensus on values ✗ Assume all delinquency is a group activity

Crime and Deviance 197

8. INTERACTIONIST CONTRIBUTIONS

THE PROCESS OF RULE AND LAW CREATION – the way people create deviance by making the rules and laws that define deviant behaviour

1. Meaning – a particular behaviour is perceived to be a threat to social values.		**2. Motive** – a moral entrepreneur takes up the cause as the result of • a conflict of interests • moral indignation • humanitarianism

4. Outcome – depends on the relative power of the different interest groups in the negotiation process.		**3. Action** – a moral crusade is organised by enlisting support from experts, religious leaders, mass media, law enforcement etc.

THE PROCESS OF BEING LABELLED 'DEVIANT'

PRIMARY DEVIANCE – is committed by the majority of people at some time but it is normalised, i.e. ignored, tolerated, or rationalised. It is marginal to the identity of the individual.

Drift – the movement in and out of deviant behaviour without commitment.	**Labelling** stigmatises the individual and those who have power can make the label stick.	**No labelling** – those who escape apprehension despite repeated rule-breaking.

Falsely accused	True deviants	Secret deviants

Rebuttal and attempt to re-establish conformist identity – seeks to re-integrate self into community	Experience similar consequences to true deviants in addition to the sense of injustice	Rejected, excluded, degraded, coerced. This group are most likely to move to next stage	Some may move into secondary deviance by anticipating the reactions of others and attempting to keep their deviance secret

or

Secondary deviance follows from the stigmatising force of the label. This social reaction leads to changes in relationships between the labelled and the labellers.

The person is treated in terms of a **master status**, i.e. past and present actions of the deviant are seen only in terms of the deviant label and are reconstructed to fit with the new identity.

Reconstruction of a positive image of their deviance by offering an alternative view based on their own experiences.	**Adoption** of deviant identity and acceptance of the negative stereotypical view others have. Accepts the master status	**Rejection** of this identity does not protect the deviant from the fact that others see him/her in this way which can be an influence on future behaviour.

Role deviance occurs as the individual conforms to the deviance that is a central feature of a person's identity.	**Moral career** involves a sequence of roles and learning experiences that are part of the adaptation to the new identity.	**Deviant collectivities** – the shared identity of membership can provide a supportive and safe environment in which the necessary learning can take place.

9. DEVIANCE AMPLIFICATION

ROLE OF THE POLICE

1. Action by the police unites the deviants and makes them feel different from the wider society.

2. Segregation from the rest of society means the deviants lose informal social controls of family etc.

3. Evolving deviant norms of dress and style reduce the chance of re-entering wider society.

4. Deviance becomes more secret and a symbol of defiance that is an essential activity for membership.

5. Increased risks of arrest mean a larger profit is asked for by those who service the deviants' needs, this attracts organised criminal business.

6. Diverse deviant groups may feel a sense of identity as victims of police harassment.

7. Deviant cultures begin to overlap and police arrest more deviants in response to public pressure for action.

ROLE OF THE MEDIA

1. Over-reporting an event of deviance (exaggerating numbers, emotive language) to increase interest.

2. Identification of those involved and associating with distinctive styles of dress, music and transport etc.

3. Sensitising police and courts so that swift action is taken and trouble is dealt with punitively.

4. Pre-publicity for an event in a way that might appear attractive to others inclined to deviance.

5. On-the-spot attention from journalists as an incentive to misbehave.

6. Exploitation by the press asking suitably dressed deviants to pose for photographs.

7. Mass media incite public opinion causing a moral panic and demands are made for more police action.

AMPLIFICATION SPIRAL

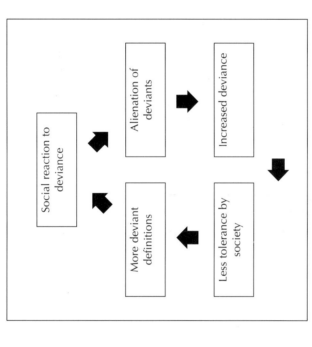

Social reaction to deviance

More deviant definitions

Alienation of deviants

Less tolerance by society

Increased deviance

Positive contributions from interactionism

✓ Recognises that crime and deviance are socially constructed

✓ Draws attention to the consequences of labelling

✓ Shows how moral panics can be created by the police and the media

✓ Ideas can be applied to many forms of deviance, e.g. drug users, youth sub-cultures, football hooligans, 'mugging'

✓ Analyses the process of becoming a deviant

✓ Explains marginal acts of deviance

Criticisms of interactionism

✗ Overplays the role of labelling by portraying the deviant as a passive victim

✗ Implies that deviance does not exist unless someone observes it

✗ Gives no explanation for the origin of the deviant act

✗ Does not explain how the spiral of amplification ends

✗ Ignores the importance of power sources in the social system

✗ Ignores the pleasures/satisfactions deviants may gain

✗ Gives too much concern for the offender

10. TRADITIONAL MARXIST THEORIES

THEORY OF SOCIAL CONTROL

Law creation

The state as an agent of the ruling capitalist class defines criminal activities so that their own interests are served.
- Most laws concern the protection of private property.
- Dog-fighting and badger-baiting (working-class) are criminal, fox-hunting (middle/upper-class) is not.
- To maximise profit, e.g. death caused by exposing workers to danger is not treated as murder.
- The workforce is controlled by e.g. anti-union laws.
- Certain forms of social life are legitimated.

Law enforcement

Biased application to less powerful groups.
- Corporate manslaughter charges rarely brought despite catastrophic industrial 'accidents'.
- Police effort directed at working-class by prioritising certain crimes and areas of towns.
- Differential sentencing biased against lower classes.
- Occasionally rich and powerful people are prosecuted to maintain the illusion of a fair legal system.
- Anti-trade union laws rigorously applied.

SUPPORTS AND LEGITIMATES

Dominant ideology
- Ruling class sets the standards of acceptable behaviour.
- Ruling class sets the agenda on which debates about law and order take place.
- Through socialisation people accept the naturalness and values of the capitalist system.
- Problem of crime is equated with the working-class who are made the scapegoats despite the trivial sums involved compared to the costs of white-collar crime.

THEORIES OF CRIME CONTRASTED

	Functionalist	Traditional Marxist
Causes of crime	Some members of society do not internalise the rules or are socialised into deviant behaviour; some are 'natural' deviants who push against social constraints.	Capitalist society emphasises individual gain and the need to win at all costs. Greed explains crimes for financial gain. Frustration caused by the dehumanising features of the capitalist mode of production explain crimes against the person.
Reasons why the working-class are more criminal	• Family, neighbourhood, peer groups are less likely to work effectively as agencies of socialisation. • Working-class more likely to be arrested because they commit more crimes.	• The law is created by the ruling class and only acts which grow out of working-class life are defined as criminal. • Everyone breaks the law, but biased law enforcement means it is mainly the working-class who get caught.
Consequences of crime for society	• Sets the limits of tolerance of deviant behaviour. • Offends everyone's conscience thus creating a tighter bond among them. • Makes people aware of common interests.	• Creates false consciousness by making the working-class think their own interests are the same as the ruling class. • Diverts attention from the exploitation the working-class receive. • Permits greater control of the proletariat.
Prospects for the future	• Societies need and produce crime to set limits to behaviour.	• Logic suggests there would be no crime in socialist societies.

11. NEO-MARXIST THEORIES

A FULLY SOCIAL THEORY OF DEVIANCE

APPLICATIONS OF THEORY TO FORMS OF DEVIANCE

(Taylor, Walton and Young, 1973)	'Mugging'	Black crime	Skinheads
1. **Wider origins**, i.e. the way wealth and power are distributed in society	West Indians were brought to this country in the 1960s to do menial jobs which were not being filled.	The African and Caribbean communities carry the scars of imperialist violence.	Youth are the age group least trapped by ruling class values, e.g. family commitments and mortgages.
2. **Immediate circumstances** surrounding the deviant act	The recession of the 1970s fell heavily on the black population and the unemployed turned to petty street crime and drugs.	The black population are subject to police harassment, racial discrimination, and racially motivated attacks.	In the 1960s the young working-class were responding to the loss of jobs, housing and their communities.
3. **Deviant act itself** and the meaning it has	These activities were not new but were given a new name 'mugging' by the media.	Crime is a political activity against injustices experienced by an exploited black population.	The skinhead style is imbued with meaning as the youth symbolically tried to recapture their lost origins.
4. **Immediate social reaction** – the way the family, police and public respond	Calls for strong police presence and a crackdown on offenders who newspapers implied were predominantly black.	Police operate on the basis of negative stereotypes, e.g. West Indians are lawless, Asians are illegal immigrants.	Skinheads were seen as a threat to authority and to the stability of society. Public responded to the outward symbols of being a skinhead.
5. **Wider social reaction** explained in terms of who has the power	Capitalism was facing a crisis and the government was suffering a loss of control because of strikes, Northern Ireland troubles, and inner city unrest.	Black people are the scapegoats for the economic crisis of capitalism and are blamed for high levels of unemployment with calls for repatriation.	Opposition reflected the cultural contradictions and divisions which existed in society especially the disadvantages of the lower working-class.
6. **Outcome**	Acceptance by the public of repressive policing measures and an amplification of the problem.	The myth of black criminality increases the sense of injustice felt by the black community.	Ideological resistance did not solve their problems or change anything but it helped the youth to make sense of their marginality.
7. **Totality** – the nature of the deviant process as a whole	Mugging presented as symptom of breakdown of law and order and the public were persuaded that the problems in society were caused by immigrants rather than by capitalism.	Black crime is part of the political struggle against a white racist society and can be seen as a legitimate resistance to discrimination.	The transition from childhood to adulthood affects each generation and class differently. Youth sub-cultures provide a ritual solution that challenges the dominant ideas and hence is a form of political activity.

12. WHITE-COLLAR CRIME

The term 'white-collar crime' was coined by Sutherland (1949) to indicate that not all crime was committed by the working class, as the crime statistics would suggest. Rather, crime was 'ubiquitous' – carried out by members of all social classes, including the most powerful in society.

✓ Shifted focus away from 'lower class' forms of crime, such as violence, towards other types of law-breaking activity, such as fraud.

✗ Did not distinguish between types of white-collar crime, so that the concept included very different activities by many different groups.

This has led sociologists to suggest different types of 'middle-class' crimes, carried out by those in positions of varying status and class, and to extend the concept to include the upper class.

Occupational crime	Professional crime	Corporate crime	State crime
Carried out in work. • Ranges from minor theft of organisation's property to large-scale fraud. • Increasingly found lower down hierarchy. • Betrayal of social capital of 'trust' by employee. • Increasingly appearing as computer fraud.	• Carried out as a lifetime career. • Ranges from large-scale operations such as drug-running to petty theft. • Often done in criminal organisations that are stable 'employers'. • Criminal organisations often have legal aspects to their activities.	• Carried out by members of organisations to increase profit. • Ranges from pollution episodes to selling of harmful products. • Not result of negligence but pressure to make money. • Increasingly global as capitalism expands.	• Carried out by agents of state in pursuance of often ideological ends. • Range from torture of citizens to denial of human rights. • Resources of state used for illegitimate purposes. • Has global aspect as concern for human rights increases.

STRAIN THEORY (PASSAS, 1990)
Members of organisations under 'strain' of pressure to make profits. Participants may choose to cut corners to meet targets set by organisation.

✓ Sets problem in an economic and psychological context.

✗ Assumes that strain is felt by all in a similar structural location, but that responses are different to it.

CONTROL THEORIES (WEISBURD, 1991)
White-collar workers are over-integrated into materialist ideologies of capitalism and seek to maximise their own financial gains. This neutralises any concern over law-breaking.

✓ Sets problem in an ideological framework and includes explanation of why law-abiders become law-breakers.

✗ Does not explicate why some will neutralise objections to law-breaking and others keep them.

EXPLANATIONS OF WHITE-COLLAR CRIMINALITY

NEO-MARXIST (BOX, 1983)
Capitalism is crimogenic, in that the system pushes members of firms towards crime to maintain profits for the owners to expropriate.

✓ Places corporate crime into a structural setting of economic and ideological forces.

✗ Mechanism whereby the interests of the owners are translated into law-breaking by executives is not laid out.

SOCIAL CAPITAL THEORY (HAGAN, 1994)
Those in positions of power in firms have too much social trust (a form of social capital) invested in them, which gives the freedom from social control to commit white-collar crime.

✓ Stresses the nature of inter-relationships between members of organisations as a source of power which allows the committing of crime.

✗ Does not explore why all those with social trust do not commit crime.

Criticism of idea of white-collar crime (Nelken, 1994)
Represents a simplified view of the behaviour of people in business, whether private or public. Assumes that many executives happily break the law, when many are as law-abiding as rest of population. Also treats all organisations as similar, when many, such as the army or the police, do not face same competitive pressures as business organisations. Environmental pollution by communist states suggests that law-breaking by the state is not confined to capitalism.

13. REALIST THEORIES

REALISM

Crime is a serious problem which requires practical solutions, hence research is policy-oriented.

RIGHT REALISM

Assumptions

- Offenders are selfish and wicked people undeterred by the criminal justice system.
- They have a poor upbringing or biological/genetic defects.
- State has become ineffective and inadequate in constraining and controlling the criminal, hence the need for more penal sanctions.
- Poverty/unemployment does **not** cause crime as crime rates have gone up in times of economic prosperity.

Cause of crime – culture of permissiveness

- Decline in respect for authority linked to fatherless families.
- Decline in family values and discipline.
- Welfare state has undermined the morality and destroyed the virtues of self-restraint and self-control.
- Collapse of sense of community.
- Control theory suggests people take part in crime when the benefits outweigh the potential costs.

Solution

Policies based on an understanding of human nature which deter people from crime by increased risks and decreased opportunities:

- target hardening, e.g. property marking, security devices
- surveillance, e.g. making people feel more responsible for what is happening in their neighbourhood
- zero tolerance policing, i.e. keeping streets clear of potential trouble to encourage the operation of informal social controls
- active citizens taking responsibility for their own environment.

LEFT REALISM

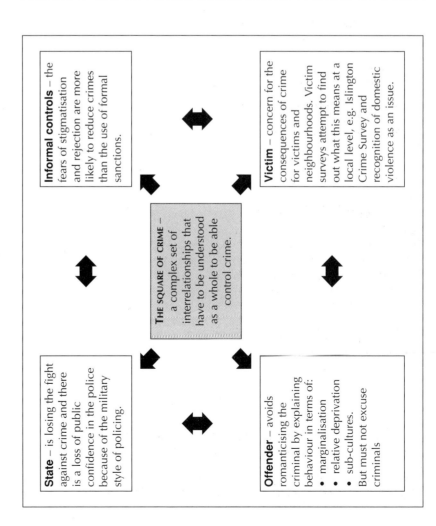

Informal controls – the fears of stigmatisation and rejection are more likely to reduce crimes than the use of formal sanctions.

Victim – concern for the consequences of crime for victims and neighbourhoods. Victim surveys attempt to find out what this means at a local level, e.g. Islington Crime Survey and recognition of domestic violence as an issue.

THE SQUARE OF CRIME – a complex set of interrelationships that have to be understood as a whole to be able control crime.

State – is losing the fight against crime and there is a loss of public confidence in the police because of the military style of policing.

Offender – avoids romanticising the criminal by explaining behaviour in terms of:

- marginalisation
- relative deprivation
- sub-cultures.

But must not excuse criminals

14. WOMEN AND CRIME

REASONS WHY WOMEN DO NOT COMMIT CRIME

Differential socialisation
- Girls are not brought up with the values of toughness and aggressiveness.
- Girls not taught the skills and technical knowledge to enable them to commit crime.
- Girls brought up to see private space, not public, as main arena.

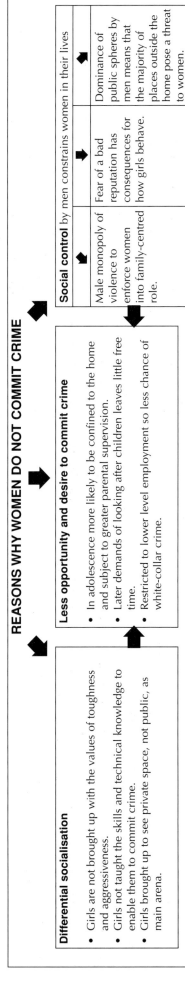

Less opportunity and desire to commit crime
- In adolescence more likely to be confined to the home and subject to greater parental supervision.
- Later demands of looking after children leaves little free time.
- Restricted to lower level employment so less chance of white-collar crime.

Social control by men constrains women in their lives

Male monopoly of violence to enforce women into family-centred role.	Fear of a bad reputation has consequences for how girls behave.	Dominance of public spheres by men means that the majority of places outside the home pose a threat to women.

PATTERN IN OFFICIAL STATISTICS
- Males 5 times more likely to appear in the statistics.
- Female crime has increased by 3 times but still very small (male by 2 times).

 Accurate

 Inaccurate

Invisibility of women in early research.

Absence of women in traditional research due to malestream bias of sociology.

REASONS WHY WOMEN DO COMMIT CRIME

Biological	Functionalist	Feminist	Poverty
• Abnormal women lack 'natural' female traits. • PMT stress can make women act irrationally. • Unmarried mothers (deviant!) are more likely to be neurotic extroverts.	Derives from role expectation: • Shoplifting from the role of family provider. • Prostitution from role of provider of sex or from desire to attract a mate. • Shop lifting make-up.	• Patriarchal legal definitions, e.g. provocation requires an immediate response which does not allow for the 'slow fuse' effects of abuse. • Women commit 'powerless' crimes such as prostitution.	• Women are marginalised in society and when they also lose faith in the welfare system they are more likely to commit crime. • Poverty can force women into victimless crimes, e.g. prostitution.

EVIDENCE THAT STATISTICS ARE INACCURATE

Treatment by police and courts		Self-report studies	Ethnographic studies
Harshness	**Leniency**		
• Women penalised because they flout gender expectations as well as normative ones. • Women imprisoned for non-violent crimes, e.g. failure to pay fines or non-payment of TV licence. • Girls more likely to be placed in protective custody.	• Prostitution and shoplifting not reported to police. • Chivalry factor by courts. • More discharges and cautions because domestic responsibilities taken into account. • Assumption that females have been led astray by men or are sick.	• High rates for trivial offences reduce M/F ratio. • Involved in domestic violence against children, partners and elderly.	• Women central to gang life, providing essential support services. • Female gangs are the subject of studies on violence.

15. ETHNICITY AND CRIME

EXPLANATIONS FOR THE ASSUMED ACCURACY

- Experience of anomie in a society where aspirations for financial success are blocked by prejudice and discrimination.

  ✗ Does not explain why the young turn to crime rather than alternative responses.

- Accumulation of anxieties and frustrations with limited opportunities of airing grievances (see Scarman enquiry)

  ✗ Does not explain why only a small number of blacks engage in crime.

- Higher levels of deprivation and unemployment have resulted in crime as a survival strategy.

- Subcultural differences, e.g. smoking of cannabis as part of a Rastafarian way of life.

- Afro-Caribbeans more involved in street crimes because they are more likely to embrace British culture and therefore experience relative deprivation compared to Asian youth.

- Age profile of ethnic minorities as younger means that higher crime rates might be expected.

- Black crime represents a form of political struggle for those who have been excluded from normal channels of political dissent.

- Differential exposure – more likely to live in inner-city areas where attacks take place.

- Victim precipitation as the result of vendetta and gangland crimes.

- Minorities are often the main victims of 'mugging' despite media portrayal of a black crime on a white population.

- Anti-discrimination laws have had little effect and resulted in very few prosecutions.

PATTERNS IN THE OFFICIAL STATISTICS (NB NO NATIONAL FIGURES)

1. OFFENDERS

- More black arrests.
- Charged and with more serious offences for similar behaviour.
- More likely to plead not guilty.
- Afro-Caribbeans more likely to be given a custodial sentence.

BUT variations by ethnic group

- South Asians not disproportionately represented.
- Chinese conviction rates very low.

2. VICTIMS

- Afro-Caribbeans and Asians twice as likely to be victims than whites.
- Asians more likely to believe the crime to be racist in character.
- Inter-racial incidents show blacks are more likely to be the targets.

STATISTICS ARE INACCURATE

over represented because

- Negative stereotypes held by police force pathologise black culture and lead to biased law enforcement.

  ✗ Victims identify approximately 36% of assailants as black.

- Victim bias may make people more likely to report crimes committed by blacks.

- The racist state is pursuing a policy of oppression against blacks using their criminality as a scapegoat for other problems.

  ✗ This argument is made by the same people who claim that black crime is a political statement.

  ✗ There is little evidence to support this conspiratorial theory.

- Police targeting of black communities.

- Police targeting particular types of crime, e.g. mugging.

- Some members of the black community are suspicious of police motives and so may challenge the police authority which may result in an arrest.

- Media distortion of black crime creates a moral panic and demand for greater police surveillance.

under-represented because of

- Institutional racism within the police, e.g. as demonstrated in the Lawrence enquiry.

- Racial harassment not taken seriously by police.

- Police adoption of victim-blaming approach deters reporting.

- Lack of faith in the police may discourage black communities from reporting crime and taking the law into their own hands.

- Statistics show that there are similar rates of reporting as in the rest of the community.

- Use of stop and search operations despite low arrest rate.

16. VICTIMOLOGY

VICTIMOLOGY

EXTENT estimated by victim surveys

National Surveys, e.g. British Crime surveys 1981–1993 Results criticised for under-representing some groups.
- Victims may not be aware or fail to remember.
- Average figures understated the number of victims in inner city, and the proportion of female and young.

Area studies, e.g. Islington Crime Survey, dealt with
- what concerns people
- uneven levels of victimisation

Fear of crime
Myth – exaggerated by the media causing increased fear of crime. *Reality* – differential exposure shows that in some areas there are real dangers and women's fears are justified.

Sensitivity to crime varies by geographical area – the more crime the less sensitive.

Consequences of being a victim:
- intrusion
- potentially long-lasting effects
- loss of possessions.

SELF-REPORTING
The victim is usually responsible for reporting the crime hence the role is self-defined.

Incidents not reported:
- fear of further violence
- embarrassment
- woman blames herself
- lack of faith in police, who are perceived as indifferent to female plight.

Domestic violence

Explanations:
- perpetrators are different
- violence is part of the sexist culture
- perpetrators come from a sub-culture of violence.

GENDER ISSUES

Protective custody
- used for young girls

Rape

Traditional explanations:
- male sexual desire in abnormal circumstance
- females lead males on
- abnormal or deviant male.

Feminist explanations:
- as a means of social control
- as an extension of normal male values
- inequalities in power and wealth
- sexist male culture.

VICTIM PRONENESS
- household characteristics may cause them to be picked on, e.g. racial attacks
- geographical area
- age and sex
- pattern of routine

Multiple victimisation
70% of offences are against repeat victims.

Offender success

Vulnerability
Certain property may be selected by different thieves because of its suitability for burglary.

Victim precipitation
Shifts responsibility onto the victim.

Victim–offender relationship is not random
- crime against the person – related or known to each other
- burglary – geographical proximity of residence

17. SUICIDE

THE HYPOTHETICO – DEDUCTIVE METHOD APPLIED TO THE STUDY OF SUICIDE
DURKHEIM'S STUDY

Stages	Application
Observation	*Patterns observed:* • Within societies the suicide rate remains relatively constant over time. • Suicide rates vary between societies and regions within countries. • Suicide rates vary between different groups in the same society.
Conjecture	The incidence of suicide will vary according to the way people are affected by their society, in particular by forces of integration and regulation.
Hypothesis formation	Higher rates of suicide are related to the level of cohesion in society:

		Level	
Social cohesion	**Inadequate**		**Excessive**
Integration	Egoistic		Altruistic
Regulation	Anomic		Fatalistic

Stages	Application
Operationalising concepts	**Concept** **Social indicators** **1.** Egoistic suicide (inadequate integration) → religion and family status **2.** Altruistic suicide (excessive integration) → army affiliation **3.** Anomic suicide (inadequate regulation) → divorce law, economic climate **4.** Fatalistic suicide (excessive regulation) → not studied, assumed to be of no contemporary relevance.
Testing	Comparison of the suicide rates of groups of: **1.** Protestants/Catholics, unmarried/married, childless/children **2.** soldiers/civilians, volunteers/conscripts, officers/men **3.** countries allowing divorce/not allowing divorce, changes in economic circumstances/stability **4.** not studied
Data analysis	The pattern confirmed the hypothesis so the conjecture stands as a theory.

Internal evaluation i.e. from within positivism		External criticism i.e. from an anti-positivist perspective
✓ Demonstrates the sociological dimension of a very individual act	✗ Integration and regulation are not directly observable	✗ No shared social meaning of suicide
✓ Use of highly complex statistical techniques before the advent of the computer	✗ Some of the comparisons involved very small numbers of suicides which may not be statistically significant	✗ Ignores the role of the coroner in defining deaths as suicides
✓ Confirmed by other studies, e.g. Sainsbury	✗ Ignored evidence that did not fit his theory, e.g. gender patterns in suicide	✗ Ignores the errors in reporting and recording statistics
✓ Stimulated research, e.g. Gibbs & Martin (1964)	✗ Social indicators may not be valid	✗ Ignores the meanings behind the suicidal act
		✗ Assumes that an act of suicide is obvious, when it may not be

18. INTERPRETIVIST APPROACH TO SUICIDE

1. DOUGLAS (1967) – THE SOCIAL MEANINGS OF SUICIDE

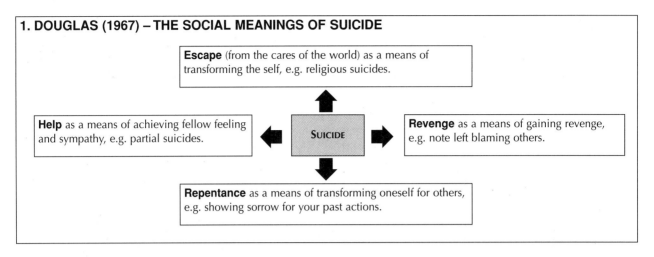

Escape (from the cares of the world) as a means of transforming the self, e.g. religious suicides.

Help as a means of achieving fellow feeling and sympathy, e.g. partial suicides.

SUICIDE

Revenge as a means of gaining revenge, e.g. note left blaming others.

Repentance as a means of transforming oneself for others, e.g. showing sorrow for your past actions.

2. ATKINSON (1978) – SOCIAL CONSTRUCTION OF DEATHS AS SUICIDES

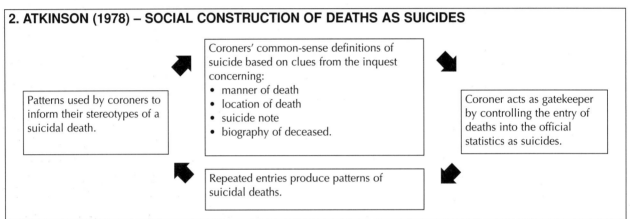

Coroners' common-sense definitions of suicide based on clues from the inquest concerning:
- manner of death
- location of death
- suicide note
- biography of deceased.

Patterns used by coroners to inform their stereotypes of a suicidal death.

Coroner acts as gatekeeper by controlling the entry of deaths into the official statistics as suicides.

Repeated entries produce patterns of suicidal deaths.

3. STENGEL (1973) – SUICIDAL INTENT

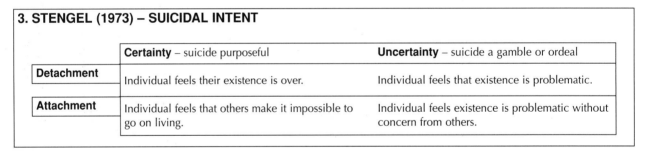

	Certainty – suicide purposeful	**Uncertainty** – suicide a gamble or ordeal
Detachment	Individual feels their existence is over.	Individual feels that existence is problematic.
Attachment	Individual feels that others make it impossible to go on living.	Individual feels existence is problematic without concern from others.

4. BAECHLER (1979) – SUICIDE A STRATEGY TO ACHIEVE PARTICULAR ENDS

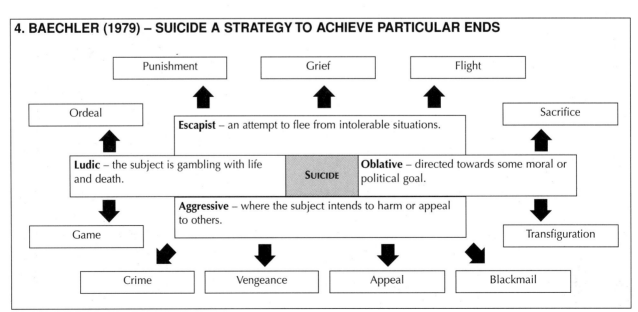

Punishment

Grief

Flight

Ordeal

Escapist – an attempt to flee from intolerable situations.

Sacrifice

Ludic – the subject is gambling with life and death.

SUICIDE

Oblative – directed towards some moral or political goal.

Game

Aggressive – where the subject intends to harm or appeal to others.

Transfiguration

Crime

Vengeance

Appeal

Blackmail

19. SYNOPTIC OVERVIEW

CONNECTIONS WITH CRIME AND DEVIANCE	TOPIC	EXAMPLES OF LINK STUDIES	METHOD	THEORY
• Maternal deprivation and single-parent families have been suggested as causal; domestic violence and child abuse.	Families and Households	West & Farrington (1973) isolated five factors related to family background associated with delinquency.	Longitudinal study	Functionalist
• Status frustration from educational failure; peer group influence; truancy and low educational achievement.	Education	Hargreaves (1967): pupils labelled as trouble-makers gained prestige and status from breaking the rules.	Overt participant observation	Labelling
• Portrayal of violence; stereotyped representations of criminals and victims; myths about rape that recur in the press.	Mass Media	S. Cohen (1972) looked at the role of the media in the process of deviance amplification.	Secondary qualitative data	Interactionist
• Poverty and relative deprivation as the cause of crime; portrayal of welfare recipients as scroungers; social policy for offenders and their dependants.	Wealth, Poverty and Welfare	Shaw & McKay (1942) showed much higher crime rates in the deprived inner city zone of transition.	Official statistics	Ecological
• Unemployment rates correlate with crime rates; white-collar and corporate crime; 'black' economy.	Work and Leisure	Ditton (1979) discovered that bread salesman regularly cheated the shops on their rounds.	Covert participant observation	Sub-cultural
• Sick role as deviance; mental illness defined as deviant; drug-taking may create health problems; suicide as a cause of mortality.	Health	Rosenhan (1978) demonstrated the power of a deviant label to those who displayed the symptoms of mental illness.	Field experiment	Anti-positivist
• Lack of moral values as the cause of crime; religious cults defined as deviant; religious conversions of criminals.	Religion	Hirschi & Stark (1969) explored the connection between religion and deviance.	Self-report questionnaires	Right realist
• Political dissidents labelled as deviant; the role of the state in law creation and enforcement; laws change that are frequently broken or impossible to police.	Politics and Power	Chambliss (1978) showed that a major crime syndicate in Seattle included political leaders and that economic and political power determined who got arrested.	Interviews	Marxist
• Relativity of crime and deviance; corporate crimes committed in Third World; child slave labour; sex tourism; global drug cartels; international police operations; United Nations and 'pariah states'.	World Sociology	Fattah (1997) showed that investigators found 10 irregularities at the Union Carbide plant in Bhopal, India, which were responsible for the toxic gas leak, killing 15,000+.	Case study	Conflict
• Socialisation and learning of deviant roles; homosexual identities and definitions of deviance; deviant sub-cultures.	Culture and Identity	Sutherland (1930) showed how the professional thief has to be recognised and received by other professional thieves.	Life history	Differential association
• Class, gender and ethnic patterns of criminal activity, convictions and victimisation.	Stratification and Differentiation	Hall (1985) found that one-third of her respondents had been raped or sexually assaulted.	Postal questionnaire	Feminist

14 Stratification and Differentiation

1. TYPES OF STRATIFICATION SYSTEM

Type of system	Hydraulic	Age-set	Feudal	Caste
Basis of divisions	Control of water	Age of the individual	Ownership of land	Caste born into
Main divisions	• Priests • Bureaucracy • Traders • Peasantry	• Gerontocracy (the old) • Married men • Warriors (young men) • Herders (pre-adult males)	• King • Nobles • Gentry • Freemen • Villeins • Serfs	• Priests (Brahmin) • Warriors (Kshatriya) • Merchants (Vaishya) • Workers (Sudra)
Examples of system	• Ancient Egypt • Mesopotamia	• Aborigines • African herding societies	• Medieval England • Rural Nepal	• India • Aspects of Japan
Degree of openness	Priests and nobility were closed, but others could advance through trading	Open as a male grew older and changed status	Fairly closed, though occasionally talent could rise	Very closed, with little chance of mobility in lifetime

Advantages of these systems

✓ Everyone 'knew their place'

✓ Provided stability

✓ Had strong identities

✓ Unified by strong religious bonds

✓ Established division of labour

✓ Encouraged 'capital accumulation'

·✓ Some had social movement included

✓ Local loyalty strong

Disadvantages of these systems

✗ Very rigid

✗ Lack of social mobility

✗ Often reliant on force

✗ Conformity could be stifling

✗ Did not encourage individuality

✗ Great inequality built in

✗ Disregard for lower orders

✗ Slow social change

2. TRADITIONAL APPROACHES TO CLASS SYSTEMS

	MARXISM AND CLASS	WEBERIANISM AND CLASS	FUNCTIONALISM AND CLASS
Class structure	Two main classes: bourgeoisie and proletariat. Other classes exist, but are not important in unfolding of history.	Four main classes in society: the upper class, petit bourgeoisie, white-collar class and manual working class. Other classes exist as sub-divisions of these four.	Many class divisions in society, organised hierarchically, and generally having seven or sometimes more divisions, from the upper class to the unskilled manual class.
Reason for divisions	Ownership and non-ownership of the means of production are the most important division in capitalist societies. Classes are mutually antagonistic.	Economic divisions are important, but market situation (the rewards people received) are more important than ownership. Status is therefore an important dimension of class.	Class divisions reflect the functional importance of different occupations. As the importance of different jobs can be expressed as a gradient, then there will be several class divisions.
Relationships between classes	History is created by the conflict between the two main classes, as they struggle to control society.	Classes and status groups compete in different ways to increase their share of rewards. Competition may be violent or peaceful.	Classes are mutually dependent. For society to function effectively, classes must co-operate to deliver the good things in life for all.
Subjective dimension of class	People in similar class positions tend to develop consciousness that they hold interests in common. When an economic class such as the proletariat act together to further their own interests, they are 'class-conscious'.	People identify more with those who follow a similar lifestyle, than those sharing the same economic position. Though these two are related, class consciousness is unlikely to develop.	People are motivated to 'get on' in a system that is generally seen to be fair and where anyone with talent and drive can climb the class hierarchy.
Main strengths	✓ Draws attention to importance of conflict as the 'motor of history' ✓ Emphasises economic relations ✓ Theory of social change ✓ Draws attention to the exploitation of the proletariat by the bourgeoisie	✓ Acknowledges divisions other than class ✓ Recognises the importance of consumption as well as production ✓ Individual consciousness is seen as important ✓ Has 'predictive power' in charting society's development	✓ Draws attention to the interdependence of groups in complex society ✓ Allows for social mobility in society ✓ Provides a justification for inequality ✓ Emphasises the importance of education and qualifications in capitalist societies
Main criticisms	✗ Determinist theory ✗ Over-emphasises economics at the expense of status ✗ 'Privileges' role of the proletariat ✗ History has shown Marx to be wrong in many aspects	✗ Underestimates importance of class divisions in society ✗ Assumes that status consciousness exists rather than demonstrates it ✗ Unclear about the relationship between classes and status groups	✗ No more than a legitimation of American society ✗ Many problematic concepts such as 'talent' ✗ Accepting of the status quo ✗ Does not explain satisfactorily who decides what are the 'functionally important' positions
Historical time	Marx was writing in the second half of the nineteenth century.	Weber was writing in the early part of the twentieth century, as a response to Marx.	Davis and Moore wrote their seminal account in the United States in the 1940s.

Underlying the traditional theories of class is the conception of a capitalist society, in which there is inequality and where groups and individuals are organised hierarchically from a relatively small group at the top of society to the bulk of the population lying towards the bottom.

3. CHANGES IN CLASS STRUCTURE IN THE TWENTIETH CENTURY

	Processes of change	Description	In favour	Against
UPPER CLASS	**Managerial revolution**	Separation of ownership and control, so that managers now form a distinct subsection of the upper class, with different interests to owners of capitalist firms.	✓ Firms too big to be controlled by owners ✓ Managers must look to consumers, not owners	✗ Many managers also own shares ✗ Profit still main criterion for managers' success
	Fragmentation	There are real differences between elites, e.g. financial, commercial, industrial and the intelligentsia.	✓ Upper class too big for a common interest ✓ Intelligentsia often hostile to capitalism	✗ Elites are committed to capitalism ✗ Elites identify with each other
	Changes in ownership	Globalisation; large employers have become internationalised, and different to small employers and the petty bourgeoisie.	✓ Big firms are now multinational ✓ Small employers have own organisations	✗ Ownership remains in hands of the few ✗ Small employers are dependent on large employers for work
MIDDLE CLASS	**Rise of the service class**	Growth in tertiary industry; a new grouping has emerged, which 'services' the capitalist economy, for example, technical experts.	✓ Face of industry has changed ✓ New occupations have emerged based on knowledge	✗ Who is the service class servicing? ✗ 'Experts' still work for capitalist enterprises
	Fragmentation	'Old' middle class has joined the upper class, leaving a divided 'intermediate' class of supervisors, self-employed, clerical workers etc.	✓ Professions are now high status ✓ No common identity among rest	✗ Professions are themselves proletarianised ✗ Rest have poor salaries in common
	Proletarianisation	As routine clerical work has become more like manual work, so white-collar workers have become more like the working class.	✓ Clerical salaries have fallen sharply ✓ Working conditions have deteriorated	✗ Clerical work still retains status ✗ Lifetime earnings are better than manual workers'
WORKING CLASS	**Embourgeoisement**	As manual workers have become more affluent, they have taken on the attitudes and behaviour of the middle class.	✓ Affluent workers voting Conservative ✓ Improved wages for skilled workers	✗ Affluent workers are floating voters ✗ Differentials with middle class remain in wages and perks
	Rise of the new working class	Division between workers in private industry, the South, who own their homes (new working class) and their opposites in the North, council tenants working in public sector.	✓ New working class vote differently from old ✓ New working class in favour of privatisation	✗ New working class voted Labour in 1997 ✗ Most workers want own homes
	Immiseration and the underclass	Growing poverty and unemployment among some working class has split them off from mainstream working class.	✓ State-dependent population grown ✓ Underclass no longer identifies with working class	✗ Is scape-goating the poor ✗ Underclass retains aspirations

4. MODERN CLASS THEORIES

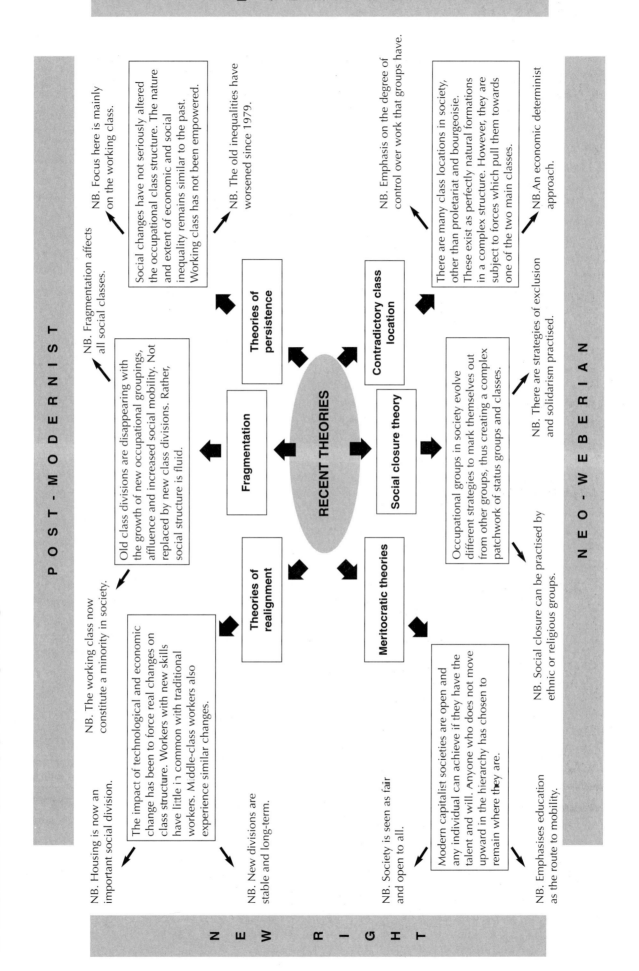

MARXIST

POST-MODERNIST

NEO-WEBERIAN

NEW RIGHT

NB. Focus here is mainly on the working class.

Social changes have not seriously altered the occupational class structure. The nature and extent of economic and social inequality remains similar to the past. Working class has not been empowered.

NB. The old inequalities have worsened since 1979.

NB. Emphasis on the degree of control over work that groups have.

There are many class locations in society, other than proletariat and bourgeoisie. These exist as perfectly natural formations in a complex structure. However, they are subject to forces which pull them towards one of the two main classes.

NB. An economic determinist approach.

NB. Fragmentation affects all social classes.

Old class divisions are disappearing with the growth of new occupational groupings, affluence and increased social mobility. Not replaced by new class divisions. Rather, social structure is fluid.

Theories of persistence

Contradictory class location

Fragmentation

RECENT THEORIES

Social closure theory

NB. There are strategies of exclusion and solidarism practised.

Occupational groups in society evolve different strategies to mark themselves out from other groups, thus creating a complex patchwork of status groups and classes.

NB. The working class now constitute a minority in society.

NB. Housing is now an important social division.

The impact of technological and economic change has been to force real changes on class structure. Workers with new skills have little in common with traditional workers. Middle-class workers also experience similar changes.

Theories of realignment

Meritocratic theories

NB. New divisions are stable and long-term.

NB. Society is seen as fair and open to all.

Modern capitalist societies are open and any individual can achieve if they have the talent and will. Anyone who does not move upward in the hierarchy has chosen to remain where they are.

NB. Social closure can be practised by ethnic or religious groups.

NB. Emphasises education as the route to mobility.

5. POST-FORDISM AND THE CLASS STRUCTURE

FORDISM

Features of Fordist production

- *Mass production:* industry produces large numbers of standardised goods for large numbers of people.

- *Focus on quantity:* industry aims to produce cheap and reliable goods for mass consumption.

- *Centralised management:* decisions are taken mainly at the top of a firm.

- *Manual workforce:* the majority of employed people are semi- or unskilled manual workers.

- *Repetitive work:* manual labour engaged in boring routinised tasks.

- *Conflictful labour relations:* managements keep control by divide and rule, separating workers with different tasks.

- *Regulatory systems:* focus of management is on controlling the actions of workers.

Features of Fordist class structure

- Class structure is *rigid* and divided into large social classes.

- Society is *hierarchically* organised.

- Elites are *closed* to lower classes.

- Social mobility is *limited* to mainly one class up the social class hierarchy.

- The majority of employed people are *manual workers*, with similar interests.

- Capitalism is *highly organised*, with high levels of state intervention.

- Society is dominated by professional and managerial *elites*.

- Relations between classes are full of *conflict*.

- While skills divisions in classes are evident, they are not as important as *class identity*.

POST-FORDISM

Features of Post-Fordist production

- *Segmented production:* industry produces a diverse range of goods for niche markets.

- *Focus on quality:* industry aims to produce quality goods for consumption by diverse groups in society.

- *Decentralised decision-making:* decisions about production are taken mainly at the point of production.

- *Flexible workers:* labour is multi-skilled and adaptable to a variety of tasks.

- *Co-operative labour relations:* workers are integrated into management, with one common purpose.

- *Empowering systems:* focus of management is co-ordinating semi-independent actions of workers.

Features of Post-Fordist class structure

- Class structure is *fluid*.

- Society is organised as a *network* of social relations.

- Traditional elites *no longer hold power*.

- There is a great deal of *social mobility*, both short and long range.

- Manual workers are divided into *core and periphery*, with different interests.

- Capitalism is *highly disorganised*, with multinational companies creating uncertainty for home-grown industries.

- Elites have become *fragmented* and no longer dominate.

- Relations between groups are *co-operative*.

- *New skills divisions* emerged in all social classes.

ARGUMENTS AGAINST THE DEVELOPMENT OF POST-FORDIST SOCIETIES

✗ Cannot explain social changes on basis of economic changes (economic determinist argument)

✗ Dominance of Fordist features in twentieth century is over-emphasised

✗ Flexible workforce existed under Fordist production

✗ Flexible working is exaggerated in post-Fordist arrangements

6. CONVERGENCE AND ALLIED THEORIES

WHAT IS CONVERGENCE THEORY?

Convergence theory argues that, as societies industrialise, they must take on board similar social, economic and political arrangements, if they are to be successful economies. That is, all industrial societies must adopt similar arrangements for performing important social functions.

Different types of convergence

One-way convergence	Two-way convergence
This sees the United States as the most advanced industrial society and thus the end-state for all industrialising societies.	This sees both socialist and capitalist economies becoming like each other, with enterprises becoming independent of the state and private owners.
Arguments against convergence	**Arguments in favour of convergence**
✗ It is a technologically determinist theory, which over-simplifies the processes of change involved as a society industrialises ✗ It ignores the different starting points and cultural traditions of different societies, which are retained as they industrialise ✗ There is limited empirical support for the proposition that industrial societies adopt similar social arrangements, such as democracy	✓ Advanced industrial societies face similar problems and tend to choose similar solutions ✓ Regardless of issues of ownership, advanced societies need highly skilled and flexible workforces ✓ Collapse of communism suggests the final victory for convergence theory as previously socialist societies adopted capitalist social arrangements ✓ Theory based on a close comparative analysis of the routes to industrialisation taken by different societies

ASSOCIATED THEORIES

END OF IDEOLOGY THESIS	POST-INDUSTRIAL SOCIETY THEORY	LOGIC OF INDUSTRIALISM THESIS
This theory suggests that • The Cold War between communism and capitalism will end with a victory for Western democratic values. • The great ideological disputes of the twentieth century will disappear, as societies adopt common values. • Class conflict will come to an end.	This theory suggests that we are moving towards a new kind of society based on: • services not manufacturing • planning not enterprise • technical knowledge • professional dominance • new ways of problem-solving. These are features of all advanced industrial societies.	This theory suggests that all industrialising societies need: • a highly skilled workforce • scientific innovation • a highly mobile population • an open society • a strong state. The adoption of these features means that advanced industrial societies will be similar in core aspects.
✗ Ignores the emergence of new ideological forces such as fundamentalism of various kinds.	✗ Ignores the continued dominance of the owners of capitalist enterprises in the global economy.	✗ Ignores empirical data which suggests that advanced societies retain distinctive core features of their own.

7. RURAL AND URBAN DISTINCTIONS AND THE LOSS OF COMMUNITY

THE IDEOLOGY OF LOSS OF COMMUNITY
Sociologists who have drawn sharp distinctions between urban and rural life reflect a powerful ideology, which still operates in contemporary society. That ideology suggests that, in the move from rural life to urban life, society has 'lost' something valuable – its sense of belonging to a community. Individual identity is somehow weakened by this move from rural to urban, as people no longer identify with the collective to the same extent as they did.

CONTRAST BETWEEN RURAL AND URBAN LIVING

Rural society	Urban society
Offers security, certainty, strong identity, authenticity, in a pastoral setting, often described lyrically.	Offers crime, violence, loneliness, isolation, in a squalid setting. Often described negatively.

FIRST PROBLEM: WHAT IS THIS COMMUNITY THAT HAS BEEN LOST?
Three different ways in which community is supposed to have been lost:

1.Changes in relationships	2.Loss of locality	3.Loss of neighbourhood
Loss of identity and affection based on personal contact between people who knew their place in society.	Disappearance of self-sustaining village and small town locations as independent entities.	Rather than villages, disappearance of working-class communities in urban areas.

SECOND PROBLEM: EMPIRICAL CONTRADICTIONS
A large number of community studies were carried out on the loss-of-community thesis. While many supported the dichotomy of community-minded villages and soulless cities, others did not find what they were 'supposed' to find.

Discovery of community in the city
- Cities did have aspects of the village within defined locales – the 'Urban Villages' (Gans 1968).
- Working-class areas of cities had strong community features.
- Had long history of solidarity to fall back on.
- Families formed focus of community life.
- Often strong gender segregation in social life.
- Urban villagers often hostile to official society.
- Strong social organisation maintained urban communities over generations.

Criticisms
✗ Such communities undergoing change from 1950s in wake of urban redevelopment programmes.

✗ Often communities are fragile rather than robust, especially where dependent on single industry.

✗ Degree of inter-connectedness of relations may be exaggerated.

✗ Communal life leads to tensions and divisions as well as to solidarity.

Discovery of conflict in the country
- Rural areas also found to have aspects of urban living within the rural setting (Pahl 1970)
- Class divisions just as important in rural as in urban life.
- Village life often conflictual rather than harmonious, especially over economic issues.
- Tensions exist between commuter inhabitants of villages and those who earn their living there.
- Commuting leads to 'empty village syndrome' when they are deserted during day.
- Rural poverty and exploitation existed in the past as well as present day.

Criticisms
✗ Community life in many villages still vibrant, and based on local organisation.

✗ Integration of newcomers can occur quickly.

✗ Mutual support systems in villages and rural areas strong, especially in times of need.

✗ Problem for villages is lack of amenities, not lack of community spirit.

Conclusion
Problems with concept of community has led sociologists to other, less value-laden concepts to deal with spatial issues:

Locale (Giddens, 1990)	Locality (Cooke, 1989)
The space that provides the setting within which social action takes place – can range from a room to geographical regions. Locales are not fixed like communities but vary according to the nature of the social interaction taking place.	Avoiding the romanticism of community and neither urban nor rural, locality is the space within which individuals carry out most of their social lives. It can be seen as a distinct geographical area, but is also the space within which people act.

8. MEASURING SOCIAL CLASS

Name of measure	Registrar-General's classification	Hall-Jones scale	Runciman scale	Goldthorpe and Hope scale	Erik Olin Wright's classification

DISTINCTIVE FEATURES

Features					
	• 5 social classes • based on jobs • manual/non-manual in class 3 • changes made as status of jobs change • government-derived • been used over long period • 7 social classes	• based on perceived status of jobs • manual/non-manual distinction • derived from panel method • claims consensus support	• 7 social classes • based on degree of ownership, control and marketability • provides a more fragmented view • incorporates an underclass • dismisses high-paid 'entertainers'	• 7 social classes • collapsed into 3 groupings • service class distinct • based on Weberian theory • suggests intermediate class is fluid	• 3 main classes • contradictory class locations • Marxist classification • takes ownership into account • recognises ideological influences on class position

WHO IS MISSING FROM THE SCHEMES?

Occupationally based schemes	**Ownership control and marketability based schemes**
• Women (based on male head of household) • Owners (shareholding is not represented) • Unemployed (those without occupations ignored) • Military (R-G's scheme ignores these)	• Those whose wealth is not disclosed • Women (assumes the head of household is male) • Socially mobile (class of origin is ignored)

WHY ARE THESE SCHEMES USEFUL?

✓ Relatively straightforward/represent the complexities of class in an understandable way	✓ Have been used as operationalised schema by many sociologists
✓ Idea is familiar to the public	✓ Therefore comparisons can be made over time
✓ Occupations are a good indicator of other social dimensions of inequality	✓ Where market, ownership and control issues are incorporated, inequality is represented in a systematic way

CRITICISMS OF THE SCHEME

✗ Changing structure of occupations makes it difficult to make comparisons over time in any reliable way	✗ Most schemes make sexist assumptions about class position of married women, even when they are working
✗ Is a static analysis of class position, not accounting for people moving up and down during their careers	✗ The match between income and occupation at the heart of the schemes is not perfect – income can be hidden
✗ The boundary problem – all make some arbitrary decisions about who should be included in which category	✗ All attempts to reduce complex class relations to a single indicator, or trio of indicators, do not capture the reality
✗ As descriptions of social class, they ignore the relations between classes and processes of interaction between them	✗ With the exception of Wright, all attempts to show class as a gradient mask real and great gaps between classes
✗ For those outside paid employment, they either have to be included through past jobs or ignored altogether	✗ Class groupings often include occupations that commonsensically are seen as belonging in differing categories

CONCLUSION

Often seen as arbitrary in the way that occupations are divided into groups, they do reflect, in a limited way, the way that society is conceived by many people. They can be simplistic and hide the very complexities which sociologists are seeking to explore. Too often devised for administrative rather than sociological purposes, even more sociologically informed attempts end up with very different groupings. However, they are useful for operationalising class in an empirical way.

Other classifications used:
1. Standard Occupational Classification – a 'non-class' scheme, developed to replace the Registrar-General's.
2. Advertising Industry Standard – a tool for marketing.
3. Surrey Occupational Scheme – incorporates women into classification.
4. Subjective classifications – based on asking people which class they belong to.

9. SOCIAL MOBILITY

GROUP UPWARD MOBILITY

EMBOURGEOISEMENT

Arguments in favour	Arguments against
✓ Manual workers voting Tory.	✗ Little evidence of equal lifetime earnings.
✓ Similar consumption patterns between middle and working class.	✗ Voting is instrumental rather than loyal Tory.
✓ Growing interaction across class boundaries.	✗ Middle class do not accept affluent workers as equal.
✓ Growth of consensus between middle class and affluent workers.	✗ Consumption patterns do not represent class.
✓ Growth of divisions within working class.	✗ Always been a section of working class 'embourgeoised'.
✓ Growth of ideology of individualism.	✗ Collectivism varies according to economic circumstances.

The idea that growing affluence after the Second World War has made a section of the working class increasingly like the middle class in behaviour (voting patterns), attitudes (towards welfare) and values (belief in individuality).

INDIVIDUAL MOBILITY

Processes
Absolute mobility rates had increased but relative rates remained the same.
Upwardly mobile routes
- qualifications
- marriage
- good fortune
- occupation

Changes in mobility patterns
- In 1940s, mobility was mainly short-range, across one class boundary. At the top and bottom, little mobility could be detected (Glass 1954)
- In 1972, there had been a substantial increase in the amount of long-range mobility, with more openness at the top of society (Goldthorpe 1980)
- This seemed to suggest that educational opportunities since 1945 had opened up the class system and created a more open mobile society.

Comments
Goldthorpe concluded that changes in the occupational structure were the main reason for the increase in relative rates of mobility. The implication was that those left in the manual working class were likely to remain there, unless occupational structure continued to change.

Implications for class structure
- no longer stable classes
- demise of class interests
- people not identified with class
- class formation difficult

Changes in occupations
1. The globalisation of the labour markets threatened the lifelong career patterns of middle-class workers and led to increased levels of downward mobility. This may be counteracted by increased entrepreneurialism in the middle class (Handy 1984)
2. New technologies have also impacted upon manual work, so that many blue-collar workers have been ejected into the underclass and young working-class males have much reduced chances of obtaining employment (Bagguley 1991)

Downwardly mobile routes
- being sick
- falling on hard times
- declassed individuals
- deskilled workers

There is an important gender division emerging in this, with the labour market becoming increasingly feminised, and men finding it more difficult to obtain work.

Is Britain meritocratic?
It is still difficult to gain entry to the upper class, though movement is possible through the rest of the structure. However, it is not certain that position is now determined by talent, rather than background.

Ethnicity, region and gender still important

GROUP DOWNWARD MOBILITY

PROLETARIANISATION
The idea that, as working conditions of middle-class workers change, they become increasingly like the working class in behaviour (voting), attitudes (towards TUs) and values (collectivism).

Arguments against	Arguments in favour
✗ Middle class do not identify with working class.	✓ Technology has deskilled clerks and professionals.
✗ Salaries over lifetime much larger.	✓ Falling salaries towards levels of working class.
✗ Mechanisation has freed middle class from drudgery.	✓ Increasing routinisation of middle-class work.
✗ New skills emerged which are dominated by middle class.	✓ Larger union membership and militancy in middle-class.
✗ Trade union activity aimed at maintaining salary differences.	✓ Managers increasingly control middle-class workers.
✗ Evidence for deskilling limited.	✓ Growth in collectivist ideologies amongst the middle class.
✗ White-collar work fragmented.	

10. THE UNDERCLASS

Social policies advocated
- Reduction of benefits to encourage participation in work.
- Re-emphasis on the traditional family.
- Reduce child support to discourage housing list jumping.
- Increased control and patrol of underclass areas.

Social policies advocated
- Tax and benefits harmonised to make it easier to get work.
- Welfare-to-work programmes.
- Re-emphasis on fairness and opportunity.

Arguments against

1. Is based on stereotypical views of the poor.
2. Evidence for a dependency culture is limited.
3. Many individuals born into poverty move out of it.
4. Often based on assumed inheritance of intelligence.
5. Is often racist in its links to ethnic minorities.

1. Assumes only important link of the underclass is to the state.
2. Often underpinned by a disapproval of the underclass.
3. Split between the working class and underclass is unproven.
4. No clear dividing line between primary and secondary labour markets.

mainly   but also   mainly

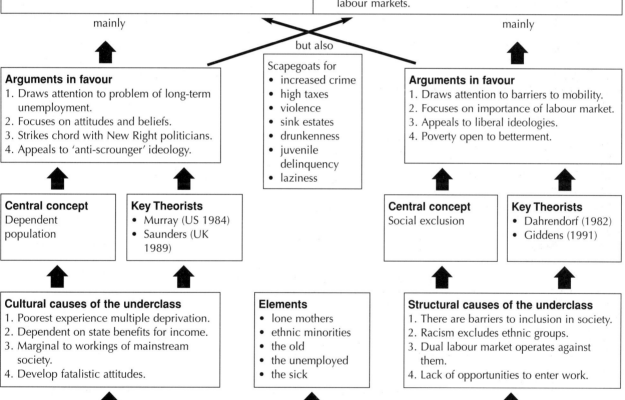

Arguments in favour
1. Draws attention to problem of long-term unemployment.
2. Focuses on attitudes and beliefs.
3. Strikes chord with New Right politicians.
4. Appeals to 'anti-scrounger' ideology.

Scapegoats for
- increased crime
- high taxes
- violence
- sink estates
- drunkenness
- juvenile delinquency
- laziness

Arguments in favour
1. Draws attention to barriers to mobility.
2. Focuses on importance of labour market.
3. Appeals to liberal ideologies.
4. Poverty open to betterment.

Central concept
Dependent population

Key Theorists
- Murray (US 1984)
- Saunders (UK 1989)

Central concept
Social exclusion

Key Theorists
- Dahrendorf (1982)
- Giddens (1991)

Cultural causes of the underclass
1. Poorest experience multiple deprivation.
2. Dependent on state benefits for income.
3. Marginal to workings of mainstream society.
4. Develop fatalistic attitudes.

Elements
- lone mothers
- ethnic minorities
- the old
- the unemployed
- the sick

Structural causes of the underclass
1. There are barriers to inclusion in society.
2. Racism excludes ethnic groups.
3. Dual labour market operates against them.
4. Lack of opportunities to enter work.

CHANGES IN SOCIETY SINCE MARX'S TIME
While absolute poverty in the capitalist West has declined, there remain strong pockets of relative poverty, alleviated by state welfare provision. The existence of benefits is argued to change the nature of the lumpenproletariat to an *underclass*.

LUMPENPROLETARIAT
Marx originally designated the poorest and unorganised section of the working class as the 'lumpenproletariat', who were possessed of individual consciousness and were marginalised from the rest of society. In a time of no state benefits, this section existed in abject poverty, too concerned with day-to-day survival to engage in revolutionary activity of any kind.

THE UNDERCLASS

11. GENDER AND INEQUALITY

TRADITIONAL APPROACHES – THE INVISIBILITY OF GENDER
Stratification theorists have tended to ignore women in their approach to inequality because they have:
- taken the family as the unit of stratification
- assumed that the head of the family is the male breadwinner (and only in exceptional circumstances is this not the case e.g. the Queen)

Objections to this:
- ✗ Not everyone lives in a family
- ✗ 'Normal' family of male breadwinner, domestic wife and kids is minority
- ✗ Wives have social and economic standing of their own

Early attempts to deal with gender:
1. Collins (1972) saw women as 'sexual property' with gender stratification based on male aggressiveness and female attractiveness. Attacked as sexist nonsense.
2. Parkin (1972) argued that only if women saw selves in non-family terms could they be counted in stratification theory. Attacked as a tautology.

WOMEN AND THE DIMENSIONS OF INEQUALITY

- Traditional role of women as home-makers have kept them in the private sphere and away from the public sphere of work, where their stratification status might be measured.
- In labour market, women can be found disproportionately in the less well paid or secure jobs.
- There operates a 'glass ceiling' for women in work, so that even very talented women find it difficult to penetrate the upper reaches of the workplace.

Spheres in which inequality is reinforced
- wealth
- income
- housing
- health and illness

but
- advances made in the position of women
- not all women experience the same degree of inequality
- women are divided from each other in terms of class, ethnicity etc.

Women and the secondary labour market
Women (along with other groups) take low paid, insecure, routine jobs in disproportionate numbers, because (it is argued) they are:
- more dispensable than men
- less likely to have had training
- seen by employers as being willing to work for less money
- less likely to join trade unions and engage in industrial action
- used as part of a segregated labour force.

Women as a reserve army of labour
Women offer labour which industry brings into work when times are good, but dispenses with in economic downturns. Thus women:
- act to divide workers and help keep wage bills low
- are employed in jobs that have been de-skilled, so that they do not need high levels of training to enter the labour market
- are seen as more willing to carry out part-time work than men are.

Problems with this approach
- Women not just confined to the secondary market.
- Women earn less through all levels of the hierarchy.
- Many men also work in the secondary market.

Problems with this approach
- if women are cheaper bosses would let expensive men go first in an economic downturn.
- relies on a 'conspiracy'-type explanation.

Men are gendered too!
In the debate about women's indisputable inequality in the stratification system, it should be remembered that many men also suffer from exploitation and unfairness. Stratification patterns consist of complex interconnections between gender, class, ethnicity, region, age, sexuality and disability – female inequality does not exist on its own.

12. THEORIES OF GENDER STRATIFICATION

THEORIES

FEMINIST

Basic theory: women as a group experience inequalities in the stratification system and these should be explored sociologically in their own right.

Variations in feminist theory

Patriarchy theory (radical feminism): power in all societies resides in the hands of men. Women are united globally by their common oppression by men.
Dual-systems theory (Marxist feminism): there are two causes, independent but linked, of women's oppression – capitalism and patriarchy.
Three-systems theory (Black feminism): ethnicity should be added to the dual-systems theory to emphasise the different experiences of black women in a racist society.
Difference theory (post-feminists): feminism has tended to treat all women as a single category and to define femininity in one specific way. Post-modern societies exhibit a great variety of ways to be female as women explore and construct their own identities.

Criticisms
- ✗ Feminism no longer a unified theory
- ✗ Tends to treat women in undifferentiated way
- ✗ Relegates class issues to unimportance
- ✗ Privileges gender over other forms of oppression

SOCIO-BIOLOGICAL

Basic theory: biological causes are the main factor which decide differences between men and women.

Variations in socio-biological explanations

Hormones: levels of male and female hormones determine aggressiveness in males and passivity in females.
Bio-grammar: evolution has programmed men and women into different roles, based on hunter-gatherer behaviour.
Sociobiology: human behaviour is governed by need to pass on genetic inheritance, which leads to the promiscuous male and home-making female.

Criticisms
- ✗ Based on controversial science
- ✗ Gender divisions vary
- ✗ Legitimates male power
- ✗ Biological mechanisms unclear

TRADITIONAL SOCIOLOGICAL

Basic theory: focused on the family as the 'natural' sphere of women, gender issues were demoted to a less important level than issues of class. Gender was marginalised.

Variations in traditional sociological theories

Functionalist: viewed female role in domestic terms and thus did not incorporate gender issues into theory.
Marxist: did not see gender as part of central dynamic of society, which was driven by class divisions.
New Left: saw women as 'softening' male revolutionary urge.

Criticisms
- ✗ Made women invisible
- ✗ Were deterministic
- ✗ Too focused on family
- ✗ Treated women as the 'Other'.

SOCIAL CONSTRUCTIONIST

Basic theory: social and cultural factors shape ideas and behaviour about gender.

Variations in constructionist explanations

Gender order: every society develops its own division of labour and conceptions of femininity and masculinity.
Gender identity: socialisation leads to patterns of behaviour which are seen as feminine or masculine.
Gender attribution: our bodies are 'constructed' as male and female by our ideas about gender.

Criticisms
- ✗ Tends to be deterministic
- ✗ Ignores gender changes
- ✗ Compartmentalises gender from other identities
- ✗ Ignores structural inequalities

13. ETHNICITY AND CLASS STRUCTURE

Difficulties in exploring ethnic minorities and stratification
- Traditional use of 'race' challenged because it has no scientific basis.
- Not always clear what is meant by ethnicity and who belongs to which groups.
- Notions of race and ethnicity deeply bound in racist assumptions of colonial times.
- Conflict between objective notions of ethnicity and subjective feelings of individuals.

Divisions within ethnic minorities:
- between 'white' (e.g. Irish) and 'black' (e.g. Afro-Caribbean and Indian sub-continent)
- between migrants (other country of origin) and second/third generation (black British)
- between different ethnicity of origin, e.g. African and Indian sub-continent
- between different religious traditions, e.g. Hindu, Sikh and Muslim.

Areas of disadvantage

- work
- pay
- hours
- health
- poverty
- housing
- prison
- education

Different patterns of

MODELS OF MIGRATION

IMMIGRANT-HOST MODEL
Optimistic view of race relations which offers a host society which will gradually assimilate immigrant groups. Thus, patterns of inequality will disappear as immigrant communities adapt to the host's values and culture and gradually become assimilated within it. The host population will accommodate the new cultures.

MARXIST MODEL
Pessimistic view of race relations which demonstrates that migration serves the needs of the capitalist class for labour, and is used to divide workers from each other on account of ethnic differences. While capitalism prefers conflict between ethnic groups, the existence of diversity opens up a culturally plural possibility in society.

Evaluation of the model

✓ Emphasises dynamic nature of ethnic relationships

✓ Looks at interactions between groups

✓ Offers a complex view of conflict and co-operation

✗ Ignores racism as part of the dynamic

✗ Tends to an essentialist view of assimilation

✗ Takes assimilation as the ideal end-product

✗ Assumes that the host society is unidimensional

Both assume that the reaction of migrants to their situation is the same, but there are many different ones.
Different groups of migrants carry their specific cultural and historical associations with them. It is unsurprising that they therefore respond to similar situations in differential ways.

Evaluation of the model

✓ Emphasises the global nature of migration

✓ Places migration in historical context

✓ Details the economic imperatives of migration

✓ Focuses on racism as a divisive force.

✗ Assumes a conspiracy by capitalists

✗ Downplays co-operation between groups, for example in the trade union movement

✗ Ignores cultural factors in favour of economic

✗ Assumes hostility is the norm.

Ethnic traditionalists
Mobilised around issues of tradition and preserving their culture.

Ethnic manipulators
Mobilised around ethnicity for political and economic purposes.

Ethnic militants
Mobilised around separate identity and political separation.

Symbolic ethnics
Mobilised weakly on special occasions and following outward conventions.

These categories of ethnic groups also serve to divide the minority population within itself.

14. THEORIES OF RACIAL INEQUALITY

Basic theory: biological causes are the main reason for differences between ethnic groups and/or races

BIOLOGICAL EXPLANATIONS

Variations in theory
Physical features theory: innate differences in physical characteristics indicate real differences in performance.
Genetic explanations: the genetic inheritance of different 'races' is different and account for variations in achievement.
Sociobiology: biology together with culture governs behaviour. Ethnic groups are compelled to preserve the group's genetic inheritance.
Underclass theory: certain ethnic groups inherit a lower range of intelligence than others and thus appear more frequently in the underclass.

Criticisms
- ✗ Biological factors are assumed, not proven
- ✗ Mechanism of influence of biology not shown
- ✗ Ignores similarities between groups

Criticisms
- ✗ Downplays structural factors with focus on level of ideas and discourses
- ✗ Often very abstract analysis
- ✗ Stresses identity not inequality

STRUCTURAL EXPLANATIONS

Variations in theory
Marxism: dividing workers from each other through racial divisions benefits capitalism.
Weberian approaches: racial disadvantage is linked to the class and status position but separate from them.
Functionalist: present racial disadvantage will melt away as the meritocratic society is established.
Symbolic interactionist: racial prejudice emerges out of the competitive interaction of different ethnic groups, competing over the same scarce resources (see Ethnicity explanations).

Criticisms
- ✗ Marxism marginalises race by stressing class
- ✗ Weberianism devalues class position of ethnic groups
- ✗ Functionalists assume a meritocracy
- ✗ Symbolic interactionism concentrates too much on individual

THEORIES OF RACIAL INEQUALITY

RACIAL FORMATION EXPLANATIONS

Variations in theory
Cultural theory: both black and white nationalism should be examined as ethnic groups form around their ideas and values.
Political theory: stresses the way that the political and legal processes are involved in the creation and maintenance of ethnic categories.
Neo-Marxist approaches: tend to see racism as relatively autonomous from other aspects of social relations.
Post-modernism: there is no single ethnic identity or uniform experience of disadvantage and thus ethnic minorities are not victims.

Basic theory: there is no single form of racism and no monolithic block of ethnic minority people, rather racial discourses create patterns of exclusion and disadvantage differentially among groups.

ETHNICITY EXPLANATIONS

Basic theory: there are structural reasons for ethnic disadvantage, not just attitudes of prejudice.

Basic theory: that racial disadvantage emerges from the interaction between different groups and the way that reality is socially constructed from this interaction.

Variations in theory:
New racism: the nature of racism has changed towards an obsession with 'British' identity.
Situational: ethnic identity is not fixed but fluid and changing.
Foucauldian: institutions have power to categorise and define groups and individuals along ethnic lines.

Criticisms
- ✗ New racism implies permanent exclusion of ethnics
- ✗ Situational sees identity only in positive forms
- ✗ Foucauldian does not spell out how this happens

15. GENDER, ETHNICITY, SEXUALITY, AND DIFFERENCE

GENDER

Cities as a 'landscape of fear'
- Suburbanisation removed many women from centres of cities for significant parts of the day.
- Women became less 'acquainted' with central public spaces.
- Control of cars often male, restricting opportunities for women to be mobile.
- Lone mothers in inner cities have little income to spend on safety.
- Women able to identify areas of high risk and avoid them.
- Women who experience violence in cities often seem suspect for venturing into these areas in first place.
- Leisure venues often male dominated, where women seen as available.
- Bingo is female-dominated leisure activity of choice for working-class women and is carried out in restricted time and space.

Differences in way men and women experience the City
- Use of urban space more constrained for women, because of fear of attack and sexual violence in certain areas and at certain times.
- Women still primarily concerned with private rather than public space.
- Design of cities is 'man-made', being concerned to control women in part.
- Different categories of women experience cities in different ways, e.g. ethnic minority women go to fewer areas than white women.
- Similarly for men, categories such as 'employed' or 'unemployed' affect way men experience the cities.
- Women paid less than men and thus have fewer opportunities to take advantage of the city.

ETHNICITY

Ethnicity as source of identity:
- Provides strong basis for formation of communities
- Assisted when minority has migrated to new location
- Furthered where members experience similar discrimination and practices of exclusion
- Often form in distinctive geographical areas
- Cultural symbols and spaces develop which signify ethnicity e.g. saree shops
- Community identity more likely where language is different from majority
- Solidarity assisted where occupations broadly similar
- As a rule, the greater the degree of otherness, the greater the amount of residential segregation.

BUT ethnicity is not fixed. Subject to change as assimilation, adaption, rejection or absorption occurs.

Multi-cultural living
- 'Race relations' is central concept for official approach to multicultural living.
- Community organisations involved in mediating between ethnic and religious groups.
- Relationships typified by both conflict and cooperation.
- Cooperation more likely where different groups have interests in common and can work together.
- Government policies important in avoiding or encouraging competition between ethnic groups.

Ethnicity and conflict
- Most conflict between ethnic groups occurs over access to scarce resources such as housing.
- Conflict is not always between whites and non-white groups, but can be between ethnic minorities.
- Conflict can be based on religious tribalism (Belfast) as well as skin colour.
- Housing is main cause of long-term conflict as 'territoriality' comes into play.

SEXUALITY

Emergence of gay urban spaces
- 'Hollowing out' of cities has left room for emergence of new communities.
- Greater tolerance and decriminalisation created opportunities for development of gay identity.
- AIDS precipitated withdrawal into own urban spaces.
- Gay villages developed (Manchester) with emphasis on leisure and 'pink pound'.
- Gay urban spaces provide protection from gay-bashers.

16. HOUSING PATTERNS AND TRENDS

KEY CONCEPT
Housing classes: social class no longer encapsulates social divisions sufficiently, so need to look at other ways in which populations are divided. Housing is one way in which segregation between social groups occurs.

Types of housing
- Owner-occupied, either mortgaged or owned outright
- Public-rented housing – council housing, often on estates built specifically to provide low-cost housing for poorer sections of community
- Private-rented housing, mainly from private landlords, but also from institutions (Church) or housing associations.

Criticisms of housing classes

✗ Confuses cause and effect – income and wealth is more important than housing in determining lifestyle.

✗ Housing is an important aspect of lifestyle not the cause of a particular lifestyle.

✗ Categories are too open to be of analytical use – need constant amending.

✗ People's subjective views of what is desirable housing is very varied, e.g. closeness to family might be more important than having three bedrooms.

Effects of government policy on housing stock and urban locations
- Political power at local level held by business elite, able to out-manoeuvre part-time councillors. Policy operates in favour of this elite.
- Government policy functions to aid capitalists to make profit, by providing urban infrastructure for operation of commerce and industry. Taxation policy geared towards business interests.
- Privatisation of local services, begun under Tories and continued under Labour, impact upon urban spaces:

Sale of council housing under 'right-to-buy' legislation	→ popular amongst buyers, effect is to limit new house building by councils
Deregulation of transport services, especially buses	→ little improvement in transport or reduction in car use by commuters
Compulsory competitive tendering for council services	→ costs kept low, wages for workers fall, profits for services increase, some loss of service
Privatising public spaces (more in US than UK)	→ transfer of responsibility for parks to private companies, creation of walled communities, private patrolling of housing areas.

- Planning regulations for development of shopping areas important. Led to growth in large shopping malls on outskirts of towns, which led to decline in city centre shopping and acted as a focus of industrial development. In turn this led city centres to develop as entertainment centres, with growth of café culture. Shift away from large shopping complexes as impact on city centre became known.

Housing classes (Rex and Moore 1982)
Housing segregation not just result of low income, but way in which rules of housing market are operated. Housing classes struggle with each other for favoured urban locations, and are important in determining lifestyle and associations:
1. Outright owners, large houses, desirable areas
2. Mortgage payers, large houses, desirable areas
3. Council tenants in houses built by authority
4. Council tenants in slums awaiting demolition
5. Tenants of private house owners
6. Owners who take lodgers to meet repayments
7. Lodgers in rooms.

Effects of planning on housing stock and urban locations
- Slum clearance programmes led to 'high-rise living', which proved to be unpopular with tenants.
- Garden cities versus radial cities – small decentralised green belt areas versus large populations with green spaces.
- Road planning impacts upon urban housing and land use, both destroying homes and creating new commercial centres e.g. growth of out-of-town shopping malls on urban ring roads.

Sociological views on housing
1. Role of urban managers
   Focus on activities of mortgage lenders, public housing officials on the distribution and allocation of housing – for example, reluctance of mortgage lenders to lend to ethnic minority applicants, or rules for time on waiting list favouring one-parent families and lone mothers.

   ✗ Focus is on middle-ranking officials, when it should be on wider policy implications.

2. Housing market operates to increase gap between wealthy and poor as financial gains of ownership outstrip benefits of renting

   ✗ Negative equity shows not all benefit from ownership.

3. Need to focus on activities of property developers and speculators to understand housing markets. These skew the housing market because they prefer to invest in commercial developments rather than housing, because former is more profitable.

   ✗ Speculation in property brings benefits as well as unwanted office space like Centrepoint in London.

4. Environmental issues should be taken into account, such as the loss of green spaces through back-fill developments.

   ✗ One person's back-fill is another person's home – leads to NIMBYism ('Not in my back yard').

5. Need to look at impact of high urban land values on housing stock. As pressure on limited urban space grows, trend is towards smaller houses, built in small 'batches', often according to standardised design, or at least standardised variations.

   ✗ Full extent of land restriction on architecture not been explored, but design seen as 'artistic' not sociological.

6. Move towards 'brown site' building and reclaiming of derelict land for housing rather than intruding on the green belt. Claim that will solve 'housing crisis'.

   ✗ Availability of brown sites has been exaggerated.

17. OTHER DIMENSIONS OF STRATIFICATION

Marxist sociologists have focused on the way that the logic of capitalism has led to the construction of industry in different locations at different times. They see the dominance of the South as in part a consequence of the increasing importance of finance in capitalism, but that this is itself threatened by processes of globalisation.

Consideration of regional inequalities has led to the fruitful interaction between sociology and both geography and history, as theorists have attempted to explain the growth and persistence of regional inequalities.

Traditional sociology has long accepted that there are regional inequalities in Britain, but they were largely seen as the almost accidental result of decisions about investment and the location of industry. A more systematic approach was neglected.

LOCALITY AND REGION

More recent debates have focused on the social construction of disability and the social reaction to it, as elements of disadvantage experienced by those so labelled. The reaction of the disabled to this stigmatisation has been investigated, especially the attempts by disabled groups to assert their citizenship rights through legislation and integration.

Traditional sociology tended to accept a medical model of disability (see **Health 7**), which had the effect of silencing the voices of the disabled themselves, as their condition was socially constructed by doctors and other important gate-keepers of disability.

Until recently, sociology and society ignored the issue of disability, despite its prevalence in the population. Sociologists have since begun to explore disability in a sociological fashion.

DISABILITY

The different dimensions of inequality interact with each other to form multiple forms of disadvantage. While the major forms of class, gender and ethnicity are the most influential, other aspects of inequality can be important in individual lives.

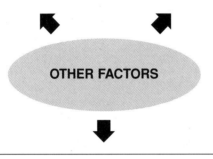

OTHER FACTORS

When different forms of inequality exist for the same person or group, they are said to be 'nested', that is, the individual or group will experience different forms of disadvantage in different situations.

AGE AND GENERATION

Theory	Strengths	Criticisms
Functionalism	✓ Age groups help integrate society ✓ Emphasises transition to age group	✗ Dismisses potential for conflict between generations ✗ Focuses mainly on the young
Marxism	✓ Argues that retirement is seen negatively ✓ Compares retirement to unemployment	✗ Underplays importance of the elderly in society ✗ Focuses mainly on the elderly
Weberianism	✓ Argues that age cohorts are status groups ✓ Emphasises long-term processes	✗ Ignores importance of class differences within a cohort ✗ No explanation of why cohorts differ over the long term
Life course	✓ Argues that ageism operates in society ✓ Stresses that individuals resist inequality	✗ Over-estimates control people have in their lives ✗ Not clear which inequalities are the important ones

Factors affecting age inequality

Young people
- lower wages
- greater social control
- greater unemployment

Old people
- lower incomes
- poor pensions
- lack of involvement

18. SYNOPTIC OVERVIEW

	MODERN SOCIETY	SOCIETAL CHANGES	POST-MODERN SOCIETY
Nature of society	• World is controlled by the West • Developing democracy • Strong social cohesion • Bourgeois values dominate • Industry is Fordist	• Collapse of communism • Managerial revolution • Decline of manufacturing • Growth of global trade • New information technologies • Greater democracy • Effects of two World Wars • Feminist and other social movements • Growth of service sector of economy • Switch from manual to non-manual work • Development of mass communications • Greater educational opportunities • Dominance of meritocratic ideologies • Growth of individualism leads to new dimensions of stratification • gender • ethnicity • status groups • disability • locality • age cohorts • sexuality	• Decolonisation leads to new independent countries • West democratised and communist authority destroyed • Strong centrifugal forces such as nationalism operate • Proliferation of value systems in any one society • Industry is post-Fordist
Stratification system	• Society highly hierarchical • Class divisions sharply drawn • Working class is largest group • Social mobility is limited • Occupational change is slow • Social values reflect dominant class interests • Traditional social divisions are important		• Society is more networked and less hierarchical • Class divisions are less clear-cut and rigid • Working class no longer major group • Social mobility increases as occupational structure changes • New technologies transform opportunities • Social values are many – no one system of thought dominates society • Different social cleavages become important
Important theories	• Functionalism • Structural Marxism • Symbolic Interactionism		• Post-modernism • New right • Neo-Marxism
Important issues in stratification	• Importance of educational achievement in mobility • Where the boundaries of classes are • How many classes exist • Function of ideology in a class system • How changes in classes come about • Conflict between capitalist and communist systems • Ownership of the means of production		• What is the nature of identity in post-modern societies? • Is class still important at all? • How do different dimensions of stratification fit together? • What is the impact on social cohesion of developments? • Is there a new world order emerging? • End of class conflict?
Examples of links to other areas	*Class effects on:* Health – lower classes have greater morbidity/mortality Housing – differential patterns of home ownership Education – differential levels of achievement Life-chances – differential opportunities Family – different child-rearing effects Crime – concentration of crime in working-class areas Culture – different values and attitudes.		*Other-dimensions effects on:* Health – specifically health of women, ethnic minorities and the disabled Work – discrimination against minorities in the workplace Religion – diversity of value systems in multicultural society Politics – growth of nationalism and parochial politics Family – growing diversity of family forms.

SPECIMEN QUESTIONS AND INDICATIVE ANSWERS

UNIT 1: CULTURE AND IDENTITY

OCR AS LEVEL UNIT 2 OPTION 4: YOUTH AND CULTURE

7(a) *Identify and explain two ways in which youth cultures may differ from mainstream cultures.* **[20]**

Culture and Identity 7 and **8** may be used here. The two factors could include 'mechanistic' factors such as the speed of social change after World War 2, the extension of education, consumption patterns changing as new leisure industries focus on youth markets. Middle-class counter-culture in the 1960s might also feature.

7(b) *Outline and discuss the view that class remains more important than age as a source of social identity.* **[40]**

Here you will need to be clear what is meant by social identity, see **Culture and Identity 1**. As for (a) above, **Culture and Identity 7** and **8** will be relevant together with **Culture and Identity 4**. Emphasis should be placed on the ideas that class and age are not mutually exclusive, youth sub-cultures are also class sub-cultures.

UNIT 2: FAMILIES AND HOUSEHOLDS

AQA AS LEVEL UNIT 1 SECTION A: FAMILIES AND HOUSEHOLDS

1(e) *Using information from Item B and elsewhere, examine the relationship between industrialisation and changes in the family.* **[20]**

Families and Households 8 will provide information on different theoretical perspectives concerning changes to family structure, whilst the social construction of the housewife role in **Families and Households 11** and historical changes in the concept of childhood in **Families and Households 14** will show how family roles have changed.

1(f) *Using information from Item A and elsewhere, assess the claim that the increase in the divorce rate since World War 2 has been mainly due to changes in the law.* **[20]**

Families and Households 10 shows a variety of causes for divorce which can be organised into paragraphs around the four different levels represented by the concentric circles. Be careful not to wander into the consequences of divorce which is not asked for in this question. The best answers will explain how the causes have led to an increase.

OCR AS LEVEL UNIT 2 OPTION 1: THE FAMILY

Either:

1(a) *Identify and explain two ways in which the extended family remains important in contemporary society.* **[20]**

1(b) *Outline and discuss the view·that recent changes in the nuclear family contribute to marital instability and high divorce rates.* **[40]**

(a) **Families and Households 1** identifies different types of extended family. These could be used to help structure your answer. **Families and Households 13** show how wider kin and elderly in the family can be seen to have important positive and negative consequences.

(b) Use **Families and Households 10** to distinguish between different types of marriage breakdown and then show how the loss of extended family might impact on the factors in the individual and partners' ring of the causes half of the diagram.

Or:

2(a) *Identify and explain, using two examples how family life may be influenced by ethnicity.* **[20]**
2(b) *Outline and discuss the view that there now exists a range of family types in contemporary society.* **[40]**

(a) You could take one of the cross-cultural examples from **Families and Households 2** and some contemporary variations to the traditional family model from **Families and Households 4**.

(b) **Families and Households 1** provides illustrations of the range of family types and **Families and Households 15** offers a debate between modern and post-modern views of family types.

UNIT 3: HEALTH

AQA AS LEVEL UNIT 1 SECTION B: HEALTH

2(e) *Explain why some sociologists argue that medicine and the medical profession have made little or no contribution to improvements in the general health of the population in industrial society.* [20]

The middle column of **Health 7** offers a number of criticisms of the medical model and **Health 10** gives four perspectives excluding the functionalist that are critical of the power of the medical profession.

2(f) *Using material from Item B and elsewhere, assess the view that class inequalities in health and illness are the result of cultural and behavioural differences.* [20]

Health 3 provides an account of the behavioural argument and offers criticism of this. The alternative explanations can also be used to challenge cultural and behavioural theory.

OCR A2 LEVEL UNIT 5 OPTION 3: HEALTH

Either:

3(a) *Outline and assess sociological explanations for class differences in health and illness.* [90]

Health 3 provides an account and criticism of five different explanations.

Or:

3(b) *Outline and assess sociological explanations of the view that the practice of medicine functions as an agency of social control.* [90]

Health 10 examines five explanations and their role in social control, **Health 9** develops the functionalist analysis further and this can be put in the context of the bio-medical model in **Health 7**.

TION C: MASS MEDIA

n people might be influenced by the output of the mass media. **[6]**

...fying not describing in detail. You might refer to a theoretical approach such as Marxist, feminist etc. ... You might refer to studies such as those on moral panics, see **Mass Media 4** and you might also look at representation portrays various social groups, see **Mass Media 10–12**. The violence debate might also be *Mass Media 7*.

...ne the sociological arguments and evidence for the view that the reporting of news by the mass media ...ctive. **[20]**

This will involve the examination of the news-making process and specific examples to demonstrate how it operates, see **Mass Media 8**.

3(f) *Using material from Item A and elsewhere, assess the arguments for the view that the media perpetuate stereotypes of gender.* **[20]**

You must be clear about the nature of gender, this is not simply a question about women. **Mass Media 10** examines representation of gender with reference to men and women and to changes in representation, i.e. gender liminality. You might also look at **Culture and Identity 6** which refers to gender and culture.

OCR AS LEVEL UNIT 2 OPTION 2: MASS MEDIA

EITHER:

3(a) *Identify and explain two ways in which sociologists have increased our understanding of the production of news.* **[20]**

Mass Media 8 can be used to examine news production. You could use **Mass Media 10–12** to select aspects of representation within the media and **Mass Media 6** which looks at moral panics as part of the process of news production.

3(b) *Outline and discuss the view that the mass media are able to influence their audiences.* **[40]**

This question can be answered in several different ways. You would need to look at the theories of the role of the media in society, see **Mass Media 3**. Audience effects models are shown in **Mass Media 5** and **7**. Moral panics also demonstrate effects, see **Mass Media 6**.

OR:

4(a) *Identify and explain two ways in which the consumption of mass media has changed in the last decade.* **[20]**

Mass Media 13 on new technology examines some of the recent developments in media hardware. **Culture and Identity 13–14** on post-modernism and consumption could also be used.

4(b) *Outline and discuss the view that globalisation has had a major impact on the content of the media.* **[40]**

Mass Media 14 outlines aspects of globalisation and its relationship to the media.

UNIT 5: EDUCATION

AQA AS LEVEL UNIT 2 SECTION A: EDUCATION

1(e) *Explain how the hidden curriculum and processes within schools help to produce inequalities between children of different social classes.* **[20]**

Education 6 gives the theoretical background to school processes and this can be illustrated with studies of social class identified in **Education 7** school section.

1(f) *Using material from Item A and elsewhere, assess the contribution of functionalist sociology to an understanding of the role of education in society.* **[20]**

Education 2 provides a functionalist perspective on the role of schools in socialisation and this can be assessed by using the Marxist view as an alternative. For the functionalist view of the selection role, see **Education 5**, the ladder of opportunity and the Marxist alternative – reproduction.

OCR A2 LEVEL UNIT 5 OPTION 2: EDUCATION

Either:

2(a) *Outline and assess the contribution of studies of classroom interaction to sociological accounts of gender differences in education.* **[90]**

Education 6 gives the theoretical background to classroom interaction and this can be illustrated with studies of gender identified in **Education 9** school section.

Or:

2(b) *Outline and assess how sociologists might explain the growth and development of vocationalism in education in the UK since the 1970s.* **[90]**

Education 3 provides alternative views on new vocationalism.

UNIT 6:WEALTH, POVERTY, AND WELFARE

AQA AS LEVEL UNIT 2 SECTION B: WEALTH, POVERTY, AND WELFARE

2(d) *Identify and discuss two reasons why 'older women' are more likely to be in poverty than 'older men'.* **[8]**

Use the women and elderly rows of **Wealth Poverty and Welfare 9** and select two of the columns to give two reasons.

2(e) *Examine some of the different ways researchers have attempted to measure poverty.* **[20]**

Measurement cannot be discussed without reference to definitions so the whole of **Wealth, Poverty and Welfare 5** is relevant here.

2(f) *Using information from the Items and elsewhere, assess the usefulness of 'individualistic' theories of the causes of poverty.* **[20]**

Wealth, Poverty and Welfare 6 gives two individualistic explanations and both are evaluated, but you can also assess them by using alternative explanations provided in **Wealth, Poverty and Welfare 7** and **8**.

OCR A2 LEVEL UNIT 5 OPTION 5: SOCIAL POLICY

Either:

5(a) *Outline and assess how recent changes in welfare provision have affected any one social group.* **[90]**

The recent changes in welfare provision could be discussed in terms of the provider of welfare (**Wealth, Poverty and Welfare 4**), the delivery of welfare (**Wealth, Poverty and Welfare 11**), or the philosophy of welfare provision (**Wealth, Poverty and Welfare 12**), or in terms of the debate between community and institutional care (**Health 13**). Whichever approach you adopt you must apply the material to the group chosen.

Or:

5(b) *Outline and assess the view that social policy has tended to promote a culture of dependency rather than a culture of enterprise.* **[90]**

Wealth, Poverty and Welfare 6 gives two individualistic explanations and both are evaluated, but you can also assess them by using alternative explanations provided in **Wealth, Poverty and Welfare 7** and **8**.

UNIT 7: WORK, ORGANISATIONS, AND LEISURE

AQA AS LEVEL UNIT 2 SECTION C: WORK AND LEISURE

3(e) *Using material from Item A and elsewhere, examine the influence of the role of work and other social factors on patterns of leisure.* **[20]**

You will see the basic definitions of work and leisure in **Work, Organisations, and Leisure 1**, along with some of the difficulties in defining each of these activities. The relationships between work and leisure are examined in **Work, Organisations, and Leisure 14**, with three different approaches identified. The main ideas are given but also some strengths and weaknesses to assist you in your evaluation of them. Some other issues associated with leisure are included and these will be useful for looking at other social factors, such as globalisation.

3(f) *Using material from Item B and elsewhere, assess sociological explanations of the nature and causes of alienation.* **[20]**

The issue of alienation is a complex one and is often discussed in relation to other forms of dissatisfaction with work. You will find these different forms, as well as alienation, in **Work, Organisations, and Leisure 7**. The importance of alienation is assessed on this page and empirical examples are also given. You should also look at **Work, Organisations, and Leisure 8** on 'Technology and Work', where issues to do with alienation are also examined. For a more specific example of the relationship between technology and alienation, **Work, Organisations, and Leisure 9** looks at automation and its effects on work as a whole, but an impact on alienation is also included.

OCR A2 LEVEL UNIT 8: SOCIAL INEQUALITY AND DIFFERENCE

1(d) *Using your sociological knowledge from any one area of social life with which you are familiar, show how 'racist assumptions are built into the rules and routines' (Item A, lines 3–4) of this area of social life.* **[30]**

Work, Organisations, and Leisure 13 includes a section on rules in organisations and the way that participants in organisational practices use them. In **Work, Organisations, and Leisure 11**, 'Gender, Ethnicity and the Workplace', the position of ethnic minorities in the workplace is examined, with some theories identified for explaining disadvantage. A combination of these two pages would assist you in answering this question.

UNIT 8: SOCIOLOGICAL METHODS

AQA AS LEVEL UNIT 3 AND A2 LEVEL UNIT 5 (SOCIOLOGICAL METHODS ASPECT)

1(e) *Using material from any studies with which you are familiar, explain why interviews and observation could be said to be 'more sensitive techniques' than questionnaires.* **[20]**

From **Methods 1** you could contrast the qualitative sources of participant observation and unstructured interviews with the quantitative technique of questionnaires, then use **Methods 9** and **10** selectively to show the features that make the qualitative techniques sensitive and the quantitative technique less sensitive. You could also challenge the question by using **Methods 8** to argue that not all types of observation are sensitive and from **Methods 10** that some interviews are more sensitive than others.

1(f) *Using material from the Items and elsewhere, assess the view that practical issues are the most important factor in deciding which research method(s) to use.* **[20]**

Methods 2 provides details of a range of practical, theoretical and ethical factors that influence choice of method. These are shown to be important at different points in the decision process. For the best answer illustrate with studies.

OCR A2 LEVEL UNIT 6: APPLIED SOCIOLOGICAL RESEARCH SKILLS

1(d) *Identify the limitations of the quantitative and qualitative methods used in the Items.* **[24]**

NOTE: Item A describes a postal questionnaire survey. Item B is an overt participant observation study.

Methods 1 gives the general disadvantages of both quantitative and qualitative data. This can be combined with **Methods 10** to consider the specific limitations of postal questionnaires and **Methods 9** to consider the specific problems of overt participant observation.

UNIT 9: POWER AND POLITICS

AQA A2 LEVEL UNIT 4 SECTION A: POWER AND POLITICS

Part Two

Either:

2. *Evaluate the contribution made by Weber to an understanding of power and authority in contemporary society.* **[40]**

Power and Politics 1 gives you basic definitions of power and authority and summarises the main ideas of Weber on these concepts, especially on authority. You could use the idea of ideology in **Power and Politics 2** to criticise the Weberian approach. Also **Power and Politics 3** and **4** give alternative approaches to power and authority in contemporary societies. **Power and Politics 16** highlights issues about the nature of power at the turn of the twentieth century and could be used to assess the contemporary relevance of Weber's ideas.

Or:

3. *'From the early 1970s, there have been changes in both voting behaviour and other forms of political participation.' Assess sociological explanations of these changes.* **[40]**

The traditional view of voting behaviour is contained within **Power and Politics 10**. This will provide you with a base-line from which to analyse any changes in both voting behaviour and political participation. In the case of voting behaviour you will find descriptions of the main changes in **Power and Politics 11**, organised around theoretical positions. For participation, **Power and Politics 12** provides you with an account of New Social Movements as political vehicles. For an overview of the theories of democracy which underpin the debates about voting behaviour and participation, look at **Power and Politics 15**.

OCR A2 LEVEL UNIT 5 OPTION 6: PROTESTS AND SOCIAL MOVEMENTS

Either:

6(a) *Outline and assess theories of new social movements in relation to any one social movement with which you are familiar.* **[90]**

Power and Politics 12 is about New Social Movements and you will find a comparison between Old and New there. Some examples are also given, as well as evaluative points about them. A theoretical view of NSMs is also included.

Or:

6(b) *Outline and assess sociological explanations of riots.* **[90]**

Power and Politics 13 looks at urban disorder, with a particular focus on the 1980s to begin with. You can also use the information to identify similarities and differences between different types of riot and have a basic understanding of the different positions taken by sociologists in seeking to explain them. You will need to use the information to assess each of the

UNIT 10: RELIGION

AQA A2 LEVEL UNIT 4 SECTION B: RELIGION

4(b) *Examine some of the problems involved in measuring the extent of religious beliefs and activity in modern society.*   **[8]**

Define religious beliefs carefully as either exclusivist or inclusivist as in **Religion 1**. The indicators of secularisation and the relationship between modernity and religion are outlined in **Religion 11** and **12**. Problems of actual measurement need to be addressed as different religious organisations measure membership differently.

Part Two

Either:

5. *Assess different sociological accounts of the role and functions of religious institutions and movements in contemporary society*   **[40]**

You will need to refer to theoretical positions in **Religion 2–4**. Religious movements are addressed by **Religion 6** and **7** and for fundamentalism, see **Religion 13**.

Or:

6. *'There are many types of religious movement in modern societies but they all act as an influence against social change.'* *Assess the sociological arguments and evidence for this view.*   **[40]**

This question implies that religious movements are inevitably conservative and invites a debate. Arguments for the conservative aspect come from feminists, Marxists and functionalists, but neo-Marxists see religion as a change agent. See **Religion 2–4**, **7**, **8** and **13**.

OCR AS LEVEL UNIT 2 OPTION 3: RELIGION

Either:

5(a) *Identify and explain two aspects of secularisation.*   **[20]**

Religion 11 outlines the major definitions of secularisation, but be clear that you identify only two aspects, and explain these.

5(b) *Outline and discuss the view that we now live in a secular society.*   **[40]**

Religion 12 will be useful here in examining the factors involved in the debate. **Religion 13** on Fundamentalism can be used to challenge the view, as can **Religion 7** on New Religious Movements.

Or:

6(a) *Identify and explain two ways in which religion reinforces social order.*   **[20]**

In this answer, you might examine the Marxist idea that religion is the opium of the people, see **Religion 3**, and/or the Functionalist view that religion reinforces social solidarity, see **Religion 2**. You might wish to argue the feminist case that religion is essentially a patriarchal institution controlling women, see **Religion 8**.

6(b) *Outline and discuss the view that religious organisations play a conservative role in contemporary societies.*   **[40]**

Each of the sections cited for question (a) will be appropriate again here, but in more detail. The challenge to the view may come from the Weberian position, see **Religion 4** on religion and social change, and the Neo-Marxist position on religion as a potential challenge to social order, see **Religion 3**.

UNIT 11: WORLD SOCIOLOGY

AQA A2 LEVEL UNIT 4 SECTION C: WORLD SOCIOLOGY

Part One

7(b) *Examine some of the problems faced by sociologists in defining 'development'.* **[8]**

You can draw on a number of sections here to highlight the different approaches to development which have been advocated by sociologists. **World Sociology 1** looks at the classical sociologists and their different views on the nature and direction of development. **World Sociology 2**, **3**, **4** and **5** also contain information and assessments, which will help you address this question.

and

Part Two

Either:

8. *Compare and contrast the contributions of modernisation and dependency theories to our understanding of development.* **[40]**

Modernisation theory is detailed and evaluated in **World Sociology 2** and dependency theory in **World Sociology 3**. However, you should also look at **World Sociology 4** and **5**, which bring these theories into a more contemporary focus and seek to evaluate them.

Or:

9. *Evaluate the view that education is the most critical factor in the shift from underdevelopment.* **[40]**

The issue of education is dealt with in **World Sociology 6**. However, in order to evaluate whether it is the most critical factor or not, you need to examine other factors which may have been put forward as important or critical factors in the process of development. You can find these in **World Sociology 2** on modernisation theory and **World Sociology 3** on dependency theory. You should also look at **World Sociology 11**, which details strategies for development and identifies factors that are important in the process of development. One particular factor is dealt with separately in **World Sociology 12** and that is aid.

UNIT 12: SOCIOLOGICAL THEORIES

AQA A2 LEVEL UNIT 5: THEORY AND METHODS (SOCIOLOGICAL THEORIES ASPECT)

Section B

Either:

2. *Assess the influence of feminist perspectives on sociological research.* **[40]**

This question invites both theoretical and empirical evidence. The theoretical position is outlined in **Sociological Theories 7**, whilst application of feminism may be found in many different sections. For example:
Education 9
Religion 8
Mass Media 4
Crime and Deviance 12
Work and Leisure 11
Culture & Identity 6
Stratification and Differentiation 10, 11.

Or:

3. *Evaluate the ways in which scientific thinking and methods have influenced sociological research.* **[40]**

This is an interestingly worded question, slightly different from the question of whether or not sociology is a science. You will need to examine the nature of scientific thinking, however, and that will necessitate an exploration of positivist and realist thought. As it asks for the influence on sociological research, you will need to compare those sociologists who opt for a more scientific approach with those of an interpretivist stance. You might conclude with the relevance of realist approaches for both natural and social science. See **Sociological Theories 12**, **13** and **14**.

UNIT 13: CRIME AND DEVIANCE

AQA A2 LEVEL UNIT 6 SECTION A: CRIME AND DEVIANCE

1(b) *Examine some of the problems involved in using official statistics to measure the suicide rate.*   *[12]*

Apply the problems identified in **Methods 3** to the content of **Crime and Deviance 17**.

1(c) *Evaluate Marxist explanations of crime.*   *[40]*

Crime and Deviance 10 provides an account of traditional Marxism and functionalist views can be contrasted with this as an assessment. Neo-Marxists are examined in **Crime and Deviance 11** and these can be assessed by opposing sub-cultural theories (**Crime and Deviance 7**) that explain youth crime and deviance from a functionalist perspective, interactionist theories (**Crime and Deviance 8** and **9**) or realist approaches (**Crime and Deviance 13**).

OCR A2 LEVEL UNIT 5 OPTION 1: DEVIANCE AND CRIME

Either:

1(a) *Outline and assess the strengths and weakness of labelling theory as an explanation of criminal behaviour.*   *[90]*

Crime and Deviance 8 and **9** give strengths of labelling theory and some criticisms. Other theoretical perspectives, functionalist (**Crime and Deviance 5** and **6**), Marxist (**Crime and Deviance 10** and **11**), realist (**Crime and Deviance 13**), non-sociological (**Crime and Deviance 4**) could all be used to show up the weaknesses of labelling.

Or:

1(b) *Outline and assess sociological explanations of how the operation of agencies of social control affect the representation of any one social group in official criminal statistics.*   *[90]*

Choose one of the social groups identified in **Crime and Deviance 2**. For youth look at **Crime and Deviance 7**. For class you might use **Crime and Deviance 3** to show how the non-manual workers escape entry into the crime statistics at every stage in their production. For women use **Crime and Deviance 14**, for ethnicity, **Crime and Deviance 15**. For the social construction of crime statistics examine **Crime and Deviance 3**. **Crime and Deviance 9** will give you some ideas of the role of the police in these processes.

UNIT 14: STRATIFICATION AND DIFFERENTIATION

AQA A2 LEVEL UNIT 6 SECTION B: STRATIFICATION AND DIFFERENTIATION

2(a) *Briefly discuss some of the problems of using occupation to define and measure social class.*   *[8]*

Stratification and Differentiation 8 focuses on the issues associated with measuring social class and in particular the use of occupational scales. These are evaluated through looking at the usefulness of such schemes and criticisms that have been made of them. A conclusion is also suggested. The page gives several examples of different types of occupational scales and the differences between them, to allow for a sophisticated view of this issue. You might also refer to **Stratification and Differentiation 9** on social mobility for an example of an area where much use is made of the occupational schemes.

2(b) *Examine the extent to which social class exerts an influence on different aspects of people's lives.*   *[12]*

There are many connections that can be made to other areas of social life here. **Culture and Identity 4** will help you with a general overview. More specific information can be found in **Education 7**, **Wealth, Poverty and Welfare 6**, **7**, and **8**, **Mass Media 12**, **Power and Politics 10**, **Crime and Deviance 7**, and **Health 3**, amongst others. Be careful to acknowledge that there are other social factors which cut across class divisions, such as gender, age and ethnicity. Look for the appropriate concepts in the Contents list.

2(c) *Assess the view that stratification is both inevitable and beneficial to individuals and society.*   *[40]*

You will find a general account of functionalism in **Sociological Theories 3**, with applications of the functionalist approach in **Sociological Theories 4**. There is a more detailed account of functionalism and class in **Stratification and Differentiation 2**, 'Traditional Approaches to Class Systems'. The material here on Marxism and Weberianism can be used to evaluate the functionalist approach, although specific strengths and weakness are also provided.

OCR AS LEVEL UNIT 1: THE INDIVIDUAL AND SOCIETY

1(d) *Discuss the view that the differences between masculine and feminine roles are disappearing.*   *[40]*

Stratification and Differentiation 11 provides a full account of the difference in gender roles, with particular reference to the labour market. You can also refer to **Families and Households 11** and **12** for further information on this issue.

Index